THE CHINESE REVOLUTION
ON THE TIBETAN FRONTIER

Studies of the Weatherhead East Asian Institute, Columbia University

The Studies of the Weatherhead East Asian Institute of Columbia University were inaugurated in 1962 to bring to a wider public the results of significant new research on modern and contemporary East Asia.

THE CHINESE REVOLUTION ON THE TIBETAN FRONTIER

Benno Weiner

CORNELL UNIVERSITY PRESS   ITHACA AND LONDON

Publication of this book was made possible, in part, by a generous grant from the Chiang Ching-kuo Foundation for International Scholarly Exchange.

First published 2020 by Cornell University Press

Library of Congress Cataloging-in-Publication Data

Names: Weiner, Benno, 1972– author.
Title: The Chinese revolution on the Tibetan frontier / Benno Weiner.
Description: Ithaca [New York] : Cornell University Press, 2020. | Series: Studies of the Weatherhead East Asian Institute, Columbia University | Includes bibliographical references and index.
Identifiers: LCCN 2019036104 (print) | LCCN 2019036105 (ebook) | ISBN 9781501749391 (hardcover) | ISBN 9781501749421 (pdf) | ISBN 9781501749414 (epub)
Subjects: LCSH: Minorities—Government policy—China—Tongren Xian (Qinghai Sheng)—History—20th century. | Communism—China—Tongren Xian (Qinghai Sheng)—History—20th century. | Tongren Xian (Qinghai Sheng, China)—History—20th century. | Tongren Xian (Qinghai Sheng, China)—Politics and government—20th century. | Tongren Xian (Qinghai Sheng, China)—Ethnic relations—Political aspects. | Tongren Xian (Qinghai Sheng, China)—Relations—China. | China—Relations—China—Tongren Xian (Qinghai Sheng)
Classification: LCC DS793.T7 W378 2020 (print) | LCC DS793.T7 (ebook) | DDC 323.1195/4105147—dc23
LC record available at https://lccn.loc.gov/2019036104
LC ebook record available at https://lccn.loc.gov/2019036105

For my parents

Contents

Illustrations

Maps

Figures

Acknowledgments

Long ago, while flying over the Pacific Ocean on a now long-defunct airline, I salvaged a fortune cookie from an otherwise inedible airplane boxed meal. I was on my way to China to start research for what after many twists and turns turned into this book. Feeling increasingly unsure of myself as I got closer to my destination, I cracked open the cookie, pulled out the white strip of paper, and read, "All your hard work will pay off in the end." At the time, it seemed like a serendipitous if trite omen. In the years since, however, there were more than a few moments when it appeared that the fortune inside the cookie may have been mistaken. That it was not is a testament to the remarkable support I have received from friends, family, and colleagues near and far.

At Columbia University, where this project began, I was fortunate to work with a group of wonderful scholars, teachers, and mentors. Not only did Robert Barnett introduce me to Tibetan studies, but he also was the first person to take a genuine interest in me as a scholar. Without his guidance and friendship, this book never would have been written. Madeleine Zelin has been a constant source of encouragement, patience, and sound advice. Gray Tuttle, who has done as much as anyone to make the study of Amdo a legitimate and active field of historical inquiry, has been an inspiration, advocate, and mentor. Eugenia Lean, Morris Rossabi, Guobin Yang, Thomas Bernstein, and Gulnar Kendirbai have all been more instrumental in my career than they likely realize.

I am particularly grateful to colleagues and friends who selflessly gave their time and energy to read and provide valuable feedback on the manuscript: David Atwill, Kelly Hammond, Charlene Makley, Max Oidtmann, Brenton Sullivan, and Dominique Townsend, as well as two anonymous readers. Their contributions to this book cannot be overstated. Special thanks go to Lauran Hartley, Chengzhi Wang, and Chopothar of Columbia's Star East Asian Library. Language instructors are the unsung heroes of East Asian studies. I would especially like to acknowledge Tenzin Norbu Nangsal, Liu Lening, Meng Yuan-Yuan, and all of the instructors at Tibet University.

I owe debts of gratitude to more people than I can possibly thank here. Some introduced me to a new contact, others pulled aside a useful document, many helped with a translation or cleared up a misconception, most gently nudged (and sometimes shoved) me in the right direction, and all provided encouragement and support. It is with great sadness but I hope an overabundance of caution that

I cannot thank many people in the Amdo region and beyond by name. Thank you, Ed Behrend-Martinez, Sandrine Catris, James Cook, DL, Jason Deathridge, Kristen Deathridge, Xénia de Heering, D, DT, Andrew Fischer, Joshua Freeman, Wendy Goldman, GK, Gedun Rabsal, Arunab Ghosh, Melvyn Goldstein, GT, Andrew Grant, GT, Brent Haas, Donna Harsch, Bianca Horlemann, JK, LG, James Leibold, Vincent Leung, Emily Leyava, Bill Lindeman, Jonathan Lipman, David Luesink, Covell Meyskens, Dáša Pejcha Mortensen, MW, Ruth Mostern, Thomas Mullaney, N, Carla Nappi, Paul Nietupski, "Philip," Christopher Phillips, Steven Pieragastini, Annabella Pinkin, PW, Scott Reylea, Françoise Robin, Gerald Roche, Pernille Røge, Jomo Smith, "Steven," Donald Sutton, Noah Theriault, Tsehua Jia, TT, TD, TD, Stacey Van Vleet, Ute Wallenböck, WW, WX, Molly Warsh, Jason White, Nicole Willock, Yuxiu Wu, Lan Wu, Yang Hongwei, Yongdrol Tsongkha, Zhaojin Zeng, and the faculty and staff at Carnegie Mellon University and Appalachian State University.

My editor Emily Andrew has shepherded this book to completion with a combination of professionalism and compassion that is deeply appreciated. Thank you also to Ross Yelsey, Bethany Wasik, Sarah Noell, Susan Specter, Don McKeon, and everyone at Cornell University Press and the Weatherhead East Asian Institute. The wonderful maps were created by Mike Bechthold. The cover art was generously provided by Ute Wallenböck from her personal collection.

Major funding for the initial stages of research was provided by a Fulbright Hays DDRA grant. At every stage thereafter, I benefited from a variety of fellowships and grants, including a Sasakawa Young Leaders Fellowship and a V. K. Wellington Koo Fellowship. A China and Inner Asia Council Small Grant from the Association for Asian Studies and a Falk Fellowship in the Humanities from Carnegie Mellon's Dietrich College provided essential support for a final round of research needed to complete the manuscript. A Chiang Ching-Kuo Foundation Publication Grant and a second Falk Fellowship helped in the final stages of turning the manuscript into a book.

Over many years and across continents, the friendship of Alastair Hunt and Felicia Koh, Zachary Waldman, and Dirk Eschenbacher and Lea Chen has been one of the few constants. Kelly, I am not sure I could have made it to the finish line without your companionship, encouragement, and commiseration. Although separated from me by distance, my siblings Josh, Carl, and Jessica have always been at my side. Macayla Ann and Ava, this book project is almost as old as you. Thank you for being who you are. You mean everything to me. This book is dedicated to my parents, Ellen and Dan, the most generous, loving, and creative people I know. Thank you.

Abbreviations

APC   agricultural production cooperative
CCP   Chinese Communist Party
CYL   Communist Youth League
GMD   Guomindang (Nationalist Party)
HLC   high-level cooperative
MAT   mutual aid team
NAC   Nationality Affairs Committee
PLA   People's Liberation Army
PPC   pastoral production cooperative
PRC   People's Republic of China
UFWD   United Front Work Department

A Note on Sources, Transliteration, and Nomenclature

This book is about the Chinese Communist Party (CCP) and the ideologies, policies, practices, and limitations that drove its state- and nation-building efforts in an ethnic frontier region during the first decade of the People's Republic of China (PRC). The focus is on the greater Repgong region in the eastern portion of the area Tibetan-speakers refer to as Amdo. The core is culled from the archives of the Zeku (T. Tsékhok) Tibetan Autonomous County, an administrative unit that in 1953 was carved out of the grasslands south of Repgong proper. Totaling nearly twenty-five hundred individual folios, the material is separated into the Zeku County Communist Party Committee Archives and the Zeku County People's Government Archives, each covering the years from the county's establishment up to 1960. These documents provide a history of Zeku County that moves along two vertical axes that stretch from Beijing to the provincial authorities in Xining, to Huangnan (T. Malho) Prefecture, and finally to Zeku County and its subcounty districts. On one side is a government bureaucracy that at the prefectural level and below was at least nominally headed by local Tibetan headmen. On the other is the Communist Party bureaucracy, which was dominated by Han Chinese operatives overwhelmingly from outside the region. The majority of material in both archives consists of a variety of reports generated at the district or county levels, which were then sent upward to prefectural- and provincial-level authorities. Much of the remainder are orders that traveled in the opposite direction. Taken as a whole, the two archives provide a remarkable portrait of the CCP's intentions and actions, its headway and hindrances, and its achievements, frustrations, and fiascos as it attempted to turn a culturally foreign and physically demanding corner of a former imperial borderland into an integrated component of the new, socialist nation-state.

In addition to the archives, I employ a variety of valuable primary and secondary sources, most of which were produced in the PRC and at some level were sanctioned by authorities. These sources provide important context and expand the field of examination beyond the temporal and geographic limitations of the archives. They include published and unpublished document collections, reportage meant for internal circulation (*neibu cankao*), gazetteers, Party histories, and state-sponsored oral history collections (*wenshi ziliao*). As a result, however, this is a story largely told from the perspective of the Party-state and its representatives. Even in the county archives, when local Amdo Tibetan voices can be detected, they are recorded by, and mediated through, state agents. This does not mean that the Communist Party has enjoyed carte blanche to dictate its own history. While the archives are filled with a seeming endless stream of reports and missives filed by mostly nameless CCP cadres and government functionaries, they are not the work of a monolithic Party-state. Instead, although often couched in a surface narrative of mounting successes, the files expose deep anxieties, buried imperatives, conflicting orders and expectations, admitted setbacks and failures, and a constant barrage of criticism leveled by higher-ups toward their subordinates. Taken as a whole, the archives reveal a regime that at the grassroots level—where most Amdo Tibetans actually interacted with its representatives and policies—was often floundering to reconcile programs imposed from above with local conditions on the ground.

Of course, whether qualitative assessments or quantitative reports, the information found in the archives and other sources must be read critically. Even when quotes are directly attributed to indigenous actors, we should not assume that they faithfully reflect the words or attitudes of local Amdo Tibetans. After all, informants may have been less than forthcoming when speaking with state and Party cadres, and those same cadres may at times have been similarly circumspect when reporting their findings to superiors. Misreporting might be due to any combination of a cultural or linguistic misunderstanding, a lack of trust between officials and local communities, rivalries on the grasslands and factionalism within the bureaucracies, confirmation bias on the part of Party or government cadres (a phenomenon so common the CCP had a term for it: "subjectivism" [*zhuguan zhuyi*]), and deliberate attempts by subordinates to mislead higher levels. After all, bureaucracies, in which meeting or not meeting the expectations of one's bosses often determines rewards and censures, contain built-in incentives for exaggeration or even fabrication. This may have been particularly true in the hyperpoliticized environment of Maoist China. Nonetheless, it should be kept in mind that these were internal reports circulated within the Party and state apparatuses and therefore reveal the way in which local conditions were represented by the Party-state to the Party-state. As such, they illustrate the bureaucracy's own concerns, goals, responses to obstacles and miscalculations, built-in contradictions, and internal dynamics. In the end, this may be the greatest value of the archives.

Readers will likely notice several areas for which the archival and related sources are unexpectedly quiet and, therefore, so is this book. The most obvious example is that monasteries and monastic leaders warrant relatively little attention in the Zeku County Archives, at least in comparison to the "tribal" leaders who demand so much of the Party's energies. This may reflect an assumption on the part of the CCP's local leadership that because Zeku's grasslands are not home to monastic institutions comparable in scale or prestige to those in surrounding agricultural areas, they were less important nodes of identity and authority than their secular counterparts. Another possibility is that this relative silence is a function of the Party's United Front policies, which will be described at length in the following chapters. In recognition of Tibetan religious sensitivities, Party leaders placed monasteries largely off limits to official interference, and this lack of oversight may be echoed in the archives. While there was a brief investigation into Zeku's monasteries prior to the founding of Zeku County, it would not be until they were emptied during the 1958 Amdo Rebellion that a comprehensive survey of Amdo's monastic establishments was finally undertaken.

Two other areas to which the archives pay surprisingly little attention are security and communication. The grasslands of Amdo could be dangerous. People were armed. Banditry and intercommunity feuding were both regular occurrences, and opposition to the state and its interests was not uncommon. Yet the archival sources have little to say about what type of security arrangements accompanied the establishment of Zeku County or were put in place to protect its cadres as they were sent into the grasslands to propagandize the CCP's agenda and implement its policies. Likewise, there are only scattered references to what must have been a nearly constant struggle for the largely Han Chinese cadre force to communicate with Zeku's Tibetan-speaking population. We know, for example, that the county secretariat had difficulty translating orders into Tibetan, that welfare and tax-collection efforts were hampered by a lack of Tibetan-speaking cadres, and that county leaders at one point ordered their subordinates to take elementary (six-week) Tibetan language classes, but otherwise there is little documentation of substance on this topic.

One potential way to have addressed absences such as these, as well as concerns relating to Tibetan voice and agency, might have been through interviews and oral histories. Early on, however, after conducting roughly two dozen oral histories within Tibetan and Salar communities, I decided that the political situation in Amdo was such that I could not assure the safety of my research assistants and informants. Therefore, I made the decision not to conduct further interviews.[1] As a result, this book relies on sources primarily generated by the Party-state and is therefore a book primarily about the Party-state, the vision that propelled it, and the policies and practices it employed in its ultimately failed effort to "gradually," "voluntarily," and "organically" incorporate the Amdo grasslands into New China.

There is currently no standard romanization system for phonetic Amdo Tibetan. I therefore employ the Tibetan and Himalayan Library's (THL) Simplified Phonetic Transcription of Standard Tibetan, developed under the direction of David Germano and Nicolas Tournadre. As Tibetan pronunciation diverges widely from written Tibetan and because transliteration systems that accurately transcribe Tibetan spellings are often incomprehensible to non-Tibetan speakers, the THL system was developed to provide both specialists and nonspecialists a uniform, readable representation of spoken Tibetan. However, the THL system is based on Central Tibetan pronunciation, which is incomprehensible to speakers of Amdo Tibetan and vice versa. In employing Central Tibetan orthography, scholars working on other parts of the Tibetan Plateau run the risk of further peripheralizing their subjects while reinforcing a framework of a single Tibet radiating outward from Lhasa. Nonetheless, lacking a suitable alternative, I employ THL's Simplified Phonetic System with the following exceptions: Where the initial consonant sound diverges significantly between Central Tibetan and Amdo Tibetan, I employ the latter. For example, I refer to the Hor chieftain Wagya, not Bagya, and to the Shisa chiefdom, not the Chisa chiefdom. I also convert the nominalizing suffix *ba* to *wa*, as in *tsowa* (instead of *tsoba*). While it is tempting to take it a step further and turn Wagya into Wajya, recognizing the limitless potential for fine-tuning I have tried to refrain from further corruptions to the THL system.

Full Wylie transliteration of Tibetan spellings of many of the proper nouns found in this book, along with Chinese equivalents, can be found in appendix B. As is now near universal, I employ the pinyin system for transcribing Chinese. Whether dealing with Tibetan or Chinese, however, I maintain commonly recognized variations for well-known figures such as the Dalai and Panchen Lamas, Sun Yatsen, and Chiang Kaishek. Mongol names are provided as found in Christopher Atwood's *Encyclopedia of Mongolia and the Mongol Empire*. Unless otherwise indicated, all translations are my own.

Writing about Amdo is made more difficult because of what is often the nonequivalence of the various toponyms used in Tibetan and Chinese. For example, the Tibetan place name Repgong is not historically coterminous with the Chinese county of Tongren, although in practice today they are often used interchangeably (officially the county name in Tibetan is Tungrin). These discrepancies can signify not only different spatial arrangements but may also carry lingering political implications. In this study, I try to use Chinese place names when referring to Chinese administrative units (such as Qinghai Province or Tongren County) and Tibetan when referring to a geography or polity conceived of outside Chinese statist frameworks (such as Amdo and Repgong), although the lines are not always so clear.

Similar difficulties arise over the question of how to refer to Tibetan communities. In the following pages, rather than "tribes," as they are commonly called in both English and Chinese, I refer to Amdo's larger sociopolitical units as "chiefdoms." From an anthropological perspective, the term "tribe" usually connotes segmented groups defined by common ancestry, real or imagined. There is no consensus over how well that definition fits Amdo. Fernanda Pirie, for instance, argues that pastoral communities in Amdo are "rooted more in territorial and political unity than in a descent ideology."[2] Others note the important role that notions of patrilineal descent play in the construction and maintenance of group solidarity.[3] My decision to use the term "chiefdom" rather than "tribe" is twofold. On the one hand, it is meant to sidestep the association of tribal with "primitive" or "backward," connotations that not only permeate Chinese writings on Amdo and many other communities inhabiting ethnic border regions of the PRC but also have a long, lingering colonial legacy in Western depictions of a variety of non-European people. Second, it points to the hierarchical, state-like nature of these confederations, which were organized either under hereditary chieftains—what David Sneath in the context of pastoral Inner Asia refers to as "noble houses"—or under the administration of the corporate monastic estates of reincarnate lamas.[4] What Chinese sources refer to as tribes (*buluo*) are these larger confederations, under which normatively are found several tsowa (C. *cuowa, caowa*), sometimes imprecisely glossed as clans (*zu*) or small tribes (*xiao buluo*). Within each tsowa are smaller herding groups (T. *rukhor*, C. *quanzi*) and finally individual households or tents (T. *dra*, C. *zhangfang*).

This neatly nested structure simplifies and standardizes what certainly was, and remains, a far more internally diversified sociopolitical landscape. In practice, for instance, tsowa can also refer to the chiefdom as a whole. Moreover, other terms such as *shokwa* and less often *dewa* might be used more or less interchangeably with *tsowa* or can be more prominent in different parts of the plateau.[5] While recognizing that it is imprecise and based largely on Chinese categories, for the sake of readability I refer to the large confederations, such as the Hor or Gönshül of Zeku County, as "chiefdoms." Lacking a suitable English equivalent that would distinguish them from the chiefdom, as in Chinese publications I retain the word *tsowa* to describe the larger subunits—for example, the five tsowa of the Hor chiefdom.[6]

On a final note, as many have remarked before me, the Chinese term *minzu* is particularly fluid, contested, and malleable. James Leibold writes that *minzu*, a neologism borrowed from Japanese in the last years of the Qing dynasty, would come to "connot[e] a cluster of meanings and associations similar to those captured in English by race, nation, people, ethnic group, and nationality."[7] In my estimation, however, by 1949 the term was not ambiguous to Communist Party leaders or theorists whose understanding of minzu grew from—but, as shown by Thomas Mullaney, did not ape—the Soviet concept of nationality (*natsia*).[8] More recently, some Chinese scholars have objected to this correspondence. They argue that by mistakenly equating nationality and minzu, the state actually has hindered the coalescence of a strong, unified national community. Instead of referring to a country made up of many nationalities (*duominzu guojia*), they insist that the singular Chinese nation (*Zhonghua minzu*) consists of multiple *ethnicities.*[9] The point is not to weigh in over which formulation is more correct. After all, any such effort to categorize is inherently subjective and political. Nonetheless, during the 1950s, minzu was consciously and purposely understood to mean something akin to the Soviet notion of nationality. I therefore retain that terminology, with all its thorny connotations and knotty complications.

THE CHINESE REVOLUTION ON THE TIBETAN FRONTIER

AMDO, EMPIRE, AND
THE UNITED FRONT

Midsummer is a busy time on the grasslands of southern Amdo. For the pastoralists who inhabit the high plateau, the long, sunny days and moderate temperatures provide a brief respite from the punishing conditions that predominate the rest of the year. Still, there is plenty of work to be done. Days begin well before dawn. Livestock, consisting of sheep, goats, yak (and hybrid *dzo*), and horses, must be untethered and the young separated from their mothers so that milking can be completed by sunrise. Then the herds are driven out to pasture. In good years—those without a late frost, crippling drought, insect infestation, animal epidemic, or other disruption—the animals pass the sunlit hours grazing on the lush summer grass, fortifying themselves for the onset of autumn and the long, harsh Amdo winter that would quickly follow. Throughout, herders must remain on the lookout for strays as well as predators and bandits, both common dangers on the grasslands. Meanwhile, having risen early to milk the animals, women and girls often spend the rest of their mornings and afternoons gathering fuel for fires, making butter, cheese, and yogurt, fetching water, and performing other household tasks among the black tents that dot Amdo's summer encampments.[1]

On July 5, 1958, however, in one corner of the plateau the daily rhythms of pastoral life were shattered. That afternoon, 124 members of the Wöngya chiefdom descended upon an isolated and lightly guarded government outpost in Zeku (T. Tsékhok) County. With dozens of miles of grassland separating the settlement from potential rescue, the Tibetan horsemen quickly overcame the hapless defenders, killing a district-level secretary of the Chinese Communist Party

(CCP) and six of his cadres. With a cache of newly captured weapons, including a small number of handguns and rifles, a machine gun, twenty grenades, and 1,980 rounds of ammunition, the insurgents then ambushed a reconnaissance squad of the People's Liberation Army (PLA). Soldiers of the PLA's 163rd Regiment, 55th Division, were quickly mobilized, but it would take three days before the reinforcements were able to track down the last of the Tibetan rebels and put an end to the Wöngya uprising.[2]

This was not how it was supposed to be. When PLA soldiers and CCP cadres marched into Qinghai Province nine years earlier, they claimed to be "liberating" their Tibetan, Mongol, and Muslim "compatriots" from the oppressive rule of Chiang Kaishek and his local agent, the "Muslim warlord" Ma Bufang. Almost a decade later, the relationship between the Communist Party and Amdo's "minority" communities lay in tatters, for the Wöngya revolt was not 1958's only armed challenge to CCP rule. Since early spring, one after another a string of antistate uprisings had engulfed Qinghai, leading provincial leaders to declare a state of open "counterrevolutionary armed rebellion." In response, the Party-state unleashed a wave of retaliatory violence unparalleled in the region's recent history. Over sixty years later, the legacies of 1958 still reverberate across Amdo and beyond.

This book is a close examination of the Chinese Communist Party's attempts to avoid that outcome, a description of why and how its efforts failed, and a rumination on the consequences of that failure for both Amdo Tibetans and the Chinese state. In the process, it also explores a host of broader issues connected to the end of empire and the transition to nation-state, a process that requires the adoption of new notions of sovereignty, territoriality, and identity, as it seeks to reshape disparate, often loosely governed, and relatively disconnected subject populations into a new political community, one now divided into a single majority and multiple minority populations.

The People's Republic of China (PRC) considers itself a unitary, multinational state made up of fifty-six legally distinct but equal "nationalities" (*minzu*)—fifty-five minorities and one majority—the Han Chinese. This composite nation is said to have coalesced over centuries of common struggle to form one big socialist family. Yet in recent years, popular challenges to the unitary state and its alleged pluralist political culture have occurred in several of China's ethnic minority areas. Most prominently, since 2009, interethnic unrest and violence has racked the Muslim majority region of Xinjiang, ushering in an era of unprecedented state surveillance, incarceration, and oppression aimed at Xinjiang's Uyghur and other Muslim populations. And in March 2008, the first in a series of sometimes violent demonstrations broke out in the Central Tibetan capital of Lhasa and quickly spread across much of the Tibetan Plateau. Now centered in the eastern areas of the plateau, the regions Tibetans traditionally refer to as Kham and Amdo, these disturbances continue in the form of sporadic protests and a string of more than 150 self-immolations.[3]

The immediate causes of interethnic violence and antistate protest in both Xinjiang and Tibetan regions involve a host of intertwined issues, from restrictions on religious practice to economic and social dislocation, demographic transformation, state surveillance and repression, ecological degradation, and fears of ethnocultural annihilation.[4] However, they also must be understood in the context of seven decades of failed efforts to fully integrate these regions and their populations into first the socialist and now the postsocialist Chinese state and nation.[5] After all, these were not the first waves of unrest to hit either region. Since the founding of the People's Republic in 1949, intermittent outbreaks of mostly localized protest have been fairly common in both Xinjiang and Tibetan regions.[6] From 1987 to 1989, for instance, repeated demonstrations in Lhasa, some of which turned violent, were only quashed with the implementation of martial law.[7] And, as alluded to above, in the mid-to-late 1950s, open rebellion swept across the Tibetan Plateau.

Both the Chinese state and supporters of an independent Tibet tend to frame unrest in Tibetan areas of China within the ongoing debate over Tibet's international status—namely, whether or not Tibet historically has been an "integral" part of China or a wholly independent country. That is to say, they argue over whether or not Tibet *should* or *should not* be part of China. This is hardly surprising. "History" often serves as the battleground on which competing visions of the nation are fought—who should be included and excluded, where "natural" boundaries begin and end. This almost always requires a process of simplification in which inconvenient details are forgotten and premodern logics are repurposed in the service of more recent presumptions about identity, loyalty, and sovereignty.[8] In the case of Tibet, Emily Yeh writes, "both Chinese state authorities and Tibetans have reconceptualized past imperial relationships in terms of modern territorial sovereignty, anachronistically projecting the modern nation-state form backwards in time to make their claims."[9] Of course, neither the present-day Chinese nation-state nor the stateless Tibetan nation is simply a modern manifestation of an earlier political community. Instead they are relatively recent and contested creations that only became fully realized over the course of the twentieth century. Therefore, rather than asking if Tibet *should* be part of China, more useful are avenues of inquiry that instead explore processes, strategies, and problematics of state and nation building on China's ethnocultural frontiers. In other words, *how* have state representatives tried to integrate Tibetan regions into the modern Chinese nation, and *why* has this project been less than successful? This book aims to answer some of these questions.

A central assertion of this book is that the CCP's goal in 1950s Amdo was not just state building, which presumably could have been accomplished primarily through force, but also nation building, which required the construction of narratives and policies capable of convincing Amdo Tibetans of their membership in a wider political community. It argues that Communist Party leaders implicitly understood both the administrative and epistemological obstacles to transforming an expansive, variegated, and vertically organized imperial formation into an integrated, socialist, multinational state. Moreover, the ideological underpinnings of the CCP demanded the active participation of individuals and communities in this new sociopolitical order, albeit in heavily scripted ways and as part of a distinct hierarchy of power. The CCP therefore adopted and adapted imperial strategies of rule, often collectively referred to as the United Front, as means to "gradually," "voluntarily," and "organically" bridge the gap between empire and nation. As demonstrated, however, the United Front ultimately lost out to a revolutionary impatience that demanded more immediate paths to national integration and socialist transformation. This led in 1958 to communization, large-scale rebellion, and its brutal pacification. Rather than a voluntary union, Amdo was integrated through the widespread and often indiscriminate use of violence, a violence that lingers in the living memory of Amdo Tibetans and many others.

Amdo and Empire

One of the first entries in the Zeku County Archives introduces the region by noting, "Zeku County is . . . very high and extremely cold. The people who live here are ten tribes of various sizes, purely Tibetan, who engage in pastoralism as their main pursuit."[10] Filed in November 1953 and written by hand on otherwise unmarked lined paper, this represented the boundaries of what was definite, what seemed indisputable. Prior to its "liberation" in September 1949, the CCP had no physical presence Qinghai, few allies, and limited understanding of the region's ethnic composition, political and religious cleavages, or productive forces. Four years later, Party operatives were aware that Zeku was purely Tibetan and almost totally pastoral, that it was at high elevation (averaging nearly 11,500 feet above sea level), and that it had an extreme climate (the average temperature hovers around thirty-two degrees Fahrenheit).[11] From the CCP's perspective, it was materially poor, with primitive infrastructure, difficult communications, nonexistent industry, low education levels, and a culture racked by religious superstition. Cadres arrived with a rudimentary knowledge of the region's demographic makeup that split Zeku's inhabitants into ten "tribal" groupings—what

I will refer to as chiefdoms to reflect the sociopolitical nature of these confederations (see "A Note on Sources, Transliteration, and Nomenclature")—and were
aware that deep divisions existed between and often within these units. They had
identified many of the area's leading secular headmen and monastic figures and
established relationships with several (see appendix A). And investigators were
aware that both the Geluk and Nyingma traditions of Tibetan Buddhism had an
institutional presence in the region through a collection of fourteen relatively
small monasteries (many of them mobile "tent monasteries") and the incarnate
lamas (T. *trülku*, C. *huofo*) who presided at many.[12] Beyond this, however, not
much was sure. The challenge they faced was daunting but clear—transforming
an alien, "tribal," and "backward" corner of the Tibetan Plateau into a politically,
economically, and psychologically integrated component of New China.

Today Zeku County remains a relatively remote and sparsely populated pastoral area located in the southeastern portion of Amdo.[13] Along with Kham to
its south and Central Tibet (Ütsang) to its southwest, Amdo (sometimes called
Northeast Tibet) is one of three major ethnolinguistic subregions that constitute
what is often referred to as "greater," "cultural," or "ethnic" Tibet. Covering an
area roughly the size of France, the majority of Amdo lies in present-day Qinghai, with the remainder spilling into neighboring areas of southern Gansu and

FIGURE 1.   Amdo Tibetans near a tributary of the Tséchu River. Joseph Rock,
1926, courtesy of Harvard-Yenching Library.

northern Sichuan. Despite frequent references to Amdo as one of the three traditional "provinces" of Tibet, this characterization is the product of recent nationalist reimaginings. In fact, it is doubtful that Amdo was ever governed as a single administrative entity, much less as a province of a unified Tibetan state. Instead, political power in Amdo historically has been exercised by a dizzying array of often overlapping authorities, each exercising varying degrees of autonomy while generally acknowledging allegiance to larger regional, interregional and imperial centers of power.[14]

Adding to the confusion is Amdo's considerable ethnocultural diversity. Its expansive southern and western grasslands are primarily inhabited by Tibetan and to a lesser degree Mongol and Kazakh pastoralists, while the more densely populated agricultural districts along its northeastern and eastern frontiers have long been home to a multicultural, multiconfessional mixture of Chinese, Tibetan, Mongol, and Turkic-speaking communities. While linguistic, cultural, and religious markers certainly produced affinities between local Amdo Tibetan communities and the larger Amdo Tibetan and pan-Tibetan worlds, this should not be confused for a protonational consciousness.[15] Instead, principal markers of identity might have been connected to the local landscape and its associated spirits and gods, while political loyalty may have been directed toward the local

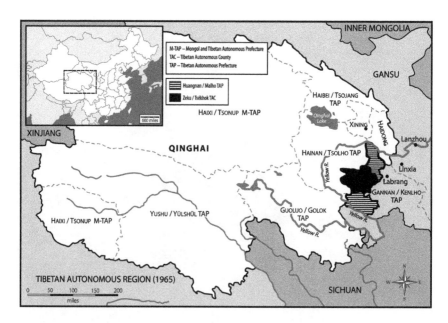

MAP 1. Qinghai Province. Mike Bechthold, cartographer.

dewa or *tsowa* (elastic terms akin to "group" but often glossed as "tribe" in both English and Chinese) under the authority of a hereditary chieftain (*gowa, pönpo*) or monastic estate (*labrang*).[16]

While intercultural conflict was common, so was cultural and commercial exchange. The boundaries between ethnocultural communities could be quite permeable and identities often indeterminate, particularly prior to their hardening (although never fully ossifying) over the course of the twentieth century.[17] For these reasons, Amdo can be thought of as a frontier zone, "a meeting place of peoples in which geographic and cultural borders [are] not clearly defined."[18] This is particularly true for several areas on Amdo's eastern marches, including Repgong (C. Tongren), Xunhua (T. Yadzi), and Labrang (C. Xiahe, T. Sangchu), each of which will make repeat appearances in the following pages. Given their porous nature, rather than fixate on political boundaries or demographic features, anthropologist Toni Huber usefully reminds us, "There is not, and there never has been, a single or discrete [Amdo] in time and space, and there is no benefit for us to invent and impose a precise one here."[19]

With Huber's warning in mind, for this study I broadly conceive Amdo as having been part of an imperial formation with China-based imperial cores for much of the past millennium.[20] For centuries, various imperial centers frequently invested Amdo's secular and religious leadership, particularly Mongol and Tibetan, with honors, titles, and rewards in exchange for expressions of loyalty and their service as intermediaries between the imperial state and local society. As will become clear in chapter 1, this is not to suggest that these imperial centers exercised direct control over Amdo, nor am I claiming that their influence was uniform over space and time. To the contrary, for long spans most of these local interlocutors remained substantially free of imperial supervision. Nor should it be interpreted to suggest that "Tibet" has been part of a historical "China," a jump in logic that assumes "Tibet" and "China" to be self-evident historical entities and presupposes a linearity in which political relationships of the past are determinant of rightful political statuses today.[21] However, as explicated below, I do hold that the broad parameters of an imperial relationship existed through unequal but reciprocal relationships between imperial centers and a multitude of Amdo's ruling institutions, secular and/or religious. While tensions were often present and considerable gaps in imperial oversight not uncommon, over the *longue durée* these structural relationships were relatively stable and mutually reinforcing. It is certainly the case that at various times many of Amdo's elite actors maintained imperial-style relationships with other centers of power, both those in Amdo (such as with Khoshud Mongols) and elsewhere (in particular Central Tibet). That from at least the eighteenth century, these competing power centers were also part of the same overarching imperial polity, the Manchu Qing Empire (1636/1642–1912), only underlines the flexibility and nonexclusive nature of sovereignty inherent to most pre- and early-modern imperial formations.

This is only one of the many ways to understand Amdo's past. After all, the coexistence of overlapping delineations of political space and concepts of sovereignty are hallmarks of both prenational polities and frontier zones.[22] Some prefer to approach Amdo through a prism that de-emphasizes statist institutions and instead stresses the fractured and charismatic nature of political and moral authority. For example, Stanley Tambiah's concept of an unbound but concentric, mandala-like "galactic polity" has been employed as a lens through which to view Tibetan political realms.[23] Others have chosen to view Amdo's various political groupings within the framework of what Geoffrey Samuel has termed a "stateless society," "decentralized polities, often with strong 'tribal' elements."[24] Wishing to transcend national borders while deperipheralizing the peoples of the highlands of Asia, in recent years some scholars have proposed the alternative geography of "Zomia" "as a political and historical entity significantly distinct from the usual area divisions of Asia."[25] By contrast, Paul Nietupski describes Amdo as a "'polythetic' phenomenon," an organic entity unto itself, despite "different taxonomies or shifting clusters of religions and associated political visions."[26] Referring to Amdo as a "contact zone," "shatter zone," or "middle ground," still others insist that it is that very diversity that makes Amdo "a center in its own right."[27]

Depending on the intellectual project, these approaches all have their usefulness. Amdo Tibetans certainly have and continue to participate in trans-Himalayan communities, for example, and the charismatic nature of authority in Tibetan Buddhist society may have helped mitigate against (if not eliminate) the consolidation of centralized, bureaucratic rule. As this study shows, however, there is little doubt that Amdo's varied and various political institutions also participated in China-based imperial formations. For instance, Max Oidtmann finds that Amdo Tibetans and others often took advantage of the legal mechanisms available to them through the Qing administrative state, even while Nietupski demonstrates the hermeneutical power of monastic charismatic-legal authority.[28] In truth, the fluidity of identities, differing notions of territoriality, and the messy, nonexclusive nature of sovereignty may not have been particularly troublesome for many people living in frontier zones such as Amdo. By contrast, in recent centuries these same conditions were often a source of considerable anxiety to nation builders of all stripes as they sought to realize their various visions of the modern, consolidated state and nation. In this vein, my approach is useful both conceptually and empirically because it focuses on the primary node through which "China-based" imperial formations constructed, conceptualized, and interacted with the Amdo frontier and therefore explicates one of the central problematics of postimperial Chinese state and nation building: the transition from empire to nation-state.

Empire and China

The literature on empire is almost as old as empire itself. Historians and political theorists have exhausted countless wells of ink, typewriter ribbons, and toner cartridges defining empire, detailing their conquests, explaining their operations, and perhaps most recurrently expounding upon the decline and fall of empire.[29] The overall effect of the preoccupation with imperial decline and collapse has been twofold. On the one hand, it has helped conceal the more enduring successes of empire in ruling over vast, diverse populations for lengthy periods of time.[30] Second, it has fed into a teleology of the nation-state in which the nation inevitably supplants empire as not just the dominant but also the most natural, desirable, and legitimate form of political organization.[31] In this framework, empire often becomes the infamous "prison house of nations," to use a phrase made famous by Vladimir Lenin, the subjugator of "long-repressed primordial national consciousness."[32]

In contrast to populist narratives of nationhood, most scholars today contend that states make nations, rather than the other way around.[33] Either way, when talking about the transition from empire to nation(s), commentators often emphasize rupture and revolution while continuities between empires and their successor states are largely ignored. Certainly rupture is an inherent and inherently important component of change. Yet postimperial nation builders never began with clean slates. Instead, they were forced to contend with what Alfred Rieber refers to as the "historical legacy" of empires, which he describes as "those elements of institutional, ideological, and cultural structures and practices that survived the demise of imperial rule."[34] They also faced many of the same challenges as their imperial predecessors, including dealing with diverse ethnocultural populations. Despite brandishing heady new conceptions of the political community, to deal with a host of complex issues nation builders—whether out of habit or desperation—often dipped into the toolboxes of their imperial forbearers.

The Chinese Revolution on the Tibetan Frontier examines one such transition from empire to nation, in this case from the Manchu Qing dynasty and its imperial predecessors to the People's Republic of China. Rather than posit the inevitable defeat of the old empire by the forces of nationhood, I argue that the transformation from imperial formation to Chinese nation has been contested, constructed, negotiated, and ultimately incomplete. Rather than fixate on historical rupture between the ancien régime and what in many ways were fundamentally new political constellations, following Rieber, I take note of "the persistent factors that confronted the new ruling elites of the successor states"— in this case, primarily agents of the Chinese Communist Party—and their reversion to imperial-style practices to resolve them, even if those practices were often reimagined and rearticulated in radically new ways.[35]

Of course, I am not the first to note China's rocky transition to nationhood. For much of the twentieth century, the seeming inability of the postimperial order to reconfigure itself as a modern nation-state was a subject of considerable anxiety for both Chinese intellectuals and outside observers. Lucian Pye has argued that the problem of nation building in twentieth-century China was the difficulty of transforming a civilization into a nation.[36] While not without merit, this conclusion is also a function of a particular lacuna in both the popular memory and, until fairly recently, scholarly treatment of China's past. Even while widely being lauded as the world's most enduring imperial formation, what in fact made the Chinese Empire an empire often was assumed rather than explicated.

In recent decades historians have jettisoned static and insular models of China's past. In the process, they have also begun to locate the "imperial" in "imperial China." This is particularly the case for studies of the Qing Empire. Rather than viewing the Qing as the last dynasty in China's more than two millennia of imperial history, as had been the norm, practitioners of what has become known as "New Qing History" approach the Qing as a composite, multiethnic empire led by a Manchu royal house operating under its own cosmological conceptions of sovereignty and identity and positioned in the larger world of early modern Eurasia.[37] In particular, these scholars pay close attention to the non–Han Chinese segments of the empire and the Qing's recognition, toleration, manipulation, and "simultaneous" dominion over vast, diverse, and largely discrete sets of ethnocultural "constituencies."[38] As such, they have relocated what in fact made the Qing an empire.

New Qing historians did not only complicate narratives of China's dynastic past but also offered clues as to how the Qing imperial formation became the modern Chinese state and nation. After all, it was the borders created at the height of Qing imperial expansion, boundaries that had "no precedent in Chinese history," that the state claimed in the early twentieth century as the natural extent of an enduring, historical China.[39] Now firmly entrenched in the historiography of late-imperial China, the New Qing turn has helped spark a burgeoning interest in China's ethnic frontiers during the Republican (1912–27) and Nationalist (1928–49) periods by scholars exploring efforts of successive Chinese regimes to counter the powerful centrifugal forces that during the first half of the twentieth century threatened to tear apart the postimperial polity.[40]

By contrast, the post-1949 conquest, consolidation, and rule over non-Chinese portions of the Qing's former imperial domains, a full 60 percent of the land-mass of the PRC, have received far less scholarly attention. Fortunately, China's socialist or Maoist era (1949–76) is currently in the first stages of a wide-ranging reassessment. The work of earlier generations tended to emphasize elite poli-tics, interest-group dynamics, and the comparative analysis of political systems. Historians and historically minded social scientists now are increasingly calling attention to everyday life, uneven experiences, and varying levels of accommoda-tion between state and society. In general, however, despite their geopolitical im-portance and the ramifications for the demographic disposition of the modern Chinese state and nation, this reevaluation has not yet been extended to ethnic minority regions in a sustained manner.[41] *The Chinese Revolution on the Tibetan Frontier*, therefore, provides a crucial link between New Qing History, "Maoism at the grassroots," and efforts to understand the CCP's ongoing difficulties inte-grating non-Han peoples into the People's Republic of China.

What Is an Empire?

In an influential study, Michael Doyle writes, "Empires are relationships of po-litical control imposed by some political societies over the *effective sovereignty* of other political societies."[42] Doyle, who is mainly interested in the noncontigu-ous European colonial empires of the early modern and modern periods, comes from a long line of theorists for whom empire, and its extension imperialism, is inseparably marked by political, economic, and/or social domination and exploi-tation.[43] Within the scholarship on empire, however, a branch has emerged that argues against formulas that define empire primarily through prisms of domina-tion. In this book, I follow theorists such as Charles Tilly and Karen Barkey who instead understand empire in terms defined by the reciprocal relationships be-tween imperial elites and the elites of multiple, distinct peripheral polities. From this perspective, Tilly provides perhaps the most useful definition. He writes,

> An empire is a large composite polity linked to a central power by indi-rect rule. The central power exercises some military and fiscal control in each major segment of its imperial domain, but tolerates two major elements of indirect rule: (1) retention or establishment of particular, distinct compacts for the government of each segment; and (2) exercise of power through intermediaries who enjoy considerable autonomy within their own domains in return for the delivery of compliance, trib-ute, and military collaboration with the center.[44]

Importantly, as Tilly notes, empires do not rule subordinate societies directly but instead rely on the mediation of intermediaries, often local elites, who "use existing practices, understandings and relationships to extract the requisite minimum of tribute, military support, and loyalty for the center's benefit."[45] Barkey elaborates further: "The imperial state does not have complete monopoly of power in the territory under its control. It shares control with a variety of intermediate organizations and with local elites, religious and local governing bodies, and numerous other privileged institutions. To rule over vast expanses of territory, as well as to ensure military and administrative cooperation, imperial states negotiate and willingly relinquish some degree of autonomy."[46] Noticeably, coercion is not absent from this formula. After all, empire is predicated on unequal and hierarchical political relationships. And, of course, the violence committed by empires and their agents over the centuries is incalculable. The point is not to suggest otherwise.

Yet, rather than domination, Tilly, Barkey, and others identify flexibility and internal variance—each itself a product of the uneven absorption of imperial domains—to be constitutive components of imperial formations. In such a system, at least in the case of more enduring empires, to varying degrees both the imperial center and peripheral elites can be beneficiaries of empire. This might occur through the actual accumulation of resources (those sent upward as taxes and tribute and/or downward as rewards and bribes), military support for the center and protection for the peripheral polity, or through the exchange of titles and ritual practices that recognize and reinforce both the universal sovereign and local authority. In this framework, the actual ability to exert direct influence over an imperial segment might at times be less "effective" than the appearance of compliance.

Whether demanding Doyle's "effective control" or, as with Tilly and Barkey, allowing for the exercise of considerable local autonomy, most agree that empire is by definition dependent on the maintenance of differentiated and unequal segments.[47] Particularly in the European maritime empires, this might mean (in theory although rarely in practice) a "binary split into colonized and colonizer." More often, "an empire could be an assemblage of peoples, practicing their religions and administering justice in their own ways, all subordinated to an imperial sovereign."[48] Ideally, these "assemblages" are vertically integrated through "distinct compacts" with the imperial center, not horizontally attached to the other imperial segments. Empire is therefore often visualized as a "hub-and-spoke network" in which each segment is connected to the imperial center but not each other.[49]

The enforcement of difference, however, should not be confused with a commitment to equality or pluralism. Instead, difference was often predicated on legal distinctions that disadvantaged certain segments of the empire in relation to others. Moreover, it was only one strategy of incorporation available to imperial centers. On the other end of the spectrum were imperial ideologies and civilizing missions that emphasized assimilation and homogenization. In truth, for most empires the choice between policies of difference and those of acculturation was never a zero-sum equation. The longevity, flexibility, and variegated nature of successful empires meant that they might employ variations of both strategies, often simultaneously.[50] This was certainly the case for the Qing, which in its northern and western domains imperfectly enforced policies of separation and differentiation, while along its southern and southwestern frontiers pursued an uneven strategy of administrative standardization and acculturation (*gaitu guiliu*).

Nevertheless, Barkey notes, "Once the multifarious settlements between state and different communities diminish and stabilize, and standardized relations apply to all segments of imperial society, we are not talking about empire anymore, and have moved toward an alternative political formation, perhaps on the way to the nation-state."[51] Rarely, if ever, has this level of simplification been successfully realized across the entirety of a former empire. Instead, when observers talk about the transformation from empire to nation, they are generally speaking of the breakup of the old imperial polity into some manifestation of its component parts, often reimagined as the liberation of preexisting and self-evident nations. What is important here, however, is recognizing the fundamental dissimilarities between empire—in which difference, inequality, and incorporation are definitive components—and the consolidated nation-state, which attempts to enforce uniformity, equality, and the exclusion of those determined to be others. While empires explicitly seek to rule multiple, distinct communities (ethnic, religious, geographical) as separate entities, nation-states, even those with pluralistic aspirations, are prone to homogenize as they demand new types of expressions of loyalty and identity from their citizens (whether in a liberal democracy or authoritarian regime), who are expected to buy in through active participation in the body politic.[52]

This, then, was the challenge faced by the CCP in the non-Chinese regions of the former Qing Empire. How to reconstitute separate populations of imperial subjects as members of a singular, horizontal, and eventually socialist political community?

Erasing Empire, Making Minorities

In the many cases in which multiple nation-states have emerged from the ashes of an empire, these postimperial entities could define themselves against the old empire as enduring, self-evident nations freeing themselves from imperial shackles. Where attempts have been made to reconstitute the geographic and demographic diversity of the former empire as a new political community, however, the discursive relationship with empire is more complex. Rather than campaigning against empire, the political calculus has to be reconfigured in a way that obscures or erases the imperial nature of the polity.

The history of the construction of the modern Chinese nation-state provides a useful example. The narrative surrounding the end of imperial China and the establishment of the republic is one dominated by radicals and revolutionaries who espoused a racialized, irredentist, and exclusivist Han nationalism. However, as in the waning years of the Ottoman and Hapsburg empires, there were also voices from within the multicultural imperial elite that sought "to construct hybrid notions of an empire-nation," essentially eliminating the hub-in-spoke organization for horizontal integration—making majorities and minorities.[53] That in all three cases exclusivist, racialized visions of the new nation initially won out over more pluralistic and inclusive ones highlights the limited resources available to those wishing, in Benedict Anderson's evocative words, to stretch "the short, tight, skin of the nation over the gigantic body of the empire."[54] Simply put, the discourses available to supporters of an empire-sized nation, with all its inherent diversity, were not as convincing or powerful as those that preached a more limited nationhood based on arguments of common culture and decent.

Chinese revolutionaries initially appealed to ancestral commonalities that set an aggrieved ethnic Chinese community apart from not only the Western imperialists who had imposed themselves so aggressively since the mid-nineteenth century but also other inhabitants of the Qing Empire—most prominently its Manchu ruling elite. However, soon after the overthrow of the monarchy, the newly established Republic of China and its champions began to rethink the boundaries of the new nation. In the main, the victors of 1911–12 chose an expanded national discourse that included all of the lands and peoples of the former empire.[55]

In order to explain this new multiethnic nation, empire had to be "erased," most often by invoking culturalist and racialist arguments to explain a multiethnic/multicultural Chinese nation as something other than the legacy of empire, especially a Manchu empire.[56] During the eighteenth century, the Qing court had employed the discourse of the "five peoples" (wuzu) to conjure an image of Qing divine dominion over a unified but internally differentiated empire in which Manchus, Han, Mongols, Tibetans, and Muslims coexisted harmoniously. After 1912, Chinese republicans redeployed the rhetoric of wuzu, this time secularized as the "five races as one family" (wuzu yijia). Rather than distinct constituencies connected along separate spokes to an imperial center, in Sun Yatsen's words it was now meant to project "the continued territorial integrity of the lands of the five races . . . in one great Republic of China."[57] As Joseph Esherick notes, however, "nobody really tried to demonstrate why they constituted a single family; nobody was able to show—especially show to the satisfaction of the Tibetans and Mongols—why they constituted one nation."[58] As far as many (but not all) Mongol and Tibetan elites were concerned, the imperial compact struck with the Manchu Qing rulers had been severed. Seeing little stake for themselves as minorities in a Han-dominated nation (and influenced themselves by the stirrings of ethnonationalism), both Central Tibet of the Thirteenth Dalai Lama and Outer Mongolia of the Eighth Jibzundamba Khutugtu quickly proclaimed themselves independent of the new republic.

The rise of the Nationalist Party, or Guomindang (GMD), under Chiang Kaishek coincided with even more assertive claims to the Qing's former imperial possessions. However, the domestic weakness of the Guomindang state and related geopolitical dynamics of interwar Asia combined to limit the Nationalists' ability to make good on their rhetoric of national unity. Lying outside Chiang's effective control, most of China's ethnic borderlands remained "complex frontiers"[59] torn between local actors, so-called warlord regimes (often but not always allied with the GMD), in several cases transnational interests, and global powers, including the Soviet Union, Britain, and Japan.

Given the demonstrated inadequacy of the ideology of nationalism, James Leibold writes that "the GMD adopted a pragmatic yet inherently conservative frontier policy that was rooted in the language and administrative precedents of the Qing court."[60] In several cases this entailed reestablishing imperial-style patronage of Tibetan Buddhist institutions, one manifestation of what Uradyn Bulag has alternately referred to as "going imperial" and "subimperialism." Bulag coined the term subimperialism to describe the modern state's "tapping into the heritage of the former empire's techniques of rule in the service of nationalism."[61] In other words, despite otherwise dedication to the modernizing, secularizing, and homogenizing tenets of the nation-state, Chinese state and nation builders were often forced to rely on imperial-style strategies to lay claim to an unwieldy and inchoate postimperial polity. These subimperial strategies included granting imperial-era titles, financial and political support for religious institutions, maintenance of administrative distinction, and indirect rule through local elites.[62] Important for this study, unlike Central Tibet, in Amdo the disintegration of the Qing imperial state did not herald a period of "*de facto* independence."[63] Instead, as detailed in chapters 1 and 2, Amdo fell under the contested control of the so-called Ma Family warlords, who themselves were often forced to revert to subimperial practices in order to govern their rump state.

When the CCP came to power in 1949, its leadership quickly made known that it, too, considered the near entirety of the Qing's geographic and demographic expanse to be inseparable parts of the new, soon-to-be socialist nation.[64] Unlike the GMD, however, the CCP possessed administrative, organizational, and coercive capacities—as well as a more favorable if still challenging international environment—that would allow it to secure far-flung borderlands firmly into the new state. The Communists also had a transformative ideology that at least on paper lent itself more readily to inclusivity than did the Nationalists' appeals to racial and (less often) civic nationalism. In practice, however, this project was not packaged within a discourse of socialist internationalism. After all, the borders of the new state conspicuously ended at the boundaries of the old empire. Like its predecessors, the CCP needed a narrative of national unity that obscured the legacy of empire. As solution, the Communist Party claimed the composite Chinese nation (Zhonghua minzu) to be the "collective creation" of "all of China's nationalities." In contrast to the CCP's characterization of Guomindang ethnic policies, which they described as discriminatory and assimilationist, Communist Party leaders insisted that this unity was the product of "reciprocal amalgamation between nationalities," "an unavoidable and progressive phenomenon" forged through common struggle against foreign aggression and domestic reactionaries.[65]

In essence, as Charlene Makley observes, lacking "divine embodiment as a way to link micro- and macrospaces in their radical vision of a new overarching political order," the CCP's leadership turned to the "secular category *minzu*" to explain membership in the new political community.[66] Yet Party leaders understood that empirical conditions on the ground often ran counter to its pluralistic vision of multinational China. Rather than ignore the chasm between rhetoric and reality, the CCP openly conceded that deep-seated antipathies existed between nationalities. This alienation was caused by the long-term existence of what, borrowing from the Soviets, the Party termed "great Han chauvinism" (*danhanzu zhuyi*). CCP leaders argued that the dominant Han nationality had exploited less advanced peoples, retarding their social and economic development and creating enmity between the nationalities. In contrast to its Russian counterpart ("great Russian chauvinism"), however, only in the Chinese case was "great nationality chauvinism" considered to have disrupted a *preexisting* multinational unity. Unlike the tsarist state, imperial China was not a prison house of nations but "had a long history [as] a unified state."[67] Empire was thus erased. Rather than functioning as the necessary linkages that help define imperial formations, the CCP reinterpreted past relations between imperial centers and local elites as markers of an indelible if damaged historical unity. Membership in the multinational People's Republic of China, therefore, was both innate and extant, although at the time of "Liberation" often unrealized.

A Magic Weapon

The primary method to repair this tear in the fabric of the multinationality nation was called the United Front (*tongyi zhanxian*). In its broadest definition, the United Front is the theoretical justification *and* bureaucratic method for bringing non-Party and nonproletarian elements into the political process and thus defining them (at least for the time being) as allies rather than enemies of the CCP and the people. The tendency in scholarship has been to assume that the United Front as deployed in ethnic minority areas was little more than a short-term expediency or cynical ruse meant to placate certain segments of society until the CCP was in position to forcibly implement its radical agenda.[68] If we begin at the end of the 1950s and work backward, it is easy enough to come to this conclusion. However, a closer examination of internal communications and actions within Amdo prior to 1958 tells a different story. In fact, among the more remarkable characteristics of the materials from Zeku County and beyond is the earnestness, dedication, and often frustration evident in the Party's own internal reports regarding its role as an institution of both state and nation building.

In recent years, the United Front has increasingly made headlines in the international press as the agency tasked with polishing China's image abroad through such "soft power" instruments as sponsoring Confucius Institutes (language and cultural centers installed on college campuses around the globe) and the co-option of overseas Chinese willing to quietly promote CCP interests.[69] However, scholars have paid relatively little attention to the role and practices of the United Front *in China* since 1949. To date, only two monograph-length studies dedicated to United Front work have appeared in Western language scholarship—one by Lyman Van Slyke in 1967, the other by Gerry Groot in 2004. This is despite Mao Zedong himself having declared the United Front, along with Party building and armed struggle, one of the "three magic weapons" (*sanda fabao*) of the Chinese Revolution.[70]

The roots of the United Front stretch back nearly to the birth of the CCP. Famously, Lenin had argued that the revolutionary fervor of the proletariat in the industrialized, Western nations had been dampened by the influx of "super profits" that monopoly capitalism earned through the exploitation of the colonial and semicolonial world. For Lenin and his supporters, the solution was to disrupt the flow of these profits by encouraging national liberation movements. Lenin determined that in colonial settings, local Communist Parties, lacking proletarian bases of their own, should unite with the most progressive, anti-imperialist, bourgeois forces.[71] Under the direction of Joseph Stalin and the Communist International, in 1923 the nascent Chinese Communist Party formed a United Front with Sun Yatsen's newly reconstituted Guomindang. Four years later, the always uneasy alliance ended disastrously for the CCP when Sun's successor, Chiang Kaishek, violently purged the movement of leftist and Communist elements.

From these darkest days at the brink of annihilation, the Communist Party re-emerged and with it the concept of the United Front. In the process, according to Van Slyke's pioneering work, the United Front developed "from tactic to strategy to ideology."[72] And to this might be added a bureaucratic institution, the Party's United Front Work Department (UFWD). During the Second Sino-Japanese War (1937–45), the Communists and Nationalists brokered an awkward and oft-broken Second United Front. The ostensive purpose was "total mobilization of the entire nation" against Japanese occupation.[73] Yet, in the longer term, the CCP also had its sights on destabilizing the GMD. For these purposes, "this Second United Front enlisted practically any conceivable group that might assist the CCP against the GMD and Japanese."[74] This included smaller political parties, intellectuals, religious groups, and even landlords, capitalists, and militarists. From its wartime base in northwest China, Party leaders also began to take notice of non-Han communities, in particular Mongols and Muslims, and launched efforts to recruit them into a patriotic United Front.[75]

Upon coming to power in 1949, Mao publicly credited the three magic weapons—Party, army, and United Front—for the CCP's victory over the Nationalists in the Chinese Civil War.[76] Despite the establishment of the PRC, however, external and internal enemies remained; therefore, the three magic weapons must continue to exist as well. Van Slyke argues that the United Front quickly became a vital component of post-1949 state building, "its function . . . changing from the isolation of an enemy to the integration of the people in support of the new regime."[77] This was possible because of Mao's concept of "New Democracy," which allowed for a transitional period of indeterminate length during which time capitalism, feudalism, and socialism would coexist under Party rule.[78] The UFWD became one of the main institutions tasked with managing this messy transition. Once again, allies were recruited from among nonproletarian classes, most famously intellectuals and entrepreneurs, their purpose to "convince their class base to accept and work towards CCP goals while modeling and acting as exemplars of such change."[79] Paraphrasing UFWD director Li Weihan, Groot writes that by uniting the greatest number of potential allies under CCP leadership, the United Front "would assist in eliminating enemies, help revive and develop a new economy and culture and help establish the conditions needed to enter the socialist stage."[80] By then, Van Slyke adds, "The united-front approach had become an almost instinctive element of the Party's mentality."[81] Far from peripheral, it was a key component of early-PRC state and nation building.

Writing nearly four decades apart, both Van Slyke and Groot are mainly concerned with non-Party intellectuals, in particular the eight so-called democratic parties (*minzhu dangpai*) that after 1949 were allowed to continue as minor part-ners in a United Front with the CCP.[82] Borrowing from Antonio Gramsci, Groot in particular views the United Front as having been institutionalized along cor-poratist lines through which the Party-state "accords some groups privileged sta-tus and access to itself in return for compliance and some influence over them."[83] Each minor party thus was reorganized in Leninist fashion and made to represent distinct categories of peoples, from the petty bourgeoisie to educators to former members of the GMD.[84]

Whatever its applicability for the democratic parties, and despite many par-allels in practice and intent, corporatism does not seem as useful a model for United Front policies in minority regions such as Amdo. Groot describes mem-bership in a corporatist unit as limited, hierarchical, and noncompetitive. For instance, only eight parties were given patent, and anyone deemed unreliable was quickly excluded or worse. In Amdo, the Party cast a far wider net because its needs were different. For one, as in many ethnic border regions, the CCP had virtually no presence in Amdo prior to 1949, a problem exasperated by the speed by which anti-Communist forces crumbled.[85] With no infrastructure, few friends, and little local knowhow, Party leaders ordered the recruitment of tra-ditional elites into a "patriotic United Front," one of three core tasks in "newly liberated minority nationality regions."[86] Second, as described in chapters 3 and 4, despite the overwhelming power of the CCP and its military, the nature of the Party's nation-building project demanded that minority peoples be integrated through persuasion rather than coercion. For the CCP, ruling over Amdo was not simply a matter of obtaining "effective control" because control was never the sole objective. Speaking of the multiethnic imaginings of the Soviet state, Fran-cine Hirsch writes, "The Bolsheviks did not wish to just establish control over the peoples of the former Russian Empire; they set out to bring those peoples into the revolution and secure their active involvement in the great socialist ex-periment."[87] This focus on voluntarism and participation was also central to the Chinese Communist project in Amdo and beyond, where physical control was a necessary precondition to the realization of a grander formula for national unity and eventually socialism.

Under these circumstances, non-Han elites were simply indispensable. For both Gramsci and Groot, the most important non-Party allies are intellectuals due to their "considerable social authority" and ability to "act as 'organizers and mediators of consent.'"[88] Although hardly intellectuals in either the Confucian or Communist cultural milieu, if anything the CCP considered the role of mi-nority secular and especially religious leaders even more vital because their stat-ure within minority communities was assumed to be greater and their influence deeper.[89] If properly nurtured, minority elites could marshal their charismatic authority to model patriotic nationality unity among the masses. As shown in chapter 2, rather than recruiting a limited number of vetted elites into a Leninist or corporatist bureaucratic institution, in Amdo the CCP therefore welcomed almost any willing influential minority figure—even those who had taken up arms against its soldiers and cadres.

In contrast to corporatist logic, this meant that the Party needed to bargain with innumerable individual interests. As a result—and despite its fervent wishes—the CCP could not easily transform Amdo elites into appendages of the Party-state. While it did attempt to build bureaucratic institutions that might better be thought of as corporatist, including various political consultative committees, the Communist Youth League (CYL), the Women's Federation, and nationality autonomous administrations, during the 1950s it repeatedly fell back, as this book shows, on the personal charisma and authority of pre-1949 religious and secular leaders who retained considerable agency and influence. These United Front "religious representatives" (*zongjiao daibiao*) and "nationality representatives" (*minzu daibiao*) did not *represent* a class but, as in earlier periods, functioned more as *intermediaries* between the state and local society.[90] Thus, rather than corporatist, the United Front in 1950s Amdo is better thought of as subimperial.

Class Struggle versus Nationality Struggle

On the one hand, Party leaders blamed the outsized influence of traditional elites in Amdo on the "backward" economic conditions, political systems, cultural traits, and especially deeply ingrained religious beliefs that (from their perspective) plagued many of China's minority peoples. On the other, they highlighted the injurious legacy of "great Han chauvinism." As today, the CCP leadership was unwavering in its insistence that China is a historical entity made up of multiple nationalities united through centuries of common struggle against external imperialism and internal reactionaries. Ostensibly, minority elites had taken a leading position in both of these struggles. Against foreign imperialism they had joined the Han in progressive patriotic resistance. Domestically, however, these same elites led their communities in resisting the exploitation of Han rulers and their interests. To an understandably wary rank-and-file concerned that the Party was pandering to class enemies, the CCP's Northwest Bureau explained that although members of Amdo's upper strata were surely agents of class exploitation, "from the perspective of the minority nationality people, . . . they are seen as heroes. The reason is simple: it is because in the past under the rule of Han chauvinism, [minority elites] played the leading role in opposing nationality exploitation."[91]

These "special characteristics" of underdevelopment and nationality oppression meant that class consciousness was particularly weak and "local nationalism" (*difang minzu zhuyi*)—a parochial response to Han chauvinism—relatively strong within many non-Han communities.[92] By eliminating nationality exploitation, the primary cause of alienation between nationalities, Party leaders predicted that local nationalism would wither and pannationality patriotic consciousness would take its place. In Maoist terms, for the indefinite future the primary contradiction in minority areas was not class struggle but nationality struggle—the struggle against Han chauvinism. Internal class divisions having been labeled nonantagonistic, indigenous elites in Amdo and elsewhere were made leaders of newly established nationality autonomous administrations where they would continue to form both a filter and a conduit between the masses and the state.

Unlike traditional imperial practice, however, the United Front was not simply a strategy for managing difference. CCP leaders considered it a *transformative methodology* of state and nation building, one that was fully theorized and integrated into the Party's work practices and bureaucratic philosophies. The Northwest Bureau, which was then under the day-to-day direction of Xi Zhongxun, father of China's current leader, Xi Jinping, was quick to add, "Today we strive to unite with these minority nationality upper strata elements, in reality this is winning over the minority nationality masses."[93] By promoting nationality equality and economic development within designated nationality autonomous areas, Party leaders insisted that nationality exploitation would end and minority communities would become "masters of their own homes" (*dangjia weizhu*). Eventually, "in accordance with the wishes of the majority of its people and of the local leaders,"[94] "democratic reforms" (*minzhu gaige*)—the final elimination of pre-1949 political institutions—could commence. Only then would each nationality make the full transition to socialism and the mission of the United Front presumably end.

These mechanics of nationality rapprochement and transformation operated through a dialectical relationship between what was often referred to as "consultation" (*xieshang*) and "persuasion" (*shuofu*). Students of modern China will recognize an approach that falls squarely within the rubric of the famous "mass line." The mass line is most often thought of as a mechanism for raising the class consciousness of the Han Chinese peasantry and cementing their solidarity with the Party. Arlif Dirlik adds that it "was intended to achieve leadership rather than domination of the masses."[95] Similar in both rationale and methodology, the object of the United Front was never simply to dominate but to raise nationality and patriotic consciousness and lead Tibetans and other minority nationalities of the Qinghai-Tibet Plateau on a gradual and voluntary path toward nationality unity and socialist transformation.

Yet, as with the broader mass line, power relationships between the Party and its United Front targets, whether Chinese intellectuals or Tibetan headmen, were highly unequal and often coercive.[96] These inequities embedded in the Leninist system all but ensured that Party leaders, not local actors, would determine when the Amdo grasslands were ready for "democratic" and socialist reforms. First, the dialectics of consultation and persuasion were inherently imbalanced. As described in chapters 3 and 4, rather than an honest give-and-take, consultation and persuasion almost always were geared to produce consensus support for the Party's predetermined objectives. In similar fashion, even while directing its agents to consider the "special characteristics and concrete conditions" of each minority area, higher levels provided little space for substantive local innovation or input. Instead, it set policies from above and expected them to be faithfully carried out below. While outcomes often fell short of expectations—as shown in chapters 4 and 5—these setbacks invariably were blamed on poor execution rather than misguided instructions.

In fact, United Front gradualism existed in constant tension with a revolutionary impatience deeply suspicious of practices that advocated allying with "feudal" elites.[97] Through most of the 1950s, the Party leadership—including Mao himself—firmly supported United Front policies in nationality minority areas. Yet the indeterminate duration of the period of New Democracy, a shifting definition of who were friends and who were enemies, and the idiosyncratic nature of the CCP, in which being accused of being too conservative was far more dangerous than appearing too radical, meant local cadres were ideologically primed and institutionally conditioned to err to the left. As shown in chapter 5, it is little surprise then that when given the opportunity, many cadres in Amdo allowed their "subjective wishes" for socialist transformation to overcome objective evaluation of conditions on the grasslands. For reasons described in chapters 6 and 7, by 1958 these tensions had reached a breaking point. That year, as the Great Leap Forward descended upon Amdo's pastoral areas, the plateau erupted into large-scale rebellion. The response was swift and brutal. Tens of thousands were arrested, and many thousands killed. With few exceptions, members of Amdo's pre-1949 secular and religious leadership were purged and jailed, in many cases dying in prison or labor camps. These, of course, were the very same United Front figures that since 1949 had been the bedrock of the Party's efforts to "voluntarily" integrate Amdo and its inhabitants into the new socialist nation. Fragile from the start, the subimperial compact struck between the Party-state and Amdo elites was shattered. The final chapter details the cost in lives and legitimacy wrought by this sudden and violent end to empire.

Nonetheless, sources from 1950s Amdo give little reason to assume that calls to make Tibetan and other minority communities "masters of their own home" amounted to either empty sloganeering or Orwellian doublespeak. Instead, the United Front might be better thought of as a component of Maoist "high modernist ideology." James Scott describes high modernism as a "strong, one might even say muscle-bound, version of the self-confidence about scientific and technical progress, the expansion of production, the growing satisfaction of human needs, the mastery of nature (including human nature), and, above all, the rational design of social order commensurate with the scientific understanding of natural laws." Scott makes clear that he is not speaking of scientific practice itself but a "faith that borrowed, as it were, the legitimacy of science," in this case interpreted through Marxist, Leninist, and Maoist ideological preconceptions and practices.[98] In 1950s Amdo, the United Front was a quasi-scientific process of organizing and making legible an alien society in preparation for its integration into the socialist state and nation.

This is not to suggest that from the start the CCP and its agents were not intrinsically hostile to the interests of Amdo's monastic leaders, hereditary headmen, and other "feudal" institutions or that the intent of the United Front was other than their eventual elimination as a privileged class. And, of course, just because it was earnestly pursued does not mean that the CCP's actions in Amdo and other minority areas were justified. It is to say, however, that in its own time and by its own logics, the United Front was considered by its advocates a legitimate, progressive alternative to strategies of nation building and the treatment of minority populations in the capitalist West. It was imagined as a nonexploitative mechanism to gradually and voluntarily reunify the historical Chinese nation, just as the People's Liberation Army had reconstructed the historical Chinese state, and pave the way for full, peaceful socialist transformation. It was fundamental to the manner in which the Party understood its *own* presence and legitimacy in places like Amdo and as such set and reflects the CCP's institutional ethos and practices of sovereignty during the first decade of the People's Republic of China.

According to Scott, things often go "tragically awry" when "well-intended schemes to improve the human condition" are implemented by hyper-self-assured authoritarian regimes animated by utopian visions, particularly where "a prostrate civil society . . . lacks the capacity to resist."[99] In Amdo and elsewhere on the Tibetan Plateau, there was determined resistance to the CCP's "high modernist designs." As will be shown, in the end it was not enough.

1

AMDO AT THE EDGE OF EMPIRE

On August 27, 1949, units under General Wang Zhen of the People's Liberation Army "traversed the rarified air of the high mountains" that separate Linxia in Gansu from neighboring Qinghai Province. By four o'clock that afternoon, Xunhua County, an ethnically mixed region on the southern bank of the Yellow River, had become the first area of Qinghai officially "liberated." As if to emphasize the impact of Xunhua's capture, that same day the "Muslim warlord" Ma Bufang, long the leading power broker in northwest China, fled the provincial capital of Xining, never to return. A week later, on September 5, 1949, vanguard troops of the PLA's First Regiment, First Corps, entered Xining, "liberating the ancient city of the plateau" and "ending the Ma Bufang family's long forty years of bloody rule in Qinghai, opening a new historical era where the masses of each nationality were to become the masters of their own home."[1]

Back in Xunhua, the leader of the Tibetan Linggya tsowa hurried south to neighboring Repgong to confer with the region's most prominent Tibetan authorities. These men had been keeping a close eye on events that for months had been unfolding over their eastern horizon. For example, the Seventh Shartsang Lama, Lozang Trinlé Lungtok Gyatso, abbot of Repgong's Rongwo Monastery, had regularly sent representatives to Gansu's capital of Lanzhou to receive the latest updates on the military situation.[2] And some days earlier, grain stored at the local military barracks had been destroyed by fire. Suspecting sabotage and fearing for his safety, Tséring Gyel, the ethnically Tibetan, Ma Bufang–appointed county head, requested a meeting with the men PRC sources would later refer to as the "three-in-one feudal rulership of Tongren County"—Rongwo *nangso* (a secular, panchiefdom leader) Trashi Namgyel, Zongqianhu Gyelwo Dorjé, and the chief steward (*chakdzö*) of Rongwo Monastery and younger brother of the Shartsang Lama, Gélek Gyatso.[3] "The provincial leaders have ordered me to return to Xining, but currently society is in chaos," Tséring Gyel allegedly exclaimed. "Please will you three take responsibility for maintaining the area's law and order and managing the granary and trade office. I will return when my business is done." The next day, having collected horses, supplies, and the county's wireless equipment, Tséring Gyel set fire to the local archives and fled with a small coterie of loyal officials.[4]

Abandoned by Xining, representatives of Repgong's elite soon gathered at the manor house of the Rongwo nangso to hear the Linggya chieftain's report. In addition to the trio of Trashi Namgyel, Gyelwo Dorjé, and Gélek Gyatso, also present were the *qianhu* and *baihu* (hereditary chieftains) of the "Twelve Tribes of Repgong," the region's eighteen *nangchen* (leading monastic figures), and the heads of Rongwo Monastery's three *dratsang* (monastic colleges), as well as members of Rongwo and Bao'an Townships' merchant communities (including Hui Muslims). Seemingly aware that momentous changes were at hand, these ad hoc representatives of Repgong's various constituencies accepted the Linggya chieftain's suggestion and quickly dispatched to Xunhua a thirty-seven-person "private" delegation tasked with welcoming the PLA to Repgong.[5]

Upon their arrival in Xunhua, the mission presented General Wang Zhen with "grain, horses, khatak [ceremonial scarves] and other gifts." Accepting the *khatak* (C. hada) but refusing the other items, Wang responded noncommittally to the delegates' purported request that troops be sent to Repgong to establish a new county government. Instead, like Tséring Gyel several days earlier, Wang Zhen instructed the delegates to ask Repgong's indigenous leadership to take personal responsibility for maintaining social order and protecting state property.[6] The general had little choice. The Chinese Communist Party was painfully aware that it had no preexisting organizational foundation in Qinghai.[7] Yet, by recognizing the authority of Repgong's traditional leadership, Wang Zhen and the CCP were also tapping into a long tradition of imperial-local relations that for centuries helped shape the region's political and social worlds.

Scholars of twentieth-century China have commented extensively upon the friction generated between champions of various versions of the Chinese nation-state and practices they perceived as backward, feudal, or traditional and therefore antithetical to their modernizing agendas. More recently they have also begun to appreciate the ways in which Chinese statesmen, many with well-known modernizing credentials, were at times forced to accommodate or appropriate what might be considered imperial strategies of rule in the service of nation building, a dynamic that Uradyn Bulag refers to as "subimperialism."[8] Following Bulag, this chapter employs the institutions of the Rongwo nangso, Rongwo Monastery, and the *qianbaihu zhidu* (system of one thousand and one hundred households) to examine the subimperial practices pursued in the Repgong area of Amdo by the Republican-era "Ma family warlords."

First, however, it provides a brief look at the development of these institutions from their founding in the thirteenth and fourteenth centuries during the Mongol Yuan Empire. Over the centuries, various imperial centers frequently invested members of Amdo's religious and secular leadership—including the Shartsang lineage of Rongwo Monastery, the Rongwo nangso, and a multitude of qianhu and baihu—with honors, titles, and rewards in exchange for expressions of loyalty and their service as intermediaries between the imperial state and local society. Rather than clearly demarcated institutions in perpetual competition, it might be best to think of authority in Amdo as operating within an integrated, syncretic, often conflict-ridden, but mutually authenticating web of personal and institutional relationships. This syncretism did not vanish in 1912 with the collapse of the imperial system. Instead, the new rulers of Amdo would reconstruct, if not quite replicate, imperial-style linkages with many members of the Amdo elite.

Lamas, Chieftains, Mongols, and Manchus

It is difficult to determine how sovereignty, territoriality, and political identity were historically experienced and understood by individuals and communities within Amdo and how these may have changed over time. However, certain generalizations can be made. Charlene Makley suggests that prior to the final destruction of Amdo's traditional political system in 1958, rulership often consisted of "patrifilial alliances between Tibetan lamas and lay male leaders."[9] Makley is referring on the one hand to the institution of the *trülku* (lit. "emanation body") and on the other to hereditary (usually) lay rulers of varying prominence and power.

Unique to Tibetan Buddhism, the trülku or incarnate lama refers to highly evolved Buddhist masters (usually understood to be earthly emanations of a bodhisattva) who—in distinction from the more mundane rebirths the rest of us experience—can both remember past lives and direct their future births "in order to continue their salvation project in a series of successive reincarnations."[10] In more temporal terms, by creating a mechanism through which religious authority is transferred across a series of lifetimes, a continuum is produced that can help preserve and expand religious prestige, political influence, and economic power that otherwise might dissipate or fragment with the death of a charismatic religious leader. Although there are sporadic recorded instances of individual trülku dating back to the eleventh century, the *trülku system*, which Peter Schwieger describes as "a fully established line of succession of ecclesiastical hierarchs," is generally considered to have emerged in Central Tibet during the late-thirteenth century. By the end of the sixteenth century, it had been adopted by all four major orders of Tibetan Buddhism, including the ascendant Gelukpa tradition—the order to which the Dalai Lamas and Panchen Lamas belong—which during the seventeenth century became the dominant sectarian force in Amdo. By then, generally speaking, the trülku had replaced the hereditary lay nobility at the pinnacle of Tibetan society.[11]

The relationship between monastic authority and lay chieftains could be quite complex and intertwined. In many but certainly not all cases, a headman and his chiefdom might owe direct or indirect fealty to a prominent trülku, such as the Jamyang Zhépa lineage of Labrang Monastery. It also was not uncommon for the reincarnation of a deceased lama to be found within an already notable noble family, thereby creating interwoven layers of monastic-lay authority. Moreover, the authority of a trülku and his monastery might be reinforced through the patronage, protection, and recognition of greater powers, including those in Amdo, Central Tibet, and, as is the focus in this chapter, the Mongol Yuan, Chinese Ming, and Manchu Qing Empires. At the same time, China-based imperial states often recognized lay headmen as hereditary leaders of their chiefdoms, what in Chinese were referred to as qianhu (T. *tongpön*), or leader of one thousand households, and baihu (T. *gyapön*), or leader of one hundred households, designations that could both reflect and affect local power relations. Although the qianbaihu zhidu is unique to Amdo and parts of northern Kham, modern Chinese sources generally consider it a subcategory of the better-known *tusi zhidu*, or "native chieftain system," a practice of indirect rule commonly deployed on China's southern and southwestern ethnocultural frontiers. Nonetheless, the qianbaihu system had distinct origins in the Mongol Yuan Empire and in turn most likely developed from the decimal-based system of military and social organization that had long existed in Inner Asia.[12]

In fact, the origins of the qianbaihu system, the Rongwo nangso, and Rongwo Monastery are intertwined and inextricably linked to the thirteenth-century inclusion of the Amdo region into the expanding Mongol Empire. In 1235, Köten Khan, second son of the great khan Ögedei and after 1241 younger brother of the great khan Güyüg, led an expeditionary force through the Sino-Tibetan border regions, reaching as far south as Sichuan. After returning north, Köten was invested with a hereditary appanage at the old Minyak trading town of Liangzhou (near present-day Wuwei, Gansu), giving the Mongols a permanent base on the edge of the Tibetan Plateau.[13]

FIGURE 2. Elderly trülku and three monks, Southern Gansu. Joseph Rock, 1926, courtesy of Harvard-Yenching Library.

As early as 1253 but perhaps not until after Köten's cousin Qubilai proclaimed himself great khan in 1260, a "pacification commission" was established at Hezhou (present-day Linxia) to oversee Amdo and neighboring districts.[14] In today's Repgong region, the Mongols invested the leader of what apparently was the area's most powerful local clan, the Awar Téu, with imperial recognition as the head of the Bili Wanhufu.[15] Meaning something akin to "Bili Ten-Thousand-Household Brigade," it had at least nominal authority over the regions south of the Yellow River in current-day Huangnan and Hainan (T. Tsolho) Prefectures. Below the Awar headman, the Mongols recognized local chieftains as qianhu and baihu, marking the introduction of the qianbaihu system into Amdo.[16]

In 1264, a Tibetan Buddhist missionary named Lharjé Draknawa is said to have arrived in the Repgong area with his three sons and as many as thirty clansmen. An "accomplished Buddhist master and medical practitioner," he had been dispatched by Qubilai Khan's newly designated state preceptor (*guoshi*) and leader of the Sakya order of Tibetan Buddhism, the Pakpa Lama, "to spread the Dharma and rule over Rebgong."[17] It appears that by dint of Lharjé Draknawa's connections with the imperial throne and the ascendant Sakya tradition, by leveraging his family's knowledge and patronage of religion and medicine, and by forging marital alliances with local leaders, under his son Dodé Bum and nine grandchildren the clan quickly consolidated authority over the Repgong region.[18]

It was from within this convergence of imperial rule, sectarian concerns, and local context that the institution of Rongwo nangso first appeared. Calling it "a completely distinctive development in the history of Tibetan regional administrative positions," Qin Shijin notes that the particulars regarding the origins, jurisdiction, and authority associated with the nangso title remain unclear.[19] The term seems to have originated in Central Tibet, perhaps coming east with Lharjé Draknawa himself, who may have functioned as an official of the Sakya state. Sonam Tsering maintains that in the early fourteenth century, Dodé Bum was invited to the Yuan capital where he was recognized as the first Rongwo nangso. However, the title would not appear in Chinese-language sources for another century, and it may be that the nangso title was used locally or in intra-Tibetan contexts but not in the bureaucratic language of the Yuan court. In any case, Dodé Bum's third son would serve as a religious adviser to the Mongol emperor and in 1333 was himself named state preceptor. In 1342, on land donated by the indigenous headman and father-in-law of Dodé Bum, Sakyil Tabéhu, Dodé Bum's eldest son founded Rongwo Déchen Chökorling (hereafter Rongwo Monastery), at that time devoted to the Sakya tradition of Tibetan Buddhism.[20]

While the qianbaihu zhidu, Rongwo nangso, and Rongwo Monastery each were established during the extension of Mongol military-administrative power over the Amdo region, each would outlive the Yuan, in part by hitching their fortunes to other sources of authority. This included but was not limited to that which emanated from Beijing. While the actual ability of the imperial center to intercede in local affairs waxed and waned from the fourteenth century to the twentieth, receiving the imprimatur of the throne apparently never entirely lost its majesty. During the Ming dynasty (1368–1644), Beijing's ability to directly intervene in Amdo was largely limited to regulation of the famous tea and horse trade, the uneven maintenance of several frontier garrisons, and the issuance of titles and rewards.[21] On four occasions (1373, 1403, 1404, and 1406), the early Ming court conferred titles on successive leaders of the Awar Téu clan, while the descendants of Lhajé Draknawa and Dodé Bum continued to receive honors throughout the Ming period, in particular as state preceptor.[22] All the while, members of the clan continued to receive titles from Central Tibetan authorities as well.[23]

By the mid-Ming, the house of the Rongwo nangso had eclipsed that of the original Bili wanhu, the Awar Téu clan. This is not to suggest, however, that it owed its position solely to Ming support and patronage. Qin Shijin, for one, suggests that the rise of the Rongwo nangso occurred not because of imperial patronage but in the vacuum left by the diminished reach of the Ming state. In other words, the Ming's recognition and rewarding of the Rongwo nangso clan was made from a position of weakness, not strength. However, Qin does note that the two were mutually reinforcing. The Ming recognized the growing power of the nangso by granting its holder the title *daguoshi* (great state preceptor), which in turn may have helped elevate the local position of the nangso and his lineage above potential rivals.[24] While perhaps not well integrated from the perspective of the modern, consolidated nation-state, from the perspective of empire the long-term relationship between imperial center and local elites largely maintained the mutually imperative objectives of imbuing local actors with imperial authority while providing the crown with imperial grace and grandeur, the ritualistic bonds of loyalty between local leaders and the imperial core that is central to imperial formations.

None of this is to imply that at any given time the relationship between Amdo elites and imperial centers was necessarily harmonious. Far from it. Amdo's history was often marked by considerable intraimperial violence. And I certainly do not contend that Amdo's history should be viewed through paradigms of stasis or equilibrium. Along with a multitude of more subtle shifts, over the centuries several significant developments sent shock waves through Amdo's political and social worlds.[25] Among them was the reintroduction of Mongol military might (Tümed and Khoshud Mongols in the sixteenth and seventeenth centuries), during which time the lineage of the Shartsang Lama was established and Rongwo Monastery converted to the Geluk tradition of Tibetan Buddhism (1630); the

establishment of the Lhasa-based Ganden Podrang government of the Dalai Lamas (1642) and the expansion and institutionalization of the Geluk order in
Amdo (seventeenth and eighteenth centuries);[26] and the tremendous violence
that accompanied the region's final submission to the Manchu Qing Empire following the rebellion of the Khoshud Mongol prince Lubsang-Danzin (1723).[27]

Faced with evidence of the loose loyalties of Amdo's monastic establishment
and pastoral population, the Qing responded to the rebellion with a scorched-
earth campaign against suspect monasteries and communities, established the
office of the *amban* (imperial commissioner) in Xining to oversee Tibetan and
Mongol affairs, and twice implemented major reorganizations of the qianbaihu
system (1726, 1822). The Qing would go on to foster a new generation of political and religious authorities while pumping vast amounts of resources into
approved religious institutions.[28] The result was to strengthen the imperial bond
between the Qing center and many among Amdo's political-religious elite, while
shoring up Gelukpa institutional strength in the region. For instance, Rongwo
Monastery may have survived the worst of the violence due to a personal connection between the Second Shartsang Lama (1678–1739) and the family of the
Khoshud Mongol prince, Erdeni Jinong, who had remained loyal to the Qing
during the rebellion. For this loyalty, in 1725, Erdeni Jinong was rewarded the
title of *qinwang* (prince of the first rank). From their homeland on the Sokpo
grasslands south of present-day Zeku County, the qinwang and his descendants
would remain important regional political and economic actors into the twentieth century.[29] Likewise, the Third Shartsang Lama (1740–94) received Qing titles
through the auspices of Chankya Rölpé Dorjé, an Amdowa trülku who became
the most influential religious figure at the court of the Qianlong Emperor (r.
1735–1796/1799). In fact, the next three incarnations of the Shartsang lineage
were discovered in Rölpé Dorjé's family. Of course, the Third Shartsang Lama
also traveled to Lhasa where he received titles from the Eighth Dalai Lama. Authority clearly flowed in multiple directions.[30] It should be noted that despite
the Gelukpa's institutional dominance, the Nyingma order of Tibetan Buddhism
would develop a significant presence in the Repgong region as well, including the
grasslands that eventually would become Zeku County.[31]

A short bureaucratic report regarding the 1875 transmission of the Gönshül
chiefdom's (present-day Zeku County) qianhu title from deceased father to his
son, Sönam Bum, helps illustrate the syncretic and often mutually authenticating nature of authority that existed in Amdo. What makes the exchange particularly interesting is that for a number of years the court had not acted to fill
the vacancy. This is unsurprising. At the time, Qing armies had only recently
put down a massive uprising in the northwest—sometimes referred to as the
Tungan or Muslim Rebellion (1863–75)—that at its height had stretched well

into the Amdo borderlands.[32] With the Qing court understandably distracted, the Gönshül situation was remedied through the lobbying of a particularly prominent Rongwo nangso, known as Nangso Khanak. In a petition sent to the Qing's Xunhua Subprefecture (which administered much of eastern Amdo, including Repgong), Nangso Khanak argued that following the death of his father, Sönam Bum had faithfully attended to all of the qianhu responsibilities, including effectively restraining members of his chiefdom from engaging in the endemic grassland feuds that over the previous decades had devastated Amdo's social and economic landscape. After an investigation into Sönam Bum's worthiness, the court presented him permits and seals as the Gönshül qianhu.[33]

The 2005 edition of the *Zeku County Gazetteer* (*Zeku Xianzhi*) contains Xunhua Subprefecture's recommendation in support of Sönam Bum, an inclusion surely meant to demonstrate Amdo's enduring submission to national sovereignty. Arguably, however, it instead illustrates the loose control, administrative flexibility, and relative reciprocity inherent to these types of imperial borderlands. As Charles Tilly and others have noted, when empires are most effective, it tends not to be because of their ability to dictate the details of rule over subordinate components.[34] While in 1875 the Qing may or may not have had the ability to aggressively insert itself into the region's local affairs, the important thing to note—at least in this case—is that it did not have to. After all, what the late-Qing court likely valued most in a local power holder was formal expressions of loyalty and the ability to deliver relative peace and order. On the other hand, even when the state was too preoccupied or incapacitated to exercise its imperial prerogatives, local leaders might seek recognition to reinforce their own claims of legitimacy.

Unsurprisingly, when the imperial system collapsed in 1912, this syncretic nexus of authority that had developed in Amdo over centuries did not immediately lose its cultural relevance, moral authority, or pragmatic appeal. Instead, as both local elites and aspiring state and nation builders maneuvered within rapidly shifting political and epistemological contexts, they often fell back on imperial-style precedents.

Amdo under the "Ma Family Warlords"

Despite the successful 1875 petition on behalf of Sönam Bum, by the latter half of the nineteenth century Amdo was party to many of the same trends affecting other parts of the Qing Empire, including the devolution of power from Beijing to regional centers. Drawing from the seminal work of Jonathan Lipman, Susette Cooke notes that one of the "paradoxical consequences" of the great Muslim rebellions that struck northwest China after 1860 was the rise of Hui Muslim military might and political power.[35] In exchange for supporting the throne against their more recalcitrant coreligionists, the Qing appointed certain local Hui leaders to civil-military offices. Most successful was the Ma clan of Hezhou (Linxia), which from the 1880s "was able to consolidate a commanding regional power-base, legitimized by imperial mandate and local prestige alike."[36] Andrew Fischer adds, "For the first time in the history of Amdo, local Tibetans were surpassed by local Muslims in strategic alliance and military strength."[37]

After 1912, with the acquiescence of the fledgling Republican government and later the Guomindang of Chiang Kaishek, one branch of the Hezhou Mas would come to dominate Qinghai. PRC sources are brimming with testimonials to the brutality of the "Ma family warlords" and their agents, particularly at the expense of the region's Tibetan population. Special scorn is reserved for the clan's third and final paramount leader, Ma Bufang, his ethnic and religious pogroms said to have severely damaged the historical unity between the nationalities. Scholars have not been especially kind to the Mas either, in general painting them as violent and petty militarists. Several have highlighted the Islamic nature of Ma-family rule, one referring to the regime as "a separate, and Islamic, state-within-a state in Qinghai under the Republic."[38]

To a large degree these portrayals are warranted. Confrontation between the Mas and their rivals, no matter the ethnicity or religion, was often marked by tremendous cruelty and bitter recriminations.[39] However, the Ma regime was also an aspiring centralizing and modernizing state that sought to do many of the things that such states seek to do. This included building schools and roads, regulating commerce, engaging in demographic, ethnographic, and geological surveys, attempting to enforce the state's monopoly on violence, and rationalizing bureaucratic rule over a contiguous territory by eliminating the autonomous spaces that often exist within premodern polities.[40] Taking particular note of Ma Bufang's ambitious sanitation, irrigation, education, and beautification programs, the American reporter and scholar A. Doak Barnett once described Ma's Xining regime as "authoritarian, militaristic, and autonomous" yet "one of the most efficient in China, and one of the most energetic."[41] A second American observer, John Roderick, a journalist known best for reporting from the CCP's wartime base at Yan'an, went even further, painting Ma as "a somewhat enlightened warlord" and even "something of a socialist."[42] Of course, not all commentators were as generous to the Mas. In what was once a well-known travel account, the spy and adventurer Leonard Clark referred to Ma Bufang as "the terrible chief of a good section of those little-known ten million Chinese Moslems."[43] Nor were all Muslims equal beneficiaries of Ma rule. One nearly contemporaneous report suggests that by "using military force to push modern social reform," Ma produced "a good deal of resentment" within local Muslim communities.[44]

Upon closer inspection, discord between Xining and local actors was as likely to be rooted in the fiscal and logistical demands of an expanding state as it was a pure reflection of interethnic or interconfessional hatred.[45] Yet, despite their centralizing instincts, time and again the Mas were forced to forge subimperial accommodations with an assortment of the region's religious and secular authorities, often the same people and institutions that for centuries had served as intermediaries between the imperial state and local communities. Most visibly, each autumn the Mas presided over a large ceremony on the banks of Qinghai Lake to placate the "god of Kökönuur." Since the Qing's suppression of the Lubsang-Danzin Rebellion three centuries earlier, this state-sponsored ritual had aimed to assure Mongol loyalty to the imperial throne. Now, in front of large gatherings of officials, lamas, and headmen, it instead sought to ensure their loyalty to the multiethnic Republic of China.[46]

In fact, under the Mas, many local elites and institutions continued to function as intermediaries in a negotiated space between the state and local society, one often subject to great levels of violence but also degrees of reciprocity. The Qing's reliance on local elites had been a quintessential example of imperial practice, in Tilly's words, "because it holds together disparate smaller-scale units without requiring much centrally-controlled internal transformation."[47] By contrast—and not unlike the frontier policies of the Guomindang more generally—the Mas often had little choice.[48] As the Japanese spy Hisao Kimura would later reflect with some astonishment when talking about Ma Bufang's procurement of a Tibetan lama's release from captivity in Lanzhou, "This in fact was a move typical of Ma, an extremely pragmatic Muslim with a large Buddhist population to govern."[49]

A particularly illustrative example was a well-known tax dispute in the early 1930s between the Ma regime and the Nangra Tibetans under their headman Wangchen Döndrup. Three times from 1931 to 1934, Ma's soldiers laid siege to the Nangra region, and three times the Nangra Tibetans forced them to withdraw after heavy fighting and significant casualties on both sides.[50] In the end, the conflict was resolved through the mediation of an influential lama, the Third Gurong Gyelsé Rinpoché, and the powerful leader of the Qinghai Lake–region Tibetans, Zongqianhu Kangtsé Welzang. In Xining, Wangchen Döndrup and Ma Bufang pledged an oath of brotherhood. The Tibetan headman then joined the Muslim warlord's government as an "adviser" (canyi) and subsequently was appointed commander of Ma's Third Defense Battalion and leader of Nangra District (xiang).[51] All of these positions appear to have been more ceremonial than substantive. The advisory position seems to refer to a seat on the Qinghai Provincial Advisory Committee, which was founded at the behest of the Guomindang leadership in Nanjing and dominated by Ma Bufang's close associates.[52] Meanwhile, the Third Battalion most likely consisted of members of Wangchen Döndrup's chiefdom, and Nangra District seems to have existed largely on Xining's drafting tables. Not unlike during the imperial period, these were gestures that acknowledged and reinforced Wangchen Döndrup's local prestige while ostensibly co-opting him into the regime.

To take another example, in 1924, six hundred and fifty years after his ancestors first settled in the Repgong region, establishing both the office of the Rongwo nangso and Rongwo Monastery, Trashi Namgyel was born into the hereditary nangso family. His elder brother then serving as nangso, in 1945 Trashi Namgyel was sent to the provincial capital. There he joined Ma Bufang's retinue as a military officer and translator. Trashi Namgyel would later insist that his presence in Xining amounted to little more than human collateral.[53] In truth, Ma's goal was likely twofold. On the one hand, he did use physical control over the scions of Amdo's noble houses to assure their families' continued compliance. On the other, through institutions such as Xining's Mongol-Tibetan School (est. 1937; Meng Zang Xiaoxue) and the subsequent appointment of graduates to positions within his administration and military, Ma also hoped to groom a loyal generation of indigenous leaders. For instance, Chöbum Gyel, son of the qianhu of the pastoral Tibetan Atsok chiefdom, admits that through this process he became Ma's "follower" (zuoyou; suicong). With Ma's blessing, Chöbum Gyel later succeeded his father as Atsok qianhu.[54] Likewise, when his elder brother passed away, Trashi Namgyel returned home to become what turned out to be the last in the nearly seven-century line of the Rongwo nangso.[55]

These encounters are representative of a broader pattern in which Xining retained the imperial prerogative to grant titles, offer recognition, and at times provide material support to Amdo's secular and religious leadership in exchange for varying degrees of cooperation and compliance. This does not imply that these relationships were equitable or noncoercive. To the contrary, many local elites likely would have preferred to stay distant from the Ma regime. In the far south of Amdo, for example, the Mas waged years of bloody campaigns against the determined resistance of some Golok communities.[56] Yet, as this possibility became increasingly untenable in the course of the early twentieth century, others often discovered that reaching an accommodation with Xining was not only preferable to confrontation but could also bring tangible benefits to themselves as well as their various constituencies.

While the details remain hazy, this seems to have been the case with Rongwo Monastery and the Shartsang lineage. In 1919, Ma Bufang's father, Ma Qi, had detained the recently discovered Seventh Shartsang Lama, subsequently ransoming the four-year-old lama "back" to the Twelve Tribes of Repgong. For this and future offenses, CCP sources portray the Shartsang Lama as a victim of "the Ma clan's oppression, many times personally experiencing suffering, catastrophe and humiliation."[57] Again, this characterization is not unwarranted. As an offshoot of Ma Qi's wider efforts to consolidate his position against both local power holders and interregional rivals, throughout the 1920s Xining subjected the Repgong region to considerable violence and extortion. In the late 1930s, Repgong again found itself on the wrong end of the Ma family's bayonets. This time the proximate cause seems to have been competition over resources (especially timber) and tax revenue. Although Rongwo Monastery itself was apparently not targeted, several other monasteries were damaged or destroyed by Ma Bufang's forces.[58]

The relationship between Rongwo Monastery and Xining appears to have taken a turn for the better in the early 1940s. This was around the time of the Seventh Shartsang Lama's full ordination and his assumption of personal leadership over the monastery. It was also at this time that his younger brother Gélek Gyatso was made the monastery's chief steward, "devoting himself to assisting the Shartsang Lama in managing the day-to-day political and religious affairs [of the monastery]."[59] Apparently Gélek Gyatso's duties included repairing the monastery's frayed relationship with the Xining regime, a mission that was formally consummated in 1946 when Gélek Gyatso officially joined the Ma Bufang–affiliated Guomindang.

A short anecdote regarding the third member of Tongren County's "three-in-one feudal rulership," Zongqianhu Gyelwo Dorjé, may offer clues as to the motivations that led both Rongwo Monastery and the Ma regime to forge closer ties. The *zongqianhu* (panchiefdom headman) title was a product of the post–Lubsang-Danzin Rebellion systemization of the qianbaihu zhidu. However, in the years since, it only had been bestowed intermittently. In 1932, Ma Bufang recognized Gyelwo Dorjé's leadership of the Gyelwo chiefdom and zongqianhu of the entire Repgong region. As with the Nangra's Wangchen Döndrup, Gyelwo Dorjé was subsequently appointed "adviser" to the provincial government. And like Gélek Gyatso and many other members of the Amdo elite, soon after he is said to have joined the Guomindang.[60]

It is uncertain why, of all the region's prominent Tibetan figures, Gyelwo Dorjé was chosen as one of only two headmen recognized as zongqianhu during the Republican period (the other being the aforementioned Kangtsé Welzang). Yet it seems clear that by forging an alliance of sorts with Dorjé and his Gyelwo chiefdom, Ma Bufang intended to influence the local balance of power. Several sources note that around this time, Ma intervened in a violent, decades-long "grassland dispute" (*caoyuan jiufen*) between the Gyelwo and the Gengya Tibetans. The latter resided across the Gansu border and were traditionally considered subjects of Labrang Monastery, Amdo's largest and most prominent monastic institution.[61]

Hardly the disinterested mediator, Ma reportedly confirmed the Gyelwo's owner-ship of the disputed grassland while providing Dorjé with one hundred rifles and ten thousand rounds of ammunition.[62] Perhaps not coincidentally, Labrang had been a regional competitor with Ma's Xining regime and even longer a financial, spiritual, and political rival of Rongwo Monastery.

In fact, it is difficult to locate a prominent secular Tibetan or Mongol leader in eastern Qinghai (and only slightly less so for religious elites) who was not in some manner complicit with the Ma regime. None of this is to suggest that the Mas acted in good faith and partnership with local leaders or vice versa. How-ever, examples such as these should remind us not to assume clearly demarcated divisions between indigenous authorities and state institutions or that cultural systems are autarkic or exclusive. After all, Muslims were not a new addition to the Amdo region, even if Muslim political and military power was a relatively recent phenomenon. Instead, Ma Bufang and his government were implicitly accepted as a legitimate component of Amdo's evolving but still intact syncretic nexus, even as his authority might simultaneously have been contested.

The "Zeku Region" under Ma Bufang

The complex web of relationships between Ma Bufang and local elites such as Trashi Namgyel, Gyelwo Dorjé, Gélek Gyatso, and Wangchen Döndrup are in-dicative of a political environment in which a nascent bureaucratic structure thinly cloaked a political landscape more reflective of a prenational, imperial-style formation than that of a centralized state. Qinghai Province itself had been officially founded only in 1929 as part of the ascendant Guomindang regime's administrative reorganization of north and northwest China. That same year, Tongren County was carved out of the old Xunhua Subprefecture. Then, in 1932 Tongren was divided into subcounty districts (qu). What is often anachronisti-cally referred to as the "Zeku Region" (Zeku Qu)—an ill-defined pastoral area up the Rongwo River and across the mountains southwest of Repgong's agricultural heartland—was designated the county's Fourth District. Nevertheless, there is no indication that a parallel bureaucratic infrastructure was established. Instead, as far as can be told, the Fourth District existed largely on paper.[63]

In partial response to the threat from Communist forces during the Red Ar-my's famous Long March, beginning in 1935 the Xining government moved to tighten its control over southern Qinghai. In many agricultural districts, vestiges of the old "tusi" native headman system were replaced by subdistrict townships and rural xiang, as well as the baojia community responsibility system. However, rather than centrally appointed officials, local headmen were made leaders of these new administrative units.[64] Simultaneously, the Xining government divided Qinghai into fifteen regional defense districts. Tongren and Xunhua Counties were jointly designated the Fourth Defense District. As with the bureaucratic reforms, Ma appointed local leaders to head these quasi-state forces. Tongren County, for instance, was subdivided into four cavalry corps, each commanded by a Tibetan headman, including Gyelwo Dorjé and the then Rongwo nangso. As noted, in neighboring Guide (T. Trika) County, the Nangra's Wangchen Döndrup was named commander of the Third Battalion.[65]

In pastoral areas, the administrative and military reorganization was even more nominal. As one source explains, "at the time the baojia system was being implemented in agricultural regions, the pastoral regions continued to follow the old system of qianhu and baihu rule."[66] In the remote grasslands that would become Zeku County, Xining appointed Tibetan headman from the area's two largest chiefdoms as commander and deputy commander of what Chinese accounts call a "militia regiment."[67] The commander, Lhagyel, was both an incarnate Nyingma lama and scion of the ruling family of the largest confederated chiefdom in the area, the Hor. Lhagyel had recently traveled to the provincial capital where, like several of his contemporaries, he received the position "advisor to the provincial government" and joined the Guomindang.[68] His "deputy," Serökyap, was qianhu of the Hor's frequent rival, the Gönshül chiefdom. Despite language found in secondary sources that suggest centralized command, it is doubtful that there was much if any coordination between the two chieftains.[69] From the perspective of the nation-state, the appointments of local headmen as district heads and militia commanders demonstrates Ma Bufang's continued dependence on nonstate (or quasi-state) actors even for basic functions that are often assumed to be the sole purview of the state. The ambiguity goes both ways, however, and local elites such as Lhagyel and Serökyap were surely acting in a space between autonomy and dependence in which threats of or actual coercion, as well as the benefits of cooperation with and recognition by the Xining regime, were far from inconsequential.

In fact, nearly every major figure on the grasslands of what would become Zeku County was, in one fashion or another, associated with Ma Bufang. For example, CCP sources describe the Gönshül's Serökyap as having been born into a wealthy "herdlord" (*muzhu*) family. In 1940, he reportedly joined the Guomindang and was appointed to the now familiar position of "advisor to the provincial government." In 1945, Ma Bufang presented Serökyap with a wooden bell and seal recognizing him as qianhu of the Gönshül chiefdom. Two years later, subcounty pastoral districts having finally (if nominally) been established, Serökyap was appointed leader of Guanxiu (Gönshül) District.[70] In another instance, Zongqianhu Gyelwo Dorjé is said to have brought Lubum of the Gartsé chiefdom, the third largest in the Zeku region, for a 1936 audience with Ma Bufang. A distinguished monk of uncertain background, while in Xining Lubum seems to have joined the Guomindang and at least ostensibly served in Ma's government (*banshiyuan*). In 1946, Ma appointed Lubum leader of Guanshize (Gartsé) District, while simultaneously recognizing him as disciplinary head (T. *gékö*, C. *gegui*) of Gartsé Monastery and qianhu of the Gartsé chiefdom.[71]

As with Nangso Trashi Namgyel, Zongqianhu Gyelwo Dorjé, and others, it is difficult to determine the role Ma Bufang played in the selection of Serökyap and Lubum as leaders of their communities. To what degree was Ma either confirming candidates already chosen by internal methods or dictating their appointments? Or perhaps this is the wrong question. While it is natural to think that the Gönshül, for instance, would have chaffed at the interference of Ma's regime into their internal affairs, Gönshül headmen may have viewed Serökyap's association with Ma Bufang and the Guomindang more ambivalently. Just as in 1875 when Rongwo nangso Khanak requested that the Qing court recognize Serökyap's distant predecessor Sönam Bum as qianhu of the Gönshül chiefdom—and clearly the inclusion of both Sönam Bum and Serökyap's appointments in Chinese sources is meant to emphasize this—accepted methods of succession may have included receiving the imprimatur of state authorities, even if at times that approval may have been a fait accompli.[72] After all, authority in Amdo was not a zero-sum equation. Instead, actors operated within a complex, evolving, yet historically rooted nexus of authority.

Approached from this perspective, Ma Bufang was one of many powerful figures working within a wider web at the liminal and temporal edges of empire. As Lipman notes, "the 'Ma family warlords' represent a new development in the Muslim worlds of northwest China, the modern nation-state's incorporative power expressed locally through cooption of existing elites."[73] In this formulation, Ma Bufang himself becomes the indigenous headman in the central elite-peripheral elite relationship that structurally defines empire. This is not to say that the Guomindang state was an empire—just that out of necessity it was drawing on imperial practices. Nor is it to suggest that relations between the Ma family and local elements were not antagonistic. Clearly, they often were—as was Ma Bufang's relationship with Chiang Kaishek and the Guomindang. Bulag notes, for instance, that at times Ma Bufang was forced to defend his nationalist credentials against accusations of feudalism and warlordism while at others he was able "play the Mongol and Tibetan card" to insist that his domination over Qinghai made him a patriot and a champion of national unity.[74] However, amity and equilibrium are not what define (sub)imperial space, nor does their absence necessarily preclude the existence of an imperial relationship. Instead, as Tilly has pointed out, it is simply the difference between a well-functioning empire and one in transition or turmoil.[75]

Hor Qianhu Wagya and Collaboration at the Edge of Empire

These tensions are demonstrated well by Lhagyel and his elder brother Wagya, qianhu of the Hor chiefdom. Not only was Wagya among the wealthiest individuals in the region, but his "prestige" (*weiwang*) was also said to extend throughout southern Qinghai and across the provincial border into nearby Tibetan regions of southern Gansu.[76] Various sources claim that in addition to his brother Lhagyel, three of Wagya's sons and at least two nephews had been recognized as "living Buddhas" (i.e., trülku), leading Chinese commentators to hold the clan up as an example of the "feudal" nature of Amdo's social and political structure that allowed for the collection of secular and religious authority in one family.[77]

Given the Hor leader's regional prominence, it is unsurprising that Wagya was deeply enmeshed in the interchiefdom politics of southern Amdo, particularly as they intersected with state interests. An official biography puts Wagya in the same circles as many of the region's top power brokers, noting, "at the time he had a close relationship with Ma Bufang, Ma Yuanhai, Ma Yuanxiang, Huang Wenyuan,[78] [the Seventh] Shartsang, [Zongqianhu Gyelwo] Dorjé, the Rongwo Nangso and other distinguished members of [Amdo's] military, political and religious spheres."[79] This reality, and the precarious situations it could sometimes lead to, is underscored by a story Wagya and Lhagyel would pen decades later. The incident in question revolved around Wagya's attempts to mediate a 1937 tax dispute between the Xining regime and a subunit of the Hor, the Détsang tsowa. In short, when the Détsang refused to pay arrears they felt Xining had levied unfairly, the commander of Ma Bufang's southern forces, Ma Yuanhai, approached Wagya with an ultimatum. Ma Yuanhai ordered the Hor qianhu to convince the Détsang to surrender. Otherwise, he warned, the Détsang would be "exterminated." True to his word, when the Détsang leadership rebuffed Wagya's efforts, Ma Yuanhai unleashed his soldiers. The battle lasted a full day, with both sides suffering heavy casualties. The Détsang's spirited defense apparently enraged General Ma. The following day, forty Détsang prisoners were executed. According to the account, among them were men, women and children, including Wagya's own son-in-law, whose severed head was presented to his parents for identification.[80]

The Détsang incident is included among Chinese sources to emphasize the depravity and greed of Ma Bufang and his lieutenants as well as the subordination of the region to their rule, all of which it accomplishes quite well. Conversely, however, the narrative ends with a passage that manages to highlight the incomplete status of Ma's state-building ambitions and instead reveals the broad contours of an ongoing subimperial relationship between Amdo's local leadership and Ma Bufang. A month after the confrontation, Lhagyel led leaders of the Hor to Xining for an audience with Ma Bufang. There, through a reversion to tactics more familiar to imperial borderlands than modern, centralized states, a conclusion to the Détsang incident was reached. The Hor delegates admitted the guilt (*renzui*) of the Détsang and presented Ma with horses and Tibetan carpets of the highest quality. Then, in exchange for allowing the downtrodden Détsang to return to their pastures, Lhagyel and the other Hor headmen offered to pay the Détsang's tax arrears and fines. This act of contrition apparently appeased Ma, who presented each chieftain with a rifle and arranged the release of the sole remaining imprisoned Détsang headman.[81]

While Wagya and Lhagyel use the Détsang incident to retroactively assert "the increasingly cruel rule of Ma Bufang and Ma Yuanhai over us headmen and the masses," other sources would note Wagya's involvement with the Ma Bufang regime that continued up until the eve of "Liberation."[82] In late August 1949, as the PLA prepared to ford the Yellow River, Wagya did not send representatives to Xunhua along with the Rongwo delegation. Instead, he personally traveled to Labrang, the great monastic center, trading depot, and cultural crossroads located across the Gansu border. There, in an act of submission that was being played out time and again across Amdo and elsewhere, Wagya bestowed gifts upon victorious units of the PLA, much as his brother had done a decade prior in Xining.[83] As detailed in the subsequent chapters, for the next decade Wagya would work closely with the CCP, acting as the primary conduit between the Party and the Zeku grasslands.

Like Repgong's "three-in-one feudal leadership," Nangra qianhu Wangchen Döndrup, and so many others, Wagya has been canonized in reform-era narratives of Amdo's "early-Liberation period." In these treatments, Wagya's cooperation with the CCP is celebrated as a great victory for the Party's nationalities policy, while his earlier association with Ma Bufang and the GMD is excused as the result of the poisonous influence of Ma's reactionary rule. This neat bifurcation, however, ignores the political acumen of people like Wagya who had long experience dealing with multiple interests and powers across the region. Moreover, it obfuscates the contentious and delicate relationship between the Party and local leaders that would exist throughout the 1950s.

Since at least the Second World War, when various European governments or puppet regimes came to terms with Nazi Germany, "collaboration"—the act of betraying one's nation to another—has become something of an ultimate sin.

However, it only becomes necessary to think in binary divisions between collaboration and resistance when uneven temporalities and overlapping sovereignties are replaced by unitary notions of the nation-state. As Rana Mitter has pointed out when speaking of the vast gray space in which imperial power intersected with lived experience in Japanese-occupied northeast China, collaboration occurred within a context in which many Chinese elites were still operating in broadly imperial terms. Instead of anomalies that belie and betray more common society-wide patterns of resistance—as national remembering would often have it—Mitter argues that collaboration is in fact the "'bargain' between two sides at the empire's periphery."[84] To put it another way, without collaboration there cannot be empire.

Given the necessity of procuring the cooperation of non-Han elites, in the years after 1949 the CCP could not hope but strike similar imperial-style "bargains" on its peripheries. This collaboration, which from the Party's perspective transgressed not national loyalties but class loyalties, would be codified and justified under the rubric of the United Front. More problematic for some observers is the post-1949 collusion between minority elites and the Chinese Communist state. Yet, as this chapter shows, a longer-term frame of reference suggests that men such as Wagya, Wangchen Döndrup, Trashi Namgyel, Gélek Gyatso, Gyelwo Dorjé, and many others were neither patriots nor quislings but instead were fulfilling roles that had traditionally been both their prerogative and responsibility. As explored further in the following chapter, perhaps to understand the participation of many indigenous Tibetan leaders in the "post-Liberation" regime, their actions must too be understood within the logic of empire in which collaboration, shorn of its unequivocally pejorative associations, was a strategy of survival that was fully integrated into the operable mechanisms of authority that existed in Amdo and elsewhere. In this sense, Wagya—and other "collaborators" like him—might instead be considered "rational actors in the dynamics of empire."[85]

IF YOU KILL THE COUNTY HEAD, HOW WILL I EXPLAIN IT TO THE COMMUNIST PARTY?

Like Wagya, Lhündrup Gyel had a complicated relationship with the Ma Bufang regime. Born around 1903, he was the only son of the headman of the Kéwa tsowa, a politically weak and economically distressed Tibetan chiefdom in present-day Guide County. According to his own account, for decades a more formidable neighbor had preyed upon the Kéwa. During the late imperial period, this had required the Kéwa to forge patron-client alliances with other Tibetan chiefdoms. In the Republican era, it meant seeking the protection of "the prince of Guide," Ma Yuanhai.[1]

A cousin and subordinate of Ma Bufang, Ma Yuanhai was the most powerful figure in the vast territories south of Qinghai Lake. Protagonist of the Détsang incident outlined in the previous chapter, not only did Ma command the area's largest military force, but—through his control over vast tracts of grasslands and herds of livestock—he was also the dominant economic power on the grasslands of southern Qinghai. Like his cousin Ma Bufang, Ma Yuanhai is uniformly portrayed in PRC sources in the darkest terms, accusing him of massacring pastoralists, looting monasteries, extracting natural resources for his personal gain, and "causing great misery to the great majority of the pastoral region's peoples."[2] And, as with his cousin, the allegations undoubtedly have much merit. However, Ma Yuanhai was also Lhündrup Gyel's benefactor and protector, an integral component in the web of authority that existed in Republican-era southern Amdo.

Of course, Ma Yuanhai's support for Lhündrup Gyel came with reciprocal obligations. This included tax collection, road construction, and militia duties. In 1936, for example, as part of a larger mobilization meant to counter movements of the Red Army, Ma Yuanhai ordered Lhündrup Gyel to lead a Kéwa militia south into the grasslands of present-day Zeku County. After a month spent on the banks of the Tséchu River, Lhündrup Gyel and his fighters returned home, having never set eyes on their mysterious foes.[3]

Nearly fifteen years later, Ma Yuanhai again ordered Lhündrup Gyel to lead a militia against approaching Communist forces. This time, well before his men reached the front lines, word came that the battle was already lost. Ma Bufang fled on August 27, and Ma Yuanhai was captured two months later.[4] As objectionable as Ma Yuanhai may have been, Lhündrup Gyel had lost his patron. What were his options now? He could flee, fight, or hope to reach a tolerable accommodation with the incoming regime—much as he had previously with the Ma clan. This was not a quandary Lhündrup Gyel faced alone. The arrival of the Chinese Communist Party meant that complex regional dynamics needed to be renegotiated as an imperial frontier slipped toward final incorporation into the modern Chinese state. Despite the suspect class background of people like Lhündrup Gyel and their prior collusion with the Mas, this was possible because of the CCP's guiding policies in minority regions like Amdo—policies that de-emphasized class struggle in favor of forming a "United Front" with indigenous secular and religious leaders.

This chapter examines efforts by the CCP in the very early months and years of the PRC to consolidate its control over Amdo's vast terrain and attract the support of its diverse inhabitants. Far from a comprehensive history of Qinghai during this transitional period, it focuses on the CCP's immediate motives and methods for wooing Tibetan elites—who not only were members of Amdo's "feudal ruling class" but with few exceptions had been implicated in the Ma regime—into a "patriotic United Front." In doing so, CCP leaders made a distinction between hardline "bandits and spies" (i.e., former Muslim officers and officials engaged in a last-gasp struggle to protect their privileged class status) and Tibetan and Mongol chieftains and religious leaders. Even in the case of headmen "hoodwinked" into taking up arms against the CCP, Party leaders insisted that open resistance should not be treated as a manifestation of class struggle but as the residual effect of centuries of nationality exploitation.

It also considers the responses of several members of the Tibetan elite to the Party's United Front overtures. Many headmen and monastic leaders, including Rongwo Monastery's Shartsang Lama and the trio of Gélek Gyatso, Trashi Namgyel, and Gyelwo Dorjé, chose to cooperate with the Communists. After some hesitation, others, including the Nangra's Wangchen Döndrup and the Kéwa's Lhündrup Gyel, cast their lot with predominantly Hui Muslim insurgents. The point is not to project reified categories of "collaboration" and "resistance" into a volatile, frontier setting. As Timothy Brook points out, "collaboration" as it has been widely understood since the Second World War, is a value-laden appellation "constructed entirely in nationalist terms."[5] Yet nationalism, an ideology that demands territorial sovereignty be clearly demarcated, identities be neatly defined, and loyalty to one's nation override all others, simply did not hold particular resonance in most of Amdo at the time of "Liberation." More than that, I suggest that these types of decisions were familiar to elites in borderlands such as Amdo, long accustomed to forging political alliances with a variety of actors in exchange for various considerations. Shorn of the totalizing expectations of the nation, collaboration itself might even be considered a strategy of resistance to the hegemonic demands of the more powerful. This is all to say that when the PLA marched into Amdo, it encountered astute political actors faced with a range of potential choices as local elites sought to secure their positions of authority and relative autonomy within a rapidly changing political calculus.

"Liberating" Repgong

On September 12, 1949, after a hazardous eight- or nine-day journey from Rongwo Township, a Tibetan named Dorjé arrived in Xining. He had been dispatched by his uncle, the Seventh Shartsang Lama, to "pay respects" to the new provincial leadership. Dorjé (no relation to Gyelwo Dorjé) was the type of transcultural agent often found in frontier regions. A young bilingual Tibetan, Dorjé had recently graduated from Qinghai's Provincial Normal School. Having returned to Rongwo, he was studying Tibetan with his uncle in anticipation of taking entrance exams for Lanzhou University's Minority Languages Department. While his relationship to the Shartsang Lama was certainly critical, it was his ability to operate in multiple cultural milieus that specifically recommended him for this duty.[6]

In the capital, Dorjé was greeted by the senior-most figures in the regional PLA and CCP leadership, including army chief Liao Hansheng, provincial Party secretary Zhang Zhongliang, and Qinghai's ranking ethnic Tibetan CCP official, Trashi Wangchuk.[7] On behalf of his uncle, Dorjé presented Qinghai's new leaders with khatak, rugs, and other gifts. Formalities complete, he writes that he "reported in detail the yearnings of the Shartsang and the masses of each nationality and all walks of life for the early liberation of Tongren."[8]

While PRC sources all suggest that it was the desire of the Shartsang Lama, Repgong's monastic and secular elite, and the masses that a "people's government" be quickly formed, it seems clear that the immediate concern of both the Party and Repgong's leading actors was the collapse of political and social order that accompanied the fall of the old regime. Before his late-August flight from

Repgong, the former county head, Tséring Gyel, had entrusted temporary leadership to the men whose traditional authority and prestige transcended both Repgong's many internal divisions and nascent state structures—Nangso Trashi Namgyel, Zongqianhu Gyelwo Dorjé, and Rongwo Monastery steward Gélek Gyatso. Having dispatched representatives to Xunhua to offer Repgong's surrender, the trio subsequently demonstrated their usefulness to the CCP by organizing supplies and provisions for General Wang Zhen's forces, then readying their assault on the provincial capital. Simultaneously, they instructed each of Repgong's twelve chiefdoms to provide five to ten young men for a self-defense corps. Under the command of another of the Shartsang Lama's brothers, this ad hoc force patrolled the granary, wool factory, state-owned Dexinghai trade company, county school, government offices, and elsewhere.[9]

Despite these efforts, later accounts emphasize the chaos that the collapse of the Ma regime had unleashed. One witness recalls, "At night everywhere there was the sound of gunshots, during the day lawless people scurried all around, threatening the property of Rongwo's inhabitants at gunpoint and setting fire to Rongwo's buildings. Residents stayed behind closed gates not daring to go out."[10] Adding to the uncertainty, intercommunity tensions quickly surfaced as groups of Tibetans gathered in the streets threatening to drive Rongwo's Han Chinese and Hui Muslim shopkeepers out of town. In response, the merchants raised their own self-defense organizations. With the security situation collapsing, the Shartsang Lama is said to have personally led his monks down from the monastery to the Dexinghai offices. Declaring, "The Hui and Han merchants are under my monastery's care," he purportedly allowed people of all backgrounds to store their grain and wool in the monastery for safekeeping.[11] "Monk patrols" (*sengren xunluodui*) then joined what seems to have been a separate fifty-plus-man self-defense force organized by Gyelwo Dorjé from among his own tsowa.[12]

It was in this context of the collapse of social order that the Shartsang Lama had sent his nephew to Xining. Perhaps to the shock of many, when on September 19 Dorjé returned to Rongwo, with him was Tongren's former county head, Tséring Gyel. Having surrendered to Communist authorities in Xining, Tséring Gyel quickly found himself reappointed to his old post. The reason was simple. As Dorjé would later matter-of-factly admit, "there was no one more suitable who could immediately be dispatched [to Repgong]."[13] With security Xining's primary concern, few resources at its disposal, and no indigenous base of support upon which to build, de-Maification was not an option.[14] Three days after Tséring Gyel's surprise return, the Tongren County government, or People's Committee, was established with Ma Bufang's former county head as its new leading official. Underscoring the CCP's tenuous position in Repgong and throughout much of Amdo, the Party simultaneously recognized the three men to whom Tséring Gyel

FIGURE 3. The Seventh Shartsang Lama, Lozang Trinlé Lungtok Gyatso.
Photograph est. 1950s, photographer unknown.

had entrusted the county in his absence, Gélek Gyatso, Gyelwo Dorjé, and Trashi Namgyel, as canyi, or advisers to the new county government.[15] This, of course, is the same term Ma Bufang's regime often employed to co-opt the authority of local elites.

Despite the show of support from the Shartsang Lama and the three canyi, Xining's plans were quickly hijacked by local intrigue. Days after the inauguration of the People's Committee, villagers from nearby Sokru village abducted Tséring Gyel and two of his aides, carrying the captives across the river to a small temple where they were suspended from a beam and beaten. Upon hearing the news, Gélek Gyatso rushed to the scene. There the monastery steward purportedly lectured the villagers, declaring, "We longed for the Chinese Communist Party, so we must employ the person sent by the Chinese Communist Party as county head."[16] Properly chastised, the Sokru villagers are said to have released the prisoners into Gélek Gyatso's care. As brother and adviser to the Shartsang Lama, Gélek Gyatso previously had served as a facilitator between Rongwo Monastery and Ma Bufang's Xining government, his mediation seeming to help ease long-standing tensions between the two. Now Gélek Gyatso leveraged his local standing to save the life of Tséring Gyel and his companions.[17]

What we know about Tséring Gyel's kidnapping comes from retrospective accounts published in the PRC decades later. These sources uniformly attribute the abduction to the simmering hatred of the Tibetan masses for the old regime. Of course, this treatment of the Sokru incident should not be taken at face value. Instead, it can be read as an anecdote meant to reveal both the nationality exploitation of the former regime and the ideal intervention of a patriotic United Front personage. Yet Gélek Gyatso's success in rescuing the Party's appointed administrator also might be seen as an unintentional metaphor reflecting tensions between statist impulses and subimperial practices embedded in the CCP's early state- and nation-building efforts. While the selection of Tséring Gyel had been a concession to the administrative structure of the Ma Bufang state, the appointment of the monastery steward, nangso, and zongqianhu was in some ways a more fundamental compromise. After all, while Tséring Gyel's collusion was perhaps more direct, few indigenous leaders in this part of Amdo were without connections to Ma Bufang and his government. What Tséring Gyel seems to have lacked was a parallel indigenous source of authority that might have made legitimate his position as intermediary between state authorities and local communities.

In effect, Tséring Gyel represents the limits of the United Front. In implicit recognition of this fact, soon after being released from captivity, Tséring Gyel was transferred out of the region. With few other resources at the Party's disposal, the three canyi had their advisory positions exchanged for permanent posts. Gélek Gyatso replaced Tséring Gyel as the county's top official, while Trashi Namgyel and Gyelwo Dorjé became his deputies. Tongren County's "three-in-one feudal rule" had been elevated to county leadership within the new revolutionary government.

Ultimately, we do not know if it is true, as Gélek Gyatso's biographers would claim decades later, that the Sokru villagers had been motivated by hatred for the Ma regime and fear of the warlord's return. But the delicate position in which

Gélek Gyatso found himself can be appreciated, one that was not unlike that which Wagya had faced during the Détsang incident. In 1937, Wagya had unsuccessfully counseled the Détsang leadership not to flee into the grasslands, reasoning, "Crows throughout the world are all black. No matter where you go it will be the same."[18] Over a decade later, Gélek Gyatso similarly pleaded with Tséring Gyel's abductors, this time making explicit his compromised position by exclaiming, "If you kill the county head sent by the Chinese Communist Party, how will I explain it to the Chinese Communist Party?"[19] From the perspective of the frontier, the Sokru incident serves as a reminder that in the 1950s many elite actors were still operating in broadly imperial terms. Freed from its pejorative associations, "collaboration" was a strategy of survival that came with both potential benefits and hazards but was one that was fully integrated into the mechanisms of authority that had long prevailed along imperial borderlands like Amdo.

Unity and Friendship I

This predicament must have been on the minds of many when, toward the end of 1949, Gélek Gyatso, Gyelwo Dorjé, and Trashi Namgyel, now officially serving as Tongren County's top officials, were invited to Xining for an All-Province All-Nationalities People's Representative Unity and Friendship Conference (Quansheng Gezu Renmin Daibiao Lianyihui). Organized under the auspices of the provincial United Front Work Department, this was political outreach of the utmost importance to the new regime. After all, Gélek Gyatso was not the only one caught in a delicate bind. Sources freely admit that the meeting's main purpose was to "eliminate the fears and apprehensions of [minority] representatives" and attract their active participation in building the new state.[20]

After five days on horseback, in early January the Repgong delegation arrived in the provincial capital. Having spent the night in Xining's most luxurious hotel, the following day Gélek Gyatso, Trashi Namgyel, and Gyelwo Dorjé were escorted to the garden meeting rooms located behind the provincial government headquarters. There they exchanged khatak with Qinghai's senior leadership, including Party secretary Zhang Zhongliang, military chief Liao Hansheng, UFWD director Zhou Renshan, and Trashi Wangchuk, the Tibetan provincial vice secretary.[21] Emissaries from elsewhere in Qinghai received similar treatment. Provincial authorities instructed government and Party attendees to "humbly listen" to the concerns of minority representatives while emphasizing the CCP's progressive nationality policies.[22]

Despite the importance Party leaders attached to the conference and the attention they lavished on their guests, when the meeting convened on January 10, only eighty of the expected five-hundred-plus attendees had arrived. Nonetheless, during opening ceremonies organizers declared the gathering to be an "unprecedented demonstration of the great unity of the people of each nationality, possessing great political and historical meaning."[23] In his keynote speech, Zhang Zhongliang celebrated the dawn of a new era by proclaiming, "The Three Big Mountains [i.e., imperialism, feudalism, and bureaucratic capitalism], which under Ma Bufang had pressed down upon the heads of Qinghai's various nationalities, have been toppled; the old era of ruling through bullying and cruelty is gone and will not return; and the people of Qinghai's various nationalities are constructing a home in which they are their own masters."[24] Liao Hansheng followed by admitting that serious distrust continued to divide Qinghai's various nationalities. This, he claimed, was a legacy of feudalism enforced under the exploitative rule of past dynasties. Yet Liao insisted that internationality hostility had become most acute under the "great nationality chauvinism" of "the bandit Ma Bufang" and his Guomindang allies. As a result, Liao told attendees, the current task was to eliminate this historical legacy of nationality exploitation.[25]

Later in the proceedings, United Front director Zhou Renshan proposed a "unity pledge" (*tuanjie gongyue*). Attendees jointly promised to conduct themselves in the spirit of nationality equality, unity, mutual respect, mutual aid, and cooperation; to resolve disputes through consultation and dialogue; to eliminate enemies and restore social order; and to follow the leadership of the government and act as "good citizens." Echoing the sentiments expressed by the new provincial leadership, speaker after speaker then promised to work to end ethnic discrimination and exploitation, eliminate bandits and spies, and "construct a happy, new Qinghai."[26] Before concluding, attendees chose Rongwo's Gélek Gyatso one of six Tibetan representatives to a thirty-two member executive committee (*zhuxituan*).[27] Closing the conference on January 15, Liao Hansheng triumphantly announced that the meeting demonstrated "Qinghai's seven nationalities are not divided by language, are not divided by region, are not divided by religious belief, and are not divided by customs but are united together under the flag of Mao Zedong. They are like brothers in an intimate and harmonious family."[28]

The central (and eponymous) message of the Unity and Friendship Conference was clear. Yet, despite the celebratory rhetoric, it is difficult to know what impact the heavily scripted meeting had on those attending. Trashi Namgyel, who during a previous trip to Xining had been held as human collateral by Ma Bufang, would reminisce that his most lasting impression of his time in the provincial capital, as well as subsequent trips to Lanzhou and Beijing, was of the warmth and respect with which Communist Party authorities treated him. He wrote, "It really was like two different societies, two different worlds. . . . I immediately realized the difference between the CCP and Guomindang. At a GMD conference, every time they just wanted money and resources. Moreover, we had to bring generous gifts. The burden on the masses was very heavy."[29] Of course, Trashi Namgyel is telling his story within a prescribed narrative published many years later through official PRC channels. Nonetheless, it is not hard to imagine that the Rongwo nangso might have been impressed, honored, and, perhaps most important, cautiously relieved by the reception and assurance he and his peers received.

Soon after returning to Repgong, Gélek Gyatso was chosen to serve as secretary on a mission of utmost importance to Party leaders. The CCP's Northwest Bureau had selected the Seventh Shartsang Lama as one of three senior lamas—in CCP parlance, "prestigious religious patriotic figures"—to lead a delegation to Lhasa. Their assignment was to convince the Dalai Lama to agree to the "peaceful liberation of Tibet and the unification of the motherland." Setting out in mid-May with an entourage of more than twenty, the Rongwo delegation did not return until November 1951.[30]

In Gélek Gyatso's absence, Trashi Namgyel was chosen acting head of Tongren County, a position soon made permanent. While Trashi Namgyel had in theory become the county's chief executive, all indications suggest that his political role remained more akin to that of nangso. Certainly, the line between the two was permeable, and perhaps people did not think in such binary terms. Nevertheless, in many respects his responsibilities to the Communist Party were not unlike what they had been under Ma Bufang, albeit repackaged and remessaged. He was expected to serve as intermediary between the rapidly encroaching Party-state and local society by raising militias and maintaining social order, providing logistical and material support to state security forces, collecting taxes, mediating intercommunity disputes, and serving as a conduit for the implementation of Party programs. While the CCP would place great attention on the cultivation of minority cadres, in these early years what it needed more than bureaucrats was the charisma associated with preexisting secular and religious authority.

Perhaps nowhere was this prestige relied upon as heavily than in the CCP's efforts to resolve "grassland disputes," a catch-all phrase referring to intercommunity conflict over the plateau's limited resources.[31] Party leaders considered these seemingly incessant clashes particularly harmful to its goals of restoring social order, fostering *intra*nationality unity, and increasing production. They therefore expended extraordinary energies mediating these sometimes generations-long feuds. In doing so, CCP higher-ups deemed the intervention of indigenous religious and secular leaders vital. For instance, when mediating disputes, Gélek Gyatso purportedly would invoke his authority as representative of the Shartsang Lama.[32] This was a level of legitimacy that the state could not hope to muster, a reality that for the time being Party leaders seemed to acknowledge and accept.[33]

A short autobiographical account by Trashi Namgyel includes descriptions of mediation work and the roles Tibetan elites were expected to play during the "early Liberation period." This included CCP-sponsored efforts to resolve the protracted conflict mentioned in the previous chapter between Zongqianhu Dorjé's Gyelwo and the Gengya chiefdom. At negotiations brokered in 1951, Trashi Namgyel served as the chief representative from Tongren County. His opposite was Apa Alo (C. Huang Zhengqing), the longtime strongman of the Labrang region, elder brother of the recently deceased abbot of Labrang Monastery, and soon to be head of Gannan (Kenlho) Prefecture. Trashi Namgyel recalled:

> During this mediation I primarily did the Tongren aspects of the work. I implored [the Gyelwo to remember] that the roots of the dispute were created at the incitation of the reactionaries of the old society. We [mediators] acted as the representatives of the masses, and hence spoke on behalf of the masses, and adopted a correct viewpoint, which was to defer to the big picture, [and adhere to the principle of] mutual understanding and mutual compromise, in order to earnestly and sincerely facilitate a new neighborly, friendly relationship.[34]

With local elites acting both on behalf of the state (as leaders of Tongren and Xiahe Counties, respectively) and concurrently representing their traditional constituencies (as panchiefdom headmen in the Repgong and Labrang regions with intimate links to their main monastic institutions), a resolution was eventually reached.[35]

In essence, the CCP did not have direct access to the Tibetan masses, a considerable deficit that it hoped to gradually redress through the careful construction of government and Party organs, the training of minority cadres, the fruits of economic development, and a campaign of focused propaganda. In the meantime, relying on subimperial practices, it sought to appropriate the charismatic authority and local know-how of traditional elites. Trashi Namgyel provides several other examples of his successful mediation of grassland disputes.[36] The inclusion of these passages and similar accounts in other PRC-published sources is clearly meant to contrast the policies of the old regime, which purportedly stoked the flames of intercommunity violence, to those of the Communist Party. In the process, however, Trashi Namgyel also demonstrates the limits of state power and the vital role traditional elites continued to play in the maintenance of order among and between the peoples of southern Amdo. For his part, whether out of conviction (as he would later claim), self-preservation, ambition, or a sense of responsibility in his position as nangso, Trashi Namgyel seems to have played the role quite dutifully. After all, although never before faced with such a transformative, interventionist regime, Trashi Namgyel and countless others across Amdo were continuing to fulfill their accustomed roles at the confluence of state power and local society.

A Little Taiwan on the Sino-Tibetan Frontier

The courting of non-Han elites at the January 1950 Unity and Friendship Conference was in lockstep with the CCP's approach to the nationality question during the "early Liberation period." For the indefinite future, class struggle was explicitly left off the agenda. The focus instead was on securing social order and promoting nationality unity, goals that would be unreachable without the cooperation of Amdo's traditional power brokers. In a lengthy report appearing in the *Qinghai Daily*, for example, Qinghai Military District commander Liao Hansheng lauded the appointment of the Repgong trio of Trashi Namgyel, Gélek Gyatso, and Gyelwo Dorjé to leadership positions in the new Tongren County government, calling it a model for constructing new governing administrations in areas inhabited by minorities.[37]

Of course, neither the victorious declarations that accompanied the Unity and Friendship Conference nor the decision by Repgong's former "feudal" leadership to cast their lot with the CCP should obscure the fact that in the chaotic days and months following "Liberation," the Communist Party was not the only viable option available to local elites. These were often seasoned political operatives whose formative experiences had been tempered in the furnace that was Amdo under the Ma family. As the PLA bore down on northwest China, Ma's agents had spread rumors of the Communists' radical agenda, claiming that the CCP would kill all government functionaries and advocated "communal property and communal wives," and especially highlighted the Communists' avowed hostility toward religion.[38] The CCP countered with its own propaganda, declaring that the new state would be built not upon the nationality exploitation of the past but instead upon the principles of equality, mutual respect, and nationality unity. Party leaders and PLA commanders pointedly promised to protect mosques and monasteries, respect the customs of each nationality, uphold freedom of religious belief, implement minority autonomy, and form a United Front with all classes of each nationality.[39]

Despite such overtures, regional leaders were aware of the difficult road that lay ahead. On the eve of Qinghai's capture, Peng Dehuai, commander of the PLA's forces in northwest China, had cautiously predicted a warm welcome from Amdo's non-Muslim communities, particularly Tibetans who were said to have borne the brunt of the Mas' reactionary reign. On the other hand, Peng and his colleagues warned of potential trouble from the region's Muslim inhabitants, who presumably had received favored treatment under the Ma family. They therefore warned cadres and soldiers to be prepared to counter deep-seated anxieties among Muslims fearful that a CCP takeover would benefit Han interests at the expense of their own communities.[40]

Peng's concerns were reinforced by some of the PLA's initial experiences as it marched into the region. For instance, in Linxia, Gansu—a gateway to Amdo as well as the ancestral home of the Ma clan—sources assert that Han Chinese residents welcomed the Communist troops as liberators. By contrast, Linxia's Hui Muslim majority purportedly viewed the PLA as a Han army and feared reprisals from both its soldiers and their Han neighbors.[41] Likewise, as the First Army crossed from Linxia into Qinghai's Xunhua County, commanders reported that many among the Turkic-speaking Salar majority fled into the mountains or across the Yellow River. The latter covered their retreat by destroying a rope bridge and burning boats. Secure for the time being, they then formed an anti-Communist militia. By contrast, these same reports insisted that Xunhua Tibetans eagerly welcomed the Communist troops, providing their soldiers with food, provisions, and logistical aid.[42]

Events in Xunhua, however, also seemed evidence of the efficacy of the Party's nationality policies. Within weeks, the anti-Communist Salar militia had disintegrated, and most Salar returned to their villages. Witnessing the goodwill

FIGURE 4.   Salar soldier on the southern bank of the Yellow River, east of Xunhua's county seat. Joseph Rock, 1925, courtesy of Harvard-Yenching Library.

and good actions of PLA soldiers and CCP cadres, a contemporary PLA report contends that they, too, gradually came to have faith that the Communists were a new kind of Han Chinese—one unlike those the Salar had experienced in the past. Soon Salar community leaders joined their Tibetan neighbors in establishing Xunhua County's People's Government.[43]

Yet a variety of sources concede that the behavior of Communist soldiers and cadres did not always live up to the rhetoric. For instance, June Dreyer notes that an October 1 editorial in the *Gansu Daily* (*Gansu Ribao*) admitted that Muslim suspicions of the CCP's pro-Han agenda seemed justified when two-thirds of those appointed to a newly organized militia in Linxia (sometime referred to as China's "Little Mecca") were Han. In a neighboring county, Hui were not only excluded from government positions but also apparently barred from entering the county seat altogether. In some areas, security forces even had arbitrarily executed Hui suspects. "This was not, the editorial warned, the way to win the trust of the masses or Hui converts to Communism."[44]

Most worrisome, scattered evidence suggests that these types of transgressions were not unique to Linxia or its environs. Contemporary reports obliquely allege that across Qinghai repeated lapses in Party and military discipline also were having negative effects on the CCP's efforts to court Muslim communities. With little accompanying detail, they indicate that in many instances cadres and soldiers had prioritized class struggle over nationality unity—causing Muslim elites to fear losing their privileged positions or even their lives.[45] Spurred in part by these violations of Party policy, contemporary sources make clear that resistance to the PLA and CCP among some Hui Muslims continued into late fall 1949.[46]

In December these tensions burst into the open. A statement from the public security bureau of Datong County contended that former officers in Ma Bufang's military, exploiting both longstanding intercommunity anxieties and more recent deficiencies in the Party's work, were spreading rumors that the CCP had seized power on behalf of the Han and were taking revenge on Hui residents. There were even reports that in Datong, an agricultural area adjacent to Xining with a large Muslim population, entire Hui families had committed suicide rather than face violence purportedly perpetrated by Communist soldiers. Finally, on December 5, over seventeen hundred men—most armed only with knives and axes but wearing white hats and red armbands identifying the combatants as purported members of Ma Bufang's Eighth Cavalry Brigade—attacked multiple sites within Datong County. Security forces quickly crushed the uprising, although considerable losses were reported on both sides.[47]

Just as quickly, however, rebellion spread to neighboring Menyuan County, then Ledu, Hualong, Xunhua, Linxia, and beyond. Like a whack-a-mole game, as soon as one threat was eliminated, another popped up elsewhere. As in Datong, contemporary reports allege that the various revolts were organized and led by former officers of Ma's army, in many cases acting in league with Muslim religious and community leaders. For example, despite earlier assertions that Xunhua's Salar population had come to support the Party, a deposed Salar official named Han Yinu and a Ma Bufang–affiliated Hui battalion commander raised a force of fifteen hundred fighters. On December 13, the insurgents launched a surprise attack against a company of the PLA's First Regiment. One hundred and four were killed in the ambush, among them a district leader, its Communist Party secretary, and ninety-four soldiers. The military region command immediately dispatched reinforcements and after three days of intense fighting put down the uprising. Inexplicably, however, Han Yinu "escaped the [PLA's] net." He would not resurface for nearly a decade.[48]

Not until fall 1950, after thirty-six battles and numerous casualties, could commanders report that rebellion in the "eastern agricultural districts" of Qinghai had been nearly extinguished.[49] Yet resistance continued. Some fighters fled into the vast grasslands of southern Amdo where they purportedly formed sleeper cells within Tibetan and Mongol communities.[50] Others remained hidden in plain sight. And, as PLA troops overwhelmed rebel bases north of the Yellow River, "Ma Bufang remnants, bandits, and local despots" escaped into the forested, mountainous area south of the river that was home to the Nangra Tibetans and their headman, Wangchen Döndrup.[51]

At first glance, the Nangra region seems an unlikely refuge for Ma partisans. After all, among the incidents often cited in CCP sources to illustrate Ma Bufang's predatory nature and ethnoreligious oppression were his clashes in the 1930s with the Nangra Tibetans. In the years since, however, Wangchen Döndrup appears to have maintained generally amicable relations with the Xining regime, eventually even joining the GMD. By the late 1940s, he controlled a large "self-defense army" that CCP sources describe as "southern Qinghai's mightiest tribal armed force."[52] Yet as the PLA swept westward in early September 1949, Wangchen Döndrup refused Ma's orders to mobilize his fighters against the Communists. Instead, as in neighboring Repgong, the Nangra headman sent representatives to offer his support for the new regime. As reward, the regional leadership quickly reconfirmed Wangchen Döndrup's dual roles as Nangra qianhu and administrative head of the Nangra region.[53] In the process, the Party essentially reaffirmed the subimperial relationship he previously had negotiated with Ma Bufang.

Much as it had been with the Ma regime, however, Wangchen Döndrup's loyalty to the CCP should be considered strategic and conditional. In January 1950, he rebuffed invitations to attend the Unity and Friendship Conference. By then, fleeing insurgents had begun trickling into the Nangra region, and the Nangra

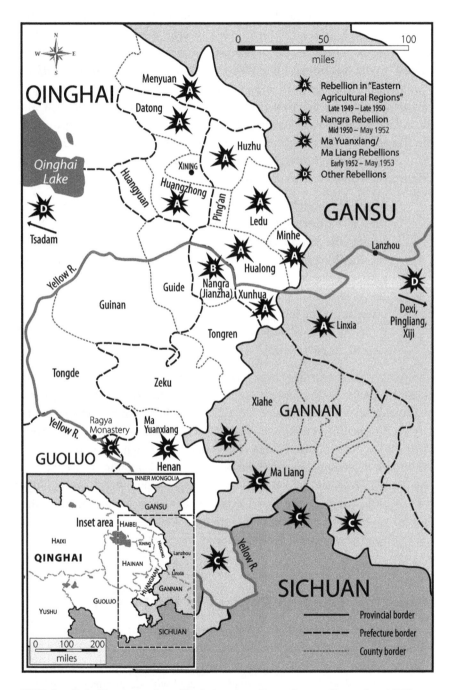

MAP 2. Rebellion in eastern Qinghai and southern Gansu, December 1949–May 1953. Mike Bechthold, cartographer. Sources: *JFQH, JQSX, GSSZ JSZ*.

Tibetans may have engaged PLA detachments in sporadic skirmishes. Over the first half of 1950, as security forces overran rebels elsewhere in Qinghai, the stream of refugees became a flood. Eventually, more than three thousand "outside bandits" would seek protection in Wangchen Döndrup's Nangra stronghold.[54]

Amid these developments, in August 1950 Wangchen Döndrup finally traveled to the provincial capital to attend the funeral of provincial vice chairman Ma Pu. In Xining, United Front director Zhou Renshan took the opportunity to press the Nangra headman to separate himself from reactionary elements that were then taking shelter in his territories. According to a Chinese source, Wangchen Döndrup reassured Zhou by declaring:

> After Liberation, I did not understand the government's policies. . . . In particular I listened to the rumors of the evildoers. . . . Today I have come to the government and have been warmly received by senior cadres. They have sincerely explained the policy of nationality equality and unity and the policy of the freedom of religious belief, [and this has] caused me to recognize the value that the Party and the government places on us minority nationalities, [by which we] genuinely are regarded as fraternal nationalities. From now on, I definitely will remain close to the government.[55]

Immediately upon returning home, however, the authors contend that Wangchen Döndrup "broke his word" by stockpiling weapons, fortifying roads and passes, and stirring up his people against the CCP. Then, in November, he joined former Ma Bufang officers to formally establish the China Guomindang Northwest Revolutionary Committee. Calling their mountain stronghold "Little Taiwan," the Nangra chieftain became commander of the Anti-Communist Save the Nation Second Army, said to consist of over twenty-one hundred "tribal militiamen." A Little Taiwan on the Sino-Tibetan frontier having been established, the insurgents then launched what one source refers to as "Qinghai's longest and most influential rebellion of the early Liberation period."[56]

Wangchen Döndrup Returns to the People

It is unclear what exactly might have pushed Wangchen Döndrup into active rebellion. However, the experience of Lhündrup Gyel may offer clues. Like elsewhere in Amdo, in Guide/Trika, the collapse of the Ma regime had thrown local society into disorder. With the roads scattered with desperate, demobilized Ma soldiers, Lhündrup Gyel and others hunkered down in the county seat and waited with trepidation for the coming of the PLA. When a few days later the first

Communist soldiers arrived, to Lhündrup Gyel's surprise they did not plunder the town. Instead, their commander, Li Xibo, invited Lhündrup Gyel and other prominent local figures to a meal. Over dinner Li reassured his guests by promising, "We are the people's army; there is a fundamental difference between us and the Ma-family army. Our soldiers serve the people."[57] Lhündrup Gyel writes that the good behavior of the occupying troops—who quickly restored social order—and high-minded promises of its officers and officials soon won him over. On September 27, Commander Li, now newly appointed Party secretary of Guide County, convinced the Kéwa headman to join the reconstituted county government as a *xiangzhang* (district head), the same position he nominally held under Ma Yuanhai. Lhündrup Gyel had become a United Front representative.

The honeymoon did not last. Despite assurances that local elites would not be subject to class struggle and that their wealth would not be redistributed, as the months wore on Lhündrup Gyel became increasingly concerned about his prospects under the Communists. In autumn 1951, amid a campaign to "reduce rents, oppose local despots, and suppress counterrevolutionaries," a regional qianhu and his son were executed by firing squad. Rumors began to swirl among the area's prominent indigenous figures, most of whom in some capacity had acted as agents of the Ma regime. Lhündrup Gyel later recalled, "In the past not only was I a local official, but I was a district leader, my relationship with Ma Yuanhai was also very good, and it was also true that I had blockaded the Red Army. . . . I began to think that the CCP's knife might already be closing in on my neck."[58] Finally, guns and ammunition in hand, in early 1952 Lhündrup Gyel and a handful of loyal followers fled on horseback into the nearby mountains. As word of their location spread, the small band sought the protection of Wangchen Döndrup's much larger insurrection.

From the start, Party and military leaders treated Qinghai's Little Taiwan differently than the string of uprisings that had erupted north of the Yellow River. The latter were described as manifestations of the final stage of class struggle, one report comparing the largely Muslim-led insurgencies to the struggle against Japanese fascism. In those instances, commanders pledged to "firmly, thoroughly and completely eradicate whoever dares oppose the people's government and wreck the revolutionary order."[59] Yet, rather than instruct its fighters to "sharpen knives and polish guns"[60] as it had elsewhere, in response to the Nangra Rebellion Xining engaged in eighteen months of protracted diplomacy aimed at winning over Wangchen Döndrup. This is despite the Nangra chieftain's own long, if complicated, relationship with the Ma Bufang regime. An open letter signed by Qinghai's governor and vice governors and delivered by a United Front emissary explained the Party's position. It read, "Mr. Wangchen, considering your crimes, you should have already been punished according to state law, but the people's government believes that you have been hoodwinked by outside spies and ban-dits."[61] If he were to break with Ma Bufang partisans and "return to the people," the letter continued, the Nangra headman's personal safety would be guaranteed, his property protected, and his position as qianhu reconfirmed.

The decision to distinguish "outside spies and bandits" from "hoodwinked" headmen like Wangchen Döndrup was connected to the CCP's a priori assump-tions about great nationality chauvinism. As members of an exploited nationality, even Tibetan leaders could and should be won over through patient propagan-dizing of the Party's nationality policies of equality, mutual respect, and auton-omy. The immediate task, then, was to employ United Front tactics to separate these men from their erstwhile allies. None of this meant that Muslim landown-ers or religious leaders were necessarily to be treated as enemies. Time and again Party and military leaders reminded subordinates that the insurgencies were not "Hui rebellions." They contended that most Muslim rebels also had been tricked into joining the uprisings (often under the cloak of religion) or had joined in response to "some shortcomings and specific mistakes that exist in our work." In these cases, leniency was called for. Instead, Commander Liao Hansheng ordered that security forces target the "backbone" of the insurgency, those "remnant Ma bandits unwilling to accept the demise of their power."[62] This all but precluded Tibetans. Instead, the CCP leadership viewed Tibetan elites—even those engaged in active rebellion—as potential allies and vital emissaries to the Tibetan masses.

In this vein, from late 1950 to early 1952, Party leaders sent seventeen sepa-rate diplomatic missions into the Nangra region. Just as it had dispatched the Shartsang Lama to Lhasa as part of a delegation meant to secure the Dalai Lama's peaceful surrender, the CCP enlisted influential Amdo Tibetan religious and sec-ular figures to head many of these efforts. This included representatives of the Tenth Panchen Lama and Kumbum Monastery (C. Ta'ersi), the famous Buddhist scholar and educator Geshé Shérap Gyatso, the Third Gurong Gyeltsé Rinpoché, and Zongqianhu Kangtsé Welzang.[63] Notably, the final two were the same men who two decades earlier had helped negotiate Wangchen Döndrup's truce with Ma Bufang, once again highlighting continuities between the subimperial prac-tices of the Ma regime and the CCP's United Front agenda.

At the same time, the CCP's commitment to the United Front did not keep it from making military preparations. During the months of diplomatic stalemate, the PLA reconnoitered the region, built supply lines, and amassed its forces. Nor was its patience limitless. On May 1, 1952, commanders finally mobilized over ten thousand soldiers in a massive assault on the Nangra region. Although the Nangra headman and a small number of his fighters managed to escape into the surrounding hills, Wangchen Döndrup's home village and members of his family were quickly captured. By the following afternoon, Qinghai's Little Taiwan had been destroyed.[64]

The next day, provincial leaders issued a proclamation. Despite his transgressions, if Wangchen Döndrup "stepped back from the precipice and ended his relationship with the bandits, the People's Government still would treat him leniently, and his life, property and qianhu position would be protected."[65] Nangra religious leaders and headmen also were told that if they surrendered, they would not only not face punishment, but also both their wealth and positions would be preserved. On the ground, PLA officers instructed their soldiers to protect monasteries and unite with Tibetan officials, headmen, and "especially the great high lamas of the monasteries."[66] The Nangra region itself was promised a two-year tax holiday and the delivery of emergency grain relief, medical provisions, and expertise so that "production can be restored." A Chinese source claims that captives (including Tibetan headmen but not "outside counterrevolutionaries") were quickly released, over three thousand people were provided medical attention, and 395 households received a portion of an initial shipment of 37,000 *jin* (approximately 18,500 kilograms) of emergency grain.[67]

On July 11, after two and a half harrowing months on the run—and with two trülku acting as guarantors—Wangchen Döndrup and several dozen compatriots finally came down from the mountains.[68] In the parlance of the Party, the Nangra qianhu "received a new life and returned to the people." Senior CCP leaders feted Wangchen Döndrup first in Xining and then Lanzhou and for a second time confirmed his position as Nangra qianhu. At a banquet hosted by the Northwest Bureau, Xi Zhongxun personally entreated the Nangra headman to not again be enticed by the lies of spies and bandits, remarking, "Only by following the CCP will the path forward be bright." Soon afterward, provincial authorities named Wangchen Döndrup head of the newly created Jianzha (T. Chentsa) Tibetan Autonomous County and vice chairman of Huangnan Prefecture.[69]

While the military operations were certainly more decisive than the diplomatic overtures, the agreeable conclusion of the Nangra insurrection was heralded as a stunning success for the CCP's United Front strategy. On September 8, 1952, an announcement appeared in the *People's Daily* (*Renmin Ribao*) celebrating the resolution of the Nangra revolt. The paper's nationwide readership was told that the agreement was a "Model of the People's Government's implementation of the policy to win over and unify with minority nationalities."[70] Specifically citing the Nangra insurrection, internal communications of the CCP's Northwest Bureau declared that armed rebellion in minority regions was not simply a case of the ruling class trying to preserve its feudal privileges (in other words, class struggle) but a function of historical antagonism between nationalities (nationality struggle) created by the Han majority's long-term exploitation of minority peoples and sharpened by the ruinous rule of Ma Bufang and Chiang Kaishek. "Because of this," the Northwest Bureau added, "in pacifying rebellion we must actively separate the nationality and religion problem from the counterrevolutionary problem and separate the outside counterrevolutionaries from the indigenous nationality upper strata elements."[71] Party leaders further boasted that they had "applied experiences resolving the Nangra problem" to settle separate insurrections among Tibetan and Muslim communities in Gansu.[72] The key takeaway was the vital importance of forming United Front alliances with minority elites.

At the end of 1952, Wangchen Döndrup addressed a conference attended by many of Qinghai's leading "nationality" figures. During his speech, he urged attendees, especially "the [Mongol] nobility and [Tibetan] qianbaihu," to heed his experience, concluding, "The bandits and spies are like birds in the sky. If there are no rocks on which to stand, they cannot land. Therefore, if none of us act as a rock, there will be nowhere for the spies and bandits to land."[73] In a few short months, Wangchen Döndrup had been transformed from a rebel leader into a model United Front personage.

Despite Wangchen Döndrup's avowed newfound commitment to internationality unity, the confrontation between the Nangra and the CCP-state also can be viewed as an extension of earlier efforts to define center-local relations. Speaking of the Nangra drama, Mark Stevenson writes, "The [Nangra] region had never been under *effective* (Tibetan or Chinese) state control. . . . The Tibetan renegades were doing what they had it seems always done, resisting outside control and acting on the principle of local loyalty."[74] While Stevenson is correct, like Doyle he fails to note that the definition of "effective" control might not be static or self-evident. When faced with an increasingly belligerent Ma regime in the 1930s, Wangchen Döndrup had been able to negotiate a mutually agreeable settlement that maintained the broad outline of an imperial relationship between himself and Xining. Two decades later, even from a position of considerable weakness, Wangchen Döndrup again was able to leverage his geographic position and personal prestige to obtain what he must have viewed as concessions, guarantees, and titles from the new state power. Like the Kéwa's Lhündrup Gyel, who after a short stay in the Nangra base area also returned home to reclaim his position in the new regime, Wangchen Döndrup's insurrection in part was an attempt to maintain some semblance of an imperial relationship. For the time being, the United Front allowed for that possibility.

Liberation's Last Act

When in December 1952 Wangchen Döndrup exhorted his fellow headmen to resist the entreaties of outside agitators, he was specifically referring to a rebellion that was brewing in the Gansu-Qinghai-Sichuan border region. Just as Wangchen Döndrup had much longer relationships with the Ma Bufang stalwarts who flocked to his stronghold than with agents of the Communist Party, the leaders of this insurrection were hardly newcomers to the southern grasslands or its inhabitants. In the mid-1930s, Ma Liang and Ma Yuanxiang had commanded Ma Bufang's southern defenses against the Red Army, working closely with local headmen such as the ninth qinwang of the Sokpo Mongols, Künga Weljor. By contrast, in the summer of 1952, provincial UFWD director Zhou Renshan noted that the area was the very last part of Qinghai to which the Party had dispatched its cadres.[75]

The story of the self-proclaimed "Qinghai Commander," Ma Yuanxiang, is itself a lesson in the syncretic nature of pre-1949 Amdo. Several sources claim that Ma was a Hui Muslim from Linxia or perhaps a Salar from Xunhua County. Befitting the transcultural world that exists on the eastern edge of Amdo, however, the commander of the PLA "bandit suppression" forces organized to oppose the rebellion asserts that Ma Yuanxiang was actually born a Tibetan named Lozang (C. Lamuzang). In this narrative, among the Chinese-speaking population of his southern Gansu birthplace, he went by the "Hui name" Ranmuzan. As a young man, Lozang served as a herdsman and farmhand in the Linxia area for Ma Bufang's uncle and predecessor, Ma Lin.[76] Later, "because [Ma Yuanxiang] was fluent in the Tibetan language and intimately familiar with the conditions of the pastoral regions, he became Ma Bufang's close and trusted follower."[77]

Whatever the truth, the man now known as Ma Yuanxiang would rise through the ranks to become one of the most powerful figures on the grasslands of southern Amdo. On October 28, 1949, well after the capture of Xining, Ma Yuanxiang surrendered to the Communist forces and was sent to a PLA camp for political reeducation. Eight months later, he was released. Despite promises of leniency, Ma returned home to find that security forces had captured and killed his son, brother, and nephew. Fearing for his life, Ma donned a disguise and made his way south into Sokpo, the territory of the Four Mongol Banners.[78] Although Künga Weljor had since passed away, Ma Yuanxiang and his old colleague Ma Liang exploited long-standing connections to leading indigenous figures—including the late Mongol prince's Tibetan brother-in-law (and son of Labrang's Apa Alo), Huang Wenyuan (T. Gönpo Namgyel, a.k.a. Amgon)—to spread anti-Party sentiment, organize a counterrevolutionary militia, and establish a "guerrilla base area" on the southeastern edge of the Qinghai Plateau.[79] Calling themselves the Anti-Communist Save the Nation 102nd Route Army, the insurgents had grown by the end of 1952 from a small band of twenty-five compatriots to a force of nearly two thousand fighters supported by GMD airdrops of machine guns, rifles, ammunition, radios, and six GMD agents.[80] From his sanctuary situated in the vast grasslands between the Sokpo Mongol territories and Labrang, Ma Yuanxiang and his allies sent agents throughout southern Amdo who reportedly "deceived and won over reactionary elements from among the qianhu, baihu, [Mongol] nobility, incarnate lamas, and old military officers." Among his targets was the Hor chieftain Wagya, Ma Yuanxiang hoping to set up a second base of operations within his territories.[81]

With the suppression of the Nangra Rebellion as a guide, Party leaders quickly sought to distinguish local Mongol and Tibetan "tribal" and religious elements implicated in the insurrection from "outside counterrevolutionaries." The provincial Party committee announced, "The former generally are targets to unite with and win over. The latter are targets to be resolutely and completely eliminated," adding that "counterrevolution must be strictly separated from the nationality and religion question; we absolutely must not confuse them as we have in the past." In other words, at times Tibetan headmen and religious elites had been targeted as class enemies, leading some to join this and other insurgencies. Xining now reiterated that any resistance from these elements should not be interpreted as a manifestation of class struggle but as a consequence of great nationality exploitation. In no uncertain terms, Qinghai's leadership declared, "No matter how large their crimes, [they should be dealt with under] the principle of firmly educating and winning over; we cannot waver in the slightest."[82]

In March 1953, troops under the command of Qinghai Military District vice commander Li Shumao spilled into the region. In mid-April, scouts located Ma Yuanxiang's main force in a mountainous area near the intersection of Gannan, Henan, and Golok. His forces badly mauled in the subsequent PLA assault, Ma was driven northwest toward Tongde (T. Ba) County. Trapped near Ragya Monastery on the banks of the Yellow River, in May 1953 Ma Yuanxiang was killed and his insurrection crushed.[83] If the capture of Xunhua on August 26, 1949, is commemorated as the first salvo in the "liberation" of Qinghai, the May 7, 1953, defeat of Ma Yuanxiang and the eradication of his band of loyalists is officially remembered as the drama's final act. "After this, our province's last remaining political bandits were extinguished."[84] Nearly four years, ninety-eight "bandit extermination engagements," and fourteen hundred PLA casualties later, the CCP finally could proclaim, "a great victory in the whole province's bandit extermination struggle."[85]

While the tendency to romanticize resistance—particularly on behalf of a seemingly weak minority in the face of overwhelming state power—is understandable, many have pointed out that this may have more to do with our own proclivities than those we are championing. Borrowing from Lila Abu-Lughod, Bulag reminds us that rather than a moral absolute, resistance should "be seen as a diagnostic of power within the society concerned."[86] Given the acrimony that marked relations between the Ma regime and many Tibetan communities prior to 1949, the CCP assumed that most Tibetans would eagerly support the overthrow of Ma Bufang. Many Tibetans (and Mongols) did in fact throw their lot in with the CCP. Perhaps some did so out of pure hatred for the Ma family. For most, however, a realpolitik grasp of the rapidly changing balance of power almost certainly entered the equation. On the other hand, whether due to past relationships with the Mas or misdeeds of Communist soldiers and cadres, others joined Ma Bufang–affiliated rebellions.

In other words, given the extant power dynamics and limited alternatives available to elites within Amdo, working with the Communists was a rational decision with precedents dating back centuries—just as was allying with remnants of the Ma Bufang regime. However, the elimination of Ma Yuanxiang meant that by 1953 a viable counter to the CCP no longer existed. For most members of Amdo's indigenous leadership accustomed to striking bargains at the edge of empire, the only option remaining was to cooperate with the Communist Party. For its part, both practical concerns and the philosophical roots of the Party's dual project of nation building and socialist transformation determined that its representatives had little choice but to consult, negotiate, and compromise with Amdo's pre-1949 power brokers, almost irrespective of past connections to the Ma family warlords. In the coming years, these United Front representatives would find their ability to act autonomously severely circumscribed. Yet as long as the United Front remained intact, they would not simply become cogs in the Party machinery. From their positions at the gateway separating the Party-state from the masses it hoped to one day lead, Amdo's pre-1949 leadership retained considerable influence and authority. The military conflict was over; the political struggle was just beginning.

3

BECOMING MASTERS OF THEIR OWN HOME (UNDER THE LEADERSHIP OF THE PARTY)

On September 11, 1953, a dozen Chinese cadres arrived on the northern bank of the Tséchu River. They were led by a veteran Communist Party official named Guo Min, who at the age of thirty-six had already spent more than half his lifetime in the revolution. A native of the CCP's legendary base area of Yan'an in Shaanxi Province, he and his County Establishment Preparatory Work Group (Jianxiang Choubei Gongzuozu, hereafter County Work Group) had been sent from Rongwo township with orders to construct a new county-level administration in what had been Tongren's southern pastoral districts.[1] This was the territory of Wagya's Hor, Serökyap's Gönshül, Lubum's Gartsé, and seven other federated chiefdoms later to be referred to as the "Ten Tribes of Zeku." There, on the Shadar grasslands in the territories of the Sonak chiefdom, the small band joined a rudimentary encampment of four to five dozen cadres who for the past two months had been laying the groundwork for establishing what was not yet officially known as the Zeku Tibetan Autonomous County.[2]

This chapter first examines the CCP's practical and ideological motivations for creating Zeku County and Amdo's other autonomous nationality administrations, within which—Party leaders repeatedly promised—minority communities would at last become "masters of their own homes." Scholars have largely dismissed nationality autonomy as empty rhetoric, the fiction of autonomy acting as a thin disguise for Chinese Communist domination.[3] While true political autonomy was never a possibility, this assumption misses a fundamental point. In 1950s Amdo, nationality autonomy was considered *the* key mechanism by which non-Han people would be both administratively and psychologically integrated into the

MAP 3.   Huangnan (Malho) Prefecture with the ten chiefdoms of Zeku (Tsékhok). Mike Bechthold, cartographer.

new state and nation. It was a central component of the Maoist "high-modernist" project, its aim to reterritorialize ethnocultural frontiers into component parts of a unitary nation-state, a process Dru Gladney refers to as "minoritization."[4] To paraphrase Qinghai's United Front director Zhou Renshan, if properly implemented nationality autonomy had the power to build trust, overcome ethnic prejudice, eliminate tribal division, develop productive capacities, isolate counterrevolutionaries, win over the indigenous elite, arouse both mass awareness and patriotic consciousness, consolidate nationality unity, and pave a path for socialist transformation—all under the leadership of the Chinese Communist Party.[5]

As director of the provincial United Front Work Department from 1949 to 1954, after which he served as vice secretary of the Qinghai Provincial Party

Committee until his 1956 transfer to Central Tibet, Zhou Renshan was not only one of a handful of senior provincial-level Party officials in Qinghai but also the province's leading voice on nationality affairs. A native of Gansu Province, he had moved to Beijing in the mid-1930s to attend law school. There he became radicalized under the influence of the Mongol Communist Su Jianxiao, and, in 1938, Zhou made his way to the Communist base area of Yan'an. In Yan'an, Zhou quickly made a name for himself in nationalities work, first in policy formation and later as leader of a work committee sent into Inner Mongolia.[6]

Given his portfolio, it is tempting to assume that Zhou represented a relatively moderate wing of the provincial leadership. However, contemporary sources contain no indication of a "two-line struggle" between advocates for more gradual and more immediate paths to socialist transformation. There were almost certainly disagreements among Qinghai's senior cadres over the practical advisability and ideological correctness of the United Front, and, as noted in chapter 8, these differences may have played out during the Great Leap Forward (1958–61) and the Cultural Revolution (1966–76). Notably, however, during the bulk of the 1950s, these debates simply did not make their way into either public statements or internal directives issued by Qinghai's Party or state bureaucracies. Regardless of the personal feelings of any individual sitting in Xining or trudging through Amdo's grasslands, for most of the decade the United Front represented the institutional ethos and operating principles of Party work in Qinghai's minority nationality areas.[7]

Afterward, I trace efforts by Guo Min's County Work Group to build a consensus among the region's divided headmen for founding Zeku County. This almost certainly was to be the first time in its history that the region would be territorialized and administered as a whole and distinct entity. Party leaders were aware that this not only demanded drawing boundaries and building administrative organs where none had previously existed—it also necessitated creating a county-level constituency from the disparate interests and loyalties of the region's divided population, a process deeply informed by the mass line principles of "consultation" and "persuasion." Encapsulated in Mao's famous phrase "from the masses, to the masses," the mass line was a method of leadership, an application of theory, and a strategy of mobilization designed to draw from local experience, check the arbitrary power of the Party, and enlist the masses into the revolution. As Mao explained, "This means: take the ideas of the masses (scattered and unsystematic ideas) and concentrate them . . ., then go to the masses and propagate and explain these ideas until the masses embrace them as their own."[8] Thus, consultation and persuasion existed in a highly imbalanced dialectical relationship. In privileging its vanguard position to interpret, synthesize, systemize, and implement the will of the masses, in Leninist fashion the Party maintained ultimate authority. Yet it also necessitated encouraging the active participation of the very people it sought to transform. Therefore, at every juncture the CCP's agenda had to be deliberated, endorsed, and implemented by newly created participatory governing bodies. With the Party having little direct access to the "pastoral masses," for the time being these committees would be led and populated mainly by secular headman and religious elites, figures that from the perspective of the CCP leadership had the political acumen and charismatic authority needed to both implement the Party-state's political and economic programs and model patriotic unity for the masses.

Less clear is how the CCP's repeated promise to make Tibetans and other minority communities "masters of their own homes" was received by the inhabitants of Zeku and others living on Amdo's high plateau. Pledges to promote equality, autonomy, and economic development aside, it surely was not lost on Tibetan elites and others that the new, ostensibly autonomous governing apparatuses allowed for far more direct, intrusive, and centralized oversight than any that had previously existed. And this is in addition to the linguistic and cultural difficulties cadres must have faced in communicating their high modernist agenda to local Amdo Tibetans, obstacles only hinted at in available documents. Zeku was to become an autonomous county in which Tibetan pastoralists would at last become "masters of their own home." And this would demand a significant degree of consultation, negotiation, and compromise with local leaders. Ultimately, however, Zeku would be constructed according to blueprints brought to the grasslands by the Chinese Communist Party.

What's in a Name?

When in late summer 1949 the CCP first arrived in Tongren County, rather than push deeper into the grasslands, Party leaders chose to consolidate their position in Repgong's agricultural heartland. There simply was no infrastructure, resources, or personnel with which to govern the vast, sparsely inhabited pastoral areas that lay to its south. Instead, the CCP attempted to bring the grasslands north by reconfirming "former qianhu and baihu to their old positions," now under the "leadership of the People's Government," and inviting local headman to join various governing and consultative bodies meeting in Rongwo Township.[9]

This was always considered a stopgap measure. However, Ma Yuanxiang's insurrection—particular his outreach to pastoral elites such as Wagya—exposed the CCP's tenuous position in southern Amdo. It is unsurprising, then, that in June 1953, just one month after Ma's defeat, the Tongren County government hastily dispatched several dozen cadres into the Zeku region to lay the groundwork for founding a new pastoral county.[10] Among them was a young Tibetan medical worker named Gyelyön. A rootless teenager seemingly with few prospects, he had joined the county government two years earlier. Gyelyön later would describe being attracted by the relative egalitarianism and sense of purpose displayed by the small cadre force then based out of Rongwo (although the prospects of earning a small monthly salary certainly helped). As he recalls, "Most were demobilized soldiers, some still wearing their army uniforms and boots, dragging their bandaged legs to work." So spartan were the conditions, Gyelyön writes, not even Tongren's Party secretary, Du Hua'an, could get more than a single fifty-pack of Starlight or Liberation brand cigarettes.[11]

Gyelyön admits that his political consciousness initially was not high. This started to change when as a member of an agricultural work team he was ordered to accompany an ill cadre out of the countryside and to a medical clinic in the county seat. Inspired by what he witnessed, Gyelyön claims to have decided to devote his life to using medical science to "battle" (douzheng) the "superstition" (mixin, i.e., religion) that he now felt plagued Tibetan society. Soon afterward, Gyelyön received permission to transfer to the clinic, where he began training with a small group of medical workers.[12]

Ma Yuanxiang's rebellion now over, county leaders assigned Gyelyön as pharmacist, accountant, and in all likelihood translator to a three-person medical team attached to the vanguard force being sent into the southern grasslands. Despite being given just three days to prepare for the arduous three-day march, he would later recall the good spirits of his company as they traveled up the Rongwo River, over "the great Wöngya Mountain, and into the Topden grasslands within the [future] borders of Zeku County." Marching through the high plateau, some sang mountain songs; others played games. At times, "March of the Liberation Army" would break out. On the third day, however, when word came down that the column had nearly reached its destination, the enormity of the task that lay ahead suddenly became apparent. Expecting to find at least a small village where they might be welcomed with firecrackers, Gyelyön writes, "Everyone rushed their animals to get there first. . . . Who could have guessed that when we arrived at the county seat, it would turn out to be complete wilderness?"[13]

Despite the initial shock, Gyelyön and his companions quickly went about setting up a rudimentary base of operations. Before the county could be founded, a tremendous amount of work needed to be done—political work among the pastoral leaders and common herders but also the strenuous physical labor of constructing living quarters and office space, securing the site, establishing communications, and eking out an existence on the harsh, high plateau. Despite being situated in the territory of the Sonak chiefdom, Gyelyön gives no indication of what type of reconnaissance work, security precautions, or negotiation may have preceded their arrival.[14] On the other hand, he describes at length the physical hardships faced by the small contingent. Lying at twelve thousand feet above sea level near the convergence of the Tséchu and Shadar Rivers, even in summer the nighttime temperatures could dip below freezing.[15] With no trees and few other resources at hand, nearly everything needed to build and supply the "county seat" would have to be carried in from the outside. Nonetheless, by the time Guo Min's County Work Group arrived two months later, the ramshackle collection of approximately twenty tents had been encircled by a 2.5-meter-high, 1.5-meter-thick earthen wall, providing its residents a modicum of protection against the elements and a measure of security against more sentient threats. As the season turned to autumn, however, Gyelyön remembers that the grass turned yellow and great winds "enveloped us in blackness, making the sky dim and the earth black, so that people could not open their eyes. In the early morning," he recalls, "the ice on the grass was like a layer of white snow."[16]

Given these extreme conditions, it is not surprising that as Guo Min and his cadres got to work in the days and months after their September arrival, they reported encountering a number of setbacks, several of which are detailed in this chapter. Although on the surface perhaps not the most substantive, a disagreement that emerged in late October is particularly instructive for what it suggests about the processes and problematics of state- and nation-building on the Amdo grasslands. The impasse revolved around a fundamental yet seemingly trivial question: what to name the new county? Du Hua'an, a native of Sichuan and a Long March veteran who in addition to serving as Party secretary of Tongren County was the leading United Front representative in the region, suggested that the new administrative entity be called Zeku County. However, the gathered chieftains strenuously objected. According to the County Work Group's own contemporary account, several reasoned that because the region had formerly been under the jurisdiction of Tongren County, the new appellation should include the character "Tong." Yet Du Hua'an held firm, explaining, "'Ze' is the 'Ze' from 'Mao Zedong.' 'Ku' is the 'Ku' from 'treasure house' [baoku]. So the name 'Zeku' is a great one." Allegedly Du's argument swayed the gathered headmen, and the issue of the county name was successfully resolved.[17]

This otherwise inconsequential anecdote is striking for at least two reasons. First, that there was no self-evident name (in Chinese) by which the new county should be known helps illustrate the degree to which Zeku was a construct of the new state. According to the county gazetteer, Zeku is a transliteration of the Tibetan place name Tsékhok, which it imprecisely renders "the basin between the mountains" (shanjian pendi).[18] By extension, this implies that prior to the arrival of the CCP, a cohesive region called Tsékhok already existed. This does not seem to be the case. In his Great History of Amdo (Mdo smad lo rgyu *chen mo*), for example, Hortsang Jigme explicitly states that the toponym Tsékhok was an invention of the Chinese Communist authorities without historical precedent.[19] More important than the name itself is the implied lack of preexisting regional cohesion. While PRC sources refer to the "Ten Tribes of Zeku," there is little to indicate that there was a shared affinity that either united them or set them apart from other peoples across still invisible borders.

Second, the manner by which Du Hua'an settled the issue of the county name is instructive for what it reveals about the relationship between the mass line methodologies of consultation and persuasion. Given several other of Du's pronouncements—as well as those of his superiors—regarding the importance of consultation and the promotion of nationality unity, rather than spend political capital over an issue of little practical consequence, it seems Secretary Du would have been better served to concede to the objections of the headmen. If Du wished to convince local Tibetans that the CCP truly intended to make them "masters of their own home," as was loudly and repeatedly proclaimed, this would seem to have been a symbolically powerful opportunity to make good on that promise at little cost. Yet Du insisted on naming the new administrative region Zeku County. The reason was simple. The decision had been made well before the process of consultation had begun. More than a year before Guo Min and his work group stepped foot in the region, the term "Zeku County" was already being used in official communications.[20] The dialectical imbalance between consultation and persuasion was in full force. Not even the county's name was up for genuine discussion.

A Powerful Weapon

In both internal documents and open sources, the argument for separating the southern pastoral districts from Tongren proper was made primarily in economic terms. By severing the Zeku region, which was "purely pastoral" and where "the people all live in tents," from Tongren's agricultural heartland, where people live in "earthen houses," a work report reasoned, "it will be easy for government leaders to create plans to promote production and improve people's livelihoods."[21] While there is little question that economic factors played a significant role in the decision to create Zeku County, the pastoral economy did not exist in isolation. Economic concerns were irreducibly wrapped up in a host of political, security, and philosophical considerations crucial to strengthening Party rule in Qinghai. Party leaders understood pastoralism to be part of a particular political economy that in many ways seemed inimical to the CCP's vision of a modern, unitary, socialist state. Like sedentary states across time and space, the CCP considered pastoral peoples particularly backward, difficult to govern, and prone to violence. Filtered through the lens of Chinese Communism, pastoral regions were identified as zones of acute economic and political exploitation in which not only class consciousness but also ethnic/nationality consciousness were basically absent. In place of these two central markers of modern identity, Party leaders such as Zhou Renshan asserted, existed an almost primitive tribalism and slavish devotion to monastic leaders and hereditary chieftains who controlled both the means of production and unbridled political authority.[22]

Yet rather than smash these class enemies and "liberate" the pastoral masses, it was precisely in pastoral regions that United Front principles were judged to be most vital. Provincial planners divided Qinghai into three strategic zones: those in which the primary economic activity was agriculture, those that had mixed economies, and those that were purely pastoral. It was in this latter category that Party leaders instructed their cadres to proceed most cautiously and deliberately. In 1950, for example, Xining stipulated that the qianhu and baihu of pastoral regions retain their traditional titles and positions, albeit now under CCP leadership.[23] More consequently, in a 1951 speech to the provincial Party committee, Zhou Renshan declared Qinghai's pastoral districts exempt not only from land reform, which was then being initiated within Han and Hui farming communities north of the Yellow River, but also from more moderate reforms such as rent reduction.[24]

Most significantly, Zhou announced that all work in pastoral regions must adhere to the guiding principle of the "Three Nos" "no division of property, no class struggle, and no class delineation" (bufen budou buhua). The Three Nos policy had originated in Inner Mongolia, where the Mongolian Communist Ulanhu (C. Wulanfu) asserted that pastoral class relations were marked not by exploitation but symbiosis.[25] Despite Zhou Renshan's previous posting in Inner Mongolia, he and other Party leaders in Qinghai did not suggest that pastoral class relations were unique or that class exploitation did not exist. Instead, the Three Nos were deemed a matter of practical necessity dictated by the backward socioeconomic order and nationality exploitation that had long prevailed in pastoral regions.[26] As in agricultural areas, the ultimate goal remained collectivizing production. However, Party leaders in both Beijing and Xining conceded that a considerable amount of time might be needed before pastoral collectivization could commence. By guaranteeing that their positions would remain inviolable and their wealth untouched, the Three Nos was an explicit attempt to secure the cooperation and support of Amdo's pastoral leadership during this transitional period.[27]

With socialist reforms delayed indefinitely, Qinghai's leadership prioritized the implementation of regional nationality autonomy. Perhaps voicing the concerns of his audience, at a 1951 provincial-level pastoral work conference, Zhou

Renshan rhetorically asked, "Why do we want to energetically establish nationality autonomous regions?" In response to his own question, Zhou replied, "[Be-
cause] nationality autonomous regions and nationality democratic coalition
governments are the political forms that best embody nationality equality and
are therefore the best methods to consolidate nationality unity."[28] A year later, he
described nationality autonomy as a "powerful weapon" for enlisting the active
participation of pastoral peoples into the CCP's nation-building project. Only
through a commitment to aiding minorities to establish nationality autonomy
administrations, Zhou asserted, could the Party gain the "trust" of non-Han
communities.[29]

   Within broader United Front work, regional autonomy was thus considered
to be the specific mechanism for winning the support of minority communities.
Pitched as a democratic institution "diametrically opposite from the reactionary
rule [of the past],"[30] Party leaders insisted that nationality autonomy had the
power to overcome the legacy of Han chauvinism, considered the root cause of
internationality estrangement.[31] Zhou explained, "Because nationality autonomous areas are the best paths toward all-around unity, whatever historical an-
tagonisms minority nationality people have toward the Han nationality, after the
correct implementation of nationality autonomous areas, can be properly dealt
with and eliminated."[32] The first step, however, was enlisting the aid of pastoral
elites. Chen Sigong, another senior provincial Party official, elaborated further:

> Previously because of the control of the upper strata, the pastoral masses
> had apprehensions [toward the CCP], and we had a lot of difficulty di-
> rectly connecting with the pastoral masses. Since the establishment of
> nationality autonomous region governments, this situation has begun
> to change. On the one hand, by taking part in the governance of na-
> tionality autonomous areas, upper-strata figures and midlevel pastoral
> representatives go and spread the Party's policies and implement [na-
> tionality] work. On the other hand, through nationality autonomous
> area preparatory committees, we can organize work teams, dispatch
> them to localities, penetrate the broad pastoral masses, and meet the
> pastoral masses directly.[33]

More simply put, according to Zhou Renshan, "the implementation of nationality autonomous areas begins with uniting with the tribal leaders, and all other
work is also done by persuading the tribal leaders."[34] Only through the intercession of these figures could grassroots cadres make inroads among the pastoral
masses.

   The CCP therefore was engaged in a long-term battle for the hearts and
minds of pastoral Tibetans. Yet it was also preoccupied with immediate security

conditions, a consideration that likewise necessitated the speedy erection of na-tionality autonomous areas. Dividing southern Qinghai into three zones, Zhou Renshan directly correlated declining local support for anti-Party elements with the founding of nationality autonomous administrations. First, he noted, were regions such as Tongren in which cadres had been dispatched early and the or-gans of nationality autonomy quickly had been established. Next were places to which cadres had been sent later and still were in the process of fully establish-ing autonomous administrations. Last were regions to which cadres had only recently been deployed and preparations for establishing nationality autonomy had yet to begin. In these latter areas, Zhou suggested, "the relationship between some of the important headmen and counterrevolutionaries has not yet been completely severed, and the line between enemies and friends has not yet been completely demarcated. Therefore, the center of work in these areas still is to vigorously strive to unify the headmen, distinguish a clear line between enemies and friends, and consider how to prepare to establish [nationality autonomy] administrations."[35] Strikingly, alone in this third category were the contiguous territories of southeastern Qinghai—identified as Guoluo, Henan, and Zeku—the areas that served as the base of Ma Yuanxiang's insurrection. In fact, Zhou singled Zeku out as the very last "county" to which cadres had been sent. It there-fore is no surprise that Gyelyön and his comrades were dispatched into the Zeku grasslands so quickly after Ma Yuanxiang's defeat. The restoration of social order and the development of nationality unity were dependent on the promotion of the Party's minority policies, the core of which was the implementation of na-tionality autonomy through United Front alliances with the pre-1949 leadership.

Why Preserve Feudalism?

Han chauvinism was not the only sentiment that led to acrimonious relationships between nationalities. The "parochial attitudes" (xia'ai guandian) commonly dis-played by members of minority communities—more commonly known as "lo-cal nationalism"—had to be eliminated as well. For most of the 1950s, however, officials both in Xining and Beijing considered Han chauvinism a far greater concern.[36] CCP leaders repeatedly emphasized not only the nonequivalence of Han chauvinism and local nationalism but also drew an explicit causational link between them. Declaring "local nationalism to be the product of past national-ity exploitation," Zhou Renshan insisted, "After nationality autonomy is imple-mented, [and national minorities] become masters of their own homes . . ., the political conditions for [local nationalism] will be completely eliminated."[37] In other words, local nationalism only existed as a response to the exploitation of the Han majority. The onus therefore was placed squarely on the Party and its representatives: local nationalism would disappear only after great nationality exploitation had been eradicated.

Ridding the borderlands of Han chauvinism, however, proved easier said than done. Higher levels routinely accused grassroots cadres of lacking trust in, displaying arrogance toward, and showing disrespect for the non-Chinese people among and with whom they now worked. In a stinging 1953 report issued jointly by the Northwest Bureau's UFWD and NAC, these concerns were expressed in the strongest possible language. Quoting a recent broadside penned by Mao Zedong himself, the missive referred to Han chauvinism as "the expression of the reactionary thought and Guomindang thought of the landlord and capitalist class," adding, "It impedes the proper implementation of Party policies, damages the intimate unity of the nationalities, and causes the various nationalities to suffer a huge loss of faith in the Party."[38] The Northwest Bureau noted, for example, that Han cadres often criticized the "backwardness" of Tibetan women's dress, their elaborate hairstyles and headpieces considered to be particularly wasteful.[39] The same allegation was leveled at attitudes toward Tibetan Buddhist practices, such as lighting butter lamps and burning juniper branches. Islamic traditions, including the prohibition on eating or raising pigs, were often derided as well, and cadres were known to openly criticize imams as purveyors of superstition. These viewpoints, the report succinctly concluded, "make the masses unsatisfied" and "do not benefit unity."[40]

It was not only alien cultural practices that many Han cadres found distasteful. According to the CCP's own reports, there also existed considerable ambivalence and even hostility toward policies that appeared to abandon all pretense of class struggle in favor of reconciliation with the feudal elite of minority nationalities.[41] Bulag notes that the reversion to imperial-style strategies often creates a backlash among champions of the modernizing nation-state, adding that because it "violates the very sensibility of nationalist ideology, . . . subimperialism is often mired in tension with nationalism."[42] For many cadres, the Party's United Front policies seemed to betray the homogenizing and transformative tenants of both nationalism and socialism.

The standard response of CCP leaders to such criticism was to emphasize that these attitudes were themselves remnants of Han chauvinism, an expression of poor political consciousness, and betrayed a fundamental misunderstanding of the specific conditions of minority regions.[43] Zhou Renshan explicitly denied that the exercise of nationality autonomy amounted to the protection of feudal structures and class enemies. Instead, he maintained that nationality autonomy was a method through which socialist democracy, already enjoyed by the Han majority, would be extended to the special characteristics of non-Han regions.

FIGURE 5. Three women from the Labrang area display their braids and hair ornaments. Joseph Rock, 1925, courtesy of Harvard-Yenching Library.

As Amdo's upper strata was co-opted into the new system, now as leading members of local autonomous government committees, its "nationality form" would be maintained while its "essence" would gradually change.[44] In other words, Zhou declared, "the single person rule of the baihu system would move toward the rule of the many."[45] Rather than abdicating the promises of the revolution, as it seemed to some, provincial leaders insisted that the United Front was itself a path to socialist transformation.

In this way the Party's subimperial practice of allying with indigenous elites was reimagined as a transformative process of socialist nation building. In his 1951 address, Director Zhou proclaimed, "If we do not pay attention to the special nationality characteristics [of Qinghai], we cannot achieve success." Yet he qualified this statement by noting, "Of course the purpose of attending to special characteristics is to make it easier to produce a revolutionary force and *gradually* implement all types of socialist reforms."[46] The following year at the 1952 pastoral work conference, Zhou hammered the point home, asking an apparently skeptical audience, "Why no division [of property,] no [class] struggle, no [class] delineation, [why] preserve feudalism . . .?"[47] Zhou's answer, simply put, was that nationality autonomy was not just a means to win over and energize local people but was also itself a "*social reform* that fit the special characteristics [that exist] among [minority] nationalities."[48]

How to Make Friends and Serve the People

Nowhere was the transformative potential of nationality autonomy more apparent than in its presumed ability to undermine "tribal" identities and replace them with the logic of the nation-state. Declaring that "by their nature tribes are backward," Zhou Renshan equated nationality autonomy with "the process of moving from tribal division to democratic unity." As the benefits of autonomy became clear, he predicted that "tribal attitudes will gradually be reduced and move toward disappearing on their own accord."[49]

Moreover, nationality autonomy had the purported power to not only extinguish *inter*ethnic animosity but also end the *intra*ethnic conflicts that threatened unity and disrupted social and economic order. Of particular concern to Party leaders was Amdo's high incidence of intercommunity conflict. As noted earlier, these "grassland disputes" came to almost metonymically represent the internal disunity that seemed to plague pastoral society. Through the ideological lens of the CCP, these feuds were considered a by-product of the "contradictions in the old system's grassland management and pastoral production."[50] In other words, by replacing the exploitative political and economic relationships of the Ma

Bufang regime with the nationality unity, equality, and autonomy promised by the CCP, grassland disputes would be effectively eliminated.[51] Speaking in summer 1952, Chen Sigong even claimed that in areas in which nationality autonomous administrations already had been established, cases of "retaliatory banditry and armed feuds had basically stopped."[52]

Still, none of this would happen overnight. Because the structure of Amdo's pastoral society was the consequence of long-term economic, social, and political conditions, provincial leaders conceded that the old system could not be eliminated through dramatic Party-imposed mass campaigns and certainly not through force. Change must instead occur through a process of "organic transformation" (*youji de tuibian*) in which "the old gradually weakens and the new gradually takes root." Director Zhou instructed his cadres to let the old system die out on its own, remarking, "Do not rescue the dead, but do not cast off the living." Only when the masses themselves ceased to recognize the authority of the qianhu, baihu, and other pastoral nobility (*wanggongzhe*) could they effectively be eliminated as an economic and political class. In this manner, a provincial Party committee report declared, "backward nationalities" would gradually be transformed into "vanguard nationalities" marching down a shared path to socialism.[53]

Emphasizing the pragmatism that formed the foundation of United Front work, Zhou Renshan made it clear that during this preliminary period of state and nation building, "getting results is most important."[54] Yet the line between pragmatism and deception is a thin one. For instance, at the 1952 pastoral work conference, Zhou reminded his cadres, "In work methods, we only emphasize the intention of developing nationality autonomous regions and do not raise the issue of the backwardness of the tribes and their future [disappearance]."[55] Implied is that this was a covert effort, the ramifications of which were to be withheld from all but the most dedicated activists. In the same vein, Zhou informed his audience that despite the support and sanctuary that religious elements allegedly had provided counterrevolutionaries, security forces were not to conduct operations in monasteries, nor were political committees to be set up within their walls.[56] These considerable concessions were made in recognition of the religious sensitivities of local populations. Zhou noted, albeit patronizingly, that guarantees of freedom of religion and respect for local customs were what the average minority person "cared most about" and were therefore the primary method for gaining their trust.[57] Ultimately, he explained soberly, "This will benefit unity."[58]

Elsewhere Zhou insisted that among Qinghai's nationalities, "religious belief is very deep," adding, "Presently they would rather sacrifice their lives than sacrifice religion."[59] As long as minority peoples continued to entrust their fate to lamas and imams rather than the CCP, the Party would encounter formidable

obstacles to implementing its programs of nation building and socialist construction. Zhou admitted that the leadership wished to avoid a scenario in which
they might "win the battle but lose the war." He therefore instructed cadres to
concentrate on "making friends and collecting information," adding, "Only after
the majority of religious figures within the monasteries wholeheartedly trust us,
can we alter this passive approach to religious work." Speaking of "religious and
tribal representatives who have relationships to counterrevolutionaries," Zhou
insisted, "We will continue to win them over through the principle of unity education; this will cause them to voluntarily separate themselves from counterrevolution and lean toward us. We will not adopt the method of attack."[60] Thus,
the Party's approach to religious institutions and activities was both pragmatic
and, in a sense, hostile. Yet in its internal logic, this did not make it cynical or
incompatible with the United Front focus on voluntarism and reliance on consultation and persuasion. Instead, Zhou would remind his cadres, "Methods are
not goals, yet the relationship between the two is extremely close. If the methods
are not good, then we certainly will not be able to reach the goal *which is how to
serve the people.*"[61]

This collision between voluntarism and compulsion, pluralism and paternalism—
expressed in the well-used couplet "to become masters of their own home, under
the leadership of the Party"—in a sense embodies the high modernist sentiments
embedded in the United Front and mass line. The outwardly irreconcilable principle of nationality autonomy under CCP leadership was internally consistent
when the Party's self-appointed position as the vanguard of the proletariat *and*
vanguard of the multinationality nation is kept in mind. Of course, there was
little true autonomy (i.e., self-rule) possible in this arrangement, particularly
given the oft-cited intersection of ethnonationalism and socialism that under
the CCP has combined to assume most of China's minority peoples to be further
back on a scale of social progress and in need of being actively transformed by the
more politically, culturally, and economically advanced Han nationality.[62] Zhou
illustrated this dynamic well when he declared,

> Our policy is to attend to [nationality] special characteristics, respect
> special characteristics, and through [respect for] special characteristics
> do a good job of eliminating antagonisms, increasing mutual trust, rais-
> ing consciousness, and developing the cause of each nationality. [How-
> ever, it is] *absolutely not* to cultivate special characteristics and develop
> special characteristics (such as backward customs and religious beliefs,
> and so on) that would result in unconsciously traveling down the road
> to protecting backwardness and strengthening antagonisms.[63]

Thus, despite rebuking cadres for expressions of Han chauvinism, little inherent value was to be found in the "special characteristics" of minority nationalities. Instead, showing respect for local customs and practices was itself a pragmatic means of nation building.

However, it is also clear that within the limited parameters that mass line politics allowed, Party leaders in Qinghai *did* intend nationality autonomy to be an instrument of democratic unity, nationality equality, and socialist transformation. Calling it a major work defect, Zhou criticized the tendency among his cadres for "the guests to usurp the role of the host" and "not respect the authority of Tibetan office holders." Using Tongren as an example, he censured a cadre named Wang Jinyou for not allowing the county's Tibetan chairman and vice chairmen to preside over a meeting celebrating the "liberation" of Central Tibet.[64] A provincial report likewise declared that too often cooperative elites had not been properly consulted nor given appropriate positions and *real authority*. It continued, "There is a general lack of understanding that the upper strata of the pastoral regions are targets for our long-term cooperation and not targets of attack. [They are not] 'for temporary use,' and [this is not] 'a changing of the guard.'"[65] A year later, the Northwest Bureau roundly criticized cadres for displaying a pattern of chauvinistic attitudes toward the non-Han leaders who now served as chairmen and vice chairmen of nationality autonomous administrations. This had caused minority representatives "to feel that they have positions but no authority." Instead of becoming masters of their own home, the report admitted, local people feel that they "built a home in which they have no say."[66] While genuine self-rule was clearly not possible within the Party's United Front framework, neither was nationality autonomy simply a ruse meant to mollify minority peoples until the CCP was in position to implement the new order by force. To put it another way, what the leadership in Beijing and Xining stated publicly about minority policy and the United Front is mirrored almost without exception in internal CCP directives sent to county-level cadres and below.

It comes as little surprise, then, that as the PLA moved into position against Ma Yuanxiang in the spring of 1953, provincial leaders began to make preparations for establishing Party rule in what would become known as Zeku County. As would be expected, the decision was said to have been made in consultation and even at the behest of local headmen, an internal report remarking, "Since Zeku is a wholly pastoral county, different from Tongren County, which is semiagricultural and seminomadic, after the tribal leaders consulted with the Tongren government, they decided to establish a separate county."[67] What is interesting is not so much that the Party claimed it had procured the agreement of "tribal leaders" but that this language is maintained in its classified communications, emphasizing once again the manner in which consultation and persuasion were internalized within the CCP's operating practices. In fact, when in the spring of 1953 discussion officially began over the fate of Tongren's southern grasslands, local headmen were surely consulted. However, the decision to form a new autonomous county had been made at least a year earlier. And although the expected benefits to the pastoral economy were certainly real, increasing the productive capacities of the pastoral highlands and raising the living standards of its inhabitants were irreducibly intertwined with a host of other practical and philosophical concerns, all of which were central to the Party's efforts to "gradually," "voluntarily," and "organically" transform an imperial borderland into an integrated component of the new socialist nation-state.

Friendship and Unity II

While plans to establish Zeku County had been in the works since at least the summer of 1952, secondary sources note that the subject of the administrative future of Tongren's southern pastoral districts was only officially broached in March 1953 at the Fourth Joint Committee (*lianwei*) meeting of the Tongren Tibetan Autonomous Region Government and Consultative Committees. Convened during the height of anti–Ma Yuanxiang military operations, the meeting was attended by sixty-seven committee members and thirty-one nonvoting observers from among the "nationality headmen" (*minzu touren*).[68] Although no list of participants is provided, it seems certain that several members of the Zeku region's secular and religious leadership would have been expected to be in attendance, among them Wagya, hereditary chieftain of the Hor chiefdom. Having been recognized as one the most prominent figures in the greater Repgong region and the most powerful headman on the Zeku grasslands, for the past year Wagya had served as one of four vice chairmen of the Tongren County People's Government Committee. Similarly, Lubum, the qianhu of the Gartsé chiefdom, had been selected a vice chairman of Tongren's consultative committee. Several other headmen, including Wagya's brother Lhagyel, were also members of either of the two bodies.

The Fourth Joint Committee was convened specifically to deal with issues of pastoral production and administration, including exploring the possibility of establishing what was to become Zeku County. When the committee met again at the end of July, the question of Zeku County was once more on the agenda. However, by that time only the details were left open for discussion. With the recent defeat of Ma Yuanxiang, Gyelyön's vanguard detachment had already been sent over the mountains and into the grasslands. Outstanding issues such as where to set the county's boundaries, where to place the county seat, and how to allocate the cadre force necessary to will the new county into existence were all that remained for the committee to deliberate.[69]

The immediate goal was to hold a people's representative conference that could formally endorse the creation of the Zeku Tibetan Autonomous County. Before then, however, a foundation had to be laid. Propaganda needed to be disseminated, a consensus built, and delegates carefully selected. Yet, with minimal access to the masses and little region-wide cohesion, the process would have to be mediated by Zeku's preexisting leadership. Following established practice, the first step was to convene a Headman Unity and Friendship Conference (Touren Lianyi Huiyi). On September 21, just ten days after Guo Min's arrival, twenty-seven representatives from the region's ten chiefdoms (a considerable achievement in its own right) met with the twelve-man County Work Group for "communal consultation on restoring social order, building the new administration, developing the economy, improving peoples' livelihoods, and handling all types of disputes between the people."[70]

Demonstrating the importance CCP leaders attached to this preparatory meeting, Tongren Party secretary and United Front director Du Hua'an apparently traveled to the Shadar grasslands to personally lead the proceedings. As suggested by Du's keynote address, "How to Raise Unity," the conference was akin to an interchiefdom summit brokered under the auspices of the CCP.[71] In fact, in 1950s Amdo, the familiar phrase *minzu tuanjie*, or nationality unity, had dual connotations. The first, more intuitive meaning, and the one it retains to this day, was unity *between* nationalities. Contrary to initial expectation, however, at the time minzu tuanjie more often than not referred to "internal relations within the tribes."[72] A County Work Group report described deep divisions between and within Zeku's ten chiefdoms. For instance, the Hor was involved in ongoing conflicts with the Gönshül, Gartsé, and Sonak chiefdoms, while the Gartsé was also engaged in disputes with the Sonak and Shisa. Intercounty feuds included hostilities between the Méshül and chiefdoms in Tongde, the Wöngya with rivals in Guinan, the Hor in both Guinan and Xiahe, the Shawonar with Xiahe and Guinan, and just about everyone with the Four Mongol Banners of what would become Henan County. Disputes within chiefdoms were even more common and as debilitating.[73]

The circular issued on the final day of the Unity and Friendship Conference, "Decision on Strengthening Nationality Unity and Protecting Social Stability" (hereafter "the September Decision"), gives a clear indication of the CCP's priorities at this early date. From the perspective of the Party-state, cultural norms rooted in the backward socioeconomic conditions of the grasslands needed to be turned into criminal behaviors governed by a set of rational laws, delineated

FIGURE 6.   "On August 6, 1952, Qinwang Trashi Tséring welcomes the Henan Mongol Banner Work Committee." Detail from painting "Thangka of the Mongol History South of the Yellow River," by permission of Ute Wallenböck. © Ute Wallenböck 2019.

jurisdictions, and statutory punishments. In particular, the September Decision sought to replace cycles of retributive violence with a system of regular punishments and compensations. For example, it stipulated penalties for animal rustling (various terms of forced labor), while "harming unity resulting in the injuring or death of another" would be punishable by three or five years of imprisonment, depending on the level of culpability. An article even dictated that the owner of a dog that had bitten and injured another person was responsible not only for medical costs but also for expenses associated with inviting monks to chant sutra.

Yet the September Decision implicitly recognized that the "tribal" signatories, not security officials, remained the key guarantors of stability and unity.[74] Other than the issuance of the September Decision, the main task of the Unity and Friendship Conference was the selection of a Zeku County Preparatory Committee. While a full name list is not provided, the conference selected a twenty-nine-member committee consisting of seventeen local Tibetan leaders and all twelve members of Guo Min's work group. Wagya was chosen committee secretary, with Guo Min as his first vice secretary. Wagya's younger brother (the Hor baihu and incarnate Nyingma lama) Lhagyel, the Gönshül chieftain Serökyap, and the Shawonar's Lhakba were selected the second through fourth vice secretaries respectively. At the same time, attendees inaugurated a political consultative committee. Its cochairmen were Lubum, headman of the Gartsé chiefdom, and the Méshül "monk official" Tsintar.[75] It should be noted that with the possible exception of Tsintar, each of these Tibetan officeholders had been implicated in the Ma Bufang government. Lhagyel, Serökyap, and Lubum all had joined the Guomindang, while sources identify Lhakba as a "sworn brother" to the recently defeated Ma Yuanxiang. Again, the Party was reassembling the broad parameters of the subimperial relationships forged by past regimes, albeit in a radically reimagined and immensely more penetrative form.

Down to the Tribes

With a set of rudimentary legal codes promulgated and a new leadership chosen, the Unity and Friendship Conference concluded on September 23. However, any conceit Du Hua'an, Guo Min, and the County Work Group may have assumed from the apparent success of these initial talks was certainly dampened when only seven of the seventeen "tribal representatives" (buluo daibiao) showed up on October 20 for the county's Second Preparatory Conference.[76] Among the many no-shows was committee secretary Wagya, his brother Lhagyel attending in his place. With participation unacceptably low, the County Work Group essentially scrapped the conference's agenda. The one substantive issue successfully dealt with was the question of the county name, which as described above was pushed through by Du Hua'an himself. Thus, when reports claim that Secretary Du convinced local headmen that Zeku was indeed a suitable name, it apparently referred to only seven of the preparatory committee's seventeen Tibetan representatives.

While Du was able to get his way when it came to the relatively trivial question of the county name, he was unable to resolve a second, more consequential issue. Other than a handful of fixed-place monasteries and the small hamlets that grew around them (referred to in Chinese sources as *tawa*, T. *dewa*), few permanent structures existed on Zeku's grasslands.[77] An administrative center would have to be built literally from the ground up. Yet, with interchiefdom relations already tense, the location of the future county seat was a question of considerable sensitivity. Guo Min and his County Work Group favored the spot within the Sonak chiefdom on which Gyelyön and his colleagues had pitched their tents earlier that year. Not only did this site provide access to the Tséchu River, but it also was near the geographic center of the proposed county. On behalf of his brother, however, Lhagyel insisted that the county seat be built in the Hor territories in the far west of the county. The reason given was that "the Hor's climate is better suited [for Han cadres] than the Sonak's, and vegetables and trees can be grown."[78] The other headmen strenuously objected. Concerned that the already powerful Hor would dominate the new county, some even reportedly threatened to relocate to Tongren or Guinan Counties. The work group saw through the self-serving nature of Wagya's offer as well, reporting, "Obviously this would be beneficial for his tribe and himself."[79] Given both the contentious nature of the disagreement and the meeting's low attendance, Guo Min postponed a final decision for a later date.

Noticeably frustrated by the poor turnout and sensing hesitancy if not outright obstruction on the part of the local headmen, Secretary Guo next turned his attention to expanding the Party's reach beyond the region's traditional elite. In a handwritten report penned under his own name, Guo set a goal of increasing representation from the forty-five "tribal representatives" already chosen to attend an eventual inaugural conference to one hundred and seventeen. Of the additional seventy-two delegates, he insisted that fifty-one be chosen from among the masses and the remainder from government work units. Guo further noted that not a single woman had been included among the original slate of representatives. He therefore stipulated that twenty-five female tribal delegates be added. Demonstrating an accelerated pace of state building that contradicted more general instructions to avoid proceeding too "rashly" or neglecting "democratic process," Guo announced that the one hundred and seventeen delegates would meet in less than three weeks to inaugurate the county. While socialist transformation had been postponed for a later date, Party leaders were already exhibiting revolutionary impatience toward their state-building project.[80]

Time running short, Guo urged Tibetan members of the preparatory committee to return to their chiefdoms to select representatives from the masses for the upcoming county representative conference. While "democratic methods" were stressed, Secretary Guo added that the candidate list must be carefully vetted. Headmen were told to identify trustworthy delegates willing to work for the benefit of the people, able to contribute to the development of pastoral production, capable of elevating nationality unity, competent to perform all types of tasks, and therefore qualified to represent the people.[81] Yet the work group doubted that successful elections could be held without Party guidance, a suspicion that was surely heightened by the Second Preparatory Conference's dismal turnout. In accordance with mass line procedures, it therefore resolved to send work teams "down to the tribes" to instruct local communities on voting methods, discuss the concept of nationality autonomy, and explain to the masses the meaning of political representation.[82]

On October 26, the County Work Group deployed the first of four work teams on a ten-day assignment to Wagya's Hor. A week later it sent the three remaining teams into the grasslands, each assigned to multiple chiefdoms. Work teams were instructed first to consult with tribal leaders in order to enlist their aid. Headmen would then introduce the work teams at mass meetings, after which the team leader would address the gathering and representatives would be chosen. In Hor, for example, eight hundred people reportedly met for two days of mass meetings at which Wagya himself relayed the "spirit" of the Second Preparatory Conference and spoke about the importance of establishing an autonomous county. Afterward, according to a preset quota, twenty-seven Hor delegates were selected, including five women and two representatives from Hor Monastery.[83]

Glowing reports issued by a second work team suggest that a similar procedure was followed among the Wöngya chiefdom. Located in the far northwestern corner of the proposed county, the Wöngya leadership had responded to the new political order with unease, complaining, for instance, that the Tongren-based tax collectors continued to employ the exploitative tactics favored by the Ma regime. As a result, the Wöngya did not send a representative to the previous preparatory meeting and were disinclined to choose delegates for a future representative conference. However, the report claims, after the work team explained the benefits of nationality autonomy and assured the Wöngya that the tax situation would be investigated, a headman named Losar came forward, declaring,

> In the old society, Chiang Kaishek and Ma Bufang suppressed us so much that our anger knew no bounds; the amount he cheated us was also incalculable. After Liberation, Chairman Mao and the Communist Party saved us Tibetans from the fire. Our position has been raised. Establishing Huangnan Prefecture and here establishing Zeku County, these are our people's governments; they are the governments given to us to handle [our own] affairs. So, we must select our representatives well, and when the [people's representative] conference convenes, we must send our representatives.[84]

The blessings of autonomy now clear, a member of the Wöngya's masses allegedly proclaimed that herdsmen must protect the grasslands and livestock, eliminate bandits and spies, correct mistaken behaviors, and seek the government's redress for those who did not mend their ways. Three thieves even were said to have voluntarily turned themselves in. [85]

Of course, neither the sincerity of the Wöngya informants nor the validity of the report itself should be taken at face value. They might be better thought of as aspirational, reflecting the Party's normative expectations filtered through the grassroots cadres sent to fulfill those ambitions. By contrast, a separate summary report noted that because Zeku's sparse population was scattered across the grasslands, work teams only reached four of Zeku's ten chiefdoms—the Hor and Wöngya along with the Khéri Chunga and the Shawonar.[86] Within the four, delegates were purportedly chosen through democratic process, a vote of hands from a prepared list of candidates. Elsewhere, however, the report admitted that headmen chose delegates without input from the Party or the people. Moreover, it noted that among common herders, particularly women, it was often difficult to find willing delegates. Predictably, the County Work Group viewed this reluctance in historical terms, explaining, "In the old society, nationality oppression was felt most deeply by the oppressed pastoral masses; they did not have any rights, especially women. After Liberation, although nationality policy protects the equality of all nationalities, awareness is still not high. Because of this, they are extremely confused about the meaning of convening a people's representative conference. They believe that being a representative is similar to being a servant."[87] A third report summarized, "This shows that people do not have a clear understanding of their political right to choose representatives. There is a danger that the representatives are only being chosen by lottery. This is unsuitable for the spirit of elections."[88] Couched in the bureaucratic language of the CCP, the missives acknowledge the distance in both trust and outlook that continued to separate the Party from the people it hoped to transform. They also confirm that it was up to local officials—most of whom were Han Chinese, and all of whom were from outside the area—to close the gap. Failure to do so, the third report concluded, "is a deficiency in our work."

Consultation and Persuasion

For Guo Min and the County Work Group, the failure of the Second Preparatory Conference and mixed results generated by subsequent efforts to recruit delegates for a representative conference served as something of a wakeup call. More concentrated efforts of consultation and persuasion with Zeku's headmen were needed before the Party could hope to extend its reach among common pastoralists. The selection process mired in uncertainty and outstanding issues from the second preparatory meeting still unsettled, the representative conference planned for November 9 had to be postponed. On that date county leaders instead convened a Third Preparatory Conference. According to the county committee's own assessment, the previous meeting's failures were due to poor preparations. Therefore, the November conference was preceded by what documents describe as intensive political work (i.e., propaganda), efforts that seemed to be rewarded when all but three representatives traveled to the Shadar grasslands to attend the meeting.[89]

The immediate impasse remained the dispute over the site of the county seat. Through "informal discussions" and investigations, Party representatives had obtained advanced knowledge of the position of each chiefdom. Wagya and the Hor remained adamant that the county seat be established within their lands. The Wöngya, whose territories bordered the Hor in northwestern Zeku, were noncommittal. The other headmen, however, were firmly insistent that the county seat be built at its present location. Determined to avoid mistakes that had helped scuttle the October conference, rather than immediately convening the full meeting Party leaders divided the delegates into several "small groups." The Hor representatives were sequestered together in a single group, while the remaining headmen were dispersed among several others. Working within each, reports suggest that cadres quickly brought the Wöngya over to the majority opinion. Undeterred, Wagya again reasoned, "Even though the Hor tribe is located relatively far away from the other tribes, the climate is good, it has good prospects for the future, and it would be beneficial for the livelihood of the Han cadres." If the report is to be believed, Wagya had even absorbed some of the terminological tricks of the new regime, concluding, "These are the opinions I have brought with me from the masses."[90]

Yet Wagya was not the only chieftain already becoming adept in new expressions and rationales. In the other small groups, headmen were said to have expressed the need for Wagya to consider the interests of the entire county and to act in the spirit of "serving the people." Party intermediaries then returned to Wagya, relaying the message that the other headmen were unanimously opposed to erecting the county seat within his lands. That evening, after again being urged to keep the benefit of the entire county in mind, Wagya finally conceded to the demands of the other headmen—the Party's agents all along ostensibly acting as honest broker.[91]

The next morning, the small groups were reconvened. County leaders announced Wagya's change of heart, urging the gathered chieftains to "learn from Wagya's spirit of selflessness, unity, and mutual aid." Having provided the Hor headman an honorable exit, and all but guaranteeing a favorable resolution to the question of the county seat, the full conference finally convened. There Wagya accepted the "people's suggestion" that the county administrative seat be erected along the banks of the Tséchu River. Secretary Guo formally introduced the proposal, after which the preparatory committee unanimously voted to "build the county seat in the middle of the county."[92]

Having brought the issue of the county seat to a satisfactory conclusion, Guo Min's County Work Group framed it as a lesson in the proper implementation of the principles of consultation and persuasion. Unlike the October conference, the work group summarized that "(a) prior to the meeting, preparatory work was done well, ideas were made clear to the cadres, and the conditions [in the county] were thoroughly researched and appraised [i.e., consultation]" and that, following textbook mass line procedures, cadres, "(b) adhered to the principle of cautious implementation, won over the center [i.e., the Wöngya] and isolated the mistaken [i.e., the Hor]." Once Wagya accepted the majority position, he received commendation from Party representatives and his peers (i.e., persuasion).[93] A report summarized, "In this way, the issue was resolved," adding, "The agreement on the county seat is the beginning of developing unity among the ten tribes in Zeku."[94]

The saga of the county seat starkly illustrates the manner in which the mass line demands "meaningful participation" without relinquishing the Party's decision-making authority.[95] As with the case of the county name, the decision over where to establish the county seat had almost certainly been made long before Wagya's political epiphany. As described in Gyelyön's short memoir, by fall cadres already had built a rudimentary government seat with work units separated by earthen walls and the entire encampment enclosed behind a sturdy rampart. Now, just three days after the conclusion of the conference and several weeks before the First Zeku County People's Representative Conference would formally endorse the decision, Guo Min personally sent a report to the provincial finance office. In it, he divulged that the County Work Group already had asked an engineer to survey the area and design the new township. Guo went on to detail difficulties procuring building materials on the desolate grasslands and attached a blueprint and proposed budget for consideration. Instructively, the report was signed not by the Zeku County Preparatory Committee, which officially was led by Wagya and the indigenous county leadership, but by Guo Min as head of the CCP's Zeku County Preparatory Work Group.[96]

Learning from Lhakba

Having resolved the dispute over the county seat, delegates to the Third Preparatory Conference discussed several other outstanding issues, including grain shortages and the problem of the Tongren tax collectors brought to the work team's attention by the Wöngya.[97] A matter of particular concern was the contin-ued prevalence of grassland disputes and the damage they did to intranational-ity unity. Per the September Decision, legal statutes stipulated punishments for animal rustling and other provocative actions. However, it seems clear that the chief weapon for policing intercommunity violence was not law enforcement but "patriotic education and political propaganda."[98] Party leaders urged disputes be resolved "according to the principles of fairness, unity and mutual aid" and on the basis of "mutual understanding" and "mutual accommodation." Stopping short of offering specific remedies, mediators were ordered to "take the present situation as the starting point, show consideration for history, pay attention to the overall situation, and benefit production and unity."[99]

Predictably, Ma Bufang received the majority of blame for the pervasiveness of intercommunity violence, Amdo's high incidence of grassland conflict being "inseparable from the crimes of his bandit gang."[100] Yönten, a leader of the Hor's Shokmang tsowa, explained, "In the past the bandit Ma Bufang gave us guns, bullets, and horses to rob people. And we got rewarded for sharing with him. With this kind of instigation, he [destroyed] our unity."[101] The roots of animos-ity and disunity now extinguished, Tibetan elites were reminded that national-ity unity was a precondition for increasing production and improving people's livelihoods. Wagya summarized the new imperatives by declaring, "In the old society we had a home but were not the masters. That is to say the bandit Ma Bufang was the master of our home. Now, we are liberated. Chairman Mao has given us a home and made us its masters. In the future we need to take good care of our home and manage our own affairs well."[102] Headmen were urged to impress upon common herdsmen the importance of respecting grazing rights and territorial boundaries. Widely reported-upon cases—such as the resolution of a century-long dispute mediated by Rongwo nangso Trashi Namgyel, Nangra chieftain Wangchen Döndrup, Rongwo Monastery's Gélek Gyatso, and other leading Tibetan figures—were held aloft as victories for nationality unity and models of the correct implementation of the CCP's nationality policies.[103]

Zeku's county leadership also cited Lhakba's personal example. Upon hearing that Ragya Monastery (in present-day Maqin (T. Machen) County) had been ransacked, the Shawonar baihu organized sixty members of his chiefdom to pur-sue the "bandits." After a successful two-day chase, Lhakba returned the monas-tery's property without reward. The preparatory committee enjoined its audi-ence to "learn from the spirit of Lhakba, who took initiative solving problems in order to further consolidate nationality unity."[104] The former sworn brother of Ma Yuanxiang had become a revolutionary exemplar. In the same tenor, the committee praised the Gönshül's Serökyap for offering to share his chiefdom's grasslands with smaller, less prosperous neighbors. In a third case, Yönten and

a second Hor headman were lauded for helping to peacefully resolve a grassland conflict by ceding winter pastures to a rival chiefdom from adjacent Guide
County.[105] Following these examples, reports claim that by mid-November 1953
a remarkable 130 internal disputes had been settled.[106] A year later the number
purportedly had risen to 315.[107]

"Mediation of disputes" (*tiaojie jiufen*) would quickly become an official
work category, the number of successful resolutions—often in the hundreds—
dutifully detailed in yearly county work reports. However, the seeming inex-
haustible number of settlements and the admission, sometimes explicit and
sometimes implicit, that new feuds continued to crop up and old ones resurface
suggest that efforts to strengthen intranationality unity were less successful than
often claimed.[108] For instance, Serökyap's altruistic example notwithstanding, a
1954 investigation criticized the Gönshül leader for repeatedly breaking grassland regulations to advance his own interests. Likewise, despite the celebration
of unity that would soon surround the First Zeku County People's Representative Conference, conflicts between Wagya's Hor and both the Sonak and the
Gartsé continued to fester.[109] And although the county's 1955 work report would
celebrate the "equitable and satisfactory settlement" of another 165 grassland
conflicts, that same year the Zeku County Party Committee sent an "urgent" directive to its work teams. It declared the outbreak of ten large disputes, including
an armed conflict between the Hor and a Mongol chiefdom that resulted in nine
deaths, to be a reflection of its cadres' poor work style and lack of understanding
of local conditions.[110]

An Event Unparalleled in History

As detailed in the following chapters, the alarming persistence of grassland disputes is just one example of the many struggles the Party would encounter as it
designed, built, and furnished "Mao's Treasures House." In fact, up to the eve of
the 1958 Amdo Rebellion, communications between Zeku County officials and
their superiors would be more notable for admissions of setbacks and mistakes
than successes. In what can only be assumed to be an understatement, a 1953 year-
end summary report issued by the county Party committee's secretariat admitted,
"We began to build Zeku County in July. On December 5 the county was formally
established. Since there was no material base, it was difficult work."[111] The secretariat noted that the overall quality of the cadre force was low, individuals having
been thrown together from different work units with little relevant experience
or knowledge of the region. As a result, over the previous half year an enormous
amount of manpower and resources had been wasted. According to "incomplete

statistics," in that short time span, ten million yuan (old currency) had been mis-used. Not all was inadvertent. Two Han cadres, Xie Tianxiang and Ren Shiying, were accused of embezzling 2.12 million yuan and over three hundred thousand yuan, respectively.[112] And cadre malfeasance was not limited to outright theft. The Hor Work Group noted that although its cadres lacked experience in minority regions, most were willing to "bear hardships and endure physical labor" (chiku nailao). Nonetheless, some feared making leftist or rightist political mistakes and were therefore reluctant to engage in propaganda work. Others, however, did not think the work important and therefore did not take it seriously.[113]

Just as worrying was the case of a cadre surnamed Du. Du had been in charge of procuring and managing the cadre force's food supplies. According to the sec-retariat's findings, he worked hard but lacked training. As a result, the accounts were in disarray, and Du himself was under considerable stress. During a political study session, he allegedly exclaimed, "I am willing to work as a soldier taking care of the horses for no pay, as long as I do not have to be the food manager." Using Du as an example, the secretariat concluded that morale was low. It noted insufficient guidance, regulations, and planning from upper levels and poor po-litical consciousness among grassroots cadres. In addition, unfamiliarity with pastoral regions had resulted in the persistence of both Han chauvinism and lo-cal nationalism, leading to poor cooperation between cadres and local headmen. Noting its inability to effectively translate directives and the need for better com-munication and more accurate information, the office requested the deployment of an additional Tibetan-language secretary.[114]

None of these concerns were specific to Zeku County or even to the Amdo grasslands. A 1953 communiqué issued by the national-level NAC rebuked cad-res assigned to China's pastoral regions for a series of offenses, including im-porting methods used in agricultural regions into pastoral districts, resorting to coercion rather than persuasion, misunderstanding local conditions, promoting agriculture over pastoralism, and harboring Han chauvinistic attitudes. Underly-ing the NAC's complaints was the admission that Han cadres sent into the grass-lands were often dissatisfied with their postings and generally ill-equipped to deal with the physically demanding and culturally alien conditions that existed in China's remote pastoral areas.[115]

Undeterred, on November 29, 1953, the First Zeku County People's Repre-sentative Conference finally met to formally inaugurate Zeku County. Per Guo Min's October instructions, exactly one hundred and seventeen delegates were chosen—ninety-two men and twenty-five women (five of whom were state rep-resentatives).[116] With twenty-seven representatives, by far the largest contingent came from the Hor. Next was the Shawonar and Gönshül with ten and nine dele-gates, respectively, followed by the Méshül, Gartsé, Sonak and Wöngya, each with seven representatives. Based on admittedly imprecise figures, this amounted to roughly one delegate for every two hundred inhabitants. Adhering to Party guidelines, smaller chiefdoms were allotted a slightly higher representation. Still the Khéri Chunga received only three representatives, and the Shisa and Ködé Karing five each. Additionally, nine spots were reserved for the monasteries. Delegates were therefore allocated fairly evenly by population, if not between the chiefdoms—with one notable exception. Records identify twenty-one members of the representative conference as state delegates, giving the Party-state a presence at the conference that badly outweighed its still small physical presence on the Zeku grasslands.[117]

Still, not everything proceeded according to plan. When the conference convened, only ninety-five delegates were present. Assuming that all of the state representatives participated, sixty-two male and just twelve female Tibetan representatives would have been in attendance. Moreover, it was subsequently discovered that several of the delegates were not even who they claimed to be, thus affecting the purity (*chunjiexing*) of the conference.[118] Keeping in mind the demographic and topographic conditions of the high plateau (in December, temperatures on the Shadar grasslands average around seven degrees Fahrenheit, or minus fourteen degrees Celsius), these missteps suggest the incredible newness of the political order that the CCP was trying to create after just three months of dedicated preparation.

Despite the complications, over seven days of meetings speeches were given, the location of the county seat officially approved, and a county government committee chosen. Unsurprisingly, when the dust settled, the new leadership looked a lot like the old. The Hor's Wagya was selected to lead a twenty-one-member county government committee, with Guo Min (CCP), Lhagyel (Hor), Serökyap (Gönshül), and Lhakba (Shawonar) as vice chairmen. A consultative committee was also chosen, also with twenty-one members. Guo Min was elected chairman, while Lubum (Gartsé) and Tsintar (Méshül) were named his deputies. Members of Zeku's indigenous leadership rounded out each committee, along with a sprinkling of Han cadres.[119]

On the conference's final day, speaker after speaker declared the gathering to have been a great "triumph" and an event "unprecedented in history."[120] In a speech by a Tibetan delegate, likely Wagya, the audience was reminded, "We must take the affairs of Zeku County as our own. We should advocate for unity between the cadres and ourselves and exercise the right to be masters of our own home. We must understand that only under the leadership of the Communist Party do we Tibetans enjoy political power. In the past, we did not have any power. Therefore, we must talk about how we lived in the past and how we are now masters of our own home. We should convey this message to the tribes."[121] A summary report noted that among the delegates were many who previously had been wary of the Party and its programs, including the elderly, "living Buddhas," monks, and women. Now, the report claimed, these same people were beginning to "understand the benefits of Chairman Mao and the CCP's policies of nationality equality."[122]

On December 5, 1953, almost exactly six months after Gyelyön and several dozen cadres had first pitched their tents on the banks of the Tséchu River, the Zeku Tibetan Autonomous County was formally founded.[123] Before year's end, the Huangnan Tibetan Autonomous Prefecture would also be established, with the Shartsang Lama as its chairman and Wagya as one of his six deputies. The others included Gélek Gyatso, Trashi Namgyel, Wangchen Döndrup, and Du Hua'an.[124] Zeku's Tibetan pastoralists had become "masters of their own home." Yet, while the construction foremen may have been the leaders of Zeku's ten chiefdoms—people like Wagya, Lhagyel, Serökyap, Lubum, Tsintar, and Lhakba—the architects and project managers were representatives of the Chinese Communist Party. Again, this is not to suggest that seeking input from the local population amounted to subterfuge or that building consensuses among Zeku's elite was simply a pretense employed to mask the fiction of autonomy. Instead, it underlines the inherent imbalance between the mass line principles of consultation and persuasion. Nationality autonomy was a formula by which Zeku's pastoral population would become "masters of their own home, under the leadership of the Party." Within the Leninist logics and mass line methodologies that helped define the CCP's operating principles, these seemingly contradictory concepts were both interdependent and philosophically unproblematic.

Of course, the creation of the Zeku Tibetan Autonomous County was not an end in itself. As Director Zhou had made clear, nationality autonomy was not an institution designed to protect the "feudal" structure of pastoral society. Instead, it was conceived as a transformative mechanism, a social reform that would inexorably lead to the disappearance of the old system and creation of the new. Reliance on traditional elites was a compromise born out of necessity of the CCP's nation-building project, a means to gradually, voluntarily, and organically bridge the gap between empire and nation—what I have described as subimperial practice.

Ultimately, the objective was to gain the trust and support of common herders. County leaders declared that the representative conference had been the first step in establishing a "foundation among the masses."[125] In its work plan for 1954, also unveiled at the December meetings, the county Party committee continued to stress nationality unity but now began to turn its eyes to increasing pastoral production, raising living standards, and building subcounty administrative organs. In the short term, these tasks would still need to be mediated by local headmen, the people who now made up the official leadership of Zeku County. Given both time and the discipline to follow the CCP's United Front policies, however, Party leaders anticipated that this work would enable their cadres to penetrate more deeply into Zeku's grasslands, allowing them to build upon the tenuous foundation they claimed to have laid among the pastoral masses.

4

ESTABLISHING A FOUNDATION
AMONG THE MASSES

On December 5, 1953, following just a three-month "preparatory period"—and only six months after the Chinese Communist Party had gained its first permanent foothold on the grasslands southwest of Repgong—the Zeku Tibetan Autonomous County had been established. Despite the celebratory pronouncements that accompanied the county's inaugural conference, however, as 1953 came to an end the plateau remained far from unified. Not only did intercommunity grassland disputes continue to smolder, but eight months after Ma Yuanxiang's defeat the region also remained on high alert for counterrevolutionary threats. Before adjourning, attendees were therefore urged to "uncover rumors, trace their roots and extinguish them, educate the pastoral masses to look out for enemy planes and report them immediately, and eliminate the [conditions] that produce bandits and spies."[1] A year earlier, United Front director Zhou Renshan had ordered monasteries off limits to security operations. Nonetheless, soon after Zeku County was formally founded, county leaders dispatched security forces (*gong'anju paiyuan*) "into the monasteries and into the tribes" to investigate the "enemy's situation" and "eliminate bandits, spies and all types of counterrevolutionaries."[2]

It was against this backdrop of guarded optimism mixed with lingering unease that the newly inaugurated Zeku County Party Committee submitted a wide-ranging work plan for the coming year. In fall 1953, Beijing had announced its "General Line for the Transition to Socialism." The result of a simmering debate within the Party's central leadership over the pace of rural collectivization, the directive signaled that a core task for the coming year would be establishing or expanding agricultural cooperatives.[3] In Qinghai, this included the Han- and Hui-majority agricultural districts that radiated outward from Xining. The Tibetan and Mongol grasslands of southern and western Qinghai, however, were explicitly exempted from collectivization plans.[4] In Zeku, goals instead ranged from building roads and schools, developing an indigenous cadre force, fixing prices, guaranteeing adequate grain supplies, providing health care and social welfare, raising a local self-defense militia, and rationalizing herding practices. In sum, county planners noted, the 1954 work plan was designed to "launch patriotic education," "develop production," and "improve the livelihood of the people."[5]

The work plan also marked a subtle shift in priorities. Back at 1953's Unity and Friendship Conference, Tongren Party secretary Du Hua'an had declared nationality unity the cornerstone of all policies. As the plateau began to thaw in the spring of 1954, a slight but substantive alteration was made to this guiding formula. Addressing a joint meeting of Zeku's government and consultative committees, none other than Gélek Gyatso—the former steward of Rongwo Monastery, brother to the Shartsang Lama, and now vice chairman of Huangnan Prefecture—declared, "In pastoral areas the development of pastoral production is the long-term center of work. Under the leadership of the Chinese Communist Party, all other work revolves around promoting the development of the pastoral economy."[6] Although unity and security would remain foremost concerns, the new maxim declared increasing production to be the benchmark from which all tasks should now proceed.

As a philosophical point, this modification did not necessitate adjusting the basic foundations upon which United Front work was formulated or altering the mass line methodologies of consultation and persuasion. As a practical matter, however, the elevation of production to a position above (albeit only slightly) nationality unity demanded an expanded state presence on the grasslands. This entailed and was also almost certainly in part motivated by the desire to push beyond Zeku's indigenous elite. James Scott reminds us of the corollary between the size of a state's transformative aspirations and the depth to which it must intervene in society.[7] The "foundation among the masses" built at Zeku's First People's Representative Conference had been just that—a starting point. If the Party wished to achieve both its short- and long-term goals, its agents needed to penetrate deeper into the grasslands (*shenru xiaxiang*) and go "down to the tribes" (*xiaxiang buluo*).

Despite these ambitions, Party leaders remained acutely aware that the intercession and mediation of indigenous elites remained vital. Instructions issued by the provincial government reminded county leaders that the principles of the United Front were still in effect, emphatically stating, "Doing good work with

the headmen is the number one requirement for guaranteeing the successful establishment of governing administrations." Adopting an orthodox mass line formula, it noted that all of Zeku's residents, including headmen, could be separated
into one of three categories: "In general, half have doubts, half have faith, and [a
few] are negative and will oppose." Concerned that elites often expressed enthusiasm but harbored anxieties, the provincial directive added that propaganda
needed to be carried out first among the indigenous Tibetan leaders. Having
secured their support "in action" as well as "in words," ordinary herdsman would
also develop faith in the Party. By paying close attention to propaganda work,
assigning local leaders to appropriate positions with real responsibility, and consulting with them in good faith, provincial leaders insisted, "We can win over the
majority and minimize resistance."[8]

For both practical and procedural reasons, before work plans could be implemented, they would need to receive endorsement by the newly formed Zeku
County Joint Committee. Chaired by Wagya under the supervision of Party secretary Guo Min, the forty-two-member joint committee included most of the
region's prominent Tibetan figures. As such, it served as the primary venue at
which the CCP recruited the critical support of Zeku's Tibetan upper strata for
its state- and nation-building efforts. What these Tibetan leaders gained in return
is harder to pinpoint. As local office holders, they received a state salary. However,
given the fractured nature of interchiefdom politics, a more important inducement for accepting government posts may have been securing a seat from which
to negotiate with the CCP and lobby for their interests. In fact, while Guo Min
generally was able to push his agenda through an often wary joint committee, as
policy formation turned to practical implementation consensuses formed at the
county seat tended to break down. In the process, some of the ambivalences and
tensions embedded in a system that combined centralized political power with
meaningful popular participation began to surface.

The joint committee would meet three times over the course of 1954. Each
time, reports were drafted, propaganda disseminated, directives issued, work
tasks assigned, and quotas set. However, each meeting revolved around a primary
work task: establishing subcounty districts, social welfare, and tax collection.
Each of these undertakings—bureaucratic administration, public welfare, and
resource extraction—is, of course, a fundamental aspect of modern governance.
In total, they also are indicative of a desire to replace subimperial arrangements
struck between the CCP and indigenous elites with a more direct and deeply felt
relationship between state and society. Although actual implementation would
overlap, in this chapter each of the campaigns will be discussed in the order of
the joint committee meeting at which it took center stage.

Köngya and the Hor Work Group

Zeku County convened its First Joint Committee in early March but only after low attendance forced a three-day postponement. Even then, just eighteen of the joint committee's forty-two members and six nonvoting delegates were in attendance. The main topic of the meeting was the construction of subcounty, district-level (qu) administrations. Weeks earlier, "at the request of the masses," the county government had organized five work groups. The intent was that each would establish one of five district-level administrations, a process that county leaders described as the next step in assuring that "our county's minority nationalities secure the right 'to become masters of their own home.'" The five districts were to be mapped onto Zeku's ten chiefdoms, either as a single-chiefdom district or by combining several under one administration. Significantly, no chiefdom was to be divided among separate districts. Instead, for the time being, Party leaders sought to graft bureaucratic institutions onto existing "tribal" structures with the intent that the former would gradually replace their hosts.[9] Citing the importance and complexity of the task, however, the joint committee now ordered that only Hor District be completed that calendar year. Without further elaboration but with the approval of the provincial government, plans to found four other districts were put off until 1955. In the meantime, the five work groups were "dispatched to the tribes" where they became de facto subcounty governing bodies.[10]

Over the next several years, the Hor Work Group would be the most active of the five, often serving at the vanguard for the implementation of new policies. It reached Hor Monastery on March 20, carrying with it a laundry list of tasks laid out in the county's 1954 work plan. Most aimed at generating immediate increases to pastoral production through such activities as hunting foxes, wolves, and other predators; cutting grass for winter feed; building animal shelters; fencing pastures; and, when available, dispensing inoculations against livestock diseases. County leaders also expected the work group to guide the development of auxiliary economic activities, such as digging up yams, fungi, and herbs; collecting animal dung for fuel; producing animal by-products, including milk, yogurt, and wool; and burning bones for fertilizer.[11] While there were no immediate plans to sedentarize pastoral populations, Beijing made clear that it considered pastoralism "good for animals" but bad for human development. It therefore promoted the construction of fixed dwellings, around which schools, health clinics, and other services could be constructed.[12] Nonetheless, the assignments that were to consume much of the Hor Work Group's personal attention in 1954 were the same tasks that would dominate the three joint committee meetings: social welfare, tax collection, and, initially, replacing the Hor's loose "tribal" rule with a bureaucratized district-level government.

The process of establishing the First District, as Hor's new administrative unit would become known, largely replicated the county-building efforts of the previous year, albeit at a level closer to the pastoral masses the Party hoped to win over. Before a district government could be founded, a preparatory meeting had to be convened and a preparatory committee chosen. Propaganda would need to be spread, delegates carefully vetted, egos assuaged, and balances of power accounted for. The Hor Work Group quickly discovered that local enthusiasm for building the district was largely driven by the predicted material benefits that the literal construction of a physical district seat might bring. To this point, Zeku's inhabitants had traveled to neighboring counties to purchase grains or manufactured goods. Perhaps encouraged by the work group itself, local people now assumed that a "vibrant and bustling" settlement—complete with a trading post, a cooperative, and a grain station—would quickly appear in the vicinity of Hor Monastery. Evoking the dual mantras of nationality unity and economic development, others talked about the benefits of district building in more formulaic language. According to a work group report, even representatives of Hor Monastery felt that banditry might be reduced or possibly disappear once the district was established. As always, the veracity and sincerity of the claims are impossible to authenticate. However, in an internal report the Hor Work Group sent to its superiors (although one that perhaps reflects the outlook of cadres more than those of the local population), it asserted, "While there are differing degrees of understanding, based on what we can see of the masses' overall feelings regarding the establishment of the district, there is a common opinion: it is supportive and welcomes the quick establishment of a Hor district government."[13]

On July 18, the Hor Work Group convened the First District Preparatory Conference. At the gathering, "in consultation with tribal leaders, religious leaders and the masses," an eleven-member preparatory committee was chosen. The newly appointed committee members purportedly pledged to resolve outstanding grassland disputes, increase production beyond targets set by the prefecture, build ten animal pens and shelters, and train five livestock veterinary personnel. At the conference's conclusion, the work group reported, "Committee members went down to the tribes to explain [the policies] to the people. [In this way,] everyone, including the important people, got to know the benefits [of establishing] the district government."[14]

Despite the self-congratulatory tone with which the Hor Work Group described its efforts, a 1955 directive issued by the Zeku County Party Committee was far less generous. It alleged that the work group had done a particularly poor job assessing the important political relationships within the chiefdom. County leaders reminded the four remaining work groups, "Before establishing a district we must assiduously investigate and understand the entire district's situation, grasp the [amount of] prestige the chieftains have with the masses, and meticulously understand the situation of religion within the tribe." The directive noted that the Hor Work Group's evaluation of the "situation of religion" had been particularly poor. It specifically criticized the work group for failing to accurately discern the relationship between the Hor's Nyingma and Gelukpa institutions as well as for misunderstanding the difference between the Nyingma monastic community and the large number of Nyingma lay practitioners who did not join monasteries but instead remained engaged in pastoral production and—in the Party's view—were only part-time religious specialists.[15] It can be assumed that the county committee was not concerned with issues of doctrine or practice but instead exacerbating existing political and social divisions that might negatively affect the establishment of the district, production, and unity.

A more immediate concern was the work group's misreading of intrapersonal politics. In particular, it had failed to appoint Köngya, another of Wagya's younger siblings, to the preparatory committee. Details are sketchy. However, it seems that only after the meeting adjourned did the work group come to understand the degree to which the district's future success was dependent on the unhappy Hor headman's support.[16] Rather than criticizing the "feudal" nature of pastoral society as an impediment to democratic governance, the county Party committee berated the work group for improperly assessing objective conditions and therefore allocating positions poorly. Forced to call a second preparatory meeting in September, at which Köngya was selected head of the First District Preparatory Committee, the work group ultimately was able to correct its mistake. United Front principles having been reaffirmed, county leaders reiterated that the upper and middle strata of society must be "consulted" and their "suggestions" sought. Otherwise, mistakes would continue to be made and the negative consequences would multiply.[17]

With a "satisfied" Köngya now on board, committee members and cadres went "down to the tribes . . . to discuss the glory of being a representative. In this manner," the report declared, "thirty-three tribal representatives, three monks, four women, and four government cadres were selected."[18] Finally, at the beginning of November, a representative conference was convened, and the First District was formally established. Delegates selected Köngya along with Yönten, leader of the Hor's Shokmang tsowa, to sit atop an eleven-person district governing committee. According to a summary report, "People [now] understand that the purpose of establishing the district is exercising the right to be master of their own home."[19] Clearly, ultimate authority in the new district lay not with Köngya and Yönten but with the Hor Work Group. For instance, a report in Chinese issued in the two Hor headmen's names was almost certainly dictated by the Hor Work Group.[20] However, this does not mean that the Hor headmen were powerless stooges or obsequious satraps. Instead, as demonstrated by the controversy over the district's leadership, they remained vital intermediaries between the Party-state and the pastoral masses and as such maintained a degree of authority and agency that should not be dismissed.

Who Is the People's Government?

More illuminating than the brief description of the First Joint Committee meeting are a series of reports from the Second Joint Committee that illustrate policy priorities, methods of implementation, and dynamics of leadership. Originally set to begin on May 13, in what was becoming a recurrent theme the conference's start once again had to be delayed when less than half of the committee members arrived at the county seat on the appointed date. When the meeting finally opened ten days later, just twenty-five committee members took part, one leaving without permission on the conference's first day. A report further noted that preparations were poor, lodging inadequate, and food for the committee members and their horses insufficient, serving as a reminder of the ever-present physical hardships and logistical difficulties that at every stage complicated the Party's state- and nation-building efforts.[21] On the other hand, repeated instances of tardiness and absenteeism might also be interpreted as a manner of resistance to the incorporative demands of the rapidly intruding Party-state.

Once the meeting was underway, Wagya, Lhakba, Guo Min, and others delivered major speeches. However, it was Rongwo Monastery's Gélek Gyatso, acting as vice chairman of the Huangnan Tibetan Autonomous Prefecture, who dominated much of the proceedings. He opened the conference by reemphasizing now-familiar themes—for example, declaring that nationality autonomy "was a happiness brought to us by the CCP and Chairman Mao."[22] Later in the week, the leitmotifs of patriotic unity and increasing production were further stressed when the abbot of Jianzha's Namdzong Monastery, the Third Gurong Gyelsé Rinpoché, arrived to address the committee. Not only had the lama recently served on several of the seventeen missions meant to convince Wangchen Döndrup to "return to the people," but two decades earlier he had also acted as mediator between the Nangra headman and Ma Bufang. Now, having recently come back from an official tour of North Korea, Gurong Gyelsé described the immense sacrifices the North Korean people and Chinese Volunteer Army had made during the Korean War. Comparing "American imperialism" to the cruelty of Ma Bufang and Chiang Kaishek, he asserted that increasing pastoral production was an inseparable component of this ongoing struggle.[23] Then, evoking Buddhist notions of compassion, Gurong Gyelsé urged committee members to actively work toward nationality unity, declaring, "We must build unity in this great spirit of self-sacrifice. If we don't unite and work hard on production, how can we answer the volunteer army when they ask us? The main reason we read scripture is to seek goodness and become better. These [Buddhist] texts also talk about unity and mutual aid. Then, why can't we come together and help each other?" He continued by urging attendees to do more to uncover spies, reassuring committee members of the state's commitment to religious freedom, and promising that lingering grain supply issues would be resolved. Finally, repeating a common refrain that laid bare the CCP's Han-centric paternalism, the Gurong Gyelsé Rinpoché encouraged the Tibetan headmen to trust Han cadres as they would their "elder brothers."[24]

Following the Gurong Gyelsé Rinpoché, Lhakba gave what was described as a "captivating" eyewitness account of an official six-day visit to the provincial capital. The trip appears to have been a localized version of the propaganda tours to Beijing and other eastern cities that the CCP often conducted for more prominent minority leaders.[25] Speaking "clearly and loudly" and "gesturing wildly with his hands," the Shawonar baihu described "a strange flour factory" in which machinery was used to turn grain into powder. "Seeing it I was speechless," he reportedly exclaimed. Lhakba also recounted being shuttled to mechanized lumber, wool, and milk factories, seeing tractors working in the fields (even being allowed to start an engine), and visiting a "nationality school" where Tibetan students happily greeted him. "I rode in cars to these places and to eat," he recalled. "Anyway," Lhakba excitedly told the crowd, "today's Xining is completely different from the old Xining."[26]

Lhakba's visit to Xining was part of a propaganda offensive meant to entice the Tibetan headmen with the promise of modern material development. Yet speakers were quick to remind attendees that this was only achievable with the dedicated and enthusiastic aid of a united local leadership. Audience members were told that Geshé Shérap Gyatso, the great Amdowa educator and current provincial vice governor, had urged Tibetan cadres not to shirk responsibility by pleading ignorance, inexperience, or illiteracy but instead to actively work for the people. Armed with a chart Lhakba had brought back from Xining, Secretary Guo warned delegates that Zeku was falling behind the province's other pastoral areas. He further noted that while Zeku was a long way from the wonders Lhakba had seen in Xining, Xining was even further from Shanghai. The message was clear: Zeku's United Front leadership "must take more responsibility and lead the people in improving pastoral production."[27]

Gélek Gyatso began the next day's proceedings on a similar note, urging committee members to "arm yourselves" with the corrective practices of criticism and self-criticism, declaring, "Under the leadership of the CCP and Chairman Mao, we minority people have become master of our own home. [However,] in these four years, what have we accomplished? In particular, what duties have the chairmen and county heads performed? . . . I hope everyone will appreciate the spirit of criticism and self-criticism. This way we can discover our strengths and weaknesses and improve ourselves and our work."[28]

This emphasis on criticism and self-criticism—methodologies embedded deep within the CCP's operating principles—appears to have been prompted by the perception that "under the influence of feudal ideas," Tibetans were generally reticent to accept outside criticism and unwilling to make serious self-analyses of their own attitudes and work.[29] In his own speech to the committee, Chairman Wagya reinforced Gélek Gyatso's message, enjoining his fellow headmen to "take responsibility for becoming masters [of our own home] and overcoming short-comings in our work. We must equip ourselves through the methods of criticism and self-criticism."[30] Wagya then announced that each committee member would indeed make a self-criticism. Among the first was Wagya's younger brother, Lhagyel. After noting that minorities in China had at long last become masters of their own homes, he rhetorically asked, "Have I exercised that right dutifully?" "No," he replied, "I have not. The reason is that I am not educated and have not been able to get things done. Have the Han cadres helped us enough? Yes, they have. I have nothing bad to say about them. The problem is we minority cadres have not done enough." In turn, one committee member after another offered up his own mea culpa. Vice Chairman Serökyap admitted, "My political position is quite high, but I have not made much of a contribution." In his Xining report, Lhakba had described criticism and self-criticism as a "weapon" "similar to washing our faces every day to cleanse ourselves."[31] Confessing to "ideological problems," Lhakba now disclosed that despite having been at the county seat for two months, he had accomplished little. By the same token, Lhakba acknowledged that when he was back within his Shawonar chiefdom, "I do not put my heart into my work."[32] In turn, several other committee members revealed that although they took a salary from the state, they did little actual work, were unclear of their duties, and spent only a brief time at the county seat.[33]

Underlying much of this conversation was the implicit admission of a gulf between Zeku's indigenous Tibetan leadership and the Han cadres who had been dispatched into the grasslands. On multiple occasions, Wagya, Gélek Gyatso, and others reminded the gathered headmen that Han cadres had left their "beloved homes and families" to help Tibetans build their autonomous region.[34] However, whether due to the usurpation of authority by the outsiders or a shirking of responsibility on the part of local elites, much of the day-to-day work was being shouldered by this still smallish Han cadre force. Rather than blame Han cadres for failing to give local people real authority and position—for "building a home where they have no say," as the Northwest Bureau previously had put it[35]—Gélek Gyatso encouraged committee members to assume "full responsibility" for their autonomous region. Citing his own experience, he recalled, "When I was serving as the chairman of Tongren County, I also had the tendency to rely on others. I thought that there was the Party and the Han cadres, and I did not have to be concerned." This type of attitude, he added, "is absolutely wrong." Singling out several committee members by name, Gélek Gyatso insisted that they not hide behind excuses of being uneducated or inexperienced. Instead, as directors of various county-level departments (trade, pastoral, nationalities, etc.), they must "boldly take up responsibility"[36]

The unstated implication is that Tibetan committee members had been acting more or less as figureheads, again as the Northwest Bureau had stated, with "position but no authority." Yet while the Northwest Bureau, Zhou Renshan, and others had regularly blamed Han cadres for chauvinistic work practices, Gélek Gyatso now criticized the passivity and parochialism of the local leadership. Admitting that there was a palatable level of discontent on the grasslands—and implying that his own moral authority was suffering because of it—Lubum confessed, "I don't know what to do. Recently when I talk, the masses do not listen. They complain that the government does not work properly so what else can they do besides steal." Illustrating the gap between the Party's expectations of the headmen-cum–committee members and those of local people, Lubum reported that when he returned to the Gartsé, "They ask me what we are doing sitting in government [offices]." Speaking more as an intermediary between the Party and the masses than an official of the state, Lubum went on to note that people have responded to the "leniency" of the regime not by working toward nationality unity but by purchasing weapons. Another Tibetan committee member added that when work teams went into the grasslands, some among the masses did not tie up the dogs that guarded their tents. His meaning would have been clear to anyone familiar with the plateau: the cadres were not welcome. Lubum concluded, "It is because the government does not do what it says it will."[37]

In response to these types of comments, Gélek Gyatso reiterated that it was up to the indigenous Tibetan leadership—acting as representatives of *their* autonomous region—to implement the changes needed. He proclaimed, "The masses feel they should blame the people's government for not doing work well. Of course, this is the responsibility of the people's government. But after all, *who is the people's government?* It is the county leaders, chairmen and all the committee members at this conference. Therefore, whether the people's government does its work well or not is the responsibility of all of us."[38] Gélek Gyatso finished by imploring the Tibetan headmen, "Shoulder your responsibilities. Do not think of relying on Han cadres."[39]

This pointed exchange between Gélek Gyatso and Zeku's United Front leadership is fairly unique. In the reports and directives found in the county archives,

Han cadres are routinely criticized for poor work methods and low political consciousness. In contrast, shortcomings among the Tibetan leadership are generally excused as remnants of nationality exploitation and attributed to inadequate propaganda work. Yet here Gélek Gyatso is starkly critical of Zeku's most powerful indigenous figures. Some blame is reserved for Han cadres—for example, for failing to brief Tibetan department heads and not including Tibetan committee members in work meetings. However, this criticism is tempered by the admission that headmen were often away from the county seat and generally disengaged from the day-to-day operations of government.

As the personal representative (and younger brother) of the Shartsang Lama and a member of the trio who had long exerted influence over the greater Repgong region, perhaps Gélek Gyatso was one of the few people with both the prestige and position to speak to the gathered headmen in such a direct and critical manner. Yet he was also acting as an agent of the Communist Party and the Chinese state. By most accounts, Gélek Gyatso would faithfully serve the CCP for nearly two decades, maintaining his position even after most of his coethnic elites had been deposed, jailed, and in many cases killed following the 1958 rebellion. Before then, Gélek Gyatso had been perhaps the Repgong region's leading indigenous elite advocate for the Party's reform efforts, including cooperativization. A year after addressing Zeku's Second Joint Committee, Gélek Gyatso, a monk since childhood, reportedly broached the possibility of disrobing and applying for membership in the Chinese Communist Party. Although he never was accepted into the CCP, soon afterward Gélek Gyatso did resume secular life.[40]

Yet the exchange at the Second Joint Committee meeting can also be seen in a different, less positivistic light. Gélek Gyatso's exhortation for Zeku's traditional leaders to personally shoulder responsibility for the affairs of their government might be interpreted as a desire for Tibetans to carve out legitimate and sovereign space within the new political order. Just as Wangchen Döndrup had forged an accommodation with the CCP in which some semblance of an imperial relationship might be maintained, regional autonomy offered the promise, no matter how fleeting, that Tibetans could *remain* "masters of their own home." What Gélek Gyatso may represent then is the murky space in which the old elite had to operate before such ambiguities and uneven temporalities were leveled by the transformative demands of the nation-state.

My Life Is Completely Different from Before

Having been reprimanded by Gélek Gyatso, the Second Joint Committee gave the gathered headmen an opportunity to display their newfound commitment to unity and development. The major substantive policy issue addressed was the disbursement of livestock loans (*xumu daikuan*) and direct emergency relief (*shehui jiuji*). Social welfare work, as the two programs were sometimes jointly referred to, was considered to have several interlocking benefits. First, it would raise the living standards of the poorest of the plateau's inhabitants. Second, by infusing the grasslands with resources, in particular livestock, welfare work would stimulate the overall pastoral economy. With incomes up and animal ownership extended to formerly destitute households, social stability would be consolidated (presumably because there would be less inducement for banditry). In the process of registering households, counting herds, assessing production methods, recording animal birth and death rates, and so forth, the Party would establish a mooring from which to investigate the "concrete conditions" of the grasslands and bring its cadres into direct contact with ordinary herders. Last, through the accumulated economic and social benefits that state largesse provided, herders would come to understand the CCP's concern for their livelihoods, patriotic consciousness would rise, and Zeku's Tibetan pastoralists would be further integrated—economically, politically, and emotionally—into the socialist state and nation.[41]

A report by the Hor Work Group cited the example of a "poverty-stricken herdsman" of the Détsang tsowa, which surely represents the manner in which social welfare was envisioned to improve both the livelihoods of the masses and their relationship to the Party-state. It reads in full:

> During the period of the old society of the bandit Ma Bufang, we did not own a single head of cattle or sheep, so we were often starving, freezing, beaten, and bullied. After Liberation, the Communist Party came. Now my life is completely different from before. In June 1953, the people's government loaned me two head of cattle; now a calf has been born. This January the people's government again gave me a head of cattle, [this time] as emergency relief. Now in total I have four heads of cattle. Before I did not eat butter or drink milk. Now I have both. My heart cannot express [my gratitude]. I truly thank the Chinese Communist Party and Chairman Mao.[42]

As usual, the report cannot be corroborated. Yet it is not difficult to believe that many herders, particularly those among the most downtrodden, may have responded positively to the CCP's welfare efforts.

In Zeku, sporadic social welfare and emergency relief campaigns stretched back to 1952 when Du Hua'an dispatched pastoral work teams from Repgong into the southern grasslands. However, these early efforts appear to have been conducted with little oversight and to have reaped limited benefits.[43] Therefore, at the start of 1954, an intensified welfare program was launched. Through "consultation" with local headmen, work groups organized seven- to eleven-person welfare committees (*jiuji weiyuanhui*, literally "emergency relief commit-tees"). The committees then chose 323 households, with 1,276 people, to receive subsidies—according to contemporary statistics, roughly 7 percent of the total county population of 17,036 residents. Adhering to the principle of "equal dis-tribution" (*pingjun zhuyi*, literally "equalism"), by virtue of having the largest population, the Hor received by far the largest portion of the funds—ten times what was received by the smallest chiefdoms.[44] Party leaders determined that during earlier efforts many welfare recipients had not reinvested in production. Therefore, 120 million of Zeku's 150 million yuan (old currency) initial welfare budget was specifically earmarked for animal purchases, 167 families receiving a minimum of three sheep to a maximum of two heads of cattle. The remainder was dispensed to the desperately poor—including widows, orphans, the elderly, and the infirm—in the form of 10,785 jin (5,394.5 kilograms) of emergency grain subsidies.[45]

Despite several glowing testimonials, Party leaders clearly considered the pro-gram a failure. As before, a report concluded that the campaign suffered from both poor propaganda work and supervision. Work groups were said to have simply "discussed policies" (i.e., persuasion) while not seeking feedback (i.e., consultation). As a result, they encountered difficulty drafting headmen onto welfare committees and enlisting their aid in spreading policies to common herd-ers. Quite the opposite: many among the pastoral elite concluded that the pro-gram offered them no personal benefit and therefore did not actively support the campaign. Relatedly, a dearth of reliable data, the absence of a distribution system, and weak supervision meant that cadres often misread local conditions. In some cases, welfare recipients did not receive the aid they were promised, while others complained about inequalities between and within chiefdoms. Most dam-agingly, loan animals had often ended up in the hands of unqualified recipients while the destitute were left wanting. Thus, from the Party's perspective both the economic and the propagandistic value of welfare work had been squandered.[46]

Determined to realize the predicted benefits of welfare work, in spring 1954 Huangnan Prefecture ordered county leaders to launch a renewed campaign. Breeding animals, referred to as "production livestock" (*shengchan xumu*), were to be dispensed to households that had a surplus of labor but did not possess enough animals to otherwise increase production. Officials thus hoped to ensure an immediate reinvestment in the pastoral economy through what was essen-tially a demand-side stimulus. On the other hand, the state would continue to provide emergency relief in the form of direct subsidies of animals, defined as "livelihood animals" (*shenghuo xumu*), grain, and cash to households that did not have the labor resources needed to exploit additional livestock.[47]

The major difference between the new program and earlier welfare efforts was the abandonment of equal distribution and adoption of the principle of "focused allocation" (*zhongdian fafang*). Rather than spread a limited amount of resources thinly across the grasslands, focused allocation instead prioritized select test sites. In doing so, Party leaders reasoned that benefits could be maximized, the process more easily monitored, and experiences gathered and shared.[48] Yet focused allocation dictated that not all chiefdoms or tsowa would receive equal or even proportional support from the state. Under equal distribution, nationality unity had been considered paramount, even to the detriment of economic development. Reflecting the shift toward prioritizing production, focused allocation reversed the equation.

At the Second Joint Committee meeting, Gélek Gyatso informed the gathered headmen of the prefecture's decision to concentrate the majority of its welfare loan budget on Jianzha and Tongren Counties, leaving Zeku with an already diminished piece of the welfare pie.[49] Now the joint committee was asked to choose one area of the already fragmented grasslands to receive a substantial input of state resources. Admitting, "[We] do not want negative thoughts to arise in those who are not receiving loans," Secretary Guo instructed attendees to stress the benefits focused allocation theoretically brought to the entire county, the entire nation, and ultimately each individual household.[50] This interdependency was expressed through the dictum of "mutual support of industry, agriculture, and pastoralism" (*gong, nong, mu huxiang chiyuan,* hereafter "mutual support"). Simply put, by producing hides, wool, meat, and other grassland products, pastoral regions would contribute to the nation's industrialization. In turn, industrialization would lead to the increased agricultural output necessary to provide pastoralists the grains they could not themselves produce. As summarized by a Tibetan member of the joint committee, "If we don't receive help from workers and grain from peasants, there will be no progress in our pastoral region. If we don't provide high-quality wool and skins to industry, they won't be able to produce high-quality products. So, we are interdependent."[51]

Keeping in mind the previous autumn's stalemate over the placement of the county seat, the uneven disbursement of state aid should have been a deeply divisive topic for Zeku's Tibetan headmen, each of whom presumably would have been eager to funnel resources back to his bailiwick. Instead, whether prompted by a genuine desire for unity and a commitment to the greater good or acting under the watchful eyes of Gélek Gyatso and Guo Min, committee members went to great lengths to prove their heightened political consciousness. After Gélek Gyatso officially announced the shift to focused allocation, a man identified only as Director Ge (Ge Kezhang) of the Huangnan Prefecture Committee addressed the gathering. Reporting that the "Three Goods 'water, grass, and climate'" were all available, Director Ge singled out the territory of the Hor's Ratsang tsowa as a promising welfare test site.[52] Somewhat out of character, Wagya followed by declaring his preference for a site within the Méshül, Shawonar, or Gartsé chiefdoms. Only then did he reluctantly add to the list the Ratsang of his own Hor chiefdom. Even then, Wagya preempted accusations of favoritism by admitting that the Ratsang's close connection to his brother Lhagyel rendered it unsuitable. Despite noting that Director Ge had recommended the Ratsang tsowa, several speakers later Lhagyel also declared it "inappropriate." As if the decision was ultimately out of his hands, Lhagyel then conceded, "However, it should be researched and discussed by all. If everyone decides on the Hor or another tribe as the focus area, I have no objection." In turn, Chögyong, a Hor committee member who in his indigenous capacity was baihu of the Ratsang tsowa, added his voice to those seeming to reject the Ratsang proposal.[53]

While it is impossible to know what kind of behind-the-scenes maneuvering may have predisposed the official discussions, it seems that the Hor committee members—perhaps in concert with Party officials—had laid the political cover necessitated by the joint demands of developing production and strengthening national unity. Even while acknowledging that experts objectively preferred a site within the Ratsang, the Hor leadership explicitly rejected nepotism. Yet in stark reversal from the earlier controversy over the county seat in which rival headmen quickly closed ranks to block the ambitions of Wagya and the Hor, now one committee member after another endorsed the Ratsang proposal. Citing Chögyong's responsible leadership, for example, Tsintar of the Méshül threw his support behind the Ratsang plan. The Wöngya's Losar agreed, claiming that his own experience was too limited for such a responsibility. A nonvoting attendee identified as the Ködé Karing Lama also recommended the Ratsang site, arguing (and echoing an official talking point) that if loans were spread too thin, the benefits of focused allocation would be lost. Having proclaimed his chiefdom too small and without the necessary expertise to host the program, the Shisa headman Wenté (who was concurrently director of the county pastoral office) deferred to the Hor as well, while a representative of the Sonak pledged to support the majority's decision. When no objections were raised to Lubum's call for a vote, the committee approved the proposal for the Hor Ratsang tsowa to host the inaugural animal-loan focus site.[54]

Over the course of 1954, the Hor Work Group would distribute nearly 160 million yuan worth of animals among the Ratsang, loaning an average of twenty sheep to each of sixty-two "destitute" or "semidestitute households."[55] Of the reported 230 million yuan ultimately allocated to the Hor as animal loans, 70 percent was designated as "livestock protection loans" (baoxu daikuan), which were to be paid back at the end of the year, and the remainder "breeding livestock loans" (*zhongxu daikuan*), which were not due for several years.[56] "Through these loans," the work group summarized, "the broad pastoral masses saw the policy of 'No Division and No Struggle' in practice. It further stimulated the activism of the masses and their enthusiasm for production."[57] Yet, given the admitted reluctance of many headmen to support the previous welfare campaign, it is worth considering that many may have had little interest in a program that would invite increased state intrusion while seeming to offer little personal benefit. In fact, a key criticism of previous welfare programs had been a lack of postloan oversight. By contrast, focused allocation was designed to provide cadres the opportunity to promote "scientific" animal management practices, activities such as building shelters to protect animals from the elements, cutting and stockpiling winter feed, inoculating animals against disease, and rationalizing the allotment of pastures and seasonal movement of animals.[58]

Chairman Mao's Concern Is Even Greater than a Parent's

A window into the interaction between state agents and Zeku's pastoral population is provided in reports detailing the following year's expansion of the welfare program. Building on the Ratsang experience, in spring 1955 the prefecture dispatched a "loan work group" to Zeku to oversee the implementation of the welfare program. After training local cadres, two new work groups were formed, each consisting of a mixture of prefectural and county-level officials, and sent down to new welfare focus sites within the Wöngya and Shawonar chiefdoms. Using the Shawonar as an example, the report detailed a three-stage campaign that can be summarized as consult and persuade, purchase and distribute, and manage and reevaluate. In the initial stage, after local elites were consulted, a welfare committee was formed, and a list of potential welfare recipients created. Then small groups composed of a mixture of cadres and local leaders were sent into the Shawonar's herding groups to explain the welfare program. Afterward, the various small groups reconvened at a large gathering to "democratically discuss" their findings and finalize the list of loan recipients.[59]

Propaganda work complete and welfare recipients identified, before the loans could be distributed animals had to be acquired. As far as can be told, however, the state did not have the wherewithal to subsidize the welfare program on its own. Instead, cadres were ordered to reallocate animals from Zeku's existing stocks. Yet the Three Nos expressly prohibited the redistribution of pastoral wealth, at least through coercive measures. In order to guarantee a pool of available loan animals, the loan committees were therefore tasked with coaxing well-off pastoralists into voluntarily selling their animals to the state. At one of several prechosen sites, wealthy herders were expected to announce the number of animals they would be selling. Following this example, ordinary herders would be encouraged to do the same. Evoking images of an open grassland live-stock market, the report simple notes, "When the number of animals that would be sold became equal to the amount to be loaned, the buying began."[60] Cadres would be on hand to evaluate the process, register households, issue payments, and oversee the redistribution of animals. In this manner, not only could state workers check the credentials of the loan recipients, but they could also guarantee that the funds were being immediately converted into animal loans.

Finally, in the third stage, members of the work group reevaluated the program, received feedback from the masses, and reported to their superiors. According to 1955's year-end welfare work report, the program went relatively smoothly. Now calculated in the new currency, in total 3,655 female sheep with a total value of 47,001 yuan were redistributed as animal loans.[61] Declaring that most of the loan recipients were satisfied, it quoted members of the masses enthusiastically lauding the program, one allegedly proclaiming, "The concern Chairman Mao has for us poor people is even greater than a parent's. I will take care of the loaned cattle and sheep with all my heart. I am a person who has fallen down; now I have stood up again."[62]

Yet not all were so effusive in their praise. Although the distinction is only made indirectly, it is clear that "bitterly poor herdsmen"—the loan recipients— were often keener than those expected to sell their animals to support the program. A report described livestock purchase as the "most complex and delicate task of welfare work."[63] A Wöngya herdsman, for example, expressed confusion over what seemed the irreconcilable suggestion that raising overall production demanded reducing the size of his herd, asking, "Did the people's government want me to increase the number of animals or sell them?" Another member of the Wöngya, referred to as Niri'er in Chinese, displayed his displeasure in more confrontational language. According to the report, "When Zhuotai, a [Tibetan] cadre, went to Nire'er's home to get sheep, Niri'er exclaimed, 'You came to get sheep when no one was home. You are just like Ma Bufang before.'" The report concludes, "From these two people we can see that although on the surface the sheep from the Wöngya were sold voluntarily, actually [quotas] were allocated to the people."[64]

The admission highlights tensions that lay at the point where United Front principles met policy implementation. First, although it was continually stressed that local cadres needed to investigate, understand, and account for the concrete conditions that existed in their localities, there was very limited space for those cadres to exercise innovation based on their findings. Instead, policy was formulated at higher levels and sent downward for implementation. Time and again, provincial-, prefectural-, or county-level directives rebuked those below them for contradictorily (a) not understanding the concrete conditions of the region in which they worked and (b) failing to implement policy as directed by their superiors.

Second, Party leaders expected subordinates to execute these policies and meet production targets without reverting to coercion. It was repeatedly emphasized that work group leaders, loan committees, and well-off pastoralists must all clearly understand that the sale of livestock was strictly voluntary. However, no contingency is found in the documents for the possibility that herders would refuse to sell sufficient animals to cover the promised loans. Instead, the assumption was that propaganda would be enough. The unspoken corollary was that if there was an animal shortage, it spoke not to deficiencies in the overall policy or the obstruction of the indigenous elite but to the poor work style and underdeveloped political consciousness of grassroots cadres.[65] Given these strains, it is unsurprising that circumstantial evidence—occasionally made explicit—suggests that cadres often pressured pastoralists to sell livestock to the state.[66]

In fact, nearly two years after the Second Joint Committee launched focused allocation, the work plan for 1956 would note that both local and outside cadres continued to lack sufficient understanding of welfare policies. Consequently, neither did headmen nor the masses.[67] It also conceded that many pastoralists remained unconvinced that their lives could be improved through government programs. Instead, they purportedly insisted that fate had already dealt them a poor hand, the reference to superstition itself an indictment of poor propaganda work implemented by grassroots cadres. And despite stressing that oversight of postloan animal management was the key to maximizing economic and political benefits of the welfare program, the report alleged that cadres continued to display an attitude of "paying attention to distribution and not caring about production." It concluded, "In this area, our county has done a poor job."[68]

Perhaps most alarming, was the case of a Tibetan herdsman named Tséten (C. Caidan). According to the 1955 year-end work report, "Tséten said in a pessimistic and disappointed tone, 'If you want to redistribute [my animals], then go ahead. As long as there is enough left to feed and clothe me. Sooner or later the herds will be divided anyway.'"[69] Captured in Tséten's words is an intrinsic understanding of the transitory nature of the CCP's United Front policies. Although preaching the Three Nos, the CCP was not interested in permanently protecting the status quo. Zhou Renshan had made this clear to the very cadres who were now leading the Party's efforts in pastoral areas. In redistributing animals to the poorest of the grassland's inhabitants and, it hoped, simultaneously spurring production, the CCP sought to expand its reach beyond the subimperial accommodation it had forged with the region's paramount figures. Only by breaking down traditional economic, social, and political structures would the productive capacities of the grasslands—and the pastoral masses themselves—be fully liberated.

A Glorious Task

In early September 1954, Zeku's joint committee met for the third and final time. For the third straight meeting, however, underwhelming attendance forced a several-day postponement, a failure county leaders blamed on poor "ideological education" conducted by their cadres.[70] Even then, only twenty-seven of its forty-two members and thirteen observers were present. Once the meeting began, Party secretary Guo Min delivered a speech on the soon-to-be adopted PRC constitution. Focusing on its protections for minority peoples, Guo described the constitution as an "'amulet' protecting the people's lives and property."[71] He compared the People's Republic of China favorably to the United States, where "the white race" (*baizhong*) earned 30 to 50 percent more than "the black race" (*heizhong*) for the same work and where the children of different "nationalities" (minzu) were forced to attend segregated schools. Unlike in the racist capitalist nations, Guo explained, the PRC constitution guaranteed equality, prohibited discrimination, and inscribed into law the principle of nationality autonomy for minority people.[72] Production tasks, grassland disputes, and welfare work were also discussed.[73]

However, the emphasis of the Third Joint Committee meeting was state procurement of animals and animal by-products. If welfare work in part was designed to alleviate local anxieties toward the Han-dominated Party-state, resource extraction had the potential to do just the opposite. Local informants often told investigators that the most salient difference between Ma Bufang and the Communist regime was the contrast between Ma's heavy tax demands and the welfare policies of the CCP. In one example, a Sonak herdsman purportedly proclaimed, "In the past Ma Bufang demanded money from us. In order to pay Ma Bufang, some people had to sell all their cattle and sheep. But today the people's government not only does not demand payments from us *but instead pays us*. This truly is a government that works on our behalf."[74] In the end, however, the pastoral sector was imagined as an integral (if subsidiary) part of a consolidated, industrialized socialist economy. Authorities therefore needed to remove resources from the grasslands. During the mid-1950s, it had two primary ways to do so: direct animal purchases and taxation.

Conscious that the extractive measures of the Ma Bufang regime had been among the principal causes of conflict between Xining and local communities, speakers at the Third Joint Committee sought to distinguish Ma's exploitive taxes from the "patriotic taxes" of the CCP. Taking his cue from upper levels, Wagya told committee members, "Paying taxes to the state is the obligation of the masses of all the people. It is also the concrete manifestation of patriotism. During the period of Guomindang rule, their taxes were to enrich themselves. On the contrary, in the present period of the [rule of] the people, '[taxes] are acquired from the people and used for the people.'"[75] For instance, the Hor headman noted that animal taxes and purchases underwrote welfare work, which in turn promoted production and increased standards of living.

However, it was the mutual support of industry, agriculture, and pastoralism, first emphasized at the Second Joint Committee, that became the core principle under which both taxes and purchases were to be promoted. Describing the "intimate relationship" between pastoral regions and the "socialist industrialization of the country," Wagya explained,

> By using machines to carry out production such as milking cows, shearing wool, and so forth, pastoral production will develop faster, the mechanization of activities such as shearing wool will boost the development of animal husbandry, and the lives of the people of pastoral regions will become better and better. At the same time, the people of our pastoral regions will also put a lot of effort into developing production and providing sufficient raw materials such as hides and wool for industry and meat for city people and farm animals for agricultural regions.[76]

Wagya concluded by declaring tax collection a "glorious task," part of the process of "gradually promoting our country from a backward agricultural country to a socialist industrial country."

Wagya then announced that Huangnan Prefecture had set a 1954 Zeku County procurement target of 802 head of cattle and 10,709 sheep. The county committee allotted specific quotas to each chiefdom based on their "specific conditions," presumably referring to size and relative prosperity.[77] Leaders urged the gathered headmen to lead by example—to accurately register their own livestock numbers, be the first to pay their taxes, and voluntarily sell surplus animals to the state. Committee members were reminded, "Only in this way can we raise the people's consciousness and show them that we are serving the people." Citing a clause in the tax code, headmen were told that in exchange for paying their taxes voluntarily and truthfully, and encouraging others to do so as well, households would receive praise and rewards. By contrast, those who were unwilling to pay taxes or made inaccurate reports were to be criticized at mass meetings. Importantly, however, at this time authorities did not treat tax evasion as a criminal or counterrevolutionary offense. Instead, it was considered a problem of education and awareness. County leaders therefore urged both cadres and local elites to raise the political consciousness of violators through propaganda, not punishment.[78]

Following Wagya's lead, several committee members quickly pledged their active support. Hitting upon many of the meeting's talking points, Yönten, leader of the Hor's Shokmang tsowa, purportedly declared,

> In the past one person, the bandit Ma, enjoyed good fortune, but now the people's government serves us people. Just as our Hor Ratsang tribe received lots of loans from the government this year, every year the government also sends lots of emergency relief funds, providing emergency relief to the bitterly poor herdsmen. We should pay taxes to the government; it is glorious. This year, I will accurately report my livestock numbers. And I will take responsibility to ensure that the Shokmang tribe's livestock numbers are also accurately reported.[79]

Losar of the Wöngya announced that he would sell twenty sheep and three head of cattle. As important, he promised to encourage ordinary Wöngya households to do the same. After returning to his chiefdom, the Köde Karing baihu Dargyé not only explained the connection between taxes and the mutual support of industry, agriculture and pastoralism but also personally registered households in his small chiefdom. As a result, the Köde Karing purportedly provided the state 75 percent more animals than the previous year. Explicitly recognizing the undiminished role of Zeku's indigenous leadership, a report summarized, "This success cannot be separated from committee member Dargyé's enthusiastic work."[80]

As with district building and welfare work, patriotic tax collection was first tested among the Hor. This time the campaign's three stages were divided into a period of propaganda during which committees were formed and policies disseminated by local elites at mass meetings, one of investigation during which animal numbers would be registered, and finally procurement.[81] The basic tax unit was the white sheep, with one sheep equaling two goats, three sheep equaling one cow, four one yak, and eight one horse. Several categories of animals were declared tax exempt, including monastery animals used for food production or labor, animals that had bred in that tax year, goats and sheep under two years of age, and horses and cattle under three.[82] Hoping to avoid direct confrontation with the local population, cadres left it to the local leadership to encourage individual households to accurately report livestock numbers and level criticism when suspicions of underreporting arose. To their dismay, officials reported that local headmen instead often "adopted the superstitious [method] of 'oath-taking' (chizhou)."[83] In recognition of the campaign's sensitivity, however, the work group noted that it neither approved nor disapproved what it clearly viewed as heterodox practice.

The Hor Work Group would declare animal tax collection in 1954 an overall success. Compared to the previous year, its efforts resulted in reported procurement increases in sheep of 68 percent, cattle 22 percent, and horses 16 percent. In addition, taxes collected in wool grew by 36 percent. It would not be unexpected for such a substantial rise in the state's extractive demands to have been met by local resistance. However, according to a summary report, "By doing propaganda work alongside collecting taxes, we first strengthened the patriotism of both the leaders and the masses and made it clear that the reason the state collects taxes is 'to acquire it from the people and use it for the people.'"[84] Hor chieftains such as Lhagyel and Yönten were held up as examples of headmen who had truthfully and enthusiastically registered their herd numbers and educated the masses to do the same.[85] Yet statistical improvements masked a more mixed record of success. Not only had individual work teams often been understaffed, but the work group also admitted that many cadres lacked the requisite knowledge of tax-collection policies, and few even spoke Amdo Tibetan, a reoccurring issue that merits surprisingly little explicit attention in the archival sources. As a consequence, preparations were inadequate, numerous accounting errors were made, and some animals were never paid for.[86]

Once again, implementation had proved far more complicated than anticipated. In fact, by the following year, the degree to which animal numbers had been underreported began to become clear. Unsurprisingly, self-reporting had proven inadequate. An investigation found that despite swearing to accurately report herd sizes, many herders "concealed animal numbers *with the aid of tribal leaders*."[87] Most alarming, officials determined that headmen—the support of whom had been judged so vital for the campaign's success—were themselves among the principal tax evaders, again damaging the campaign from both a revenue and propaganda standpoint. Yet CCP leaders refrained from directly criticizing the local Tibetan leadership. Shifting blame to its own cadres, Zeku's year-end report reemphasized the Party's commitment to the United Front by declaring, "Experience shows: in order to do work well in nationality regions, we must firmly proceed from top to bottom. First, if we want local leaders to shoulder responsibility enthusiastically and to report accurately, we must do a thorough job of consultation so they have command over policy, and encourage their enthusiasm to become 'masters of their own home.'"[88] Direct taxation of local populations was a significant move toward a more centralized, bureaucratic method of governance. However, the Party clearly was still dependent on the region's pre-1949 leadership and not just in their capacities as county leaders but also as local headmen with both the prestige and skills needed to mediate such a potentially explosive yet basic function of state-society interaction.

How to Become One with the Masses

In the opening paragraph of its 1954 year-end summary report, the Zeku County People's Government Committee triumphantly proclaimed that despite an extremely cold winter, "Production has improved significantly since the December 1953 establishment of Zeku County."[89] Overall, it announced, livestock numbers had risen by 25 percent—far exceeding the 10 percent target set in the 1954 work plan. These numbers are of course impossible to authenticate, and it seems certain that improved data collection—if not outright overreporting—may account for at least some of the gains.[90] Nonetheless, with growing production enshrined as 1954's core task, Zeku's leaders could declare the year to have been an overall success.

Other accomplishments were likewise trumpeted. More or less running down the list of goals highlighted in the 1954 work plan, the report detailed progress in health care and education, tax collection, social welfare, and cadre training (including the recruitment of fifty-two Tibetan cadres). It noted the number of predators killed, pens built, and hides produced; the amount of wool, herbs, and other grassland products collected; the amount of winter feed cut; the number of grassland disputes resolved; and so forth. The founding of the First District (Hor) was prominently declared to have furthered the aspirations of minority nationalities to become "masters of their own home." In conclusion, the report summarized, "social order has been restored, nationality unity has been consolidated, production has been greatly increased, and therefore the mass awareness of all of the people has risen."[91]

However, all had not gone as planned. The five work groups sent "down to the tribes" the previous spring in fact had met mixed results. In their individual year-end reports, they admitted to being understaffed, undersupplied, and often ill prepared. Several reported having difficulties simply keeping up with the paperwork, while all of the work groups mentioned substandard living conditions, food shortages, and poor cadre quality. Sickness appears to have been common, and, as suggested by cases of "disunity between the cadres" and dereliction of duty, morale was often low.[92] While details are few, the physical and mental hardships of being a Han cadre assigned to Zeku County in the mid-1950s should not be underestimated.

Moreover, although the First District had been established, plans to found the four other districts had not gotten off the ground. A year later, only Méshül District (by then called Topden and consisting of the Méshül, Ködé Karing, and Khéri Chunga chiefdoms) had been completed. Two other districts were established over the course of 1956, and one, Haidun District (Gartsé and Shisa chiefdoms), would not be founded until 1957, only to be redivided the following year as two people's communes.[93] While over three hundred grassland disputes reportedly had been resolved, dozens of others continued to fester, including a major conflict between the Méshül and Tongren's Dowa chiefdom.[94] Production and tax revenue were both up sharply, yet revenue still only covered 27 percent of the county's expenditures, the difference made up by state subsidies.[95] Despite repeated assurances, the county continued to suffer from chronic grain shortages. To make up for the shortfall, work groups had begun issuing "grain introduction letters" to be presented in neighboring counties.[96] Likewise, only a third of the planned 1.5 million jin of winter feed had been cut, "so in the cold of last winter, many calves and lambs died from a lack of grass."[97] And while the Méshül Work Group claimed that 153 animal pens had been built within the three chiefdoms under its supervision, the Hor work report admitted that none of the seventy shelters slated to be built within the Wönkhor tsowa had been completed. The reason given was that cadres had been unable to negotiate the complex rivalries that divided the plateau, in this case preventing the physical fencing of the grasslands.[98] Overall, the county committee admitted, "[We] did not investigate, research and grasp the concrete conditions in depth, and we lacked a sufficient understanding of procedures. Therefore, there was not enough planning, [which led to] the appearance of chaos and passivity." Propaganda work also had been insufficient. Rather than consultation and persuasion, county leaders confessed, "Within the tribes, coercion was sometimes employed."[99]

In 1954, the CCP had sent work teams "into the grasslands" and "down to the tribes." Party leaders intended this to be a significant step in a process that would eventually allow it to sever its imperial-style reliance on elite intermediaries and fully integrate the grasslands into the "motherland" (zuguo).[100] Yet as the work of district building, welfare allocation, and tax collection proved, traditional elites remained indispensable. This was true at both the county level, where the joint committee functioned as the forum through which the Party introduced policy, and at the local level, where work teams implemented directives through the mediation of local leaders. While official correspondences were frequently critical of the efforts of the county's cadre force, there was no sense of urgency or desperation. As Zhou Renshan had made clear, only through a patient commitment to the principles and procedures of the United Front would patriotic spirit and class consciousness gradually and organically be injected into Amdo's grasslands.[101] Yet the United Front was not to go unchallenged. Within a year the CCP's fidelity to gradualism and voluntarism would come under pressure from a revolutionary impatience that demanded a more immediate route to national integration and socialist transformation.

5

HIGH TIDE ON THE HIGH PLATEAU

In June 1955, the Zeku County People's Representative Committee gathered at the still unfinished county seat. Meeting for the first time since the county's inaugural conference in late 1953, the delegates reviewed final reports from 1954 and reassessed plans for the current year and beyond. With the benefit of the previous year's experiences, the committee determined that tax-collection efforts needed to be streamlined, while social welfare should continue according to the principle of focused allocation and paid for through voluntary livestock sales.[1] As before, grassland disputes were to be settled according to the guidelines of "mutual understanding and mutual accommodation" (*huliang hurang*). Under the less than imaginative slogan "Earn More, Spend Less," county leaders urged cadres to tighten fiscal oversight and reduce expenditures. Work plans were issued for outstanding tasks ranging from establishing unfinished district-level administrative organs, resolving difficulties in acquiring and distributing grains, developing Zeku's health-care and educational capacities, training Tibetan cadres, improving security, and completing the construction of Zeku's administrative center. Raising production remained a key concern. The committee reconfirmed the ambitious but relatively moderate year-end goal of increasing horse stocks by 9 percent, cattle by 12 percent, and sheep by 18 percent.[2]

Overall, county leaders announced, in the eighteen months since its founding, Zeku County had made significant progress. As usual, however, the plaudits came with several caveats. In particular, it was determined that some committee members (i.e., Tibetan headmen) were still hesitant to enthusiastically tackle their work assignments. In fact, as had become routine, the majority of the Tibetan delegates had failed to arrive at the makeshift county seat on the appointed date, forcing the conference to be delayed several days. The lateness was blamed on two serious grassland disputes—one the continuing feud between the Méshül chiefdom and rivals in Tongren County and the other between the Gönshül and Xiahe's Sangkhok chiefdom—demonstrating the CCP's continued difficulty promoting *intra*nationality unity. Others had to be cajoled into coming. For instance, the leader of the Shisa chiefdom only agreed after receiving a personal appeal from Wagya. Even then, when the meeting did convene, barely half of the expected 116 full delegates were in attendance (forty-six Tibetan and sixteen Han), including just nine women.[3]

Yet Party leaders again reserved the majority of the criticism for their own cadres. They admitted that investigation into the "concrete conditions" of the Zeku grasslands remained inadequate, propaganda work insufficient, and that Han chauvinism continued to harm overall efforts. As a result, work had not always been well planned or properly implemented. Most troublesome, it was determined that cadres often resorted to coercion rather than the United Front principles of consultation and persuasion. To correct these defects, cadres needed to rededicate themselves to their tasks, acquire appropriate language skills, and educate, cooperate with, and learn from local Tibetan cadres.[4] With these goals in mind, Zeku's leadership ordered Han cadres to take elementary-level classes in political theory, economics, and, in order to "vigorously eliminate the language barrier," a six-week intensive course in Tibetan.[5]

Before adjourning, conference attendees selected a new county government committee. Wagya, Guo Min, and Lhagyel each were reelected to their positions with the delegates' unanimous support, while Serökyap appeared on all but one ballot. There was, however, one significant leadership change. For unclear reasons, Lhakba, the Shawonar chieftain, was removed from his position as the county's fourth-ranking vice chairman. At Zeku County's founding conference, Party leaders had singled out Lhakba for his activism, his antibanditry efforts lauded as an exemplification of the mantra "to become masters of their own home." A year and a half later, these same officials criticized Lhakba for refusing to help convince Tibetan delegates to attend the conference and for openly challenging the CCP's commitment to the principle of nationality autonomy. Declaring that decision-making was entirely in the hands of Han cadres, Lhakba reportedly vented, "It does not matter if we become masters of our own home or not!" Yet the outburst was said to have been a reaction to his demotion rather than its cause.[6]

Despite Lhakba's censure, both in terms of successes and setbacks work appeared to be progressing almost naturally from previous years. Most noticeably, references to socialist reforms were all but absent from the June meeting's proceedings. Instead, county leaders continued to emphasize the twin maxims of nationality unity and economic development. Again, this was in contrast to Han and Hui farming communities that predominated north of the Yellow River. Despite nationwide fluctuations in rural policy that for several years had veered between relatively gradual and more accelerated programs of collectivization, by mid-1955, 876 basic-level agricultural production cooperatives (APCs) had been established in eleven counties across Qinghai's northeastern agricultural areas.[7] This was not the case in Tibetan areas, which with few exceptions had been exempted from the cooperativization drive.

On the grasslands of Zeku County, "socialism" only received its first sustained attention in 1954 when the topic was raised at that summer's Second Political Consultative Conference. At the time, however, socialism remained a largely abstract concept, and the process for achieving it was persistently unexplained. Socialism meant unity, industrialization, and prosperity. It was the polar opposite of the exploitation and brutality of Chiang Kaishek and Ma Bufang. It involved serving the people and benefiting the people, ending grassland disputes, and increasing patriotism. It necessitated guaranteeing grain supplies, regulating prices, and eliminating the black market. It depended upon "correcting our old-fashioned ways of thinking from the old society," after which "we can . . . march toward socialism and a happy life."[8] Most of all, socialism meant supporting the coalition of industry, agriculture, and pastoralism, on which basis, Wagya announced, the Zeku grasslands could "slowly make the transition to socialism."[9] What socialism did not seem to mean, except perhaps in the fine print, was a radical reorganization of the economic, social, and political order—redistributing wealth, assigning class labels, collectivizing production, and eliminating the "feudal" authority of the secular and religious elite.

A year later, delegates to Zeku's 1955 People's Representative Conference continued to sidestep the subject of socialist reforms. The one exception was a summary of remarks made the previous December by Qinghai governor Sun Zuobin. Declaring that the country was jointly traveling down the road to socialism, Governor Sun had explained, "Constructing a socialist society is the common goal of all our country's nationalities. Only socialism can guarantee that every nationality can achieve a higher level of economic and cultural development. Our country has the responsibility to help each and every nationality down this great road to happiness."[10] Yet, having established that socialism was the nation's historic mission, its "one glorious path," Governor Sun made it clear that historical circumstances dictated that each nationality would not reach it at the same time or via the same route. Instead, Sun insisted that local officials must continue to respect the "special conditions" of each nationality: "That is to say, on the questions of when to implement socialist reforms and how to implement socialist reforms, it will be different because of the different conditions of the development of each nationality. In regard to this question, the masses of each nationality and the leaders among them must be permitted to decide for themselves in due time, and we must proceed according to their wishes."[11] The Zeku delegates, most of whom were members of the region's traditional leadership, were therefore reassured, "unity is power; unity is happiness. Anything that goes against it will not be beneficial for the people but for our enemies. . . . The purpose of unity is to build one common harmonious family for all nationalities; the purpose of unity is to build a new Qinghai, a new Huangnan, and a happy socialist society."[12] As of June 1955, the foundations of the United Front had been reaffirmed. The Three Nos were still intact. Nationality unity—not class struggle—remained Zeku's operating principle. Socialist transformation would have to wait.

Yet Lhakba's outburst at Zeku's midsummer conference would prove prescient. This chapter explores the period from summer 1955 to summer 1956, a year that saw the sudden introduction of class analysis and protocollectivization into Amdo's grasslands. Spurred by the nationwide "High Tide of Socialist Transformation," which sought to collectivize agriculture at a sudden and startling pace, in fall 1955 the CCP organized "intensive investigations" into Amdo's pastoral society, efforts meant to pave the way for the staged introduction of pastoral cooperatives. By early 1956, Qinghai's leadership had made cooperativization (*hezuohua*) the year's core task in pastoral areas. Under these circumstances, the underpinnings of the United Front came under pressure as socialism itself was declared the means to achieve nationality unity and economic development. With revolutionary impatience threatening to overwhelm United Front pragmatism, the rhetoric used to describe Tibetan elites began to shift as well. Rather than covictims of nationality exploitation, headmen and monastic leaders were increasingly transformed into representatives of the pastoral exploiting class.

However, the collectivization campaign quickly encountered resistance from Amdo's pastoral population. Ignoring the downward pressure to which grassroots cadres were subjected during political campaigns such as the High Tide, Qinghai's leadership placed the majority of the blame on the mismanagement and coercive practices of overzealous local officials. This had hurt production and given rise to "chaotic" conditions, banditry, and even "armed rebellion." By late spring 1956, Qinghai's pastoral collectivization campaign had been suspended, and efforts were made to shore up the stressed foundations of the United Front.

From Nationality Unity to Class Exploitation

Throughout the first half of 1955, instructions originating in both Beijing and Xining continued to stress the core principles of the United Front. A February decree issued in the name of the Party Center, for example, reminded local officials that minority regions "continued to be economically and culturally backward" and warned that the rash introduction of collective production before conditions were ripe "could even cause mass disturbances." Contrary to the "subjective wishes of some cadres," it added, in minority regions the correct method for advancing toward socialism "is not to speed up, but instead to slow down."[13] Closer to home, in midsummer Qinghai's new Party secretary, Gao Feng, reminded his cadres that "backward conditions" still prevailed across the province's grasslands. Declaring that "some cadres do not understand the current nature of socialist reforms in pastoral regions," the Shaanxi native cautioned, "Implementing socialist reforms too early is not only [a sign of being] divorced from reality, but it is mistaken and dangerous."[14] To any but the most astute observer or Party insider, there was little reason to suspect that pastoral policies in Qinghai might suddenly shift to the left.

In fact, concerned over stagnant growth in agricultural production, over the first half of 1955 national leaders again were absorbed in a lengthy debate over the pace of rural collectivization. This came to a head at the end of July when Mao Zedong forcibly broke the deadlock between proponents of more gradual and more immediate paths to socialist transformation. Coming down squarely on the side of the latter, Mao blamed conservatism among Party cadres for dampening rural enthusiasm for collectivization. Responding to Mao's call for a "high tide of socialist transformation in the countryside," across China Party branches began scrambling to establish APCs. Mirroring nationwide developments, by November Qinghai's eight-hundred-plus APCs had risen to 2,057, doubling again to an astounding 4,028 by the end of the year.[15]

It was not until autumn that the concrete consequences of this radicalization began to manifest themselves on Zeku's grasslands. On October 13, a directive penned by the Qinghai Provincial Party Committee reached Huangnan Prefecture. It announced that on July 21, ten days *before* Mao's pivotal speech, the provincial Party committee had received plans drawn up by a Rural Work Department–sponsored "National Pastoral Region Work Conference." In mid-September, provincial leaders discussed the Party Center's orders with the CCP secretaries of Qinghai's various pastoral areas. A month later, instructions originating in Beijing arrived in Huangnan Prefecture.[16] The directive stipulated that officials conduct "intensive investigations" into the "concrete conditions" and productive capacities of Qinghai's pastoral areas, adding, "This investigation should emphasize paying attention to *class relations* and the development of production."[17] At least within Party circles, the underlying objectives of the pastoral investigations therefore were made unambiguously clear. The work was meant to pave the way for the first phases of socialist transformation in pastoral areas, namely the establishment of mutual aid teams (MATs) and pastoral production cooperatives (PPCs).

For Zeku County, the order marked a significant and sudden shift in guiding principles that had been reaffirmed as recently as the June meetings. Up to this point, the nature of pastoral class relations had been a taboo subject. The focus instead was on uniting all pastoral Tibetans in a broad alliance with the CCP and integrating them into the multinational state. Now, however, the provincial Party committee described the pastoral economy as one based on the exploitation "of the free labor of the herdsmen."[18] Xining ordered "herdlords," the pastoral equivalent of agricultural landlords, identified and divided into three categories—upper, middle, and lower herdlord—based on three sets of criteria: number of sheep owned, amount of labor hired, and "degree of exploitation" (boxueliang). First, distinctions were to be made between households with over 1,100 sheep, those with over 2,100 sheep, and those with over 3,100 sheep. Second, herdlords were to be classified based on their having employed one, two, or three or more nonfamily laborers. Last, the degree of exploitation was to be determined by the percentage of household income that was derived from hired labor. Here the dividing lines were set at 50 percent, 60 percent, and 70 percent and above. When designating class status, all three indices had to be considered as an integrated whole, the lowest common denominator—in this case meaning the lowest degree of exploitation—being the final determinant. The provincial instructions declared, "If all three conditions are applicable, then the target can be considered a herdlord; if even one is not applicable, [then he or she] cannot be considered a herdlord." Yet despite assigning ostensibly objective criteria for calculating class status, a decidedly subjective qualification was added. The provincial committee made it clear that it was "suitable to be lenient and unsuitable to be strict." In particular, herdlords were not to exceed 5 percent of any region's pastoral households. Most important, investigators were ordered to stop short of assigning class labels to individual households or redistributing their property. Instead, the Three Nos remained explicitly in effect.[19] The waters of the High Tide were rising, but they had yet to inundate the high plateau. Even so, Party leaders were clearly preparing for a not-too-distant point when class would become the operable category of social and political organization in pastoral areas and socialist transformation could begin.

The Sprouts of Socialism

Heedless of the frigid weather that by October already would have descended upon Amdo's high-altitude areas, Xining announced that pastoral investigation work would begin immediately. Each of Qinghai's six prefectures was told to select three pastoral investigation focus sites, each ideally composed of around one hundred households. Provincial leaders were aware of the campaign's delicacy, "especially as it concerns the question of class." Therefore, local Party secretaries were instructed to "personally take control of the investigations, and to implement [work] carefully." Investigations were to be completed by mid-December, at which time reports would be submitted to various prefectural Party committees. The prefectures then had a mid-January deadline to assemble the collected data, integrate it with materials that had been gathered over the previous years, and send their final reports to Xining.[20]

Given the cooperation the Hor chiefdom had provided in previous campaigns, it is unsurprising that Huangnan's leadership chose one of its five tsowa, the Shokmang, as one of the prefecture's three investigation sites. On October 27, just two weeks after receiving the provincial directive, a newly constituted Shokmang Work Team "officially entered the tents." That same day, Lhagyel called together a mass meeting. To the over two hundred members of the Shokmang reportedly in attendance, Lhagyel explained "the work team's purpose in coming" and asked for their cooperation. Per provincial instructions, Party secretary Guo Min was also on hand in order to "persuade and educate the masses and dispel their apprehensions in order to create beneficial conditions in which work could be launched." The work team's report notes that Secretary Guo, like Gao Feng a native of the dry plains of Shaanxi Province, also spoke to the Tibetan pastoralists about winter animal-protection work and other issues relating to pastoral production, tasks the Shokmang Work Team was to simultaneously promote under the principle of consolidating work efforts.[21]

Once in the field, the work team set about collecting both demographic information and data on the makeup and size of the Shokmang herds.[22] Discovering wild annual fluctuations in livestock numbers, it also offered qualitative assessments of pastoral production practices. For example, the work team examined yearly grazing patterns and associated animal diseases, going so far as to detail how greater attention to the specifics of seasonal migration could reduce the incidence of epidemics. Pursuing its objective with a self-confident rationality that conjures up James Scott's cautionary description of "high modernist ideologies," the work team concluded that dramatic reductions in herd sizes were entirely preventable. According to its assessment, poor "animal management," in particular the failure to cut winter feed and repair shelters, accounted for the majority of animal deaths.[23]

More revealing were subsequent investigations into the Shokmang's Tsébho and Gönpo herding groups. In a short report filed on November 25, the work team identified several practices among the Gönpo that it recognized as primitive forms of mutual assistance. For instance, herding cattle was described as a joint responsibility shared by all of the herding group's households. Other forms of mutual aid identified by the work team included communal methods of moving encampments and sideline production practices such as milking cows and shearing sheep. When it came time to pull yak hair, the report noted, everyone had to help regardless of the number of animals a household possessed, receiving only meals from the owner as compensation. Similarly, the entire community was expected to donate a day or two of labor to sheep shearing.[24]

Of course, documenting "existing forms of unity and mutual aid" was not some idle ethnographic pursuit.[25] Instead, it lay at the heart of the Party's transformation agenda. Considering traditional mutual aid practices to be "sprouts of socialism" (*shehui zhuyi de mengya*), provincial authorities predicted that the most efficient means to get the pastoral masses to accept collectivization was to use "scientific" methods to improve upon extant forms of mutual aid.[26] Reports from the Tsébho, for example, noted that indigenous forms of mutual assistance had developed organically as a way to combat the difficult environmental conditions of the high plateau and mitigate damage from natural disasters. Yet the work team considered these practices backward and inefficient. Speaking specifically of communal methods of cattle grazing and moving encampments, the report emphasized, "[They] are based on a foundation of existing kinship and neighborliness. They are established voluntarily and without any material reward. But based on the [distribution of] manual labor, *they do not seem rational.*"[27] By systemizing and improving upon traditional forms of mutual aid, pastoral production could be made to be more efficient, higher yielding, and more equitable and thus help convince herders of the benefits of still more advanced forms of communal production and eventually full socialist transformation. This rationale fell squarely within mass line/United Front principles and procedures of consultation and persuasion and was itself grounded in the CCP's foundational assumption that collective production was superior to individual household-based ownership.

The Tsébho report did not limit itself to the investigation of mutual aid practices. For the first time, it also analyzed local society in class terms, identifying the political economy of the grasslands as a class-based system of exploitation dictated by the monopolization of ownership over the means of production. Much as landlords exploited laborers and peasants through low wages, high rents, and high-interest loans, herdlords similarly exploited hired laborers and common pastoralists. The report asserted that despite modest increases in the compensation paid to laborers and a parallel reduction in rates charged by lenders, poor herders remained mired in a spiral of debt and poverty.[28] The clear implication was that six years after "Liberation," Qinghai's pastoral masses were still victims of *class exploitation.*

Having established that class exploitation lay at the core of the grassland economy, the pastoral investigation report offered plenty of anecdotal evidence that in the eyes of its agents suggested a growing estrangement between the pastoral masses and the herdlord class. In one of several examples documented by the work team, a member of the Tsébho herding group reportedly complained, "The government tells us to protect the grasslands in order to develop livestock. We are poor people without animals. We only can rent livestock from others. If the grass is good, the animals will fatten and produce more butter. Yet in this case, rich households demand higher rents—they do not reduce them."[29] Herders singled out several headmen-cum–county leaders for what were deemed usurious lending practices. For instance, another of Wagya's brothers was denounced for issuing loans that "oppress those below." According to the informant, the loan recipient inevitably found himself permanently indebted to the Hor headman. A third member of the Tsébho claimed that he had received a loan from still another committee member, referred to in Chinese as Zhijiu. According to the complaint, Zhijiu had surreptitiously loaned out aged yaks and horses, animals that were no longer suitable for production. However, Hor headmen—all of whom had been vested with government office—were purportedly unresponsive to demands that Zhijiu compensate his victims. "As a result," the work team alleged, loan recipients "feel that we ordered committee members to give out nonproductive animals." Similar complaints were lodged against the Hor's smallish but influential monastic establishment. In one case, a report professed that in 1952, monks had given cattle to impoverished Shokmang households—presumably as emergency relief, given catastrophic animals losses reported that year. "At the time [the monks] said, 'These cattle are being given to you so that you can have food to eat. There is no need to repay any amount of money or yogurt.'" However, the following year, what had originally been gifts turned into loans and remittance was demanded with interest.[30]

From the perspective of Zeku's Party leadership, the key to the accusations was the masses' purported willingness to challenge the exploitative practices and prerogatives of traditional elites. In the context of the radicalizing political environment, anecdotes such as these—collected and transmitted by grassroots cadres likely on the lookout for just such corroboration—were viewed by higher-ups as a sign that mass awareness and patriotic consciousness were developing. While the degree to which class-based identities had actually begun to dislodge more enduring forms of loyalty and identity is unclear, subsequent events would suggest that predictions of the imminent emergence of class consciousness were at best overstated. Nonetheless, by the end of 1955, Zeku's Party leaders were declaring that the "mass awareness of the pastoralists has significantly improved."

This allegedly had led to the weakening of bonds binding the pastoral masses to their headmen. As evidence, the county CCP committee offered the case of First District leader Köngya. It had been discovered that Köngya had falsely reported his herd numbers, likely in an attempt to avoid taxes. To Zeku's Party leadership, however, more important than the accusation itself was the revelation that members of the Hor had brought the transgressions of the chiefdom's leading family to the attention of the state.[31]

In still one more example, investigators asserted that herdlords had previously enjoyed the right to occupy pastures "without constraint." Now, however, the masses understood that this was exploitative. Even the authority of Zeku's three powerful qianhu was no longer sacrosanct. Speaking of the Gönshül headman, the report noted, "County leader Serökyap did not obey the grassland regulations and as a result the people protested. This kind of thing was not possible before Liberation." With certain embellishment, the Party committee triumphantly concluded, "In the past, herders were subject to the orders of tribal leaders. Now when the leaders speak, the herders do not listen."[32] Back in 1952, Zhou Renshan had predicted that the CCP's United Front policies would gradually and organically give rise to mass consciousness. In the process, the grassland's traditional secular and religious leadership would become isolated from the people. Even if lubricated by the expectations of their superiors, just three years later reports flowing upward from Zeku's grassroots cadres seemed to indicate that the process was well underway.

A Feudal Society with Capitalist Characteristics

That the CCP was moving from a framework of inclusivity to exclusivity—from one that defined all pastoral Tibetans as members of an exploited nationality to identifying a few among them as enemies of the people—becomes evident in internal reports that began to emerge at the end of 1955. Suddenly terminologies that over the previous years had been almost entirely absent from the Party's discourses on state and nation building appear. For example, the county's preliminary pastoral investigation report describes pastoral society as "a feudal society with capitalist characteristics," in which "religious belief is especially strong" and "there is a lot of exploitation and class oppression."[33] While the assessment is not entirely new—similar judgments had been made in the fall of 1953—the root cause of exploitation had changed in a fundamental way. No longer were there gratuitous references to the oppression of the Ma Bufang regime, long the primary metonym for nationality exploitation. Instead, although still leveled discreetly, by the start of 1956 Zeku's indigenous leadership was being

singled out as the exploitative class and the main barrier to economic development and national integration.[34] Nationality unity was still the foundation upon
which the new society would be built. However, unity's enemies rapidly were
being redefined.

Perhaps the most direct evidence of the CCP's changing attitude toward traditional elites appears in the rhetoric surrounding grassland disputes. Two years
earlier, Guo Min and his lieutenants had repeatedly cast grassland conflict as a
manifestation of the predatory practices of Ma Bufang and his allies. Now culpability was shifted onto the qianhu and baihu themselves. Despite increases in production since 1953, the Party committee conceded that incidences of grassland
conflict had risen as well. This, county leaders asserted, was neither due to environmental hardships nor nationality exploitation. Employing language never
before used in Zeku County, the committee declared, "The reason is due to the
fact that *class struggle* during the transitional period is becoming more serious
and complex. Therefore, the small nationality ruling class wants to maintain their
dominant position, and so they create these disputes. In addition, the reactionary
elements are using religion to create conflict among the people and even armed
fighting."[35] As proof, a report alleged that while attending government meetings,
headmen would pledge to cooperate with work teams. However, "afterward they
would seal off the masses, and create lots of obstacles." An example was made of
the Gartsé qianhu Lubum. Warning members of his chiefdom, "Don't carelessly
speak to outsiders about the internal affairs of our tribe," Lubum purportedly
urged the Gartsé to be wary of the work teams who had been snooping around
their encampments, asking all sorts of questions and collecting data on their
animals.[36] Although the allegation that local elites—ominously referred to here
as the "nationality ruling class" (*minzu tongzhi jieji*)—had been selfishly working
against the realization of nationality unity is notable, it also was not unfamiliar.
A year earlier, Gélek Gyatso had made similar accusations. Now, however, the
purported obstructionism was being framed in a far more sinister light. Elite
resistance was no longer a lingering residue of nationality exploitation and backward thinking. It was a manifestation of *class struggle*.

Nevertheless, the Zeku County Party Committee continued to reserve the majority of its criticism for its own cadre force but now with a twist. Party leaders
had long condemned poor work methods and attitudes among grassroots cadres
for "damaging the Party's image" and hurting its efforts to unite with the pastoral
masses.[37] In this new political environment, however, bandits, spies, and counterrevolutionaries were no longer the only ones that took advantage. It was alleged
that Zeku's indigenous leadership was actively exploiting cadres' shortcomings
to drive a wedge between the CCP and common herders. "When we see small
problems, we do not pay attention. We fail to realize that small problems are

indeed the root of big problems," county leaders asserted. "As a result, the nationality ruling class uses them as opportunities to create problems."[38] For instance, the committee accused herdlords of exploiting both their "feudal privileges" and "certain defects" in the Party's pastoral tax-collection work to sew anxieties in the minds of the masses.[39]

In addition, for the first time, documents report significant elite anxiety over the possibility of the imminent redistribution of wealth. For example, Chögyong, the Hor Ratsang chieftain, had purportedly exclaimed with alarm, "[In agricultural regions,] all of the land of the landlords has been redistributed. When socialism arrives [in Zeku,] the livestock of wealthy herders like County Leader Wagya will also be redistributed." Wagya himself quizzed the Shokmang headman Yönten, asking, "When you visited Inner Mongolia was it true that there was no 'No Division [of property], No [class] Struggle'?"[40] According to reports, monks had expressed similar concerns, for example inquiring, "When socialism arrives everyone has to work and everyone will have food to eat. But the monks at the monasteries chant prayers and do not work. When socialism arrives will we also have food to eat?" Had they been privy to it, most worrisome to Zeku's pre-1949 upper strata would perhaps have been a literal footnote to the county's pastoral investigation report. It claimed that impoverished members of the Wöngya chiefdom were now asking for the redistribution of sheep and cattle.[41] In 1952, Zhou Renshan promised his cadres that when the masses were ready for socialist transformation, the old society could at last be swept away. For the first time, it was being alleged that this point might be fast approaching.

Before then, however, a native cadre force had to be cultivated and put into positions of responsibility. Yet at the start of 1956, only 70 of Zeku's 211 government cadres were from minority nationalities (63 Tibetan and 7 Hui). Not only was this considered to be far too few, but the overall quality was also reportedly poor. Once again blame fell squarely on Han cadres. The pastoral investigation report pointedly (if paternalistically) noted, "First of all, it is Han chauvinism that deters them from training minority cadres. Many [Han] cadres fail to understand that the training of minority cadres is the consolidation of the relationship between the Party and the people. Second, they look down at minority cadres and do not use them. Third, they do not see the [good] qualities of [minority] cadres and pay attention to them. They like the progressive and loathe the backward. They do not help them [improve their] work." The report concluded, "For the development of socialism, we must train and employ minority nationality cadres, particularly local ones."[42] Until then, despite being increasingly cast as antagonistic class elements, the continued cooperation of the pre-1949 leadership remained indispensable.

Given this reality, as 1955 drew to a close, Zeku's Party leaders continued to endorse the policies of the United Front. However, they simultaneously made clear their resolve to launch pastoral collectivization. The contradictions embedded in a Leninist system that combined United Front pragmatism with revolutionary idealism were coming to a head. Without offering specific remedy in case of noncompliance, the Party committee reminded cadres, "First of all we discuss [policy] with the tribal leaders and seek their consent and only then implement a particular work task."[43] Even when directly linked to grassland disputes, the committee ordered that headmen not be removed from office. Emphasizing once again the imbalance between consultation and persuasion, it instead insisted, "Tribal leaders must organize meetings and straighten up their thinking. Let them exercise [the right to] become masters of their own home and seek solutions."[44] As before, education—not struggle, imprisonment, or elimination—was prescribed as the treatment for ideological problems among what internally was increasingly being referred to as the "nationality ruling class."

Mutual Aid and Cooperation

Qinghai had actually been experimenting with a small number of pastoral mutual aid teams since 1954. Whether genuinely impressed by the results of these trial MATs or—as subsequently suggested—responding to political pressures, in September 1955, the Qinghai Provincial Party Committee decided to expand cooperativization in pastoral areas.[45] Specifically, thirteen experimental cooperatives were established in Haiyan (T. Dazhi) County, a mixed-nationality, mixed-economy region not far from the provincial capital. By year's end, the Party committee extended the program, announcing, "If the conditions are right, pure pastoral regions can also experiment with pastoral cooperatives." But far from rushing headlong into collectivization, Xining set four preconditions. Local officials were told that prospective cooperatives must be built on a foundation of existing mutual aid practices, nationality unity must be strong and social order stable, a minority nationality cadre force must have been developed, and the majority of the upper strata must agree.[46] Before long, eleven counties—including Huangnan's Tongren and Jianzha but not Zeku—had established experimental pastoral cooperatives.[47]

In February 1956, as Qinghai's Party committee was preparing to send its own delayed pastoral investigation report to Beijing, it convened a meeting to appraise the progress of these experimental pastoral cooperatives. According to a later account, provincial leaders concluded, "Carrying out cooperativization in pastoral regions is the decisive step in using peaceful methods as the basis to transform the relationship of pastoral production, eliminate the system of exploitation, and eliminate feudal privileges and tribal division."[48] In so many words, the Party committee changed Qinghai's guiding principles toward its pastoral areas. No longer were nationality unity and economic development prerequisites for socialist transformation. Now socialist transformation was declared the primary means to achieve national integration and economic prosperity.

Despite the still-rising High Tide, Xining was quick to add that pastoral cooperatives must be implemented gradually and on the basis of voluntary participation. It warned cadres, "The time period will be lengthy, the pace will be steady, and the policies will be flexible."[49] While the pastoral masses were to be the backbone of the new order, provincial leaders made clear that herdlords were not to be eliminated but instead reformed through "unity and education." Party secretary Gao Feng admitted that during the initial stages of experimental cooperativization there had been a tendency to neglect United Front work. Gao ordered officials at all levels to hold meetings with "middle and upper-level representatives, herdlords and religious figures" to explain policies, seek feedback, and alleviate their concerns.[50] Separately, Secretary Gao emphasized that "the policies of No Struggle, No Division and the freedom of religious belief remain in place" and warned that reforming the "herdlord economy" too quickly could cause wealthier pastoralists to slaughter their animals or engage in other "destructive behaviors."[51] Nonetheless, socialist transformation now had a date. "Partial socialist cooperativization" (*ban shehuizhuyi hezuohua*) of Qinghai's pastoral regions was to be complete by 1959.[52]

Even before Xining's February order made it official, a Zeku County Party Committee work plan indicates that establishing MATs and pastoral cooperatives had been made the coming year's central task.[53] Submitted to Huangnan Prefecture on January 8, 1956, it began by describing the general situation in Zeku County. Finding that past efforts had led to increases in both production and living standards, the county committee declared that these positive developments "had caused the majority of herdsmen and people of all strata to love and cherish the Party and its policies." Consequently, the report alleged that class awareness had begun to rise. As proof, it noted that in the past when a "tribal headman" mediated a dispute, he was compensated for his efforts. Now "some of the masses raise [objections] to giving the headmen cattle or sheep, some raise [the possibility of] not discussing with the headmen the apportion [of work] within the tribe, and, through education, some have very quickly realized the benefits of moving toward mutual aid and cooperation."[54] The report concluded that this demonstrated that many members of the masses were in favor of launching pastoral cooperatives.

At the same time, the county committee acknowledged that because con-struction of Zeku's district-level administrations remained unfinished, degrees of understanding and enthusiasm for cooperativization varied. County leaders confessed that many common herders continued to have only the most cursory understandings of socialism and its goals. In one of several examples, a Hor Détsang herder asked investigators, "What is socialism? I have only heard that we are going down the road to socialism."⁵⁵ More specifically, the committee admitted that mass awareness was only well developed within the ranks of the Party and the Communist Youth League. Elsewhere the prestige of the headmen remained unbroken, and the influence of religion still ran deep.⁵⁶ Considering that, at the start of 1956, Zeku's leadership could call on only eight Tibetan Party mem-bers and eleven Tibetan Youth League members, this was a startling admission.⁵⁷ Heeding Xining's lead, however, rather than suggest that conditions were not yet ripe for socialist transformation, the county committee demanded obstacles to cooperativization be "overcome" so that Zeku could "victoriously complete the task of socialist reform."⁵⁸

The Party committee next prepared a set of instructions that sketched out a graded path to collectivization. First, the plan called for Zeku's 4,217 house-holds to be enrolled onto four hundred MATs, each consisting of approximately ten households. Described as "economic units essentially similar to the volun-tary unity of the pastoralists' familial relations," MATs were to be formed out of existing herding groups, the pastoral equivalent of the "natural villages" that formed the basic level of cooperative production in agricultural regions.⁵⁹ Echo-ing provincial directives, the county committee ordered these MATs "correct and improve" upon "existing forms of unity and mutual aid organization found among the pastoral masses." In short time, these four hundred MATs would be transformed into 187 PPCs with roughly twenty households each. Eventually, approximately eighty high-level cooperatives (HLCs), each made up of roughly fifty families, would form the primary economic and political unit on the Zeku grasslands.⁶⁰

The Zeku County Party Committee's January directive contains few specific instructions on how MATs and PPCs were to be organized. However, it did make clear its expectations for the pace of the campaign. Cooperativization would be-gin immediately. Over 1956, 1,051 households, or nearly one-quarter of Zeku's population, were slated to join MATs. Of these, however, only about 15 percent were to be year-round MATs (changnian huzhuzu). The remainder would be organized into more basic-level mutual aid organizations: seasonal MATs (jijie huzhuzu) and temporary MATs (linshi huzhuzu).⁶¹ Although the committee's instructions did not elaborate, the provincial gazetteer notes that year-round MATs were to be permanent units with strong leadership cores, "democratic management," a basic production plan, a process to evaluate work and assign work points, and in some cases a year-round system of joint-household herding. As expected, seasonal MATs would join together periodically to engage in seasonal cooperative work. This might include herding in the summer and fall and lambing in the winter and spring. Last, in temporary MATs, herders would come together on a one-off basis to perform specific production tasks.[62]

From 24 percent of Zeku's pastoral population in 1956, the county committee's plan confidently proclaimed that membership in MATs would climb to 72 percent two years later. Zeku's last pastoral households would not join year-round MATs until 1960. By then, however, 88 percent of households already would have entered PPCs, the first of which was planned for the first half of 1956. If all went well, two to three more PPCs could be organized in the second half of the year.[63] It was envisioned that these inaugural cooperatives would expand to 10 in 1957, then 45 in 1958, and 112 in 1959. By 1961, the county's entire pastoral population was to have joined PPCs. At that point the transition to high-level cooperatives could begin. Seven of these larger cooperatives were to be established that first year, nearly tripling to twenty in 1962. From 1963 to 1967, the entire county would be enrolled in HLCs, completing the "gradual" cooperativization of Zeku County.[64]

Settling the Nomads and Transforming the Grasslands

According to the Qinghai Provincial Party Committee, the primary purpose of cooperativization was to ensure that the "laboring masses of pastoral regions can overcome hardship, develop production, and travel down the road to certain prosperity."[65] However, only by demonstrating the benefits of collective production could Tibetan pastoralists be convinced to voluntarily join MATs and PPCs. To this end, the Zeku County Party Committee was tasked with raising production by implementing a "plan to effectively use the grasslands." In addition to the usual instructions about protecting livestock and improving grassland management, the January 1956 plan introduced several new initiatives. These included an ambitious but vague scheme to irrigate more than six hundred thousand *mu* of dry grassland (approximately one hundred thousand acres) through the construction of a system of reservoirs. Planners also estimated that by digging individual wells, the county would be able to support and additional fifty thousand head of livestock.[66] In order to demonstrate to the masses the benefits of collective production and scientific grassland management, county leaders also announced that over the next three years, state-owned pastoral farms (*guoying mufang*) would be established within the Gönshül, Sonak, and Hor territories.[67]

Cooperativization, however, was more than a program of economic development. Taken to its logical conclusion, it also signaled the end of Zeku's pre-1949 economic, social, and political order. In fact, among the several anticipated "methods" by which cooperativization would increase grassland production, the first mentioned by the county committee was "eliminating the grassland rights and all types of feudal privileges of the herdlord class and their representatives in the monasteries."[68] By replacing the "exploitative" practices of the feudal past with communal ownership under the leadership of the CCP, Party leaders predicted that the full productive capacity of the grasslands could be harnessed. By extension, the privileged position of Zeku's secular and religious establishment finally would be terminated.

Second, the Party committee made it clear that cooperativization entailed "settling the nomads" (dingju youmu). Constraining the movement of mobile peoples has long been a preoccupation of sedentary states. However, the decision to sedentarize Zeku's pastoralists was articulated largely in terms of rationalizing and improving production.[69] According to the plan, in 1956, first the Ködé Karing and then the Sonak, Hor, Méshül, and Khéri Chunga chiefdoms "gradually" would be settled. The following year, as the pastoral cooperativization campaign gained steam, the remaining five chiefdoms would be permanently settled as well. While the January plan offered only the vague reasoning that settlement would aid "economic and cultural construction," prefectural instructions issued the previous August linked sedentarization to both cooperativization and increased production. The directive noted, "At present in our prefecture the distinguishing characteristic of pastoral production in pastoral regions is . . . the animals' year-round dependency on natural nomadic movement."[70] However, it insisted, this put herders at the mercy of nature. Although improvements to grazing methods and grassland management had reduced the "fragility and instability" of pastoral production, the report argued that herders still had to lead their animals on seasonal migrations, considered an exceedingly "backward method of operating." Halfway measures could reduce but not eliminate the ever-present threat from natural disaster. The solution was cooperativization. On cooperatives, settled pastoralists "using modern management methods" could warehouse high-quality grass and feed, build winter pens, and store water. According to Party planners, this would allow for the age-old battle against the elements to be "basically eliminated."[71] Through cooperativization, the directive boldly concluded, "Man can defeat nature."[72]

The third sea change introduced in the Zeku County Party Committee's January 1956 work plan was in some ways the most dramatic. In December, the Communist Youth League had launched a campaign of agricultural settlement in Qinghai. Modeled in part on Soviet premier Nikita Khrushchev's Virgin Lands program, the intent was to open up additional lands to agriculture while shoring up frontier security.[73] Zeku's leadership announced that the county would become home to a number of these agricultural "immigrants" (*yimin*). To both support the newcomers and increase overall production, large portions of the grassland would simultaneously be brought under cultivation (*kenhuang*). According to the work plan, the first five thousand migrants would arrive in 1958. These Han settlers, already numbering nearly one-third of Zeku's existing population, would be provided with twenty-five thousand mu of land. Over the next three years, an additional five thousand migrants were slated to arrive annually. From 1962 to 1964, this would increase from ten thousand, to twenty thousand, and finally an astounding thirty thousand settlers per year, before leveling off at ten thousand settlers for each of the final two years of the program. For each five thousand migrants, an additional twenty-five thousand mu of grassland was to be cleared and devoted to agriculture. Back in 1953, the NAC had expressly forbidden converting grassland into fields, noting that in the past it had not only caused "a reduction in the amount of pasture [but also] led to calamities such as windstorms, sandstorms, floods, and droughts."[74] Now, buoyed by the rising expectations of the High Tide, over nine years, one hundred thousand Han migrants were expected to turn five hundred thousand mu of Zeku's grassland—over eighty-two thousand acres—into farmland. "In order to suit the nation's socialist construction and the demands of agricultural production," plans also were announced to introduce animals not normally suited for the high plateau—including chicken, ducks, and pigs—along with mechanized agricultural equipment, an aggressive tree-planting initiative, and the construction of large greenhouses.[75]

Even by the utopian standards of Maoist China, the projections seem remarkable. They called for a sixfold increase in the population of the Zeku Tibetan Autonomous County, while turning 5 percent of the usable grassland—lying at an average elevation of nearly twelve thousand feet above sea level—into farmland. No mention is made in the work plan of the potential consequences to the pastoral economy, the environment, or the indigenous Tibetan population that in a decade's time would have become a small minority in its own autonomous county. Elsewhere, however, the Zeku County Party Committee acknowledged that preparing for agricultural settlement was "particularly discreet and particularly careful work."[76] On January 31, Party secretary Guo Min personally "consulted" with several of Zeku's leading figures, including Wagya, Serökyap, Lubum, and the Wöngya's Losar, on the "question of immigration and land reclamation." According to the report, the headmen offered Secretary Guo their cautious support along with recommendations for sites within each of Zeku's ten chiefdoms suitable for agricultural settlement.[77] Then, in concert with promoting pastoral cooperativization and production, work teams were instructed to investigate prospects for land reclamation, test soil quality, check the availability of water, research the viability of irrigation projects, report on housing prospects, and determine which crops might be best suited for the region.[78]

In the end, neither sedentarization nor the migration and agricultural reclamation plans were carried out, certainly not with the speed or numbers put forth in the 1956 directive. Not until March 1959, during the heyday of the Great Leap Forward, did Zeku's first agricultural settlers finally arrive. Instead of the proposed five thousand migrants, however, they consisted of 1,006 volunteers from the Henan Province Pingyu County Support the Frontier Youth Shock Brigade (Zhibian Qingnian Tujidui).[79] In his study of agricultural resettlement to Qinghai, Gregory Rohlf writes that the CYL painted resettlement as a "voluntary, exciting, and glorious national service program for China's newest generation of patriots, young men and women who had come of age under the red flag of socialism." [80] For many, however, including the young activists from Pingyu, the glow quickly faded.[81] The day after their arrival in Zeku, they were sent to the Batang grasslands, an area within the Hor territories said to have relatively good soil, water, and climatic conditions. Under the battle cry of "mobilize production, militarize organization, democratize daily life," over the next month one hundred hectares of grassland were cleared and sowed. However, due to a combination of frost, hail, and rodent infestation, two-thirds of the crops failed. In March of the following year, a second group of young Henanese volunteers joined the Batang settlement, bringing the total number of agricultural migrants to 2,046. By summer, however, with Qinghai then in the grips of a devastating famine (see chapter 8), more than a quarter of the settlers had already deserted. In fall 1961, the Great Leap Forward now in full retreat, the program was officially ended. The county gazetteer does not mention agricultural settlement again until 1971, when twenty agricultural families from Qinghai's Ledu County moved to what was then known as Hor Commune.[82]

Why Can't the Headmen Lead like They Did in the Past?

Plans in place, county leaders convened a joint meeting of Zeku County People's Government and Consultative Committees from January 24 to February 3, 1956, at which Wagya reported on the decision to launch pastoral cooperatives. Afterward, individual work teams were ordered to draw up proposals "for the construction of mutual aid teams and cooperatives."[83] Based on these reports, county leaders submitted a recommendation to prefectural authorities that "preliminary arrangements be made to test mutual aid and cooperation work within the Hor and Méshül tribes."[84]

Within the Hor, the work team chose to launch its initial experimental cooperative within the Dobhé herding group. In accordance with provincial instructions, first among the qualifications of the Dobhé was a stable social order marked by the absence of ongoing grassland disputes. Second, the work team claimed that twenty-eight days of propaganda and preparatory work had raised the awareness of the masses and produced an environment in which many were willing to voluntarily "proceed down the path of mutual aid and cooperation." Third, the work group identified a "leadership core" consisting of two CYL members, three candidates preparing to join the Party, and six local "activists" (jijifenzi). Last, other than a single lower-mid-level family, the remaining members of the herding group were all classified as poor households.[85] Working within the Köde Karing chiefdom, the Méshül Work Team likewise targeted an impoverished community as a suitable target for its first pastoral cooperative.[86]

Although the Three Nos continued to proscribe the assignment of class labels to individual households, it is notable that the absence of wealthy families was one of the conditions that made both sites promising candidates for cooperativization. In its own work plan, the Sonak Work Team made the correlation between class base and collectivization explicitly clear, declaring, "In building [mutual aid] teams and cooperatives . . ., it is especially important to rely on poor pastoralists. Because their lives are filled with hardship, they have a pressing need to organize [cooperatives]."[87] In this sense, cooperativization was an extension of earlier policies that considered improving the material condition of the masses a central component of both state and nation building. In fact, the prefectural committee specifically instructed Zeku County to provide animal loans to poor households that joined experimental cooperatives.[88] From its inception, the Party's welfare program had been as much an effort designed to develop mass awareness and patriotic consciousness as it was an attempt to increase pastoral production and state capacity. Similarly, cooperativization was a radical campaign of economic and social reform, but it was also the continuance of ongoing efforts to undermine "tribal" divisions and integrate the Zeku grasslands into the new socialist state and nation.

On April 20, the Hor Work Group submitted plans to the Zeku County Party Committee for the establishment of Zeku's first experimental PPC, Guanghui (Glorious) Cooperative. Demonstrating once again the thin line between commandism and volunteerism, it reported, "Under the principle of voluntariness and mutual benefit, and on the foundation of existing mutual aid groups . . ., we decided on eighteen families from among [the Dobhé herding group] as targets to form the cooperative."[89] Not until May 22 did the Huangnan Party Committee finally issue its reply. Framing their comments as "suggestions," prefectural leaders expressed general agreement with the Hor Work Team's proposal. However, they also warned of the project's potential to arouse considerable local opposition. These concerns were almost certainly connected to a series of armed revolts that had recently erupted in Tibetan areas of Sichuan as well as reports of "serious outbreaks of disorder" that were trickling in from southern Qinghai.[90] In order to "minimize social resistance," Huangnan again emphasized the importance of propaganda work among both the masses and especially traditional elites.[91]

The prefecture was parroting standing orders issued by Xining. Despite having identified poor herders as the campaign's core constituency, Party leaders understood that powerful headmen and religious leaders still enjoyed tremendous influence. According to the provincial Rural Work Department, in some instances pastoral elites sought to convince poor pastoralists that collectivization would hurt the larger community. At other times, they threatened to recall loaned animals rather than allow them entered onto cooperatives. Some herdsmen had even inquired, "Why do we have to take the lead in joining cooperatives? Why can't the headmen lead like in the past?"[92] Rather than openly condemn elite obstruction as a manifestation of class struggle, however, as long as the Three Nos remained intact, Party leaders continued to insist that this contradiction could only be remedied through education. In Zeku, the leadership therefore declared, "[Propaganda] must be wide and comprehensive, deep and clear so as to resolve doubts in the minds of the masses of all social stratums and to convince all of the masses, *especially nationality representatives and religious leaders*, to trust the Party and the people's government to uphold the Party's policies."[93]

We Will Take Up Guns and Attack the Government!

Amid this uncertainty, in late spring 1956, Zeku County established its first PPC, the Guanghui Experimental Pastoral Cooperative. Soon afterward, a second PPC and eight MATs were founded within the Ködé Karing chiefdom.[94] By then, however, Xining had begun to concede that its pastoral cooperativization campaign had overreached. In its May 22 "suggestions," the Huangnan Prefecture Party Committee had given its lukewarm endorsement to the plan to construct the Guanghui Cooperative. In seeming contradiction, however, it also revealed that provincial authorities recently had ordered "the implementation of pastoral cooperatives in pastoral regions temporarily halted." No specific reason for the reversal was given other than admit it was in response to "current conditions." The directive added that local authorities should "refuse to dissolve" existing cooperatives and instead "consolidate and rectify" them. In the meantime, the prefecture ordered Zeku's Party committee to "thoroughly investigate actual conditions" and promote the development of MATs according to the "principles of voluntariness and mutual benefit, in order to lay the future foundation for experimental cooperatives."[95]

Taken as a whole, the directive was shorthand for an acknowledgment that the transition from individual herding to MATs to full pastoral cooperatives had been too rushed. This had caused production to drop and a deepening rift to develop between the Party and local society. This is confirmed by a series of reports issued over spring and into summer. Details are few and far between. Allegedly, however, "counterrevolutionaries" had exploited "the specific conditions of pastoral society and economy" and "not a few mistakes that exist in our own work" to wreak havoc.[96] Influenced by (or, as later Chinese sources claim, in league with) uprisings in northern Sichuan and southern Gansu, conditions were particularly grave in Qinghai's far southern prefectures of Guoluo and Yushu as well as among the Mongols of Henan County (see chapter 7).[97] Yet the Rural Work Department conceded that "relatively serious cases" of rebellion were ongoing in Hainan and Huangnan Prefectures as well. In Tongde, for instance, a lama allegedly inflamed tensions by publicly announcing, "If they wish to establish cooperatives, we will take up guns and attack the government!" As the county slid toward lawlessness, a report claims that "bandits who had snuck into our Party used the pretext of being drunk to assault our district Party secretary [likely Han] and activists [likely Tibetan]." In other words, the alleged assailants were members of the Chinese Communist Party. In another episode, "evildoers" in Tongren purportedly attacked Party cadres with stones.[98]

While many of the recorded incidents sound more like spontaneous protests, riots, or even drunken brawls than they do organized rebellion, the Rural Work Department insisted that "scattered bandit gangs" were operating in both Zeku and Tongren Counties. It also claimed that misinformation about collectivization had led "tribes" in several counties to flee into the grasslands. This included fifty households from Zeku who set off toward Central Tibet. Perhaps as alarming for a provincial leadership that since 1949 had linked social stability to increased production, the missive concluded by asserting that rather than enroll livestock onto cooperatives, "in all areas without exception the phenomenon [of herders] slaughtering their animals has occurred."[99]

Just as it is difficult to determine the scope of opposition—armed or otherwise—to High Tide cooperativization, it is difficult to ascertain the extent of the CCP's military response. While certainly not excusing instances of "rebellion," reports such as the one issued by the Rural Work Department were intended not so much as battle cries but as rebukes of its own cadre force. Security forces in Qinghai did conduct targeted attacks on areas of active, organized rebellion, particularly in Henan and along the border with Sichuan, and security operations were ramped up elsewhere. Rather than a wholesale military response, however, the Party's principle reaction was first to suspend then abort the cooperativization drive.

In fact, resistance to High Tide collectivization was not unique to the Tibetan Plateau. Responding to setbacks the collectivization campaign experienced in several non-Han areas, in April 1956 Mao Zedong ordered wide-ranging investigations conducted into state-minority nationality relations.[100] Following Mao's instructions, in June Qinghai's leadership launched a province-wide reassessment of nationality work. The results of the investigation were released in August. Delivered by Liu Zexi, chief of Qinghai's Rural Work Department, the report accused cadres of allowing their "subjective wishes" for a speedy transition to socialism overcome objective evaluation of current pastoral conditions. Liu insisted that these errors had led to the "rash" or "reckless" introduction of collectives, poor planning and oversight, and the use of coercion rather than reliance on the principles of consultation and voluntary participation.[101] The Rural Work Department highlighted a case in Guide where cadres had forced a "Tibetan district head" to give all his animals to the local cooperative. In response, he fled to neighboring Guinan County with fourteen armed followers. (The group was later captured, although their fate is not mentioned.)[102] Even at the height of the High Tide, the provincial Party committee had warned that propaganda work was insufficient. As a consequence, it alleged that wealthy herders and religious leaders "feared division [of property], feared [class] struggle, feared loss of their privileges, feared not being able to hire herd laborers, and feared that there would be no freedom of religious belief, along with other doubts and anxieties."[103] Worried that monasteries would soon be dispossessed of their herds, some monastic officials had begun calling in debts owed by common pastoralists. And despite that the Three Nos officially remained in force, herdlords purportedly were spending large sums on religious offerings and to have sutras chanted on their behalf.[104]

Perhaps most alarming, Party leaders were forced to admit that resistance to pastoral cooperativization had not been confined to the upper strata. This too was blamed on poor propaganda work. Officials reasoned that the masses still did not understand the benefits of pastoral cooperatives and therefore "all types of anxieties existed." Yet rather than proceeding according to these realities, cadres often resorted to coercion, thereby violating the principle of volunteerism. As a result, contemporary and secondary sources both acknowledge that many common pastoral households had sought to leave the new collectives.[105]

The High Tide Recedes

As detailed in the following chapter, in September 1956, Beijing would officially repudiate the High Tide of Socialist Transformation. By then, many of Qinghai's hastily constructed PPCs had been dismantled, including Zeku's "Glorious" Cooperative. The swell that had been building over the first months of 1956 and threatened to crash across the Amdo Plateau instead retreated. Pastoral collectivization had been a failure. The question remains, Why?

Liu Zexi's contention that Qinghai's pastoral cadre force had let its "subjective" desire for a speedy transition to socialism cloud its objective assessment of the "concrete conditions" of the grasslands is broadly accurate. Crucially, however, it ignores the pressure to perform cadres at every level found themselves toiling under during political campaigns such as the High Tide. While committed to a program of gradual and voluntary transformation, the sudden shift to a program of rapid collectivization demonstrates the institutional inability to defend the United Front when the political winds shifted. Under such circumstances, the dialectical imbalance between consultation and persuasion reached a breaking point. United Front pragmatism easily fell victim to revolutionary impatience. After all, cadres were bureaucratically conditioned—and in many cases perhaps personally inclined—to err to the left. Their careers and livelihoods could depend on it. While the evidence is circumstantial, the rapidity with which local cadres embraced collectivization, along with not infrequent admonishments for violating the Party's principles of volunteerism, suggest that at the grassroots and mid levels the (mostly Han) cadre force itself may have acted as an informal lobbying group that became more empowered in periods of relative radicalism.[106] Despite the High Tide's retreat, these tensions between United Front pragmatism and revolutionary impatience would only intensify. Less than two years later, they would help ignite a much larger conflict with far higher human cost.

In the meantime, the revelation that the "rash" introduction of pastoral collectives in Amdo resulted in significant opposition is notable. While it has become apparent that various types of resistance to rural collectivization and even "isolated rebellions" did occur in Han areas, scholars have tended to marvel at the overall lack of collective resistance to collectivization among the Han peasantry, particularly compared to their Soviet counterparts.[107] By contrast, it is increasingly clear that the High Tide led to large disturbances and even armed uprisings in several non-Han regions, including large-scale rebellion in Kham.[108] Much is still unclear about the scope of resistance to the High Tide in Amdo, including how widespread it was, what forms it may have taken, and how large a role the concurrent uprising in neighboring parts of Kham may have played. Nonetheless, coming not long after the final insurgency of the "early-Liberation period" and just two years prior to the much larger Amdo Rebellion of 1958, a decade-spanning picture emerges in which Qinghai's grasslands were racked by sustained (if diffused) resistance and an ever-present potential for violent conflict. When Qinghai's Communist Party establishment gathered in Xining in June 1956 for its Second Provincial Party Representative Congress, delegates were warned to "avoid the occurrence of leftist tendencies" (i.e., establishing cooperatives before conditions warranted). Ignoring their own culpability during the High Tide for setting unrealistic expectations, Party leaders reiterated that socialist reforms in pastoral areas could only be implemented through consultation and with "the agreement of nationality and religious representatives and the herding masses." As always, winning over traditional elites remained key. Therefore, rather than resorting to coercion or struggle, the policy toward "herdlord class elements"—itself a pejorative term—was to "unite, educate, and reform." Reaffirming Governor Sun Zuobin's 1954 United Front promise of gradual and voluntary transformation, Xining proclaimed, "If contradictions still exist in their thoughts, then we must wait. When consultations are successful, that is when we can start work."[109] In essence, Qinghai's Party establishment sought to turn the clock back to the previous summer, a time when in pastoral areas socialist transformation was still an abstract idea with an indefinite timeline. However, there was no "reset button." The High Tide had exposed contradictions embedded in both the ideology of the United Front and the operating mechanisms of the Communist Party. Although the United Front's guiding principles of gradualism and voluntarism had been reaffirmed, a turning point had been reached.

6

TIBETANS DO THE HOUSEWORK, BUT HAN ARE THE MASTERS

The High Tide of Socialist Transformation did not receive its official repudiation until September 1956, when more than one thousand Party luminaries gathered in Beijing for the Eighth Congress of the Chinese Communist Party. The first full Party congress since 1945, for more than two weeks, delegates criticized the High Tide as a "rash advance" (*jizao maojin*) that ignored "objective conditions" across the country. In its place, speakers promoted a more "balanced" plan of economic development. Coming in the wake of Nikita Khrushchev's criticism of Stalin's cult of personality, delegates to the congress removed "Mao Zedong Thought" from the CCP constitution. For the time being, "collective leadership" became the prevailing catchphrase. While perhaps a simplification, the Eighth Party Congress therefore has been considered a victory for relative moderates over advocates for a more heightened pace of socialist transformation.[1]

Although minority work was far from the congress's central concern, a host of prominent national figures, including CCP vice chairman Liu Shaoqi and United Front head Li Weihan, as well as provincial leaders whose charges included nationality minority areas, weighed in on the issue. While expressing commitment to the end goals of socialist transformation and "democratic reform," one after another these speakers stressed policies that signaled a return to the gradualist approach and United Front tactics of the pre–High Tide period.[2]

Among the United Front's many defenders at the Eighth Party Congress was Qinghai's first Party secretary, Gao Feng. Following the requisite odes to the CCP's many achievements in Qinghai, Gao admitted that in some respects little had changed since "Liberation." In particular, traditional elites—more than five thousand by Gao's count—still held tremendous sway over the province's "minority people." Harking back to earlier critiques of Han chauvinism, Gao explained that this was due to the prominent role Amdo's "noble houses," qian-baihu, and Buddhist and Islamic leaderships had historically played in opposing great nationality oppression. He noted that many Han cadres working in Qinghai still considered traditional elites to be representatives of the exploiting class. As a result, these cadres did not consult with them or respect their opinions. This hurt efforts to strengthen nationality unity and expand the minority nationality cadre force. Calling for gradual and peaceful reforms, Gao reaffirmed the correctness of the Three Nos, announcing, "No matter which nationality or area, all socialist reforms must be implemented according to the wishes of both the minority na-tionality representatives [i.e., elites] and masses." With rebellion in Kham clearly on the mind of many delegates and a palpable fear over the expansion of armed resistance hanging over the proceedings, Gao cited the agreeable conclusion of Wangchen Döndrup's Nangra Rebellion—now four years past—as an example of the undiminished necessity to win over elite allies. Repeating sentiments ex-pressed in the earliest days and weeks of the PLA's occupation of Qinghai, he reasoned, "If we unite with these upper strata figures, it will be easier to unite with local minority nationality people, immerse ourselves among the masses, carry out work, isolate and attack counterrevolutionaries, and gradually imple-ment socialist reforms." Failure to do so, however, "would bring about the op-posite results."[3] In the wake of the suppression of the 1958 Amdo Rebellion and collectivization, Gao Feng has become associated with the most assimilative and repressive aspects of the CCP's rule over Amdo.[4] In his September 1956 speech to the Eighth Party Congress, however, Gao bluntly concluded that coercion "not only will not work but is also very dangerous."[5]

This chapter explores events in Zeku County and beyond from the end of the High Tide in summer 1956 through the eve of the Great Leap Forward in late 1957. Speaking of China as a whole, Frederick Teiwes and Warren Sun refer to this period as an "un-Maoist interlude."[6] In the main, it was marked by a re-treat from plans for rapid collectivization and even saw a push during the One Hundred Flowers campaign to encourage open criticism of the Party so that its mistakes could be rectified. A centerpiece was soliciting critiques from United Front figures, particularly Han intellectuals but also leading minority nationality figures. Among the latter, many complained that the autonomy the CCP prom-ised non-Han communities at the time of "Liberation" had proved more mirage than fact. Far from a reactionary stance, in the months following the Eighth Party Congress this critique was widely promoted in Party and government circles.[7]

Of course, 1957 also witnessed the launch of the Anti-Rightist Campaign, a swift and violent reaction to the avalanche of criticism leveled at the Party during the brief period of relative liberality. By late summer, CCP secretary general Deng Xiaoping and other Party leaders were insisting that the real danger to nationality unity in minority areas was not Han chauvinism but local nationalism.[8] As the pendulum swung left, many of the figures who recently had been lauded for their honest assessment of minority policy and practices, including the Tibetan Communist Pünwang and Uyghur writer Zia Samit, were labeled local nationalists (or worse) and purged. As such, the Anti-Rightist Campaign has been viewed as a particularly harsh period in the PRC's nationality policy, one in which calls to end Han chauvinism became muted and demands for a rapid Han-oriented assimilation to socialist unity were amplified.[9]

Even while subject to national trends and pressures, on Qinghai's grasslands this "un-Maoist interlude" followed its own logic. Overall, it witnessed a return to many of the practices and discourses of the pre–High Tide period. Despite Deng Xiaoping's call, even the Anti-Rightist Campaign would mainly target chauvinism and other defects within the Han cadre force, while largely ignoring evidence of local nationalism among the Tibetan elite. This was perhaps not unique to Amdo. June Dreyer observed long ago, "The Party's response [during the Anti-Rightist Campaign] was surprisingly mild; beneath a torrent of criticism of local nationalism can be discerned a real effort to avoid destroying the fragile structure it had put together with such difficulty in minority areas."[10]

Still, the High Tide had left an indelible mark. For one, at least in pastoral regions such as Zeku, prior to 1955 socialism had been a vague concept reserved for the distant future, while class analysis had been almost entirely absent. By contrast, even as CCP leaders dialed back their post–High Tide expectations, they explicitly left socialist transformation and "democratic reforms" on the agenda. No matter the immediate policy objectives, Party leaders now openly viewed pastoral regions through a deeply class-tinted lens. For Amdo's pastoral Tibetans, the collectivization campaign could not simply be excused as a wayward "rash advance" or leftist mistake committed by overzealous but misguided cadres. Instead, it cast a lasting pall over the relationship between the Party-state, its elite intermediaries, and the pastoral masses. A return to the promises of the United Front could not assuage fears that the High Tide was less anomaly than harbinger. By year's end, these suspicions were looking increasingly like a certainty.

The Same as in the Time of Ma Bufang

In Zeku County, the Eighth Party Congress did not spur a policy shift so much as it validated retrenchment efforts that had been underway since the suspension of Qinghai's pastoral cooperativization campaign that spring. Pastoral collectivization had been a failure, that much was admitted. It not only had hurt production but also damaged the Party's already fragile standing among the region's Tibetan population. The most notable change came at the top of the county's leadership. As recently as March 1956, Guo Min had been reconfirmed as Zeku's Party secretary, a position he had effectively held since September 1953 when he and the County Establishment Preparatory Work Group first arrived on the Shadar grasslands. In June, however, Guo was suddenly transferred out of the county.[11] In his place, Hu Zilin, a Han cadre from Hubei Province, was appointed secretary of the Zeku County Party Committee. Simultaneously, Könchok, a native of Qinghai's Hualong County, was named first vice secretary, making him the first Tibetan to serve within the top echelon of Zeku County's Communist Party administration.[12]

In line with national and provincial instructions, on June 24, the Zeku County Party Committee convened a Conference of Nationality and Religious Leaders "to inspect United Front work" and collect the opinions of the county's indigenous leadership.[13] While detailed accounts of the conference are unavailable, for the remainder of 1956 and much of 1957 the core of work centered around stabilizing and expanding production, completing the long-overdue district-level administrations, and strengthening organization by training cadres and recruiting Party members from among the local Tibetan population. Under normal conditions, members of the CCP were expected to be atheists. In Zeku, however, county leaders admitted that religious belief was still so widespread that if it was used to disqualify candidates, "Party-building work would be impossible."[14] Authorities continued to loudly champion the purported benefits of mutual aid and cooperation. Propaganda aside, however, for the time being no further attempts were made to collectivize Zeku's pastoral inhabitants.

These efforts were complicated by a series of natural disasters that over the course of 1956 continued to grow in magnitude. An early frost the previous autumn had already made for a difficult winter and spring. By midsummer, persistent drought conditions combined with insect and rodent infestation to devastate large swaths of the grassland. With grass scarce and animals weak, reports state that herders were prematurely leading their livestock into fall and winter pastures. This was creating the type of land rush (*qiangmu*) that often precipitated grassland disputes. To make matters worse, during the July breeding season a serious outbreak of hoof-and-mouth disease appeared within the Gartsé's herds, killing two hundred head of cattle and two thousand sheep before spreading throughout the county and across its borders. Before it was brought under control, the epidemic affected all of Zeku's chiefdoms except the Khéri Chunga, killing nearly two thousand head of cattle. Given the dire conditions, officials warned of a potentially disastrous winter and spring, marked by a drop in production and the eruption of violent grassland conflict.[15]

As befitting the changed times, however, Party operatives did not blame the whims of the natural world alone for the worrying economic outlook. According to investigators, the troubles also had a class dimension. For example, a report alleged that within the Gartsé, "there are still some among the nationality and religious representatives who in order to protect their feudal rule and privileges obstruct the implementation of policy." When grassland regulations were transgressed, the report continued, "it is always caused by the headmen and those with lots of animals. In this year's crisis they initially blamed other tribes for eating the grass. In reality, they did the same."[16] Elsewhere, investigators accused the Logyatsang Lama, a trülku from Hor Monastery, of using the misfortune to promote superstition while reaping collateral rewards. Implying that natural disaster was punishment for unstated transgression, the Nyingma lama allegedly declared it to be "heaven's will" (tianyi). He then predicted, "If you do not chant sutra there will be heavy snows in October and November." As a result, the Logyatsang Lama was said to have received ten thousand yuan in offerings.[17] Other members of Zeku's traditional elite also came in for criticism. A report singled out the Gartsé qianhu Lubum for "taking the lead in the destruction of the grassland system."[18] Elsewhere, a Gönshül headman purportedly displayed his recalcitrance by insisting that he would be willing to spread the Party's propaganda only *after* it successfully resolved outstanding disputes and other undisclosed problems. Shawo, a Sonak chieftain, was faulted for failing to lead the masses in building enclosures to protect animals from the elements. Rather than acting as if he was master of his own home, Shawo was accused of displaying a "guest-like attitude."[19]

The criticism of Shawo's "guest-like" behavior underscores some of the inherent tensions that had always existed just beneath the surface of the Party's United Front program of nation building and socialist transformation. On the one hand, the CCP was avowedly hostile toward the interests of Amdo's pre-1949 leadership even as it continued to rely on it to meet its short-term aims. On the other, making Tibetans "masters of their own home," a process indigenous elites were expected to actively lead, ultimately meant depriving those same figures of their wealth and positions of customary authority. During the first years of the PRC, the Party's insistence on prioritizing great nationality oppression over class exploitation had thinly papered over these inconsistencies. In the aftermath of the High Tide, however, the strains were becoming increasingly difficult to ignore.

The sharpening contradictions underlying United Front policy were laid bare in an early-1957 investigation into Lhagyel's Wönkhor tsowa. The report found that in the years since "Liberation," wealthy Wönkhor households continued to live lavishly while only modestly reducing the interest they charged for loaned animals and offering hired laborers similarly small increases in wages. All the while, well-off pastoralists personally produced little, enjoyed light tax responsibilities, and provided significant support to religious institutions. "As a result of this backward production relationship," investigators summarized, "the development of new productive capacities is constrained."[20] This allegedly had led one herdsman to levy the ultimate charge. Asserting that the dogged persistence of exploitation and inequality was directly related to the maintenance of the pre-1949 class system, he purportedly proclaimed, "It is the same as in the time of Ma Bufang—there hasn't been the smallest change. We have no means to survive [other than borrowing animals]. We urgently request the government do what it can to lower the cost of animal loans."[21] The report concluded that the relationship between herdlords and the pastoral masses continued to be characterized by class exploitation, systematic indebtedness, and impoverishment.[22]

Despite such findings, county leaders admitted that they could do little to force wealthy pastoralists to change their ways—at least not under the parameters then in place. The United Front strategy of nation building was partially predicated on the assumption that as living standards improved, the patriotic awareness of the masses would rise. Simultaneously, the grip of headmen and lamas over society would loosen. Nonetheless, eight years after "Liberation" and four since the founding of Zeku County, investigators found that wages continued to be low and the rates charged for borrowing animals remained high. As a result, despite the "subjective" wishes of some cadres, the prestige of traditional elites remained largely undiminished.[23] Yet cadres could not aggressively step in on behalf of the masses. To the contrary, the High Tide had been an emphatic reminder of the dangers of advancing too hastily. The Wönkhor report explained that due to concerns raised during the High Tide over the permanence of the Three Nos, wealthy households were less inclined to take care of their herds or reinvest in production. Instead, they chose to spend what they could while they still could. In the process, a tremendous amount of resources was not reinvested into production but was wasted on what the CCP considered to be luxuries. An example was made of Wagya himself, who in 1955 reportedly spent over twenty thousand yuan on a son's wedding.[24] Under these circumstances, the Huangnan Party Committee reminded its subordinates that pressuring wealthy households to voluntarily raise wages and lessen the cost of borrowing animals could easily backfire. Alluding to rising tensions and cases of antistate violence, it cautioned that even openly praising wealthy herders who had reduced interest on loaned animals could raise "unnecessary anxieties" about the durability of the Three Nos and "give enemies an opportunity to instigate disharmony and sow destruction."[25] The United Front had entered a cul-de-sac of its own making with no obvious way forward.

Subjectivism in Thought, Bureaucratism in Work

With these constraints surely in mind, in February 1957, the Zeku County Party Committee launched a "comprehensive" internal examination of its nationality and United Front work along with "other nonproletarian behaviors." All outside cadres from the county's Party, government, and vocational units, *but not Tibetans*, were subject to investigation. Admitting that "serious problems" had damaged its relationship with Zeku's indigenous population, "important nationality cadres," including Wagya, Lubum, Tsintar, Chögyong, and Wagya's nephew Jikmé Sönam (a trülku from Hor Monastery), were invited to attend a special meeting of the Zeku County Party Committee. There they purportedly "educated" county leaders about the actual conditions in the county. What the headmen and lamas exactly told the Party committee unfortunately is not contained in the report. However, it appears that their assessments were not commendatory.[26]

On March 2, the results of the investigation were released in a blistering report that excoriated the leadership of Zeku's former Party boss, Guo Min. In the tenor of the Eighth Party Congress and the propaganda campaign that came in its wake, Guo was accused of failing to implement democracy, strengthen collective leadership, or listen to the opinions of the masses. Instead, he allegedly relied on a couple of trusted underlings while treating others abusively. In a judgment that almost certainly alluded to the previous year's pastoral cooperativization drive, the report contended that Guo had rarely "gone down to the tribes" but instead resorted to "subjective and prejudicial methods." As a result, he failed to accurately analyze or understand the actual conditions in the county. Purportedly many cadres at the county level and below likewise adopted Guo's negligent practices and contemptuous attitudes, leading to both "subjectivism in thought"—a leftist tendency in which wishful thinking replaced objective analysis—and "bureaucratism in work"—a rightist tendency that caused cadres to become conservative, self-satisfied, and divorced from the masses.[27] One consequence of this failure of leadership was that cadre morale had fallen to dangerously low levels. The report cautioned that rather than fortify themselves with revolutionary fervor, cadres, fearing the difficult conditions of the grasslands and feeling abandoned on a forlorn corner of the Tibetan plateau, often sedated themselves with alcohol.[28]

Predictably Zeku's new leadership asserted that these organizational failures had damaged internationality relations. In November 1956, Zhao Kunyuan, vice secretary of the Yushu Prefecture Party Committee, delivered a speech to the Qinghai Party Committee in which he lambasted continuing expressions of Han chauvinism for offsetting any benefits nationality autonomy otherwise produced, among them a failure to trust, consult with, or appreciate the contributions made by minority elites or cadres.[29] Investigators in Zeku registered similar complaints. For example, when a Han cadre was sent into the field, he was provided a horse. This was not the case for nationality (i.e., Tibetan) cadres. Likewise, when medicine was available, it was first dispensed to Han and only afterward to Tibetans. The report further alleged that Tibetan cadres were often treated as translators rather than colleagues. In this way, "the important and useful knowledge of minority cadres was ignored, and their opinions were not listened to sufficiently." In other cases, investigators found that Han cadres failed to conscientiously carry out their work assignments. Declaring, "Afterall you wanted to be masters of your own home," they instead left matters to their Tibetan counterparts.[30]

Although the attitudes of Tibetan cadres were not part of the formal investigation, examples of "narrow nationalism" did surface. As before, however, Party leaders dismissed these concerns by reasoning that local nationalism was a symptom of a more serious disease. It was Han chauvinism, they insisted, that caused many among Zeku's Tibetan leaders, cadres, and masses to become dissatisfied with the CCP and suspicious of its platforms. For instance, it was reported that Vice Secretary Serökyap had simply up and left the county seat in frustration while Hor District leader Köngya had offered to return whatever salary he had earned if he was allowed to resign his position. Some Han cadres confessed that local people treated them like enemies rather than guests, while a Tibetan cadre revealed that his Han colleagues regarded him more as a pack animal than a comrade-in-arms. Back in December 1953, the CCP established Zeku County with the declaration that Tibetans had at last become "masters of their own home." Echoing Lhakba's sentiments from July 1955, local Tibetan cadres now told investigators, "Tibetans do the housework, but the Han are the masters."[31]

It is difficult to determine what elements other than sober assessment drove the new leadership's denunciation of Guo Min and his followers. Shifts in political campaigns often provide a venue for personal vendettas and factional struggles, and some of that may be what occurred in Zeku County. Deservedly or not, Guo seems to have been a ready-made scapegoat: the departed Party secretary could be blamed for the failures of the cooperativization campaign, the persistence of nationality disunity, various work deficiencies, official malfeasance, and other shortcomings the CCP encountered or created in Zeku.

Of course, criticism of Zeku's cadre force was not new. Nor did the censures end with Guo's demotion, transfer, and public undressing. Most noteworthy, when in August 1957 the Anti-Rightist Campaign formally arrived in Huangnan Prefecture, it is striking to see who was and was not targeted. Referring to a "'local nationalism' scare," Zhe Wu writes that in Xinjiang the Anti-Rightist Campaign "transformed into an effort to combat local nationalism. Efforts to combat Han chauvinism, prevalent in earlier years, evaporated."[32] In Huangnan Prefecture, by contrast, Tibetan religious and secular leaders—otherwise natural targets in a campaign ostensibly aimed at uncovering local nationalists, remnant rightists, and hidden counterrevolutionaries—were explicitly placed off limits. Instead, the Huangnan Party Committee declared, "During the antirightist struggle . . . we must avoid the religious and nationality questions."[33] Anyone breaking this prohibition was to be reported both to the prefectural and provincial Party committees.

With the local Tibetan leadership excluded, in Huangnan the Anti-Rightist Campaign instead singled out Han cadres who displayed bureaucratism, subjectivism, factionalism, Han chauvinism, and capitalist or anti-Party sentiment. In particular, the prefecture claimed that many cadres had become complacent, self-serving, and unwilling to undertake the difficult task of going down to the countryside and working with the masses.[34] Even then, the *Zeku County Gazetteer* later admitted that during the campaign just eleven presumably Han cadres were classified as rightists, four of them mistakenly. Even with its much larger cadre force, in neighboring Tongren County only twenty-four cadres were targeted.[35] Huangnan's experience does not appear to have been particularly idiosyncratic. Specifically citing Qinghai's Tibetan- and Mongol-inhabited areas, in October 1957, Beijing confirmed that "antirightist struggle" should not be carried out in places where "democratic reforms" had not yet been implemented.[36] As noted by Dreyer, this relative moderation reflects a real anxiety over internationality relations, social stability, and the Party's readiness to move beyond the United Front and suggests that at least in some minority nationality areas the campaign's consequences for local people may have been less severe than suggested by the surrounding rhetoric and several high-profile purges.[37]

From Rash Advance to Right Conservatism

Even as Zeku's new leadership lamented the damage Guo Min and his supporters had done to nationality relations and the Party's prestige, it reported that repairs were underway through a renewed commitment to cadre training and a reemphasis on nationality autonomy.[38] In May 1957, Huangnan ordered Li Chunfan, newly installed vice secretary of the Zeku County Party Committee, to investigate the situation within the Hor and Sairidan (Shawonar chiefdom) Districts.[39] Li reported that after mediating a grassland dispute between the Hor and rivals in Tongde County, he spent five days within the two chiefdoms in order "to understand and help implement work." Based on this short visit with just sixteen households, Li made several specific recommendations on how to mitigate ongoing damage brought on by potentially a second year of drought, cold, and disease. Displaying an attitude that might itself be considered both chauvinistic and lending itself toward "commandism," Vice Secretary Li suggested that part of the problem was the superstitious fatalism of the masses. His solutions were hardly novel. Insisting that scientific management methods could be used to stabilize production and increase yields, Li advocated mobilizing pastoralists to build wells, irrigate dry grasslands, and eliminate rodents and other plateau pests. With fifty days remaining before animals could be moved to summer pasture, he recommended an all-out effort to marshal all available resources and "exhaust all methods to strengthen animal protection through the spring."[40]

More to the point, Li, who was yet another native of Shaanxi Province, argued that animal losses incurred over the past year had actually been caused by a combination of factors, including disease, drought, and poor herding practices. He insisted that each was a long-standing problem not specifically connected to collectivization. Yet, because natural disaster had coincided with the High Tide, these otherwise unrelated factors had become conflated in the minds of local Tibetans. Particularly within herding groups in which animal management had been poor and livestock deaths many, Li reported that a sentiment had emerged that held collective forms of ownership "not as good as individual herding." Li also pointed to worrying deficiencies in propaganda work, claiming that many herders mistakenly feared that if they joined cooperatives, they would no longer have the freedom to chant sutras, ride horses, drink milk, eat meat, or even marry the spouse of their choice. On the other hand, he asserted that some had come to the equally dangerous assumption that after their animals became the property of the cooperative, members could "eat until their stomachs were full. It does not matter if you work or not, or produce or not." However, Li noted that it was the pre-1949 elite who still harbored the most serious doubts about collective production. Some suspected that the cooperatives signaled the end of religious freedom. Others worried that they would be pressured to divide their animals into shares at artificially low prices. In conclusion, Li reported that these concerns, though unfounded, had not only damaged production but also caused a widening estrangement between the Party and the masses.[41]

As usual, Li assigned the bulk of the blame to local officials. He criticized cadres for spending an inordinate amount of time in meetings rather than in the field and asserted that out of a group of twenty cadres—including four district leaders and two district Party committee secretaries—not one truly understood the CCP's directives on mutual aid and cooperation. Li's remedy, unsurprisingly, was not a change in policy but strengthening political work within the cadre ranks and deepening propaganda efforts among the masses. This, according to Vice Secretary Li, would "cause misgivings to be eliminated and production to be developed."[42]

Back in January 1957, Xining had announced that no new cooperatives would be established that calendar year. Yet, as Li's report made clear, Qinghai's Party establishment had not given up on the socialist transformation of pastoral areas. In contrast with the period prior to the High Tide, when socialism had been only discussed through vague platitudes, now cadres were repeatedly instructed to propagandize mutual aid and cooperation with the idea that the pastoral masses were being primed for the day when conditions would make "peaceful reforms" possible. In the interim, the focus was to be on "strengthening, rectifying, and consolidating" the thirty-five PPCs still extant across Qinghai's grasslands. In theory this would give officials time to improve the quality of existing cooperatives, increase production, raise the income of participating households, and therefore make collectivization more attractive to ordinary herdsmen.[43]

Among those who had offered criticism of the aborted pastoral cooperative movement was Party secretary Gao Feng. Speaking in February 1957, Gao noted that the pastoral cooperatives set up during the High Tide had been too large, too complex, their memberships too exclusive, and their regulations too strict. Citing Glorious and Five-Star (Wuxing) Cooperatives as examples of the mechanical importation of models from Han regions, he complained that even the names of cooperatives needed to be decided upon by their members and should reflect the nationality characteristics of the region. While noting that socialist transformation was still the objective, Secretary Gao again made it absolutely clear that collectivization had to be achieved without coercion. Sounding a lot like Governor Sun Zuobin prior to the High Tide, Gao declared, "The road to pastoral cooperativization is one that will be traveled down, but how and when . . . must completely be decided upon according to the wishes of the pastoral masses and representatives; the Party and government simply cannot use force."[44] In the meantime, Xining instructed grassroots cadres to proceed cautiously and in consultation with both the pastoral masses and traditional leaders, champion the Three Nos, and avoid tendencies that might lead them to advance rashly and become divorced from the people—in other words, cause them to repeat the mistakes of the High Tide.[45]

Nonetheless, repeated assurances and warnings would prove insufficient when the political winds blowing out of Beijing shifted violently once again. In August 1957, Party leaders met in the coastal city of Qingdao for a NAC conference on minority work. It was there that Deng Xiaoping and other senior CCP officials shifted the focus from opposing Han chauvinism to attacking local nationalism.[46] Then, from mid-September to early October, national leaders gathered in the capital for the Third Plenum of the CCP's Eighth Party Committee. Calling it "a fundamental turning point in the history of the PRC," Teiwes writes, "This meeting saw the first steps towards new economic policies which emerged as the Great

Leap Forward in 1958."[47] Spurred by slowing growth rates, tensions within the Party leadership, a disintegrating relationship with the Soviet Union, and rising dissatisfaction with centralized, top-down Soviet models of economic planning, Mao and others denounced the more cautious approach to rural collectivization approved a year earlier as "right conservatism." With these tensions coming amid the purges of the Anti-Rightist Campaign, those who over the previous year had criticized the High Tide as a "rash advance" or objected to policies that would soon lead to the Great Leap Forward were all but silenced.[48]

Teiwes and Sun write that in fall 1957, the turn "was more rhetorical and philosophical than substantive."[49] Roderick MacFarquhar adds, "There was as yet no commitment to immediate leaps in output. No inspirational challenge was set to galvanize the nation into action."[50] Instead, for the remainder of the year, Beijing continued to set relatively restrained production targets. The same was not always true in the provinces. Almost immediately, one provincial Party committee after another approved more aggressive plans of rural economic transformation, albeit still far less ambitious than those that would be implemented during the height of the Great Leap. Among them was Qinghai's. Citing vastly improved conditions on the ground, authorities quickly applied for permission to restart Qinghai's pastoral cooperativization campaign. In the context of the new political environment, however, it seems reasonable to suspect that the change instead reflected a resurgent revolutionary impatience.

A week after the conclusion of the Third Plenum (October 19, 1957), Qinghai received approval from the central government. A month later, Party secretary Gao Feng, who at the Eighth Party Congress had vociferously attacked Han chauvinism, instead dedicated a good portion of his closing speech at a plenum of Qinghai's Party committee to "opposing right conservative thought."[51] In retrospect, the floodgates had opened. In December, Liu Zexi, the director of the provincial Rural Work Department, explained Qinghai's rationale for restarting its pastoral collectivization drive. In Beijing for a national-level conference, Liu declared that problems associated with the hastily created pastoral cooperatives of the previous year had been corrected. This included reducing their size (even splitting them in two), loosening restrictions on keeping animals outside the collectives for their owner's personal use, reforming the system by which cooperative shares were assigned, enforcing the edict that allowed pastoralists to voluntarily enter and freely leave cooperatives, and strengthening United Front and propaganda work. Liu asserted that where cooperatives already had been established, collective labor itself had helped heighten political consciousness and deepen unity. He was not only referring to internationality camaraderie, such as between Tibetan pastoralists and Han cadres, but also intranationality harmony. Liu made an example of Xinghai County. There members of three Tibetan chiefdoms labored on two PPCs. Rather than adding to already tense intercommunity relations, Liu claimed that during the difficult environmental challenges of the past year, co-operativization had provided an equitable and peaceful method for mediating disputes and guaranteeing access to grassland resources. In other words, pastoral cooperatives now were being pitched as an effective means to achieve two of the CCP's main goals in Amdo: the consolidation of nationality unity and increasing production.[52]

Despite his optimistic assessment, Liu acknowledged that some areas of Qinghai and some of its nationality groups were advancing down the path toward collective production more quickly than others. Liu reminded his Beijing audience that before Qinghai implemented any pastoral reforms, attention must be paid to their wider impact. For instance, he warned that in Central Tibet, where not even basic reforms had been carried out, people were keeping a wary eye on events in Qinghai. Liu therefore offered a staggered, ten-year plan to transition from individual herding to mutual aid teams and finally pastoral cooperatives (no distinction was made here between low-level and high-level cooperatives), not unlike formulas advanced at the end of 1955. In regions where preparations were already well underway, he announced that PPCs could be established beginning the following year, with an aim toward completion within the coming Second Five-Year Plan (1958–62). However, in areas such as Zeku where preparations were still in their initial stages, Liu cautioned that socialist transformation might take a decade "or even a bit longer."[53] The reality was that at the end of 1957, just 1 percent of Qinghai's pastoralists (659 households) were enrolled on forty-five PPCs.[54]

A Reflection of Capitalist Thought

In spite of Liu's warning, by the end of 1957, orders to oppose "right conservatism" had overtaken fears over "rash advance." Likewise, the perceived dangers of local nationalism had eclipsed those posed by Han chauvinism. The CCP had long considered local nationalism a reaction to Han chauvinism—a worrying but less threatening disposition that would fade as the condition that engendered it was extinguished. In November, however, the leaders of the national-level UFWD instead described local nationalism as "a reflection of capitalist thought, a manifestation of the struggle between the capitalist and socialist road."[55] Severed from its causal relationship to nationality exploitation, local nationalism had been recast as an independent and dangerous deviation. Before the end of the year, Qinghai's leadership extended an ongoing internal Party-rectification and socialist-education campaign to the province's minority-nationality CCP and Communist Youth League members, government cadres, and even "ordinary laboring masses." In pastoral regions, this meant that rather than eliminating Han chauvinism, the focus turned to "making minority cadres understand the nature of local nationalism, its root, and its dangers."[56]

The Zeku County Party Committee responded predictably to the shifting political climate by insisting that corrections to its work since the departure of Guo Min had led many among the masses to clamor for the formation of collectives. Purportedly some had even organized themselves into self-styled mutual aid groups. At an October meeting of Zeku's People's Representative Committee, Tibetan delegates reportedly offered their support for restarting the pastoral cooperativization campaign. A month later, the Party committee announced plans to establish ten MATs, three PPCs, and one state-private joint-ownership pastoral farm (gongsiheying muchang) by spring 1958.[57] Even as it renewed its pastoral collectivization drive, however, Zeku's Party committee noted that bureaucratism, subjectivism, factionalism, chauvinism (among Han cadres), and local nationalism (among Tibetan cadres) continued to hinder work. Likewise, it once again admitted that propaganda efforts had yet to produce their desired effects. For instance, a January 1958 investigation into two Gartsé herding groups would find that "superstition" remained deeply ingrained among Zeku's pastoral population. Rather than trust the Party to raise production levels, investigators instead reported that Tibetan herders continued "to rely on heaven's will to eat."[58] Moreover, cadres found that both traditional elites and members of the masses still expressed acute misgivings toward joining pastoral cooperatives. Repeating instruction issued at the start of 1956, county leaders therefore warned, "The pace will be steady, the time period will be lengthy, and the policies will be flexible."[59]

Moreover, Qinghai's Party committee continued to make extraordinary concessions in pastoral regions that in sum amounted to an admission of its limited success laying a foundation of support among the pastoral masses. In particular, and seemingly in contradiction with the spirit of the Qingdao Conference, the Third Plenum, and even its own statements, the committee admitted that class consciousness among pastoralists was no more developed than it had been prior to the launch of the High Tide. Even while warning that local nationalism was on the rise, Qinghai's leadership continued to reserve the lion's share of condemnation for Han chauvinism. As before, Xining insisted that pastoral religious and secular elites be treated with particular leniency. Whereas in agricultural areas criticism could be leveled (preferably by members of their own nationality) at members of the pre-1949 leadership, on the grasslands methods of correction were limited to "talk but no struggle"—and, even then, only in serious cases. Nearly a decade after arriving in Qinghai, provincial authorities ordered cadres working in pastoral areas to continue emphasizing rudimentary questions, including "What is socialism?" and "How can socialism be built?"[60] As late as the start of 1958, education, not confrontation, was still being prescribed to counter the ill effects of local nationalism.

In short, the United Front had yet to work its magic—to replace an imperial-style relationship between the state and local elites with a direct compact between the pastoral masses and their class allies of all nationalities under the leadership of the Chinese Communist Party. "Tribal" structures and loyalties had not given way to either mass consciousness or patriotic awareness. Despite its aggressive posturing during the pastoral investigation efforts of 1955 and subsequent High Tide, the Zeku County Party Committee continued to affirm United Front prin-ciples and procedures. The Three Nos remained in effect. Class struggle had not been carried out, wealth had not been redistributed, and class labels had not been assigned. As the calendar turned to 1958, 136 people identified as belong-ing to Zeku's "nationality and religious upper strata"—by the state's reckoning, 51 percent of the area's traditional elite—continued to hold positions on the Zeku County Government Committee, the Zeku County Consultative Commit-tee, or in other state organs.[61]

An impasse had been reached. Recognizing the damage to both production and nationality unity caused by High Tide radicalism, 1957 had begun with Party leaders expressing a recommitment to the principles and practices of the United Front. Pastoral collectivization was suspended indefinitely, and efforts were made to repair internationality relations. Even the direct impact of the Anti-Rightist Campaign on Zeku's pastoral population was limited. Rather than root out local nationalism among Zeku's secular and monastic leaders, Xining explicitly placed Tibetan elites off limits. Instead, the campaign focused on the usual suspect, Han chauvinism, for its propensity toward commandism (coercion) and subjectivism (the urge to collectivize before conditions were ripe).

As investigators discovered, putting the genie of collectivization back into the United Front bottle was not going to be easy. For Amdo's traditional elite, social-ist transformation—once a hazy concept—had become a concrete reality and even an existential threat. However, class consciousness had yet to penetrate the masses in a substantive way. While propagandizing the benefits of collective pro-duction would further alienate already alarmed headmen and herdlords, going back to the pre–High Tide order was equally untenable. Buoyed by the Qingdao Conference's explicit targeting of local nationalism and the Third Plenum's de-nunciation of right conservatism, in retrospect the stage had been set. Nonethe-less, as this "un-Maoist interlude" drew to a close, few could have guessed that 1958 would prove to be the most consequential year in the modern history of the Amdo region.

7

REACHING THE SKY IN A SINGLE STEP—THE AMDO REBELLION

In 1953, the Chinese Communist Party established Zeku County with the pledge that its Tibetan inhabitants finally had become "masters of their own home." On the evening of July 5, 1958, almost five years to the day that Gyelyön and his detachment of activists had first pitched their tents on the banks of the Tséchu River, members of Zeku's Wöngya chiefdom rose in revolt. Before the county could be fully "pacified," Chinese sources contend that more than 4,600 Tibetans—nearly a quarter of Zeku's population—would participate in "counterrevolutionary armed rebellion."[1]

Of course, the uprising in Zeku was not an isolated event but part of a series of revolts that spread across Amdo in the spring and summer of 1958. It is tempting to think of the Amdo Rebellion as a sudden outburst of violence after nearly a decade of tense coexistence. However, a closer inspection of archival and secondary materials instead reveals nearly constant displays of resistance over the first decade of the People's Republic of China. This includes the "everyday" sorts of resistance identified by James Scott, some suggested in earlier chapters: a woman who declines to serve as a local representative by pleading ignorance, a household that fails to tie up its dog for an approaching work team, various forms of tax evasion, headmen who do not appear on the appointed date for a government meeting, and many others.[2] It also includes less subtle forms of resistance. Most obvious are the series of large-scale rebellions that struck large swaths of the Amdo borderlands in the years following "Liberation." The 1953 defeat of Ma Yuanxiang's insurrection seemed to signal an end to this era of armed struggle.

Perhaps it might even be considered the final confrontation of the Chinese Civil War. Over the ensuing years, however, sources continue to obliquely refer to "bandit-suppression" efforts and warn of the ever-present danger of "spies."[3] Gansu's provincial gazetteer even alludes to the assassination of several Gannan officials during the mid-1950s, including the director of its UFWD.[4] Whether veiled indicators of organized opposition to the new Party-state or references to heirs of longer traditions of banditry, self-defense, and, to borrow from Scott once again, practitioners of "the art of not being governed,"[5] the implication is that many elements in Amdo remained acutely inimical to the incorporative demands of the CCP.

Internal documents also occasionally refer directly to outbreaks of "armed rebellion" in the years from 1953 to 1958. In particular, the grasslands that lay at the juncture of Qinghai, Gansu, and Sichuan Provinces, the same region that just a few years prior hosted Ma Yuanxiang and Ma Liang's guerrillas, remained a haven for antistate activities. After all, boundaries were porous and did not map well onto the state's administrative divisions. While rebellion in Kham during the High Tide has been well documented, in 1956 and 1957, many Amdowas living in the northern portions of Sichuan (Ngawa) and southern Gansu also rebelled.[6] Whether to escape pursuit or expand the conflict zone (details are few), Chinese sources assert that on multiple occasions fighters crossed into Qinghai, spurring "a small number of reactionaries among the religious upper strata in Huangnan, Yushu, and Guoluo to become restless, seek to liaise with them, and conspire to carry out coordinated action."[7] In one of the most serious cases, in spring 1956, members of the "nationality and religious elite" allegedly exploited dissatisfaction with the implementation of collectivization during the High Tide to launch "counterrevolutionary armed rebellion" among the Shitsang chiefdom and neighboring tsowa in Gannan's Luqu (T. Luchu) County. That summer, the fighting spilled into Henan County, where members of the Mongol Datsen chiefdom attacked a PLA convoy, killing sixteen soldiers. The Mongol fighters were then joined by more than eighty Shitsang horsemen, and together they ransacked the local garrison and plundered the township granary. The exact chronology of events is unclear. However, according to a testimonial collected by Françoise Robin, security forces responded to the uprising with a predawn attack on a Datsen encampment. In the assault, ninety-six members of the Serlung tsowa were killed, many of them in their sleep. Attesting to the logistical difficulties of fighting small groups of mobile combatants in the vast grasslands of southern Amdo, it still took two weeks for the military district to deploy a force sufficient to put down the revolt. Even then, the PLA lost thirteen more men and suffered another twenty-eight wounded.[8]

Following the defeat of the "Datsen Area Rebellion," Xining assigned "pres-tigious" religious figures (presumably Tibetan and Mongol) to work groups, which, along with medical teams, were deployed to Henan and other areas of unrest. Their orders were to spread the Party's religious policies, treat "without compensation" those who had been "mistakenly wounded," aid in economic re-covery and development—which in Henan reportedly included investments of over sixty thousand yuan—and uncover the "true situation" along the Gansu-Qinghai-Sichuan frontier while strengthening military preparations.[9]

Despite these efforts, tensions continued to mount. Speaking specifically of Huangnan Prefecture, Chinese sources admit that "rumors circulated from all directions, and there was a growing feeling of insecurity."[10] They also assert that a number of prominent members of Repgong's religious and secular leadership, in-cluding Zongqianhu Gyelwo Dorjé, went on pilgrimage to Lhasa. There the Am-dowas allegedly purchased large quantities of "British Indian goods" and weapons and secretly transported them home in preparation for armed rebellion.[11] The charges are unsubstantiated. Nonetheless, allusions to both heightened states of fear and distrust and actual armed confrontation—although often frustratingly brief—help throw into sharper relief the tense stalemate that had materialized in the aftermath of the High Tide. Moreover, when the various challenges to CCP rule from 1949 to 1957 are considered in sum—from "post-Liberation" rebellions, continuing bouts of "banditry," fighting in Kham and parts of southern Amdo and its spillover into Qinghai, and resistance to pastoral cooperativization—rather than a decade of relative peace shattered by a sudden eruption of violence, the Amdo Rebellion takes on an aura of increasing ineluctability.

Focusing on eastern Qinghai and southern Gansu, this chapter surveys events leading up to the Amdo Rebellion, its devastating course, and its immediate consequences. Both contemporary and secondary Chinese-language sources de-scribe the Amdo Rebellion as a principally pastoral affair prompted by elite resis-tance to collectivization.[12] Some even refer to the uprising as "Qinghai's pastoral region armed rebellion."[13] However, it is important to note that under a policy referred to as Strike and Reform (Bianda Biangai), in most pastoral regions it would be *during* the pacification of the rebellion that "democratic reforms" were finally fully implemented and socialist transformation completed.[14] In fact, at the time, Qinghai's leadership claimed that the rebellion was most ferocious in places where pastoral cooperatives had yet to be established and the power of "feudal" elites therefore was still largely intact.[15] Rather than a response to the implementation of cooperatives, as both Chinese sources and popular memory frequently suggest, it appears that the rebellion began as an attempt to preempt collectivization in pastoral areas.

A Great Leap

As discussed in the previous chapter, 1957 had begun with a recommitment to pragmatism, gradualism, and voluntarism. Yet local cadres and Party officials soon discovered that reverting to the logics of the pre–High Tide period was not easily accomplished. Investigators in Zeku reported that Tibetan headmen had become increasingly suspicious, perhaps fatally so, toward the rhetoric of the United Front, while common herders had yet to jettison their "feudal" loyalties and "superstitious" beliefs. Despite, or possibly propelled by, this impasse, when in fall 1957 criticism of "rash advance" turned into condemnation of "right conservatism," pressures to reboot the pastoral collectivization campaign quickly superseded promises of an indefinite moratorium on the formation of new pastoral cooperatives. But as the calendar turned to 1958, plans were still fairly moderate, and attention to gradualism and voluntarism was still being emphasized. In Zeku, county leaders drew up an ambitious if comparatively modest proposal that would have seen just three PPCs and ten mutual aid teams organized over the coming months.

Whether or not these relatively limited goals could have formed the cornerstone for peaceful socialist transformation would soon become a moot point. Before long, the Zeku grasslands, and indeed all of Amdo, would be forcibly integrated into the socialist state and nation. In January, the Qinghai Provincial Party Committee met for the Fifth Plenum of its Second Party Committee. Just two months earlier, the same body had initiated a ten-year plan for pastoral collectivization. Now, in a series of three reports, Party leaders declared a "Great Leap Forward" in industry, agriculture, and pastoralism. Instead of a decade-long timeline based on the specific conditions of each region, in the increasingly radical atmosphere of early 1958 provincial leaders suddenly ordered Qinghai's pastoral areas completely collectivized within five years.[16]

In mid-January, the Zeku County Party Committee convened to hammer out its blueprint for the coming year. The resulting 1958 county work plan is surprising for at least two reasons. First, production quotas were still quite modest (just a 10 percent across-the-board increase in livestock), and the methods for achieving these gains were hardly radical. In fact, much of the plan easily could have been mistaken for one from 1954. As before, higher yields were to be achieved mainly through the rational and efficient use of grassland resources, improving management of grazing rights, strengthening animal disease-prevention efforts, building enclosures, warehousing winter feed, and hunting predators.[17] Given the developing political climate, the second surprising aspect of the 1958 work plan was that cooperatives were only discussed in the latter half of the document, where they were depicted as an important but perhaps secondary objective. The report did assert that several years of sustained propaganda had generated tangible successes, declaring, for example, "The excitement of the pastoral masses for proceeding down the road to cooperativization is very high." Allegedly this newfound spirit had infected Tibetan headmen as well. It cited as evidence Wagya's announcement that he had no reservations about joining a joint-ownership pastoral farm.[18]

Along with these assurances, however, came familiar caveats. County leaders conceded that many members of the masses still entertained anxieties about collectivization, elites continued to harbor backward thoughts, the quality of Han cadres remained low, and Tibetan cadres were still too few in number. Consequently, collectivization plans for the coming year were also limited—again, at least in retrospect. The work plan now proposed the formation of three pastoral farms, thirteen PPCs, and sixty-nine MATs. Ideally, each PPC would be assembled out of a single herding group and consist of approximately ten households, thus conforming to a natural community. In order to change the "backward conditions of pastoral areas," efforts at "settling the nomads" also were to begin anew. In this, too, however, projections were comparatively cautious. Back in 1956, prefectural leaders called for the permanent settlement of entire chiefdoms and for countywide sedentarization to be completed within two years. At the start of 1958, by contrast, just three *herding groups* (including Wagya's) and the relatively small Ködé Karing chiefdom were slated for settlement.[19]

If the 1958 work plan was fairly restrained in terms of targets and quotas, in some respects its tone differed markedly from the previous fall. Most notably, in November Party secretary Gao Feng had tempered instructions to "oppose right conservative thought" with reminders to also combat an array of both rightist and leftist tendencies, including subjectivism, factionalism, egalitarianism, liberalism, anarchism, individualism, and local nationalism.[20] Nowhere, however, did the 1958 work plan warn of leftist inclinations that might cause cadres to implement reforms before conditions were appropriate. Quite the opposite, the report now railed solely against the menace of right conservatism.

This was no mistake. On January 3, Qinghai's Party committee had ordered lower levels to seek out and criticize grassroots Party members who expressed capitalist ideas, rightist thought, individualism, or similar tendencies.[21] By then, national propaganda outlets were routinely running stories that either implicitly or overtly described the proposition that some minority areas might not be ready for socialist transformation—an orthodox idea just a few months earlier—as an expression of "local nationalism" or even "splittism." For example, writing in the *People's Daily*, Apa Alo, the former Tibetan strongman of the Labrang region, cautioned that a small number of nationality elites hid behind the mask of "minority special characteristics" "to promote their own agenda, in order to thwart socialist reforms."[22] Meeting in early February, Gansu's People's Representative Conference warned that the province was experiencing a "new upsurge" in local nationalism among both Tibetans and Hui Muslims. Calling it a last-ditch effort to preserve the interests of the capitalist class, the delegates charged that in Linxia some Hui complained that the "CCP is the Party of the Han nationality" and spread rumors that Islam would be destroyed. "Some even refuse to admit that China is their motherland." Instead, they purportedly called for the creation of pan-Hui Muslim state (Huihuiguo) or sought permission to emigrate to their "Arabian motherland."[23] Allegedly, this separatist sentiment was shared by some Gannan Tibetans who wished to join Amdo and Central Tibet together in an independent state. Citing slogans such as "Tibetans do the housework, but the Han are the masters" and "nationality cadres have position but no power," the conference reported that many in both Gannan and Linxia considered "nationality cadres" to be flunkies of the CCP—in the words of one Tibetan, "a stick with which to hit a dog." In years past, charges such as these might have been viewed as evidence of the stubborn persistence of Han chauvinism. In early 1958, Gansu's leadership instead interpreted them as proof that local nationalism must be the primary target of attack.[24]

Days later, leaders of the Central Nationality Affairs Committee confirmed in the starkest terms that local nationalism should remain "the focus of the rectification and socialist education campaign."[25] NAC vice chairman Xie Fumin went so far as to warn that pandering to local nationalism threatened "to destroy the unity of the motherland."[26] Since 1949, Party leaders at every level had routinely criticized Han chauvinism for damaging relations between the nationalities and spurring local nationalism among minority populations. Now Xie proclaimed the Han to be the "leading nationality" and its "politics, economy, and culture" China's most advanced. Dismissing the idea that local nationalism was a by-product of great Han chauvinism, Xie referred to the Han as the "bulwark of our nation's revolution and construction" and insisted, "The question of seeking or not seeking the aid of the Han nationality is to a great degree the question of seeking or not seeking socialism."[27] There long had been tension between the United Front policies of gradualism and volunteerism on the one side and revolutionary impatience on the other, between respecting the "concrete conditions" of minority regions and a desire to fully and rapidly integrate them and their inhabitants into a uniform socialist state and nation. By the first months of 1958, the momentum had clearly shifted toward the latter.

In this atmosphere of increasing radicalism and unfettered Han nationalism, pressure to collectivize pastoral regions quickly became paramount. On February 13, the *Qinghai Daily* announced that Haixi Prefecture's 1958 plan for implementing a Great Leap Forward in pastoral production would now include the building of sixty-three PPCs, five joint-ownership farms, and improving or establishing 386 MATs. Haixi's leadership predicted that by the end of the year, 25 percent of its pastoral households would be enrolled in PPCs, another 45 percent would be in MATs, and 30 percent of herdlord households would be members of joint-ownership farms.[28]

The race was on. The same day as the Haixi plans were announced, the Zeku County Party Committee released its own updated production plan. Suddenly the sixty-nine MATs settled upon barely three weeks earlier were transformed into 127 year-round MATs and an additional 315 temporary MATs. During the same period, thirty-five PPCs—nearly three times the previous forecast—would be established. Less than a month later, projections were raised once more, now to forty-four PPCs.[29] At the start of 1958, Zeku County had no PPCs and just seven MATs, with a total membership of forty-four families. In less than a year's time, 2,633 households—a full 60 percent of Zeku's pastoral inhabitants—were slated to be engaged in some form of collective production (initially 90 percent on MATs). According to projections, this would reach 100 percent (60 percent on 242 PPCs, the rest on MATs) by the end of 1959. The following year, all of Zeku's residents were to be members of 432 low-level PPCs, and the transition to high-level cooperatives could begin. Significant increases also were predicted for everything from livestock numbers, to acreage of cultivable land, to the amount of animal diseases prevented.[30]

In late March, Liu Zexi—who just a few months earlier cautioned against proceeding too hastily toward collective pastoral production—told a meeting of cadres assigned to pastoral regions that Qinghai's grasslands had entered a "flourishing new period." Liu therefore announced that the province intended to enroll 25 percent of its pastoral households into cooperatives or joint-ownership farms by the end of the year. Within five years, but possibly as few as two, he added, Qinghai's pastoralists would be entirely collectivized.[31] In early May, the provincial Party committee announced that where conditions were ripe, pastoral collectivization should begin in earnest. Where conditions were not ready, they must quickly be made so. A few weeks earlier, provincial leaders had ordered Haixi and Haibei collectivized by the end of the year. This was changed to the end of the *month*. Whereas Huangnan's most recent target date for collectivization had been the end of the 1959, it now became the end of the summer. More distant locations, such as Yushu and Guoluo, were ordered to dramatically quicken the pace as well.[32]

Symbolic of the shift, in early March, Qinghai governor Sun Zuobin, who at the end of 1954 had pledged that socialist transformation in minority regions would proceed according to the specific conditions of each area and the wishes of its inhabitants—then an orthodox position—was accused of being a "spokesman for the herdlord class." Sun allegedly had proclaimed, "In pastoral areas there are only nationality contradictions—there are no class contradictions."[33] For capitulating on the issue of class, he was labeled a "rightist" and purged for "anti-Party antisocialist crimes."[34]

A Single Spark

It was also in late March 1958 that Chen Ming, newly appointed secretary of the Zeku County Party Committee, convened a meeting of 264 cadres to launch Zeku's Great Leap Forward.[35] Almost immediately, however, plans had to be suspended. On April 2, a day before the Zeku conference was set to end, Tibetan insurgents attacked a district headquarters in southern Tongren County, killing nearly five dozen cadres and soldiers. Rebellion had come to Qinghai.

The specific incident that ignited the Amdo Rebellion remains somewhat obscured. Once begun, however, Mao Zedong's famous aphorism "A single spark can light a prairie fire" seems an apt description of its evolution into a major conflagration. Given the region's volatility over the preceding decade, it is unsurprising that the embers of rebellion first flared in Gannan.[36] We have seen, for example, that unrest in 1956 among the Shitsang chiefdom triggered an armed confrontation between the state and the Datsen in neighboring Henan County and heightened tensions elsewhere. Ultimately, the Shitsang/Datsen conflict was put down with considerable violence. However, Chinese sources contend that enemies continued to plot. According to a local gazetteer, as the pastoral communization campaign ramped up again in the last months of 1957, the headmen of several of Gannan's larger chiefdoms met under the auspices of Labrang Monastery to plot rebellion. As with similar claims, the allegations are difficult to assess, particularly as the source contends that one of the rebel leaders had just returned from Lhasa where he received the Dalai Lama's personal assurance—confirmed via oracle divination—that a rebellion launched that year would succeed.[37] Nonetheless, an internally circulated contemporary report asserts that at the start of 1958, "counterrevolutionaries and backward reactionary headmen gathered fighters together and started armed rebellion activities." Then during Spring Festival, the headman of Maqu (T. Machu) County's Ngülra chiefdom invited a three-member work team to a banquet at a local monastery. It was an ambush. According to a later account, the work team members were only able to escape the clutches of a large number of knife-wielding attackers by taking a senior monk hostage.[38] In response, county leaders "immediately placed all of the headmen [tuguan touren] under 'house arrest' under the guise of '[political] study.'"[39]

The Amdo Rebellion had begun. Shouting, "No to the socialist road!," "Kill local cadres!," "Drive out the Liberation Army!," and similar slogans, Gannan insurgents launched attacks on government outposts, security forces, and infrastructure. By mid-March, the rebellion had spread to all six of Gannan's counties and several Hui and Dongxiang areas of neighboring Linxia Prefecture.[40] Troops quickly poured into southern Gansu. Nonetheless, an internal report claims that by early April, more than twenty "bandit gangs" of various sizes—over 11,400 people in all—had killed seventy-six civilians, both Han and Tibetan, including cadres, activists, and their families. An additional fifty to sixty soldiers were either killed in the fighting or (at the time of the April 21 report) missing in action.[41] While these numbers cannot be verified, when considered alongside similar figures and accounts found in other internally circulated contemporary sources, it becomes clear that a large-scale, armed insurgency had erupted on the eastern edge of Amdo.[42]

As conditions in Gannan worsened, fighters again slipped into neighboring regions of Qinghai, this time making their way into Tongren County as well as Guoluo Prefecture. On March 20 and 30, a local headman named Wéma Tséring purportedly convened two large religious assemblies at an undisclosed location in Repgong. According to Chinese sources, the gatherings were actually cover for counterrevolutionary plotting. Finally, on April 2, five hundred members of Repgong's Dowa and Awa Téu chiefdoms, along with the Gannan insurgents, laid siege to Tongren's Fifth District administrative headquarters, killing fifty-seven cadres, soldiers, and militiamen. Work teams quickly pulled back to the relative safety of Rongwo and Bao'an Townships, leaving the countryside in the hands of the insurgents.[43] Soon Rongwo, too, had descended into chaos. In a scene that harked back to the early days after Repgong's "liberation," the prefectural Party committee reported that gunfire rang through the streets as fear gripped the prefectural seat.[44]

From Repgong, the revolt quickly spread to the grasslands of Xunhua County. There the initial confrontation appears to have been spurred by fears over the fate of a prominent lama from Wimdo Monastery, the Gyanak Weltsang Rinpoché. Despite serving as a county vice chairman, since the start of the uprising in Gannan he had been sequestered in Xunhua's county seat—part of a wider policy to preempt rebellion by taking religious leaders hostage under the pretext of "study classes." On April 17, members of the Gyanak Weltsang's Kantsa chiefdom captured and beat the ethnically Tibetan Party secretary and vice secretary of the local township. Two days later, insurgents attacked the township's government facilities, killing four members of an "armed work team," including a county-level military department head. On April 22, more than seventy fighters from Repgong's Langgya and Zho'ongshi chiefdoms joined the Kantsa rebels in an

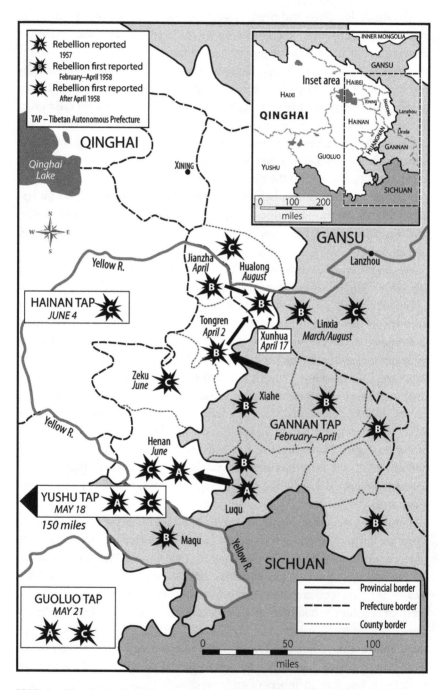

MAP 4. The Amdo Rebellion in eastern Qinghai and southern Gansu, 1958. Mike Bechthold, cartographer. Sources: *QHSZ JSZ, GSSZ JSZ, GNZZ.*

assault on Wimdo District headquarters. By then, much of the county was in a state of open revolt.[45]

Finally, in what is described as the climax to the first stage of the Amdo Rebellion, on April 23 over three thousand fighters, including the Repgong insurgents, members of Wangchen Döndrup's Nangra chiefdom, and a large contingent of local Salar, joined in a multiethnic assault on Xunhua's county seat. According to Qinghai's Party committee, what unified the combatants was Tibetan opposition to pastoral collectivization combined with a severe grain shortage that especially threatened Salar and Hui villagers. Remarkably, at the head of the hastily reconstituted "Anti-Communist Save the Nation Army" was Han Yinu, the same former Salar official who had led the 1950 Xunhua uprising.[46] According to one author, Han Yinu had avoided capture by donning women's clothing and spending years hiding in a cellar.[47]

The countryside now in the hands of the rebels, soldiers and cadres captured outside the walled county seat were shown little mercy. For instance, the leader of a state-aligned militia unit was found hanged from an electric pole surrounded by his dead fighters. However, for more than two days, the small garrison lodged behind the city walls was able to repel the attackers. On the third day, PLA reinforcements finally arrived. Following a "four-hour battle," security forces routed the insurgents and lifted the siege. In the process, Party sources contend that 3,079 "enemies were eliminated."[48] Jianglin Li, however, asserts that the "Xunhua Incident" was less a battle than a massacre. Relying on internally circulated documents, she argues that most of the armed fighters had fled in advance of the PLA assault, concluding that "the dead and wounded were all virtually unarmed."[49] In the ensuing mop-up campaign, thousands more Salar and Tibetans would be arrested or killed. Han Yinu was not among them. His home village surrounded, on April 29 Han again avoided capture—this time by taking his own life.[50]

With Xunhua back under state control, on May 4 troops reentered Tongren County, quickly arresting or capturing over nine hundred "counterrevolutionaries and evildoers." Moving south, in early June security forces routed a collection of more than eight hundred fighters who had dug in near Tongren's border with Zeku. By then, a contemporary report asserts, "pacification work [in Tongren] was basically complete."[51]

A Life-or-Death Class Struggle

As Mao noted, however, once lit, a prairie fire can be difficult to stomp out. Citing uprisings among more than ten of Huangnan's chiefdoms as well as revolts in Guoluo, Yushu, and Hainan Prefectures—virtually all of southern Qinghai—on

April 30 the provincial Party committee declared, "This is a counterrevolution-ary armed rebellion, a long-term conspiracy, planned and organized to destroy nationality unity, oppose socialism, oppose the people's government, and oppose the CCP."[52] Soon afterward, the committee described the rebellion as a "spear-head in a life-or-death class struggle." According to provincial leaders, that spear was being wielded by a litany of class enemies from the old society, including unrepentant ex-military officers and functionaries of the Ma regime, herdlords, and especially Buddhist and Islamic leaders.[53] There is no evidence to suggest that Party or military leaders purposely stoked the flames of rebellion to manufacture an excuse to rid the plateau of the old elite. Once the uprising began, however, contemporary reports referred to it as a "fortunate event, because it allowed us to completely grab the initiative, making it easier to utterly smash the feudal power [structure] and complete socialist reforms."[54] Even Chairman Mao is said to have celebrated, saying, "Qinghai's reactionary clique has rebelled. This is extremely good. The opportunity for the liberation of the laboring masses has arrived."[55]

By the end of June, twenty-two thousand people across Qinghai in twenty-four counties, including representatives of 101 Tibetan Buddhist monasteries, report-edly had risen in revolt.[56] As rebellion spread to majority Muslim areas, including Hualong County in Qinghai and Linxia, where there was a major midsummer insurrection, mosques were also singled out.[57] Asserting that lamas and imams were "exploiting weak spots in our religious work," a report declared that a com-mon thread linked the region's many uprisings: "Religion is at their core; [mon-asteries and mosques] are their headquarters."[58] For Party leaders, the complicity of religious leaders in particular helped explain why members of the masses had joined an uprising led by "counterrevolutionaries, reactionary religious elites, and herdlords." An uprising among Hui Muslims in Gansu's Zhangjiachuan, for example, allegedly was incited by an *idhn* (C. *kouhuan*, imam-granted permis-sion) issued by an Islamic authority in Lanzhou.[59] A contemporary investigation into the "Xunhua Incident" found that nearly 70 percent of the county's CCP and CYL members, including much of their leadership, had participated in the April uprising. The reason cited was the insidious influence that "religious supersti-tion" still held over both Tibetan Buddhists and Muslims. According to Qinghai's Party committee, this was proof that too much attention had been placed on the "nationality question." In what amounted to a repudiation of the United Front, the committee instead concluded, "Class contradictions are of course the pri-mary contradiction."[60]

The enemy now defined, for the first time CCP leaders ordered class struggle extended to Amdo's pastoral areas and conducted within its monasteries. In Gan-nan, authorities accused Labrang Monastery's Sixth Gungtang Lama, till then a prototypical United Front figure, of being a leader of the uprising, "perhaps in connection with Lhasa and foreign enemies."[61] He would spend the next twenty-one years in confinement. Calling them "wolves in monk's robes," Xining ordered its representatives in Xunhua to make religious figures the target of "socialist great debate and antirightist struggle."[62] Officials charged Wimdo Monastery with providing guns and material support to the rebels, while accusing its monks of inciting violence by looting public property and sabotaging infrastructure. Soon afterward, the Gyanak Weltsang Rinpoché is said to have committed suicide while in custody.[63]

In Huangnan, prefectural leaders announced that Rongwo Monastery's Shartsang Lama, Zongqianhu Gyelwo Dorjé, and the Rongwo nangso Trashi Namgyel—the men who since the fall of 1949 had been among the chief conduits of CCP rule over the Repgong region—were the "plot's chief conspirators, and organizational leaders." They identified Rongwo Monastery as the rebellion's local "command center," while accusing the area's other monasteries of acting as its outposts and charging the "resolutely antireform herdlords, landlords and upper- and midlevel reactionary nationality and religious [figures]" with serving as the "backbone" of the uprising.[64] The Shartsang Lama, Gyelwo Dorjé, and Trashi Namgyel were each placed under arrest. The nearly ten-year experiment in subimperialism had come to an end. Amdo's United Front representatives had become counterrevolutionaries.[65]

Speaking Bitterness

On April 17, the same day rebellion broke out in Xunhua, the Zeku County Party Committee released a Zeku County War Preparation Work Plan and established a War Preparation Work Headquarters. Simultaneously, Zeku's public security bureau formally expropriated the property of 149 herdlords and rich pastoralists. Work teams were quickly reorganized as "armed work teams"—"one man, one horse, one gun"—and all of Zeku's districts were ordered to "strengthen reconnaissance of the enemy's position." Outwardly, the Party committee ordered that work should proceed as usual. For the time being, cadres were to continue to consult with local headmen who would maintain their government posts. Internally, however, the now-armed work teams were told to scout the enemies' positions and evaluate developments within the chiefdoms.[66]

Although the Wöngya uprising of July 1958 described at the beginning of this book is the first specific example of antistate violence reported in Zeku County, sources suggest that by May—and perhaps earlier—various unspecified acts of counterrevolutionary plotting and sedition had occurred within its borders.[67] Whether in response to specific incidents of antistate activity or a preemptory strike against Zeku's "feudal" power structure, a Party history notes that on May 30 "rebellion pacification units" moved south from Tongren into Zeku and Henan Counties.[68] Two weeks later, Zeku's leadership announced that efforts to seize weapons and round up "counterrevolutionaries and evildoers" within the Gartsé, Shisa, and Sonak chiefdoms were "basically complete." However, security forces were only then moving into position against enemies within the Gönshül chiefdom and Topden District (Méshül, Ködé Karing, and Khéri Chunga chiefdoms). Once these operations were complete, the report obliquely noted, the Hor and Shawonar "problems," too, would be resolved. Somewhat optimistically, county leaders predicted that by the end of June, "rebellion pacification work" would be complete.[69]

Victory on the battlefield, however, was not enough. "So as to completely smash the herdlords, headmen and other feudal powers, and comprehensively implement cooperativization," provincial leaders demanded that "surrender be brought about politically" as well.[70] This specifically referred to the introduction of "Speaking Bitterness struggle" (*suku douzheng*) into the Amdo grasslands.[71] Long a staple of land reform and other political campaigns, Speaking Bitterness was a time-tested mass line methodology in which members of the masses would be encouraged—or in some cases coerced—to publicly recount the exploitation and humiliation of the old society and its ruling class, thereby arousing, or perhaps manufacturing, class consciousness and class hatred. In the process, class enemies would be identified, dragged in front of their accusers at mass meetings, made to confess their crimes, dispossessed of their wealth, and in some cases physically assaulted or even killed. In theory, as Ann Anagnost writes, "the narrative structure of 'speaking bitterness' provided a new frame for the reworking of consciousness in which the speaker comes to recognize himself as a victim of an immoral system rather than suffering as a result of bad fate or personal shortcoming."[72] Makley adds, "This was the method *par excellence* for constituting rural villagers as citizens and as members of the 'masses', the new collective political subject nonetheless dependent on the guidance of state cadres on the road to socialism."[73] Speaking Bitterness was thus the antithesis to the United Front approach to nation building and socialist transformation. It was the expression of the dialectic imbalance in the mass line methodology of consultation and persuasion taken to its logical extreme. If the United Front preached gradual transformation, Speaking Bitterness was shock therapy.

In June, provincial leaders approved Huangnan's plans for implementing "democratic reforms" alongside military operations—Strike and Reform. Once a locality had been pacified, armed work teams were to "enter the villages, tents, and monasteries to fully arouse the agricultural and pastoral masses and the poor monks of the monasteries and launch a powerful and dynamic Speaking

Bitterness campaign."[74] After all, the prefectural committee reminded its cadres, who benefited from the preservation of the "feudal" system? It was not the masses but Amdo's traditional elite. In the wake of rebellion, common herders needed to be reminded of this as well. By mid-July, the Party committee reported that across Huangnan Prefecture, over seventy-five thousand people had attended over one thousand Speaking Bitterness struggle meetings, at which six hundred targets were subjected to the criticism of over forty thousand accusers.[75]

It was in this context of open attacks on Amdo's traditional leadership and religious institutions that on July 5—a month into Zeku's Speaking Bitterness campaign and three months after rebellion had first erupted elsewhere in Huangnan Prefecture—members of the Wöngya chiefdom raided the Qiaofudan (T. Chöten) District headquarters and killed the seven cadres. The next morning, soldiers of the PLA's 163rd Regiment, 55th Division, routed two hundred Wöngya insurgents. The survivors fled west into Guinan County where, despite joining a larger group of rebels, they were surrounded on July 8 and captured.[76]

By midsummer, open armed opposition in Zeku seemed to have been eliminated. Echoing the sentiments of its superiors, however, Zeku's Party committee insisted that force alone could not defeat "the power of feudal rule." Instead the masses had to be made to recognize "the ugly face of feudal nationality and religious ruling power."[77] County leaders instructed their grassroots cadres to first uncover the "facts" about the rebellion. In the process, the "reactionary headmen, counterrevolutionaries, and evildoing criminals would be exposed." Then the masses should be encouraged "to speak of the bitterness of the old society, speak of the bitterness of the reactionary headmen and upper-level religious figures, and speak of the bitterness of the counterrevolutionaries and evildoers. . . . [Cadres must] grasp the method of comparing the old and new society, inspire and educate the masses, . . . cause them to genuinely understand the greatness of the new society and evilness of the old society. From this we can resolutely and confidently go down the path to cooperativization."[78] Penalties meted out to those exposed through the campaign could range from fines to "reform through labor" and imprisonment. In some cases, the "blood debt" owed to the masses could even be paid by execution. Otherwise, county leaders explained, "it will not appease the indignation of the people."[79]

According to the Party-state's own statistics, prior to the rebellion there had been a total of 265 "nationality and religious upper-level figures" in Zeku County. Of these, 136 served in official capacities. Over summer 1958, 129 were taken into custody, including Lhagyel, Sërokyap, Tsintar, and Lhakba.[80] By late August, a total of 29,257 people—nearly one and a half times Zeku's entire population—reportedly had attended some 230 Speaking Bitterness meetings. At these "struggle sessions," 326 "reactionary headmen and evildoers were criticized and denounced." Subsequently, 125 would be punished "according to law," presumably meaning imprisonment, while fifty-nine were sentenced to supervised labor.[81]

As rebellion engulfed Amdo, Xining had made it clear that the region's many religious institutions should be treated with particular suspicion. Each of Zeku's fourteen monasteries was now shuttered, and at least five were destroyed. By late August, according to contemporary reports, 309 of Zeku's 744 monks (40 percent) had already "disrobed and put on trousers."[82] Ultimately, forty-two of the area's fifty-one incarnate lamas were forcibly returned to secular life, and 564 monks were made to leave the monasteries and "return home to engage in production."[83] The accuracy of the state's accounting is suspect. According to Pu Wencheng, for instance, in 1958 there were fourteen hundred monks in Zeku but only twenty-six trülku.[84] Nevertheless, the implication is clear enough.

The attacks on Zeku's Buddhist establishment mirrored those taking place across the Amdo region and beyond. In November, the NAC released instructions for dealing with Islam and "Lamaism." Awakened to the falsehoods used by imams and other Islamic leaders to protect their "feudal privileges," the directive claimed that members of the Hui masses now shouted out, "Ascending to Heaven is a lie! Exploitation is the truth!" Similarly, it asserted that Tibetans had come to understand that Buddhism did not offer a route to enlightenment but instead a path to "much bitterness, deep injustice, and great hatred." Although the directive did not directly order religious institutions emptied or destroyed, the committee recommended completely eliminating the political, economic, social, and spiritual authority of both monasteries and mosques.[85] While endorsing the NAC's instructions, central authorities cautioned that superstition still lay deeply embedded in minority communities. Therefore, Beijing instructed that "some monasteries be preserved." At these protected sites, a small parcel of land and some animals should be left so that a small number of often elderly resident monks could engage in manual labor to survive. Otherwise, monasteries should be vacated and their lands confiscated.[86] An internal CCP report claims that of the 3,269 monks in residency at the great monastery of Labrang prior to "democratic reforms," over one thousand were arrested, and another two thousand were disrobed and sent home. In the end, only eighteen "old and infirm" monks were left behind as caretakers.[87] In neighboring Linxia, a similar contemporary account asserts that nearly fifteen thousand "criminals of all types" were apprehended, including 2,757 religious figures, more than half of whom were imams. The mass consciousness of ordinary Muslims having been raised through Speaking Bitterness struggle, the report claims that members of the Hui masses had enthusiastically demolished Sufi shrines and converted mosques into canteens, storehouses, nurseries, and secular schools.[88] By the end of 1958, another source boasts, 731 of Qinghai's 859 Tibetan Buddhist monasteries had been closed and nearly half of its 54,287 monks and nuns "returned to the laity to take part in production."[89]

Reaching the Sky in a Single Step

Speaking Bitterness was not only a means to break the political authority and psychological hold of Amdo's preexisting secular and religious leadership. It also aimed to "cripple the economic foundation of the feudal class."[90] With the power of the traditional leadership broken, Qinghai's final transition to socialism at last could proceed. In place of the old system of political and economic exploitation, "the absolute dominance and political authority of the laboring peasants and pastoral masses would be established."[91] Writing in the journal *Nationality Unity* (*Minzu Tuanjie*), a commentator explained, "[Because] pastoral areas had not yet gone through a systematic process of democratic reform, the two steps of democratic revolution and socialist revolution have been combined into one." This, he added, was called "reaching the sky in a single step."[92] Where uprisings had occurred or were ongoing, cadres and security forces were told to pursue a strategy of Strike and Reform to simultaneously "implement cooperativization and completely reform the political system" by eliminating the herdlords, head-men, and monastic elites from all local governments. Where rebellion had yet to emerge, authorities were ordered to seize weapons, investigate the local situation, and prepare for armed confrontation.[93]

Back in fall 1957, Qinghai could count only forty-five basic-level pastoral production cooperatives.[94] Under the policy of Strike and Reform, by the end of May 1958, 75 percent of pastoral household in Qinghai's Hainan, Haixi, and Haibei Prefectures purportedly already had been enrolled onto 1,014 coopera-tives. On June 2, the *Qinghai Daily* declared that Hainan Prefecture had "basically achieved cooperativization."[95] One month later, Tongren County announced that its entire pastoral population had leapt over intervening stages of collectiviza-tion and been enrolled onto *high-level* cooperatives.[96] The Great Leap Forward is considered a period in which statistical reporting is particularly unreliable. Nonetheless, the clear insinuation is that pastoral collectivization was occurring at an astonishing pace.

On August 1, 1958, just shy of nine years since the PLA first had entered Qing-hai, the provincial Party committee finally ordered class labels officially extended to pastoral regions. Cadres were to divide pastoral households into four broad classes: herdlords, rich pastoralists, midlevel pastoralists, and poor pastoralists. Class status would then be determined according to wealth (calculated by the number of animals owned) and degree of exploitation (determined by a variety of factors, including the amount of paid and forced labor employed, the number of animals loaned, and the rate of interest charged). In addition, cadres were told to take an individual's pre-1949 social and political status into consideration. Regardless of current economic standing, as "representatives of the herdlord class," secular headmen and upper-level religious figures were assumed to be complicit in the maintenance of the grassland's feudal system of exploitation and therefore were defined as class enemies.[97]

Two of the Three Nos—no class struggle and no class labeling—effectively had been voided. The third—no division of property—quickly followed. In order to encourage common herdsmen "to confiscate all of the property of the reactionary herdlords and reactionary headmen," Zeku's Party committee ordered rents and obligations owed to the herdlord class immediately forgiven. To visually demonstrate that the bitterness of the past would not return, it instructed each district to gather leases and loan agreements and "burn them in front of the masses." The "expropriated and cleansed" wealth of the traditional elite would then become "the collective property of the pastoral masses." Recognizing the potential for resistance, the Party committee warned the "herdlord class" to protect their herds and not kill their animals, "otherwise punishments would be increased."[98]

By the end of August, Zeku's 19,208 residents and 692,009 head of livestock were reportedly collectivized onto sixty-four cooperatives and seven pastoral farms. By then, the county Party committee claimed that eighteen permanent settlements had been established, 1,080 enclosures constructed, 950,000 jin of grass cut, 3,697 mu of land cleared, and fifteen irrigation canals built, bringing life to 29,835 mu of grassland.[99] However, an even greater leap to collectivized production already was in the works. On September 18, 1958, in conjunction with the tidal wave of Great Leap communization then washing across China, the Qinghai Provincial Party Committee announced that the province's entire rural and pastoral populations would immediately be enrolled onto giant people's communes.[100] Three weeks later, the process was proclaimed complete. Almost overnight, Zeku's sixty-four just-established PPCs were reorganized as seven people's communes.[101] With appeasing traditional power brokers no longer a concern, the communes appropriated all of the animals of the "herdlords and headmen."[102]

Finally, on October 6, in what has been called one of Huangnan Prefecture's three "main battles" of the Amdo Rebellion, twenty-two hundred members of Zeku's Shawonar (if true, virtually the entire chiefdom) rose in open revolt.[103] Led by a trio of headmen, the Shawonar insurgents purportedly killed twenty-four cadres and captured seventy-four rifles, three machine guns, eighty-two hand grenades, 7,650 rounds of ammunition, and currency and goods worth nearly thirty thousand yuan. Among the dead was the Tibetan assistant chief of the local public security office. Perhaps reflecting the Shawonar fighters' anger over his interethnic collusion, sources note that the security officer was disemboweled, his eyes gouged out, and his hands and feet chopped off before his body was thrown into a ditch. Three days later the rebels ambushed five "armed cadres" from Tongde and twenty-seven militiamen from relatively far-off Huangzhong County, killing all but one. PLA units were quickly redispatched to the region, and several weeks and seven battles later the Shawonar insurrection was extinguished.[104]

Yet the new year brought a new round of antistate activity and military responses.[105] Midway through 1959, Chinese sources contend that thirty thousand people in over ninety rebel groups still were operating in pockets across Qinghai, most in its southern grasslands. Although details remain scarce, available materials suggest a low-level insurgency relying on decentralized command and hit-and-run tactics, punctured by occasional brazen attacks on state representatives and interests. According to a contemporary report, from January to mid-March, insurgents mounted 130 ambushes, killing or wounding twenty-five, and making off with a remarkable (if accurate) ninety thousand head of cattle and over sixty thousand jin of provisions.[106] In one instance, members of a work group sent into the Henan countryside to help develop a sheep fertility program were hacked to death in their sleep. Among those killed was the Tibetan assistant head of the local township, along with several Mongol, Tibetan, and Han cadres. Their attackers, it seems, were the Mongol militiamen sent to escort the work group through the still volatile grasslands along the Gansu-Qinghai-Sichuan frontier.[107] Otherwise, official narratives only note that through the simultaneous application of military pressure and political efforts, "bit by bit [the rebels] surrendered." Nonetheless, it was not until the latter half of 1960 that Huangnan Prefecture could be declared entirely pacified.[108] Referring to a five-year insurgency, Chinese sources admit that the Amdo Rebellion was not entirely quashed until 1962.[109]

The Pastoral Masses Become Masters of Their Own Home

By then, with few exceptions, the men (and a handful of women) who had served as intermediaries between the Party-state and Amdo's pastoral population languished in jails or labor camps. Many were already dead. Nevertheless, the demise of Amdo's United Front figures did not signal the formal end of the United Front. It would survive, albeit in fundamentally altered form. In June 1958, the Qinghai Provincial Party Committee hinted at the realignment by announcing,

"United Front work is a weapon of revolutionary struggle—this absolutely cannot be ignored. However, *it must be employed to serve the fundamental objective of socialist reform.*"[110] The following year, Yuan Renyuan, the new governor and the second-ranking official in Qinghai's Party hierarchy, rhetorically asked, "Under these circumstances, do we [still] need a United Front?"[111] His answer, simply put, was yes. The reason? Despite "democratic reforms" and collectivization, Qinghai continued to be a diverse region with an essentially feudal social system in which religious belief remained strong. In the recent past these realities had dictated that the grasslands were unprepared for socialist reforms. Now it denoted the opposite. By rebelling, the herdlord class and religious leadership had shown their true colors. Instead of objects to be won over, Amdo's traditional elite had become targets for elimination as a class. Cut loose from its original method and intent, the United Front now referred to a direct alliance between the Party and the laboring masses of minority nationalities, one consummated through the dual mechanisms of Speaking Bitterness and collectivization: "democratic reforms" and socialist transformation.

Yet remarkably, even after class struggle had been enthusiastically embraced, class labels assigned, and the wealth of the "pre-Liberation" leadership appropriated, Party communiqués occasionally continued to make passing reference to the Three Nos. Less surprising, nationality autonomy remained a stated guiding principle in Zeku County and beyond. However, no longer was the goal to make Tibetans "masters of their own home." The CCP now claimed to be leading "the *laboring pastoral masses* to become masters of their own home."[112] Policies of the past that sought an alliance with pre-1949 pastoral elites were labeled "revisionist." Those who had once championed the United Front, such as former governor Sun Zuobin, were accused of wanting to eliminate the authority of the Party and make the "headmen (herdlords) 'the commanders' with the Party only serving as 'chief of staff.'" [113] Grassroots Han cadres, for years the object of their superiors' scorn for poor work practices, ideological awareness, and political commitment, were now praised without restraint. On the other hand, criticism of Han cadres—many of whom "have not hesitated to shed their blood or sacrifice their lives"—was instead interpreted as an attempt to "destroy nationality unity and obstruct the cause of liberating the Tibetan people."[114] Reaffirming that Han chauvinism was no longer a political taboo, NAC vice chairman Xie Fumin even suggested that the Chinese language be used as an instrument of assimilation, concluding, "Whatever thinking that does not recognize the progress of the Han nationality, is unwilling to learn from the Han nationality, and does not welcome the help given by the Han nationality is entirely wrong."[115] Nationality struggle had been completely eclipsed by class struggle. The embers of empire finally seemed to have been stomped out.

EMPTY STOMACHS AND UNFORGIVABLE CRIMES

In both contemporary and secondary Chinese sources, the "democratic reforms" of 1958 are celebrated as the moment of historical rupture—the point at which Qinghai jettisoned its backward, feudal past and fully entered the modern, unified, socialist nation-state. This narrative is particularly salient for pastoral regions, where nation building was deemed most difficult, progress most protracted, and obstacles most entrenched. While the *tusi* (native chieftains) of Qinghai's agricultural regions had been administratively eliminated well before "Liberation," one retrospective account notes, "the Tibetan qianbaihu of the pastoral regions . . . did not exit history's stage until the democratic reforms after the founding of New China."[1]

Of course, this sentiment is only partially accurate. By the mid-1950s, the qianbaihu had been superseded by a system of ostensibly autonomous administrations. Yet these new institutions were formally headed by Amdo's traditional secular and religious leadership. Operating in parallel as government functionaries and through the charisma of their pre-1949 positions, these figures continued to act in subimperial fashion as the primary interface between the state and local society. Ignoring grumblings from within their own ranks, Party leaders such as Zhou Renshan had defended this arrangement in orthodox Maoist fashion by arguing that as long as nationality exploitation remained the primary contradiction, the Communist Party's United Front policies were themselves a "social reform" suited to the unique conditions of minority regions. Zhou insisted that through the careful and conscientious implementation of the principles of nationality equality and autonomy, both mass consciousness and patriotic consciousness would gradually develop. Eventually the parochial and supersti-tious attitudes that undergirded the feudal domination of tribal headmen and monastic institutions would disappear, and the masses themselves would de-mand democratic and socialist reforms. Through this process, the CCP's distinct participatory method of nation building, initiated in 1949 via the recruitment of indigenous elites, would reach maturity, and Amdo's pastoral population would be "voluntarily" and "organically" integrated into the still new People's Republic of China. In essence, the transition between empire and nation would be brought to its successful conclusion.

From the start, however, this commitment to gradualism and voluntarism was at near- constant odds with a revolutionary impatience that demanded more im-mediate paths to socialist transformation and national integration, a dialectical tension built into the internal workings of the CCP. In 1958, the contest had been decided decisively in favor of the latter. This chapter surveys the aftermath of the Amdo Rebellion and its pacification. It does not purport to provide a comprehen-sive account of Amdo under high socialism. Nor does it attempt to offer an empir-ically accurate tally of the lives lost or damage done. Extant sources simply do not allow for such undertakings at this time.[2] Instead, it aims to underscore the scale of the violence committed in 1958 and afterward and considers its impact on both the lives of Amdo Tibetans and the Chinese state's nation-building ambitions.

Displaying an Ah Q Spirit

In mid-1958, the Huangnan Prefecture Party Committee boasted, "Through Speaking Bitterness struggle, we have completely defeated feudal influences, brought about pastoral socialist reforms, and caused the laboring peasants and pastoralists to completely achieve their liberation from feudal rule."[3] Almost half a century later, the *Zeku County Gazetteer* would maintain a similarly unam-biguous position toward the elimination of the "pre-Liberation" order, declar-ing, "Economically, the establishment of the people's communes fundamentally eradicated the feudal herdlord economic system and abolished the domination of the grasslands by the herdlords and headmen. . . . Politically, it extinguished the qianbaihu hereditary system and the class oppression of the pastoralists and established the political power of the laboring people." In celebratory fashion, the gazetteer concludes, "This was an earthshaking social transformation; with the force of a thunderbolt the shackles of feudal rule were smashed."[4]

Central to this narrative is the assertion that "democratic reforms"—the elim-ination of pre-1949 political institutions—were implemented at the behest of Amdo's "laboring masses." At the height of the uprising, for example, Huangnan's

Party committee announced, "Because the political consciousness of the laboring masses has risen, the reactionaries have already been completely isolated. This truly is [a case] of being opposed by the masses and deserted by friends."[5] A provincial Party committee report released the following March maintained that since the outbreak of rebellion, thirty thousand large-scale Speaking Bitterness meetings had been held across Qinghai. At these rallies, the masses purportedly engaged in "face-to-face struggle with over five thousand reactionary counter-revolutionaries, herdlords, headmen, and religious leaders, uncovering the facts, speaking the truth, calculating debts of exploitation, digging up the roots of poverty, and recalling the past and comparing it to the present, . . . speaking aloud of a thousand years of bitterness and ten thousand years of hatred." According to the provincial committee, the masses now danced with joy, calling out, "We have smashed our leg and arm shackles, the jubilant sun rises higher and higher, the pain of the dark [past] has gone and will never return."[6]

A 1963 draft history of Huangnan Prefecture makes a similar claim. Prior to the rebellion, a folk song allegedly had spread across Zeku's grasslands. In it, herdsmen lamented their continued oppression at the hands of the herdlord class—even under the leadership of the Chinese Communist Party:

> Every day the sun shines upon us
> Yet we still feel bitterly cold
> Why is this?
> Because in the sky traces of clouds remain
> Every day Chairman Mao holds us close
> But we are still poor
> Why is this?
> Because above us the headmen still ride[7]

The draft history insisted that this verse "completely reflected the hopes of the broad masses of the laboring pastoralists to speedily cast off exploitation and oppression." Democratic reforms finally having been implemented, it proclaimed that new songs now could be heard drifting across the plateau; each expressed the masses' gratitude to the Communist Party and Mao Zedong.[8] Decades later, Chinese sources continued to insist that the Amdo Rebellion had exposed the "sharpening contradiction between the needs of common pastoralists and attempts by the herdlord class to continuously protect the feudal serf system and their feudal privileges." Using language that would seem more at place in the 1960s than the 1990s, a 1996 history of Qinghai summarizes, "The basic reason for this rebellion was the existence of class struggle."[9]

Rhetoric aside, a variety of contemporary reports paint a starkly different portrait. In the months and years following the rebellion, rather than "a vast and powerful mass movement of Speaking Bitterness struggle to completely destroy feudal rule and smash the brutal exploitation of the herdlord class,"[10] much of Amdo appears to have been enveloped in a cloud of political terror and state violence that could strike irrespective of class status or prior collusion. As early as spring 1959, in fact, Qinghai's leadership already was raising concerns over the conduct of the "bandit pacification" campaign. In May, during what turned out to be a temporary retreat from the extremes of Great Leap radicalism, the provincial Party committee warned that political efforts to win over the masses lagged behind military successes in wiping out armed resistance.[11] A policy sometimes referred to as the "Four Nos" (no struggle, no arrests, no punishment, no killing) formally forbade security forces from engaging in vigilantism and demanded that members of the masses swept up in the rebellion be treated leniently. However, rather than working to win over the masses, the Party committee charged state agents with serious violations of legal codes and Party discipline, including mass arrests and even summary executions.[12] According to Governor Yuan Renyuan, security forces often made no distinction between those who surrendered voluntarily and those who were captured in battle. Inverting a Chinese idiom, Yuan explained with purposeful irony, "All were treated equally without discrimination" (*yishi tongren*).[13] Asserting that these heavy-handed security measures were creating enemies (*shudi*) rather than allies, Yuan complained that in some places if one family member joined the rebellion, the entire household would be labeled "counterrevolutionary." As Yuan noted, this meant that upward of 80 percent of the residents of some townships had been designated enemies. In these areas, he bemoaned, "there basically are no masses left" to unite with. This, Yuan bluntly concluded, "is politically very stupid."[14] The full Party committee added that transgressions such as these swelled the ranks of the rebels, obstructed the integration of others into the new commune system, and led many Amdo Tibetans to conclude that "the words of the CCP can't be trusted."[15]

As remedy, CCP leaders insisted that members of the masses coerced or tricked into joining the uprising be separated from the real culprits: tribal headmen, religious elites, and their diehard supporters. Referring to Lu Xun's famous prideful yet bumbling literary figure, Yuan Renyuan accused "some comrades" of harboring "a bit of an Ah Q spirit." Their arrogance and self-righteousness had made them unable to see that many innocent people had been erroneously punished. While Yuan conceded that errors made during the "extreme conditions" of the rebellion were often unavoidable, he insisted that those improperly arrested—or even of questionable guilt—now be released. Notably, however, Yuan offered no sympathy to the class enemies who allegedly made up the backbone of the rebellion. Primarily alluding to members of the pre-1949 leadership, he instructed that these targets be struggled against in front of the masses and then subjected to reform through labor.[16]

Of course, mass struggle required the active participation of the masses. Yet local officials admitted having difficulty convincing ordinary commune members to publicly criticize those accused of instigating and leading the rebellion.[17] In implicit admission that the massive collectives thrown together the previous fall were experiencing significant difficulties, documents instead suggest that in many cases both cadres and commune members were more concerned with hitting elusive production quotas and obtaining enough to eat than taking part in political campaigns.[18] This was in contrast to public statements that continued to praise the accomplishments of the Great Leap Forward. Echoing the rhetoric then consuming the country, Qinghai's propaganda outlets proclaimed the construction of people's communes "a decisive victory," "a revolutionary storm," "an earthshaking change." Vice Governor Sun Junyi boasted that in 1958, the number of cattle inoculated for disease had eclipsed the prior year's total by 250 percent. Eight times more canals had been constructed than during the previous five years combined, allowing for the irrigation of nearly seven million mu (1,150,000 acres) of dry grassland. According to Sun, so much land had been cleared and so much grain planted that for the first time in history some pastoral areas had become *agriculturally* self-sufficient![19]

Despite the predictable bombast, the reality was far different. In May 1959, a provincial Party committee report criticized low quality, flagging commitment, and rampant corruption within its commune cadre force. This included accusations of mismanagement, theft, extortion, embezzlement, waste, and price fixing as well as the mistreatment of both underlings and commune members. As a result, the report warned, it was not uncommon for the masses to derisively refer to commune leaders as a new form of "qianhu and baihu."[20] Among the many charges Party leaders leveled at cadres was the continued tendency to disrespect local customs and beliefs. In particular, some considered religious practice itself a counterrevolutionary activity.[21] In June 1959, Yuan Renyuan addressed a United Front work meeting by reminding his audience that the United Front was still one of the Chinese Revolution's three "magic weapons." Alluding to overaggressive officials, he argued that religious belief and local customs not be confused for active resistance, remarking plainly, "If [Tibetan women] want to have forty braids, but we tell them they only can have two braids, and if Tibetans are unwilling to wear trousers, but we insist they wear them, what is the point? And if Muslims wear caps and long robes, and they are not troubled by the heat, why can't they? What loss is this for socialist revolution?"[22] He scolded cadres for forgetting that the freedom of religious belief was a right guaranteed in the state constitution and reminded his audience that the struggle was not against religious practice per se but against the "system of religious special privileges, exploitation, and oppression and the use of religion to instigate counterrevolution."[23] Governor Yuan insisted, "It isn't to oppose the worship of Buddha and the chanting of sutra by the masses, it isn't smashing statues and demolishing temples, and it isn't opposing certain customs and habits of the masses."[24] Confusion about these and other issues, the Party committee concluded, created anxiety among the masses and had left many Tibetans unsure which side they should be on—the Party's or the rebels'.[25]

Yet instructions flowing from Xining were steeped in contradictions. Even while top officials made a distinction between the "feudal authority of the monasteries" and the everyday religious practices of the masses, religion continued to be cast in an unambiguously negative light. In February 1960, for example, provincial leaders confirmed that by destroying the old religious power structure, "the mental outlook of the people had undergone a profound change." In one county, it asserted that 26 percent of the masses "already had renounced religious belief," while doubts had entered into the minds of more than half of the remainder. Although the Party committee reminded cadres that the policy of freedom of religious belief remained intact, it insisted that state agents also protect the freedom to *not* believe in religion.[26] More to the point, it made clear to cadres that their superiors would look favorably upon a drop in religiosity among the masses.

Unforgiveable Crimes

Putting aside the conflicting messages to which grassroots cadres and security forces were subjected, it is clear that the gulf between the CCP and the Tibetan masses it claimed to have liberated was as wide as ever. The old system had been swept off "history's stage" but not by an aroused herding masses brimming with class consciousness. Instead, it had been overthrown by a Communist Party determined to erase difference by dragging the grasslands into a singular, socialist present. Rather than an "organic transformation" in which "the old gradually weakens and the new gradually takes root," as Zhou Renshan once predicted, "democratic reform" and collectivization had been achieved through the large-scale and often indiscriminate use of violence.

Evidence of this violence is littered throughout official Chinese sources and a spattering of Tibetan eyewitness accounts. If the latter are to be believed, the PLA and auxiliary security forces responded to the rebellion with a campaign similar in tactics and cruelty to many of history's infamous counterinsurgencies. This included the widespread use of torture, extrajudicial killings, the emptying of population centers, mass incarcerations, and strategy-induced famine and epi-demics.[27] State security forces were not the only ones to commit acts of brutal-ity. One report accused the insurgents of massacring livestock, looting, arson, sabotage, and even murdering and dismembering cadres and activists (especially those from minority nationalities), concluding, "Their evil knew no bounds."[28] Nonetheless, Chinese documents tend to buttress Tibetan descriptions of the state's systematic use of violence and terror against Tibetan and other communi-ties. For instance, a telling communiqué issued by the provincial Party commit-tee complained that efforts to quell the uprising in Hainan Prefecture had been severely hampered by numerous extralegal killings of prisoners, many of them innocent of serious wrongdoing. This, in turn, sent thousands more fleeing into the grasslands to join the insurgency.[29]

Figures vary widely and should probably be valued more as indicators of scale than for their statistical accuracy, but in October 1959 Qinghai's Party commit-tee reported that in the course of 1,961 "battles," security forces "annihilated" an astonishing (and unsubstantiated) 121,752 "enemies." This included the cap-ture of 41,865 "evildoers of all types," while the remainder purportedly had been killed or fled the province.[30] Referencing a "secret Chinese military document," Lama Jabb reports that in neighboring Gannan Prefecture, 21,141 "rebels were eradicated" in 996 skirmishes fought from mid-March to mid-September 1958.[31] Jianglin Li cites a classified report produced in the early 1980s that admits that in 1958 alone, Qinghai suffered 23,260 deaths due to "*wrongful* arrest, *wrongful* ver-dicts, and collective training."[32] A subsequent internal investigation would reveal that of the over 85,000 people "punished" in 1958 for participation in the rebel-lion, 64,347 were from pastoral regions. According to this report, over 18,000 ul-timately died while jailed or in reform camps (*jixun*).[33] Figures published in 1996 (and subsequently redacted) claim that in 1958 and 1959, security forces arrested fifty-two thousand people province-wide.[34] Assuming that the vast majority of those accused of involvement in a Tibetan-centered uprising were Tibetan, more than 10 percent of Qinghai's Tibetan population may have been incarcerated and/or killed during the Amdo Rebellion and its immediate aftermath.[35] Perhaps basing his estimate on similar data sets, in 1987 the Tenth Panchen Lama sug-gested that in the wake of the uprising, 10 to 15 percent of Qinghai's Tibetan population was arrested, maybe half subsequently dying in prison.[36] Of course, many Mongols, Salar, Hui, and others were also persecuted.[37]

And these figures are distinct from the devastation wrought by the Great Leap Forward. While official narratives place the majority of blame on "three years of natural disaster," from 1959 to 1961 China suffered what many observers describe as the largest policy-induced famine in human history. In 1960, at the height of the "Great Leap Famine," Qinghai's death rate trailed only Anhui's and Guizhou's and was four times what it had been in 1957.[38] Yuan Renyuan would later recall a litany of "mistakes" that contributed to the disaster, many of them common to other parts of China. These included the diversion of labor for backyard furnaces (simple blast furnaces built in the mistaken utopian belief that they could be used to produce industrial-strength steel) and land reclamation projects, the latter being particularly wasteful given the plateau's climate and topography.

However, Yuan placed particular blame on the lightning speed by which communes were thrown together with little planning, study, or training and on a repressive political environment that assured that few dared speak up as disaster loomed. This was particularly the case after the July 1959 Lushan Conference. Convened to assess the Great Leap and presumably bring the campaign to a close, an unexpected showdown with Marshal Peng Dehuai instead led Mao to call for a second Great Leap and a second Anti-Rightist Campaign. Among those attending the conference was Qinghai's first Party secretary, Gao Feng, who immediately relayed the spirit of the proceedings back to Xining. That spring, Zhang Guosheng, a member of the provincial committee's standing committee since 1949, had returned to Xining from an inspection tour in Qinghai's countryside with tales of angry, starving peasants. Now, like former governor Sun Zuobin before him, Zhang was targeted as Qinghai's most prominent rightist. At a ten-day province-wide meeting, he was forced to make repeated self-criticisms before being removed from his posts and sent to work in a factory. Yuan Renyuan would later recall that in this toxic environment anyone attempting to curb the most radical impulses of the Great Leap or ease policies toward minorities instead fell predictably in line—himself included.[39]

The consequences would be catastrophic. At a meeting called to set 1960's production plan, county leaders competed with one another to celebrate the glories of the Great Leap Forward while setting wholly unrealistic production targets for the coming year. In reality, food was already scarce. By spring, it was running out. Villagers scrambled to live off boiled weeds and roots while cases of edema became widespread. Noting that not one of Qinghai's regions escaped the famine, Yuan later admitted that many "counterrevolutionaries" arrested for sabotaging infrastructure and "attacking the socialist system" were actually desperate people scavenging bits of food to eat and pieces of scrap metal for cooking utensils. Their own had been melted in backyard furnaces.[40] Older Tibetan and Salar villagers from Xunhua that I interviewed uniformly described famine conditions of horrific proportions. Ironically, one Salar gentleman recalled that he survived the period relatively well only because he spent it in a labor camp in the far-off Tsadam Basin.

At times, contemporary documents also describe the famine in remarkably frank if limited fashion. Rather than blaming natural disaster, these sources make clear that food shortages and starvation were primarily the consequence of state actions. This unexpected candidness was made possible by political shifts that came in the wake of the Great Leap calamity. By mid-1961, the CCP was in the throes of another rectification campaign. This time, rather than right opportunism, criticism was launched against "left deviation." Among the campaign's most prominent targets nationwide was Gao Feng, Qinghai's Party secretary since 1954. The tide had begun to turn against Gao in November 1960 when a senior official dispatched by the CCP's Northwest Bureau visited a nearly deserted village in Huangzhong County. The other villagers, he was told, had died of starvation or fled.[41] That summer, the Central Committee effectively stripped Gao of his positions atop Qinghai's Party apparatus.[42]

In Gao's place, Wang Zhao, a career soldier who since returning from Korea in 1953 had served as vice minister of public security, was transferred to Qinghai. Soon after arriving, Wang addressed a "three-level cadre conference" convened to deal with the excesses of the Great Leap.[43] In front of his gathered cadre force, Wang delivered an eviscerating summary of the prior three years. Countering his predecessor's claims that Qinghai's Great Leap had spurred a rapid increase in production, Wang insisted that "leftist mistakes" under Gao Feng's "dictatorial" leadership had proven disastrous. Production had plummeted. Rather than achieving self-sufficiency, the grain situation had become desperate. Secretary Wang did not mince words: "Many people have died, births have dropped considerably, people are thin, the land is barren, and the situation with animal births is even more severe. This has seriously damaged productive forces. The people have suffered greatly, and nationality relations have become strained."[44] According to Wang, desperate rural residents had flooded into towns and cities, further damaging both agricultural and pastoral production. He also denounced the forced settlement of pastoral populations and the seizure of their animals as well as the 1959 campaign to clear grasslands for agricultural use—the same campaign that had brought the ill-fated Henan youth brigade to Zeku County— saying that it had hurt the economy by diverting agricultural resources while "destroying the grasslands."[45]

Overall, Wang charged that a "Communist wind" had infected Qinghai.[46] Strike and Reform, Wang now insisted, had referred only to the implementation of "democratic reforms," *not* to collectivization. In the mistaken rush to achieve democratic reforms and collectivize simultaneously—to reach the sky in a single step—Wang asserted that objective conditions had been ignored and minority policy disregarded. In the process, officials paid little attention to the unique conditions of pastoral regions, most of which had not even been organized into basic-level cooperatives before the establishment in quick succession of high-level cooperatives and people's communes. This had led to confusion and mismanagement and had ultimately damaged production.[47] During the previous moment of relative moderation in spring 1959, a report had bluntly admitted that since the previous fall, 25 percent of the population of a township in Xinghai County had died from lack of food. Choosing the threat of execution over the near certainty of starvation, many survivors had fled and joined the "bandits."[48] The final communiqué of the three-level cadre conference now added the remarkable admission that over the past three years, nearly *10 percent* of the province's population had perished while livestock numbers had been reduced by one half.[49]

Wang Zhao's attacks on Gao Feng's leadership were not limited to mistakes implementing collectivization. During the post-Lushan period, Qinghai's Party committee had offered a full-throated endorsement of the rebellion pacification campaign. At the time, those who claimed security forces had "gone too far" and accused soldiers of "entering with white swords and leaving with red swords" were labeled rightists "taking the herdlord class position."[50] Like Yuan Renyuan back in early 1959, Wang Zhao now criticized the antirebellion efforts for favoring purely military solutions while ignoring political outreach. Adding that state agents had committed "unforgivable crimes," Wang announced, "Under this type of mistaken leadership, some units and local work teams killed prisoners at will."[51] The final report from the three-level cadre conference charged that over the three years since the start of the rebellion, over 68,000 people had been arrested.[52] Forty years later, the editors of an official history of Qinghai reported that during the nearly five-year conflict, 16,690 "enemies" were killed in battle, 4,876 injured, 46,831 captured, and nearly 59,000 surrendered. It added that security forces suffered over 3,000 casualties, including 1,515 killed in action.[53]

Never Forget Class Struggle!

The policy shift that led to the end of the Great Leap (and Wang Zhao's appointment), included a broad pledge of support for the United Front, so much so that Gerry Groot refers to the period as a "Second Hundred Flowers."[54] In Qinghai, where the United Front primarily referred to nationality and religious policy, these changes were hinted at during a March 1961 meeting of the provincial United Front Work Department. While still extolling the "glorious" accomplishments of the previous three years, the conference's summary report pointed to "not a few serious mistakes" in minority and United Front work. With representatives of the national-level UFWD and the Northwest Bureau in attendance, Party leaders charged that under a cloud of Han chauvinism, cadres had ignored the special conditions of minority regions, disrespected local customs and beliefs, and prohibited religious practice. Suddenly "gradualism" and "voluntarism," absent from CCP rhetoric since the start of the Great Leap, returned. Science rather than coercion was proclaimed the best way to combat religious superstition. Alluding to cultural violence committed against Muslims during the Great Leap, Party leaders insisted that Hui and Salar not be made to raise pigs unless they "truly" wished to. Where halal dining halls had been abolished, they ordered them restored. The report added that the de facto proscription of religious practice had simply sent it underground. By then, only thirteen of the province's 1,698 "lama temples and Islamic mosques" remained open. By reopening select monasteries and mosques, not only would religion be brought back into the daylight, but it could also be better supervised and regulated. Likewise, by bringing minority elites back into the fold, the UFWD suggested that they could more easily be reformed through education.[55] Soon afterward, the guilty verdicts of many Party members toppled during the two Anti-Rightist Campaigns—including Zhang Guosheng—were reversed.

Of course, what mattered most to Wang Zhao (other than denouncing his predecessor) was the negative effects these actions and policies had on production, ending the insurrection—which, while in its last throes, was still ongoing—and ultimately on consolidating nationality unity. At that summer's three-level cadre conference, Wang took issue with the assimilationist sentiments promoted during the Great Leap by the likes of Xie Fumin that had privileged Han customs over minority customs. Wang once again noted that in Qinghai, minority cadres regularly found themselves victims of their Han colleagues' discrimination, exclusion, and punishment. As a result, over the past three years the percentage of non-Han cadres in Qinghai had dropped from 15 percent to 8 percent. Despite policies that ostensibly protected freedom of religious belief, Wang accused Gao Feng of implementing a program to "wipe out" monasteries, charging, "Temples have been demolished, Buddha images destroyed, scriptures burned, monks defrocked, and the masses forced to disavow their faith." "All of this," Wang understatedly reasoned, "had seriously damaged nationality unity, harmed nationality sentiment, and severely stressed nationality relations."[56] Now officials reopened 137 monasteries and 153 mosques, albeit at levels of activity far below what they enjoyed prior to 1958.[57]

Finally, Wang bemoaned the treatment of Qinghai's United Front leaders, most of whom, he admitted, had been deposed and sent for reeducation through labor.[58] The final communiqué of Qinghai's three-level cadres conference confirmed that nearly 70 percent of the province's "upper-level nationality and religious figures" had been taken into custody during the pacification of the rebellion, adding that many should not have been arrested.[59] Circumstantial evidence suggests that this tally may be low. A quick glance through the local gazetteers and similar sources from across Qinghai shows an extraordinary number of prominent figures incarcerated in 1958. Many would not survive.

By mid-1961, the Great Leap Forward was in full retreat. Along with reintroducing limited market incentives, Beijing belatedly responded to the famine by ordering reductions to the size of communes and the decentralization of their management and control over resources.[60] In line with these instructions, Qinghai's leadership declared that pastoral communes should be scaled back, agricultural land reclamation efforts halted, and limited private ownership of animals allowed, among other reforms to commune organization, management, and allocation systems. Ideally each administrative unit once again should correspond to a natural community, such as a tsowa or herding group. In particularly devastated areas, a devolution to cooperatives or even MATs was possible.[61] In Zeku, what were then six people's communes were reorganized as seven xiang-level administrations that largely mimicked the pre–Great Leap districts. Under the xiang, day-to-day operations were delegated to fifty-three lower-level communes (gongshe).[62] Significantly, the benchmarks for assigning class labels also were reworked so as to reduce the number of households designated "herdlord" and "rich herder."[63] According to an internal report, across Qinghai more than twenty-four thousand prisoners were released, included many members of Amdo's pre-1949 elite.[64] Others, however, would languish in jails and labor camps for a decade or more. Many would die in prison, inevitably of unspecified illness.

Of the men accused of being the backbone of the rebellion in the Repgong region—the Seventh Shartsang Lama Lozang Trinlé Lungtok Gyatso, Zongqianhu Gyelwo Dorjé, and the Rongwo nangso Trashi Namgyel—only Trashi Namgyel would survive to tell his own story. As the uprising spread from Gannan Prefecture to Qinghai in early 1958, members of the Gyelwo chiefdom joined the insurrection. In June, Gyelwo Dorjé was taken into custody. He died a full eighteen years later while still incarcerated.[65] According to Mark Stevenson, the cause was "complications (probably pneumonia) resulting from mistreatment during political campaigns."[66] The Seventh Shartsang Lama fared no better. Despite purportedly releasing two letters in early 1958 pleading with Repgong's population not to rebel, he was accused of personally instigating the uprising, his monastery serving as its regional "headquarters."[67] Like Gyelwo Dorjé, the Shartsang Lama spent his last two decades in prison, finally passing away in November 1978.[68] Trashi Namgyel's post-1958 fate is less clear. He was also arrested in June 1958. However, Qinghai's provincial gazetteer simply states that in 1959 he was wrongly punished, adding that throughout his ordeal the last Rongwo nangso never lost his faith in the Party.[69]

As rebellion engulfed Xunhua in March 1958, members of Wangchen Döndrup's Nangra chiefdom joined the insurrection. The Nangra chieftain had survived conflicts with Ma Bufang's Xining regime in the 1930s and again in the early 1950s against the CCP, each time managing to leverage his position and prestige to carve out space for himself within the new order. This time was different. Despite having not personally participated in the 1958 rebellion, Wangchen Döndrup was quickly arrested and stripped of his positions atop the Jianzha County government. Although released a few months later, the Nangra chieftain died the following March, reportedly from illness. He was fifty-five.[70] If in life Wangchen Döndrup represents the struggle to preserve imperial space within the shrinking confines of the modern, consolidated state, his death, symbolically at least, marks the closure of that space and the forced integration of the Tibetan Plateau into the People's Republic of China.

Among those imprisoned in Zeku that fateful summer was the Gartsé qianhu Lubum, the Gönshül qianhu Serökyap, and the Shawonar baihu Lhakba. By autumn of the following year, both Serökyap and Lhakba were dead. In September 1958, Jikmé Sönam, the Hor Monastery lama and nephew of Wagya and Lhagyel, was also taken into custody. By the following winter, he also had passed away of an unspecified illness while jailed, as had the Logyatsang Lama and at least one other Hor monastery trülku.[71] Lubum remained imprisoned until 1967, when he was released for medical treatment. Soon afterward, he, too, succumbed to his ailments.[72]

While not all members of Zeku's United Front leadership perished in prison (or soon after their release), seemingly all were deposed and incarcerated.

FIGURE 7.   Memorial to Wangchen Döndrup at his manor house in Nangra. Photograph by and courtesy of Gerald Roche.

Countywide, 854 people were officially labeled members of the "five black categories": 379 *herdlords*, 303 *rich peasants*, 103 *counterrevolutionaries*, and 69 *evil-doers*.[73] During the Second Hundred Flowers, 673 "nationality cadres, members of the masses, and religious figures" were rehabilitated. Echoing province-wide patterns, five monasteries were reopened, and eighty-seven monks allowed to reenter these monasteries. Simultaneously, twenty-two members of the old monastic and secular leadership were brought back into prefectural and county-level positions.[74]

Like its predecessor, however, this Second Hundred Flowers quickly wilted.[75] In September 1962, a resurgent Mao struck back against what he saw as revisionism within the Party. Exhorting his colleagues to "never forget class struggle," Mao proclaimed expression of local nationalism tantamount to class struggle. During the preceding period of relative openness, the Tenth Panchen Lama had submitted his famous "70,000-Character Petition" to central authorities. Based on travels to Amdo during the height of the Great Leap, it warned of widespread starvation and complained of mass arrests, religious persecution, cultural suppression, and a complete absence of genuine autonomy. At the time, senior leaders, including Zhou Enlai, Li Weihan, and Xi Zhongxun, praised the petition. Now Mao denounced it as a "poisoned arrow aimed at the heart of the Party." The Tenth Panchen Lama would spend the next fourteen years in various states of incarceration.[76] The UFWD quickly came under attack for "class capitulationism," and soon afterward its longtime director, Li Weihan, was dismissed from office. A year later, Mao effectively ended the long-simmering debate over the orthodoxy of allying with minority elites to combat the legacy of Han chauvinism by insisting, "In the final analysis, a national struggle is a question of class struggle." As both an administrative policy and philosophy of nation building, the United Front had been dismantled.[77]

Under these conditions, it is unsurprising that during subsequent political campaigns, many of Amdo's recently rehabilitated figures became targets anew. Among them was Lhagyel. After being seized during the first wave of arrests, the Hor baihu and Nyingma trülku was released in 1961. The following year, he was reappointed a county vice secretary. However, during the Cultural Revolution, Lhagyel was again branded a counterrevolutionary and subjected to criticism and struggle.[78] Despite being in the provincial capital when the rebellion broke out, the Méshül "monk official" Tsintar was labeled a counterrevolutionary and arrested. Three years later, he released and subsequently given a position in the Zeku County government. However, in 1964, during the Four Cleanups Campaign, Tsintar was "sent down to the countryside to do manual labor." Then, during the Cultural Revolution, he was again "persecuted and made to reform through labor." Tsintar would pass away at home in 1974.[79]

Alone among Zeku's headmen-cum–county leaders, Wagya weathered the initial storm of arrests. In recognition of his purported aid in limiting the spread of the rebellion within his Hor chiefdom, in 1959 the provincial Party committee even awarded Wagya a banner of commendation and appointed him acting head of Huangnan Prefecture. However, not even Wagya—for decades the Zeku region's most prominent Tibetan figure—could escape the spiraling circle of violence indefinitely. In November, he, too, was arrested. When he was released four years later, Wagya was returned to his Hor territories not as headman or county leader but to do "supervised manual labor" on a production team. During the Cultural Revolution, Wagya was labeled a member of the "black categories" and like so many others subjected to criticism and struggle.[80]

One of Amdo's few pre-1949 leaders to maintain both his position and freedom in the aftermath of the rebellion was the Shartsang Lama's younger brother, Gélek Gyatso.[81] The former steward of Rongwo Monastery, who several years earlier had renounced his vows and applied for membership in the CCP, continued to serve as a vice chairman of the Huangnan Prefecture Committee until November 1965. A month earlier, he finally was implicated in the 1958 rebellion. At the height of the Cultural Revolution, the military detained Gélek Gyatso as "protective action." He passed away two years later at the age of forty-nine. Although he ostensibly died from natural causes, in the context of the Cultural Revolution and his later posthumous rehabilitation, it seems likely that Gélek Gyatso, too, became a permanent victim of the revolution.[82]

From Counterrevolutionaries to Patriots

Most victims of the violence committed in Amdo under names such as "democratic reforms," "socialist construction," and "bandit pacification" remain nameless—at least to outsiders. By contrast, we know about the plights of many prominent figures primarily because they have been recorded in state-sponsored histories. The irony is that they are included in these volumes not because of the counterrevolutionary crimes for which they had been punished but because each was ultimately cleared of culpability, politically rehabilitated, and reaffirmed as a "patriotic democratic figure" or "patriotic religious figure." For the vast majority, this process would take two decades or longer. In 1977, Wagya became the first of Huangnan's United Front figures to be exonerated. Soon afterward, his brother Lhagyel also reappeared. Both Hor headmen would go on to accept symbolically important sinecures on prefectural and provincial consultative bodies. Lhagyel died in 1986. Wagya, who had become qianhu of the Hor chiefdom in 1932, passed away in 1995 at the age of ninety-one.[83]

FIGURE 8.   Hor qianhu Wagya in his later years. Photograph est. 1980s, photographer unknown.

The wholesale reversal of the 1958 verdicts did not begin until after December 1978's Third Plenum of the Eleventh Chinese Communist Party Committee—the event that has come to signal the dawn of Deng Xiaoping's Reform Era. At the plenum, the Maoist theory of permanent revolution was officially repudiated, and economic development replaced class struggle as the CCP's raison d'être. Soon afterward, Party leaders began the task of rehabilitating those purged and ostracized during two decades of high socialism. These tasks were intimately connected. Martin Fromm notes that in the immediate post-Mao period, the CCP faced a crisis of confidence that "required that the new leadership define itself against the previous Maoist policies of radical socialism while re-affirming the Communist Party's uninterrupted historical continuity as national libera-tor."[84] In other words, Party leaders needed to heal the wounds of a deeply scarred country while simultaneously shoring up the legitimacy of the post-Mao regime. Most famously, Mao's successors declared the Cultural Revolution to have been a great catastrophe responsible for "the most severe setback and the heaviest losses suffered by the Party, the state, and the people since the founding of the People's Republic."[85] Simultaneously, the vast majority of participants were absolved from blame, as was the Party. In their place, a small number of evil schemers, collec-tively referred to as the Gang of Four, have been assigned responsibility for the society-wide crimes of the period.

To those paying attention, it quickly became apparent that the seismic changes in the CCP's leadership and political orientation introduced at the Third Plenum would directly affect minority policy. The focus had turned from class struggle, which had alienated a large portion of China's population, to an inclusive proj-ect of national reconciliation and economic development. This necessitated a renewed commitment to the United Front. In February 1979, charges against the UFWD for "capitulationism" in minority and religious affairs work, first leveled by Mao in 1962 and then pursued ferociously during the Cultural Revolution, were unconditionally repudiated.[86] Then that summer, Deng Xiaoping delivered a speech to the People's Consultative Conference—the organ tasked with liais-ing between the CCP and non-Party elements—explicitly endorsing the United Front. While Deng avoided directly confronting the circumstances that had led to the United Front's downfall, he argued that a "pathway of words" (*yanlu*) now needed to be reopened and a "pathway of talent" (*cailu*) nourished. The time of "seizing on shortcomings, assigning political labels, and ruthlessly criticizing" was over. Past mistakes, Deng told his presumably receptive audience, "must quickly be discovered and corrected."[87]

Of course, the United Front did not only refer to nationality affairs. For most Party leaders, the primary impetus was reintegrating intellectuals, scien-tists, educators, and entrepreneurs, including overseas Chinese. As suggested by

Fromm, these were the same constituencies Deng Xiaoping's regime desperately needed to attract to aid the reconstruction and modernization of the economy.[88] However, there was also a general recognition that policies pursued since the Anti-Rightist Campaign had severely damaged both internationality relations and relations between minority communities and the CCP. Over the next several months and years, Beijing issued a flurry of policy statements and directives that at least rhetorically harked back to the heyday of the United Front in nationality work. In September 1979, for example, the Central Committee approved a resolution calling for a renewed fidelity to nationality equality and a recommitment to the stipulations of nationality autonomy. The latter had been largely gutted in the state constitution of 1975. Reviving past warnings over the hazardous effects of Han chauvinism on nationality unity, the resolution demanded cadres demonstrate respect for local languages, cultures, and religious beliefs. Insisting that particular attention be paid to "patriotic nationality and religious upper strata," Party leaders stressed the importance of the political reintegration of pre-1949 minority elites. Sidestepping the fact that the persecution of United Front figures had begun not during the Cultural Revolution but during the Anti-Rightist Campaign under the watch of Deng Xiaoping himself, the resolution added that only by following these guidelines "can the destruction caused by the meddling of Lin Biao and the 'Gang of Four' be gradually eliminated" and "the rift created between nationalities" be bridged.[89] That same month, the Central Committee ordered the removal of "political hats" for all those previously labeled "local nationalists," a designation specific to minority peoples.[90]

Public notice that the pendulum on minority policy was reversing course arrived at the start of 1980. The New Year's Day edition of the Party journal *Red Flag (Hongqi)* included a speech delivered by deceased premier Zhou Enlai at the NAC's 1957 Qingdao Conference. This was the same conference at which local nationalism had first come under concerted attack by Deng Xiaoping and others. Zhou's speech, however, vigorously defended the institution of nationality autonomy and called for local "customs and habits," including freedom of religious belief, to be respected.[91] The implications for the present were unmistakable. This was followed in July by a lengthy editorial in the *People's Daily* calling for the "indigenization" (*minzuhua*) of nationality autonomous regions. Written by Ulanhu, the Mongol politburo member and director of the reconstituted UFWD, it insisted that Mao's 1963 formula equating nationality struggle with class struggle had led many non-Han cadres, intellectuals, and elites to be erroneously treated as class enemies.[92] The following day, the paper ran a second editorial explicitly repudiating Mao's 1963 thesis. Concluding that "confusing the two types of questions was 100 percent harmful," the authors effectively elevated nationality above class as an inherently meaningful category of identity and source of historical exploitation.[93] In 1982, an amended state constitution restored many of rights associated with nationality autonomy that ethnic minorities had been promised three decades earlier.[94]

The first public indication that the new political environment had filtered down to Amdo came in a 1979 special edition of the *Qinghai Daily*. By that time, Zhang Guosheng, purged in 1959 and again during the Cultural Revolution, had been appointed first Party secretary and governor of Qinghai. In commemoration of the province's thirtieth anniversary, the paper included two editorials praising the 1950s United Front. Penned by two of the most senior members of Qinghai's 1950s leadership, Liao Hansheng and Zhang Zhongliang (Qinghai's first military governor and civilian governor, respectively), they celebrated the United Front era as a time of ethnic reconciliation and economic development disrupted by the Cultural Revolution. Neither made mention of the Amdo Rebellion or its brutal pacification. Instead, clearly looking toward the future as much as the past, Zhang Zhongliang noted the benefits gained through working with Qinghai's indigenous United Front leadership, recalling, "On many important questions, we first consulted with the elites of each nationality and were then able to satisfy [the masses of] each nationality." Reviving Zhou Renshan's long-ago prediction, he even cited the Three Nos as a key component in a strategy that enabled Qinghai's economy to grow, raised living standards, and purportedly strengthened nationality unity.[95] Not coincidentally, these were also stated goals of the post-Mao leadership.

In quick succession, virtually all of Qinghai's prominent United Front figures had their counterrevolutionary "hats" removed. Like Wagya and Lhagyel, many subsequently received postings on various consultative bodies, their presence serving as a conspicuous testament to the end of the Maoist era.[96] Of course, many others had to be rehabilitated posthumously. In Huangnan, the most visible evidence that the political winds had shifted was a special memorial held in October 1980 to commemorate the lives of the Seventh Shartsang Lama Lozang Trinlé Lungtok Gyatso, his brother Gélek Gyatso, and Zongqianhu Gyelwo Dorjé. In front of invited guests, the new prefectural Party secretary, Trashi Nyingma, eulogized the trio as "celebrated patriots" who "ardently loved the fatherland, supported the Chinese Communist Party, and supported socialism." Using the opportunity as both an entreaty to let bygones be bygones and a reendorsement of the United Front, he urged "patriotic people of all classes and all nationalities" to "turn your sorrow into strength" and to use the examples of these fallen United Front figures to reinforce the "inseparably close unity of the nationalities."[97] Such valorization was not limited to Repgong's former "feudal" leadership. With a stroke of a pen, most members of Amdo's pre-1949 elite were turned from "counterrevolutionaries" back into "patriotic nationality and patriotic religious figures." Ever since, they have been immortalized as embodiments of nationality unity—the United Front as it was dreamed up, not as it played out.[98]

Yet even while individual elites were being exonerated and celebrated, in Qinghai there was significant resistance to the *mass* rehabilitation of those accused of participating in the Amdo Rebellion. According to the since-exiled abbot of Kumbum Monastery, the Eighth Arjia (Agya) Rinpoché, local cadres were particularly reticent. After all, the wholesale reassessment of Amdo 1958 was inimical to the interests of those who had risen through the ranks in its wake. Many not only had taken part in the antirebellion efforts but also had presumably built their careers upon its wreckage.[99]

Multiple sources credit Trashi Wangchuk for breaking the impasse. Originally from Kham, in the 1930s he had become one of the first Tibetans to join the CCP. After 1949, Trashi Wangchuk served in several senior positions within Qinghai's Party and government. In 1959, he came under criticism for raising doubts about the pastoral collectivization drive and Gao Feng's prosecution of the antirebellion campaign. He later became embroiled in the charges against the UFWD and its director, Li Weihan. In both cases, Trashi Wangchuk managed to wait out the storm in Beijing under the protection of Premier Zhou Enlai. During the Cultural Revolution, he was not so fortunate. Trashi Wangchuk was purged as a "capitalist running dog" and "local nationalist," made to endure multiple struggle sessions, and sent to toil in labor camps in China's northeast.[100] After his own rehabilitation in 1979—and immediate reappointment as Party vice secretary and vice governor of Qinghai Province—Trashi Wangchuk used his nearly unparalleled revolutionary pedigree and extensive personal relationships to lobby for reconsideration of the verdict on the Amdo Rebellion. Keying on the theme of repairing the Party's legitimacy, he advised central leaders that unless "rebellion pacification" (*pingpan*) became "rehabilitation" (*pingfan*), "it will not be possible to restore the Party's reputation" among Amdo Tibetans. Reportedly, local obstruction was only overcome after Trashi Wangchuk enlisted the personal support of Deng Xiaoping. Through this intercession, Trashi Wangchuk and his supporters eventually gained access to local archives. What they found purportedly shocked even them.[101]

On March 12, 1981, Trashi Wangchuk was able to present his findings to a committee headed by Hu Yaobang, soon to be the new chairman of the CCP. A week later, the Qinghai Provincial Committee sent Beijing its own "Report on the Question of the Aftereffects of the Expansion of the Pacification of Qinghai's 1958 Rebellion." Approving the report in late March, the CCP's Central Committee ordered local officials in Qinghai to reassess individual verdicts related to the rebellion. As situations dictated, those exonerated (or their heirs) were to be provided with appropriate compensation and assistance.[102] In June, Qinghai's highest court ordered the release of all those still jailed in connection with the 1958 Amdo Rebellion.[103] Ultimately provincial authorities determined that of the more than fifty-two thousand people (officially) arrested for counterrevolutionary activity, an astounding forty-four thousand (84 percent) had been either wrongly incarcerated or were of unproven culpability.[104] Other accounts suggest that the number of people "punished" and the percentage of those eventually cleared were both considerably higher.[105]

A history of Qinghai provides two explanations for the state's overzealous response to the rebellion. First, employing orthodox Maoist discourse, "mistaken methods" are blamed for mixing up contradictions among the people (deemed nonantagonistic) and contradictions between the people and the enemy (counterrevolutionary). In other words, nationality struggle had been mistaken for class struggle, an explanation that fit squarely in line with the Dengist regime's repudiation of class struggle in favor of national(ity) unity. Second and more surprisingly, the authors admit that in some areas a desire for revenge among cadres and soldiers played a significant role in magnifying the violence. This led to "serious violations of policy," including the summary execution of prisoners—a remarkable admission to be found in a state-published history, even one subsequently removed from circulation.[106]

By invoking the need to rescue the CCP's reputation through revisiting the verdicts on the Amdo Rebellion, Trashi Wangchuk was co-opting a narrative that already enjoyed great appeal within the Dengist leadership. Likewise, in citing the crimes of Lin Biao and the Gang of Four, advocates were able to frame their support for the United Front, nationality autonomy, and political rehabilitation within one of the dominant discourses of the early Reform Era.[107] As the 1980s wore on, leading nationality affairs figures, including former United Front director Li Weihan, Ulanhu, and the Tenth Panchen Lama—all now fully exonerated—regularly leveraged the "ultraleftist errors" of the Cultural Revolution to advocate for more liberal minority policies and practices, including the reconstruction and repopulation of monastic institutions.[108]

Notwithstanding the dogged heroics of Trashi Wangchuk, in actuality neither the verdict on the Amdo Rebellion nor its pacification have been reversed. Instead, what the Party has repudiated and in theory redressed are "mistakes made during the '*expansion*' of the pacification struggle" (*pigxi douzhan zhongde "guandahua" cuowu*).[109] Despite the CCP having absolved the vast majority of alleged participants, the Amdo Rebellion continues to be considered an "armed counterrevolutionary rebellion" planned and instigated by "each tribes' qianhu, baihu, and the leading monks of the monasteries" in order to protect their economic interests and political authority.[110] Thus, the contributors to the state-sponsored *Brief History of Contemporary Qinghai* conclude, "Pacification was absolutely necessary and correct."[111] Yet in the post-Mao period, the vast majority of Amdo's pre-1949 monastic leaders and secular headmen not only have been cleared of wrongdoing but also have been commemorated (often posthumously) as "patriotic religious figures" and "patriotic nationality figures." Rather than being reviled as members of the "nationality ruling class" or as "counterrevolutionaries," people such as the Seventh Shartsang Lama, Gélek Gyatso, Gyelwo Dorjé, Wagya, Wangchen Dön-drup, and many others are instead celebrated as great patriots who helped over-come years of internationality enmity and cement the unity of the nationalities.

What is left are two offsetting crimes—the rebellion itself and transgressions committed during its pacification—a verdict that has generated many victims but almost no perpetrators; one that led to mass rehabilitation but no account-ability. Most importantly, it does little to resolve the central problem that prior to 1958 vexed Qinghai's Party establishment: how to convince its non-Chinese population of their membership in a multinational, socialist (now postsocialist), Han-dominated political community. It is far from clear that the CCP's 1950s United Front strategy of gradual, voluntary, and organic transformation could have ultimately succeeded, particularly when subject to Leninist-Maoist struc-tural pressures. As argued in the conclusion of this book, however, the violence of 1958 severed the Party's own tenuous narrative of national integration, its discursive mechanism for transforming a loose constellation of imperial subjects into an integral national body.

AMDO AND THE END OF EMPIRE?

The 1958 Amdo Rebellion and its violent aftermath were events unprecedented in Amdo's history. Perhaps the only near-equivalent is the scorched-earth violence that accompanied the Qing defeat of the Lubsang-Danzin Rebellion in 1723 and the final incorporation of Amdo into the Manchu Empire.[1] Françoise Robin refers to 1958 as an "epochal moment," and Charlene Makley as "world shattering" and "the point of historical rupture."[2] In his memoir, Naktsang Nulo only encounters the Chinese state in 1958, a year he refers to as *dülok*, or the "the turnaround of times,"[3] the moment "the earth and the sky were turned upside down."[4] According-ing to Fernanda Pirie, this is not unusual. For many pastoral Tibetans, 1958—not 1949—was "the year the Chinese came" to Amdo's grasslands.[5] So cataclysmic were the events of that year, Lama Jabb writes, "in Amdo parlance, it came to be simply known as *nga brgyad lo*, the Year of '58."[6] Additional descriptors are unnecessary.

Despite its unparalleled impact on Amdo's social, political, and economic structures—not to mention the individual lives, communities, and collective memory of Amdo Tibetans—Robin notes, "Amdo '58 has not been the object of much substantial historical research or public discussion, either in Tibet, in China, among exiles or in the West."[7] It has instead been overshadowed by up-risings centered first in Kham (1955–57) and then Central Tibet (1959), which over the second half of the 1950s set the Tibetan Plateau ablaze. Commentators have ascribed the etiologies of the Khampa and Lhasa uprisings to the different terms under which each region was initially incorporated into the PRC.[8] When during the second half of 1949 the People's Liberation Army took over Kham, as in Amdo it did so through a combination of overwhelming military might and negotiation with a myriad of local power holders of various sizes, compositions, and strengths. By contrast, Communist soldiers only marched into Lhasa in September 1951 after securing a formal written agreement with the Dalai Lama's Ganden Podrang government.

Much has been made of the legality of the Seventeen-Point Agreement for the Peaceful Liberation of Tibet (hereafter the Seventeen-Point Agreement)— whether or not it was signed under duress, for example, or whether the Tibetan negotiators were authorized to finalize the accord.[9] These questions notwithstanding, the Seventeen-Point Agreement explicitly recognized the legitimacy of the Dalai Lama and his government and promised that the region's existing political, economic, and religious systems would not be altered until "the people raise demands for reforms" and "by means of consultation with the leading personnel of Tibet."[10] As is often noted, however, the provisions of the Seventeen-Point Agreement only applied to Central Tibet or, more specifically, the areas in which the Dalai Lama's government had exercised control during the decades of "de facto independence" that followed the fall of the Qing Empire. Most of Kham and all of Amdo, therefore, were not party to the accord.

The scholarly consensus concedes that in Central Tibet, the Chinese Communist Party generally abided by the broad promises made in the Seventeen-Point Agreement—at least initially. Unhampered by a written accord, however, "democratic" and socialist reforms were introduced into Kham starting in 1955. The reforms, which included the collectivization of monastic landholdings and attacks on their political authority, soon triggered armed resistance among the notoriously independent-minded and martial-spirited Khampas. Heavy fighting subsequently led both Tibetan insurgents and refugees to flee into Central Tibet pursued by the PLA, setting off a series of events that in March 1959 culminated in a spontaneous popular uprising in Lhasa followed by the Fourteenth Dalai Lama's flight into what increasingly appears to be permanent Indian exile.

It is certainly true that the Seventeen-Point Agreement did not shield Kham and Amdo from political or social reforms. It is also true that it was in Central Tibet alone that the CCP signed a formal written compact with an existing government of a non-Han people.[11] Less noticed, however, is that despite Kham and Amdo being divided among four Chinese provinces, both United Front promises and the constitutional stipulations of nationality autonomy and equality offered eastern Tibetans many of the same protections accorded in the Seventeen-Point Agreement. These guarantees were most explicitly stated in pastoral areas where the Three Nos promised that the political and economic position of the pastoral elite would not be altered, at least not for the foreseeable future. And while pre-1949 indigenous political structures in Kham and Amdo were not given official recognition in the same sense that they were in Central Tibet, many secular and religious power holders in both regions were incorporated into the new adminis- tration, often occupying familiar positions as intermediaries between local com- munities and the state even as they acquired new bureaucratic titles and responsi- bilities alongside their traditional roles—what I have referred to as a subimperial strategy of state and nation building.

Most significantly, neither in Central nor eastern Tibet was the status quo meant to be permanent. Instead, the CCP was convinced that historical condi- tions required a transitional period during which time the masses of Tibetans (and other minority nationalities) would voluntarily shed previous political and economic arrangements in favor of membership in the new socialist, multina- tionality state. In fact, Melvyn Goldstein has recently argued that the introduc- tion of reforms into Kham in 1955 cannot simply be chalked up to a lack of writ- ten assurances. Instead, rogue Party and military officials in Sichuan imposed the reforms *against* the express orders of Beijing.[12] Just as the Lhasa Rebellion and the flight of the Dalai Lama into exile in March 1959 would officially void the Seventeen-Point Agreement, the Amdo Rebellion and the subsequent Speaking Bitterness campaign effectively nullified what for all intents and purposes had served as the subimperial compact between Amdo's indigenous leadership and the Party-state.

Although the United Front had been a core element of the Party's revolution- ary program almost from its start, most observers have described it either as an elaborate ruse or a clumsy cudgel—an illusion conjured up by the CCP to trick members of non-Han communities into cooperating with the new authorities or empty rhetoric serving as halfhearted cover for domination by the overwhelm- ingly Han Chinese Communist Party. In this book I have tried to tread a more nuanced path. In Amdo, I argue that the United Front was a primary component of how the Party understood its own relationship to non-Chinese communities, which it considered to be estranged members of a historical multinational China. It served as the CCP's institutional ethos in places like Amdo, in the sense that the United Front was manifested within the spirit, culture, and practices of the *in- stitution* of the CCP during the 1950s. This does not imply that it was a sincerely held *belief* of individual cadres, whether in Xining or those sent into the county seats, villages, and grasslands of Amdo. On the contrary, the nearly constant criti- cism leveled at grassroots cadres for their failure to live up to the principles of the United Front suggests considerable resistance to its central tenets. It is unclear whether that resistance most often was based on principled opposition to policies that seemed to protect and even elevate a host of class enemies or a more quotid- ian struggle to survive and thrive in what for many seemed a hostile physical, cul- tural, and professional environment. On the other hand, although tested in the face of widespread rebellion in the early 1950s, challenged during the High Tide of Socialist Transformation, and open to repudiation during the Anti-Rightist Campaign, the United Front in Qinghai survived for almost a decade. That the rhetoric of the United Front was still regularly employed even after the Amdo Rebellion had been effectively extinguished, Amdo's "pre-Liberation" leadership toppled, and socialist reforms implemented serves as testament to the strength of the United Front ethos, even if in practice by mid-1958 it had become divorced from its original intent and process.

As I hope to have impressed, none of this is trivial. Instead it reveals the vision the CCP had for creating a unitary, socialist, multinationality state out of the ashes of empire. At least to its advocates, it was as legitimate as the ethnonationalism and civic nationalism championed by nation builders elsewhere during the twentieth century—even more so because in principle it rejected the exploitative nature of its rivals. Rather than some Machiavellian scheme, the United Front might be better thought of as a core component of Maoist high-modernist ideology—to paraphrase James Scott, a "well intentioned plan for improving the human condition" imposed unilaterally by an authoritarian state brimming with self-confidence in its role as engine of progressive linear human development and its ability to overcome the constraints of nature, reorder society, and satisfy the needs of its population.[13] In the short term, it actually dampened the most radical impulses of high socialism but only because it was understood within the institutional ethos of the Party as a rational, scientific route to progress.

We can look at the United Front, particularly in retrospect, and conclude that the contradictions inherent within the structural dynamics of the Leninist Party-state, its Maoist high-modernist impulses, and Han-centered paternalistic nationalism were too deep to be overcome. Yet from the vantage point of the heady days at the dawn of the People's Republic of China, none of this was known, and for many anything seemed possible. Scholars have noted that the defeat of Japan in the Second World War has helped delegitimize the ideology that once propelled its imperial ambitions. Like other "defeated ideologies," pan-Asianism is often treated as a cynical rather than impassioned, even if often self-contradictory and misguided, response to Western capitalist hegemony and the Soviet alternative.[14] The same might be said about Chinese socialism under Mao, which is often reduced to a long totalitarian nightmare from which China has now awakened. Without whitewashing the monumental scale of violence the Chinese people (including non-Han communities) both suffered and committed during the Maoist period, by negating the ideologies that empowered Maoism and practices that sustained it, we not only fail to do our work as historians but do disservice to the lived experiences of millions. For many, the United Front was a central part of those experiences. In fact, unlike predominantly Han areas where it was an important but perhaps subsidiary component of Maoist practice, in Amdo the United Front set the guiding principles of all work for most of the 1950s.

Gerry Groot has referred to the United Front as a "self-defeating secret weapon." In particular, he is speaking of the corporatist structure that, he says, creates a gulf between United Front actors and the people they are meant to represent. [15] In minority regions such as Amdo, the challenge was perhaps more pronounced. Minority elites were never truly *representatives* of their coethnic constituencies. Instead, they were intermediaries and exemplars. Through the co-option of non-Han religious leaders and secular headmen, the Party intended to gain access to the masses with whom it had no prior relationship. Unlike traditional imperial practice, the United Front was not a strategy for managing and incorporating difference. From the start it was intended as a transformative vehicle of nation building and socialist transformation, one that depended on minority elites to act as agents of their own demise as a privileged class. Whether or not the United Front principles of gradualism and volunteerism could have overcome this contradiction became a moot point when they were overwhelmed by dynamics embedded in the Maoist project.

In pastoral regions of Amdo, this revolutionary impatience first appeared during the High Tide of early 1956. Although High Tide collectivization was quickly repudiated, in retrospect it marked a point of no return. In Zeku County, fears over imminent collectivization meant that indigenous elites balked at participating in United Front work. However, cadres discovered that mass awareness and patriotic consciousness among common herders were still undeveloped. Something had to give. Powered by political winds blown in from Beijing, by the start of 1958 pastoral collectivization had been made one of the year's primary tasks. A match was thus thrown into an already incendiary environment. Soon rebellion engulfed the Amdo Plateau. In the radical atmosphere of 1958, the CCP interpreted the uprising not as a response to the historical legacy of Han chauvinism or a reaction to transgression of United Front principles, as it had in the early 1950s, but as a last-ditch effort on the part of class enemies to protect their "feudal privileges" and sabotage the socialist system. Under orders to "Strike and Reform," security forces engaged in a brutal counterinsurgency campaign, and with few exceptions Amdo's pre-1949 leadership was deposed and jailed and in many cases killed. In essence, empire was extinguished before the process of nationalization was completed.

Reconciliation without Truth

Upon coming to power in the late 1970s, the post-Mao leadership faced a daunting task that demanded it reinforce the legitimacy of CCP rule while attending to the widespread violence that had been committed in its name. The imperfect solution was to declare the Cultural Revolution ten years of chaos. The lion's share of blame was pinned on a small number of troublemakers, often collectively referred to as the Gang of Four, while the vast majority of Chinese people were cleared of wrongdoing. In essence, the new Party leadership elected for a judgment of common victimization—reconciliation without truth, so to speak. While the degree to which this post-Mao narrative has achieved its objectives is unclear, the one thing it did not need to do among the Han majority was repair the narrative of nationhood itself.[16]

This was not the case in Amdo, where the Party faced a qualitatively different type of crisis of faith than it did in predominantly Han regions—one that not only brought into question the legitimacy of CCP rule but also the terms under which the region was included in the modern Chinese nation-state. On the surface, the Party's treatment of the Amdo Rebellion bears a passing resemblance to its judgment on the Cultural Revolution. A small group of evildoers were vilified, while the vast majority of participants were absolved of wrongdoing. Yet for many in Amdo, the CCP and Chinese rule had never been legitimate, at least not in the sense that Party leaders imagined. The United Front was designed to accomplish this task, to integrate Amdo Tibetans and others not just physically into the socialist state but also psychologically into the Han-dominated, multinational nation.

In other words, the violence of 1958 not only destroyed lives but also damaged the Party's mechanism of nationality rapprochement and severed its narrative of nationality unity. In order to repair this rupture, in Qinghai the post-Mao leadership sought to return to the promise of the early United Front, even as it continued to condemn the Amdo Rebellion as a counterrevolutionary putsch. While the uprising is blamed on mostly unnamed tribal and religious elites, with few exceptions Amdo's actual secular and monastic leaders have not only been rehabilitated but also memorialized in a myriad of state-sponsored publications as embodiments of nationality unity. Similarly, the "early-Liberation period" is celebrated as a time of ethnic reconciliation, economic development, and nationality unity. In this post-Mao narrative, the United Front era has been transformed from the transitional period of New Democracy—as it was contemporaneously understood—to one purporting to represent the ipso facto integration of the Amdo region and its people into the modern Chinese state and nation.[17]

Yet resurrecting the rhetoric and symbols of 1950s accommodation does little to achieve nationality unity because that period was itself intended to be transitory. The United Front Work Department not only continues to play a central role in formulating nationality policy, in recent years it also has grown in both size and influence.[18] However, the transformative potential with which the concept of the United Front was once imbued has long since disappeared. Nationality autonomy is once again the law of the land. However, a pan-Tibetan ethnic identity having consolidated both in China and in exile, instead of reinforcing state legitimacy by encouraging a sense of shared sovereignty within a multiethnic nation-state, it may have come to represent the failure of ethnic aspirations and sovereignty unrealized—a new prison house of nations.[19] Most importantly, the post-Mao narrative of nationality unity does not accord with the lived experiences and communal memory of Amdo Tibetans, not least because it elides the large-scale violence that accompanied the region's forced integration into the PRC and the decades of state repression that followed.

This does not mean that the CCP's United Front approach was wholly ineffective or that some Tibetans were not active and often willing participants in (and beneficiaries of) the campaigns of the Maoist era—including "democratic" and socialist reforms.[20] In truth, the documents simply do not allow us to determine what degree of support the Party's transformative agenda enjoyed among Amdo Tibetans or other minority communities. But Amdo Tibetans did join the government, Party, and security forces, and, like Gyelyön, some may have done so because they believed in its vision for a more equitable and prosperous future. Instead, it is to point out that for the reasons described in this book, the CCP's strategy for gradually and voluntarily transforming an imperial frontier into an integral component of a consolidated multinationality state failed. It is far from clear that the Party's 1950s United Front strategy of organic transformation ultimately could have succeeded. However, in its place the CCP has been unable to articulate a narrative that convincingly explains to many Tibetans their stake in a Han-dominated nation.

Of course, the Communist Party does not rely solely on its post-Mao United Front narrative to convince Tibetans and other minority communities of their inclusion in the Chinese nation. Beginning in the 1990s, the focus shifted to obtaining Tibetan gratitude through economic development. Most visibly, since 2000, the Great Western Development Campaign (Xibu Da Kaifa) has directed large-scale investment into western China in an attempt to raise living standards, reduce regional disparity, and strengthen economic integration. In the process, the CCP hopes to buttress state legitimacy along with the loyalty of the region's non-Han inhabitants.[21] Yet, as many studies have shown, efforts by the Chinese leadership to "buy Tibetans' love" have at best born mixed results.[22] In fact, six decades after the CCP first declared Qinghai "liberated" and almost exactly half a century removed from the outbreak of the Amdo Rebellion, there is no better evidence of the uneven integration of Tibetans into the Chinese nation-state than the uprising that in 2008 spread across the Tibetan Plateau. While the disturbances were fueled by specific grievances, at their heart, I contend, is a continued inability to persuade Tibetans of their full membership in the modern Chinese nation.

At a meeting of a subcommittee of the National People's Congress in 1987, the Tenth Panchen Lama spoke to this disconnect. Revisiting the violence committed in Tibetan regions during the Maoist period, he cautioned that the memory of those events continued to harm nationality unity. Lamenting that the warnings raised in his 1962 petition had gone unheeded, the Panchen Lama declared, "In Amdo and Kham, people were subjected to unspeakable atrocities. People were shot in groups of ten or twenty," concluding, "I know that it is not good to speak about these things. But such actions have left deep wounds in the minds of the people."[23] These words of the Panchen Lama unintentionally evoke those spoken a century earlier by the French theorist Ernest Renan. Presciently highlighting the importance that both narrative and communal memory play in the creation and consolidation of nations, in 1882 Renan referred to the nation as "a large-scale solidarity, constituted by the feeling of the sacrifices that one has made in the past and of those that one is prepared to make in the future. It presupposes a past; it is summarized, however, in the present by a tangible fact, namely, consent, the clearly expressed desire to continue a common life."[24] Yet, as Renan noted, this memory of a common past that allows for us today to desire a common tomorrow requires that we "forget" the violence—both physical and epistemological—that accompanies all transitions to nationhood.[25] To put it bluntly, in Amdo the violence of integration, represented most starkly but not exclusively by "'58", has not been forgotten.[26]

Having failed to establish a basis of organic legitimacy, the CCP instead has been compelled to rely on what Soviet historian Mark Beissinger has referred to as "coerced legitimacy."[27] In the postimperial world in which we live, where the "perception of exploitation is more important than the objective fact of empire,"[28] many observers accuse China of behaving like an empire. However, as Charles Tilly, Karen Barkey, and others point out, while empires often expand through military conquest and although the maintenance of empire frequently requires at least the threat of force, coercion and oppression are not intrinsically defining elements of empire. Arguably, it is only in the twentieth century that empire has become "a value-laden appellation" so closely associated with exploitation, domination, and by extension illegitimacy.[29] The point is not to rehabilitate "empire," which in its various manifestations has committed untold acts of violence across human history, but to recognize that the modern, consolidated nation-state acts in ways fundamentally different from traditional imperial formations.

To put it a different way, as Adeeb Khalid once asked when considering Soviet designs in Central Asia, "Where does empire end and other forms of nonrepresentative or authoritarian polities begin?"[30] In China, the question has gained newfound significance since the ascension of Xi Jinping to national leadership in 2012. Xi's rise occurred amid an ongoing and contentious debate within China's political and intellectual circles over the past, present, and future of nationality policy. With some influential scholars identifying the politics of difference—most notably autonomy and other legal makers of ethnocultural distinction—not as a pathway to unity but as a source of division, the Xi regime has pursued policies in restive minority areas that are notable for their strikingly assimilationist and coercive Han-centered nationalism.[31] This can be most clearly seen in the massive regime of security, surveillance, and incarceration that since 2016 has been unleashed against Uyghurs and other Muslim communities in Xinjiang. However, it can also be found in Tibetan areas, where several of the mechanisms of both high-tech surveillance and street-level policing that have raised concerns in Xinjiang first originated.[32] The irony is that proponents of the status quo in minzu policy, those who continue to champion the official recognition of ethnic distinction, have made their case in part by elevating Xi Jinping's father, Xi Zhongxun, to the status of primary architect of the 1950s United Front in northwest China. In a fit of fortuitous symmetry, it is the resolution of Wangchen Döndrup's Nangra Rebellion, now credited almost solely to the elder Xi, that perhaps is most often cited as the paradigmatic United Front model for the peaceful integration of Tibetans, Muslims, and other non-Han communities into the PRC.[33] Of course, this also demands an act of misremembering, of strategically forgetting that the seventeen United Front–sponsored missions sent to convince Wangchen Döndrup to "return to the people" actually failed and that the Nangra Rebellion was only settled through the mobilization of state violence.

After all, minorities, like majorities, do not just exist. They are created.[34] Whether attempting to mold them into socialist citizens or loyal neoliberal producers and consumers, the CCP makes transformative demands of its diverse subjects unimaginable to its imperial forbearers. If in the twenty-first century many Tibetans, Uyghurs, and other "minority nationalities" and their supporters consider the PRC to be an empire, this may not be a confirmation of empire so much as evidence of the failure of seven decades of nation building.

Appendix A

ZEKU'S CHIEFDOMS (CA. 1953)

CHIEFDOM/TSOWA	HEADMAN[a]	ESTIMATED POPULATION[b]
Hor	Wagya	5,600
/ Wönkhor Tsowa	Lhagyel	(992)
/ Ratsang Tsowa	Chögyong	(1,156)
/ Shokmang Tsowa	Yönten	(1,063)
/ Détsang Tsowa	Tséten/Jampa	(826)
/ Yunok Mokser	Sermo	(740)
Gönshül	Serökyap	1,920
Gartsé	Lubum	1,512
Méshül	Tsintar/Lama Bum	1,388
Shawonar	Lhakba	2,080
Wöngya	Shawo/Losar	1,448
Sonak	Gönpo	1,320
Shisa	Wenté	696
Ködé Karing	Dargyé	724
Khéri Chunga	Tséten	348
	Total	17,036

[a] ZCPG, folder 1, folio 2.
[b] ZCPG folder 1, folios 3–4. The population figures for the five Hor tsowa are either from 1955 or 1958 and taken from Chen Qingying, *Zhongguo Zangzu Buluo*, 243–66.

THL/PINYIN-CHINESE-WYLIE CONVERSION TABLE

THL/PINYIN	CHINESE	WYLIE TIBETAN
Achok	阿木去乎	a mchog
Apa Alo	黄正清	a pha a blo
Arik	阿柔	a rig
Atsok	阿粗(曲)乎	a tshogs
Awar Téu	阿哇铁吾	a bar the 'u
Ba	同德	'ba'
Bao'an	保安	mtho kya
Batang	巴滩	'ba' thang
Béri	白利	be ri
Bili Wanhufu	必里万户府	
Cao Xueyan	曹学彦	
Chankya Rölpé Dorjé	章嘉若必多吉	lcang skya rol pa'i rdo rje
Chen Ming	陈明	
Chen Sigong	陈思恭	
Chentsa	尖扎	gcen tsa
Chöbum Gyel	切本加	chos 'bum rgyal
Chögyong	切什俊/曲俊	chos sgyong
Dargyé	达日吉/他日加	dar rgyas
Datong	大同	gser khog
Datsen	达参	mda' tshan
Deng Xiaoping	邓小平	
Détsang	德仓	sde tshang
Dobhé	多白	rdo bhe
Dodé Bum	多得(代)本	mdo sde 'bum
Dorjé	多杰/多吉	rdor rje
Dowa	多哇	mdo ba
Drakkar	兴海	brag dkar

(Continued)

THL/PINYIN	CHINESE	WYLIE TIBETAN
Du Hua'an	杜华安	
Duofudun	多福顿	stobs lden
Fan Ming	范明	
Gao Feng	高峰	
Gartsé	瓜什则	mgar rtse
Gélek Gyatso	格勒嘉措	dge legs rgya mtsho
Gengya	甘加	rgan gya
Gétak	格达	dge rtags
Golok	果洛	mgo log
Gönpo	公保	mgon po
Gönpo Namgyel	黄文元	mgon po rnam rgyal
Gönshül	官秀	mgon shul
Guanshize	瓜什则	mgar rtse
Guide	贵德	thri ka
Guinan	贵南	mang ra
Gungtang	貢唐	gung thang
Guo Min	郭民	
Guoluo	果洛	mgo log
Gurong Gyelsé	古嘉赛	dgu rong rgyal sras
Gyanak Weltsang	嘉那化仓/加乃化仓	rgya nag dpal tshang
Gyelwo Dorjé	加吾多日吉	rgyal bo rdor rje
Gyelyön	賈勇	rgyel yon
Haibei	海北	mtsho byang
Haidun	海顿	
Hainan	海南	mtsho lho
Haixi	海西	mtso nub
Haiyan	海晏	mda' bzhi
Han Yinu	韩乙奴	
Henan	河南	sog po
Hezhou	河州	
Hor	和日	hor
Hu Yaobang	胡耀邦	
Hu Zilin	胡子林	
Hualong	化隆	ba yan
Huang Wenyuan	黄文元	mgon po rnam rgyal
Huang Zhengqing	黄正清	a pha a blo
Huangnan	黄南	rma lho
Huangzhong	湟中	ru shar
Jamyang Zhépa	嘉木样	jam dbyang bzhad pa
Jianzha	尖扎	gcen tsa
Jikmé Tenpé Wangchuk	久美丹贝旺旭	'jigs med bstan p'l dbang phyug
Jikmé Sönam	九麥索南/晋美索南	'jigs med bsod nams
Kangtsa	岗察	kang tsa
Kangtsé Welzang	刚察 华宝藏	rkang tsha'i dpal bzang
Kardzé	甘孜	dkar mdzes
Kelzang Rachu		skal bzang rwa mchu
Kenlho	甘南	kan lho
Kéwa	东山	ske ba
Khéri Chunga	克利其那	khe ris chu rnga
Ködé Karing	古德尕让(浪)	ko'u sde ka ring

(Continued)

THL/PINYIN	CHINESE	WYLIE TIBETAN
Könchok	官却	dkon mchog
Köngya	官加	dkon rgya
Kumbum	塔尔寺	sku 'bum
Künga Weljor	更(滚)噶环觉	kun dga' dpal 'byor
Labrang	拉卜楞	bla brang
Labuzang	拉卜藏	blo bzang
Lamo Déchen	拉某德千	la mo bde chen
Lamo Sertri	拉莫赛赤	la mo gser khri
Lamuzang	拉木藏	blo bzang
Langgya	浪加	glang rgya
Ledu	乐都	gro tshang
Lhagyel	拉加	lha rgyal
Lhakba	拉巴	lhag ba
Lharjé Draknawa	拉吉(杰/扎)直纳哇	lha rje brag sna ba
Lhündrup Gyel	兰州加	lhun grub rgyal
Li Chunfan	李春藩	
Li Shumao	李书茂	
Li Xibo	李熙波	
Li Weihan	李维汉	
Liao Hansheng	廖汉生	
Liangzhou	凉州	
Linggya	朗加	gling rgya
Linxia	临夏	ka chu
Liu Shaoqi	刘少奇	
Liu Zexi	刘泽西	
Logyatsang	罗嘉仓	blo rgya tshang
Losar	洛次日	lo gsar
Lozang Trinlé Lungtok Gyatso	洛桑赤列隆朵嘉措	blo bzang 'phrin las lung rtogs rgya mtsho
Luchu	碌曲	klu chu
Luqu	碌曲	klu chu
Lubum	冷本	klu 'bum
Ma Bufang	马步芳	
Ma Hailin	马海霖	
Ma Lin	马麟	
Ma Liang	马良	
Ma Pu	马扑	
Ma Qi	马麒	
Ma Wanfu	马万福	
Ma Ying	马英	
Ma Yuanhai	马远海	
Ma Yuanxiang	马元祥	
Machen	玛沁	rma chen
Machu	玛曲	rma chu
Malho	黄南	rma lho
Mangra	贵南	mang ra
Maqin	玛沁	rma chen
Maqu	玛曲	rma chu
Menyuan	门源	sems nyid
Méshül	麦秀	dme shul

(Continued)

THL/PINYIN	CHINESE	WYLIE TIBETAN
Naktsang Nulo	纳仓怒罗	nags tshang nus blo
Namdzong	南宗	gnam rdzong
Nangchen	囊谦	nang chen
Nangra	昂拉	snang ra
Nangso Khanak		nangso kha nag
Ngawa	阿坝	nga ba
Ngülra	欧拉	dngul rwa
Pünwang	平汪	phun dbang
Qiaofudan	乔夫旦	mchod rten
Qilian	祁连	chi len
Ragya	拉加	rwa rgya
Ranmuzan	染木赞	
Ratsang	日阿仓/拉仓	ra tshang
Ren Shiying	任世英	
Repgong	热贡/同仁	reb gong
Rongwo	隆务	rong bo
Rongwo Déchen Chökhorling	隆务德钦琼科尔林	rong bo bde chen chos 'khor gling
Rongwo Nangso	隆务昂索	rong bo nang so
Pakpa Lama	八思巴	phags pa
Peng Dehuai	彭德怀	
Sairidan	赛日旦	
Sakyil Tabéhu	萨吉大百户	sa kyil ta be hu
Sangchu	夏河	bsang chu
Sangkhok	桑科	bsang khog
Serlung	赛尔龙	gser lung
Sermo	赛日毛	gser mo
Serökyap	赛尔什加	gser 'od skyabs
Shadar	夏德日	bya dar
Sharkok	松潘	shar khog
Shartsang Lama	夏日仓	shar tshang
Shawo	夏吾	sha bo
Shawonar	夏吾那	sha bo nar
Shérap Gyatso	喜饶嘉措	shes rab rgya mtsho
Shisa	西卜沙	dpyi sa
Shitsang	西仓	shis tsang
Shokmang	豁忙/许乎忙	shog mang
Sokpo	河南	sog po
Sokru	苏乎锐/苏合日	sog ru
Sonak	唢乃亥	so nag
Sönam Bum	唢南本	bsod nams 'bum
Songpan	松潘	shar khog
Sun Jianxiao	苏剑啸	
Sun Junyi	孙君一	
Sun Zuobin	孙作宾	
Tongde	同德	'ba'
Tongren	同仁	thung rin
Topden	多福顿	stobs lden
Trashi Namgyel	扎西安嘉	bkra shis rnam rgyal
Trashi Tséring	扎西才让	bkra shis tshe ring
Trashi Wangchuk	扎喜旺徐	bkra shis dbang phyug

(Continued)

THL/PINYIN	CHINESE	WYLIE TIBETAN
Trika	贵德	thri ka
Tsadam	柴旦/柴达木	tshwa 'dam
Tsébho	才保	tse bho
Tséchu	泽曲	rtse chu
Tsékhok	泽库	rtse khog
Tséring Gyel	才仁加	tshe ring rgyal
Tséten	才旦	tshe brtan
Tsézhung	泽雄	rtse gzhung
Tsintar	曾太日	tsin thar
Tsojang	海北	mtsho byang
Tsolho	海南	mtsho lho
Tsonup	海西	mtsho nub
Tungrin	同仁	thung rin
Ulanhu	乌兰夫	
Wagya	哇加	ba rgya
Wangchen Döndrup	项谦	dbang chen don grub
Wang Jinyou	王进有	
Wang Zheng	王震	
Wang Zhao	王昭	
Welmang	阿莽	dbal mang
Wéma Tséring	完麻才让	pad ma tshe ring
Wenté	完德	ban te
Wimdo	文都	bis mdo'i
Wöngya	王加	bon brgya
Wönkhor	红科（日）	dpon khor
Wuwei	武威	
Xi Jinping	习近平	
Xi Zhongxun	习仲勋	
Xiahe	夏河	bsang chu
Xie Fumin	谢扶民	
Xie Tianxiang	解天祥	
Xiji	西吉	
Xinghai	兴海	brag dkar
Xining	西宁	zi ling
Xunhua	循化	ya rdzi
Yadzi	循化	ya rdzi
Yan'an	延安	
Yönten	羊旦	yon tan
Yuan Renyuan	袁任远	
Yülshül	玉树	yul shul
Yunok Mokser	伊吾乎莫赛日	g.yu rnog rmog ser
Yushu	玉树	yul shul
Zeku	泽库	rtse khog
Zhang Guohua	张国华	
Zhang Guosheng	张国声	
Zhang Zhongliang	张忠良	
Zhangjiachuan	张家川	
Zhao Kunyuan	赵昆元	
Zho'ongshi	双朋西	zho 'ong dpyis
Zhou Enlai	周恩来	
Zhou Renshan	周仁山	

Notes

The following abbreviations are used in the notes:

AAH   Archives of the Academia Historica (Guoshiguan), Taipei, ROC.

DZMG   Dangdai Zhongguo Congshu Bianjibu, ed. *Dangdai Zhongguo de Minzu Gongzuo*. 2 vols. Beijing: Dangdai Zhongguo Chubanshe, 1993.

DZQH   Dangdai Zhongguo Congshu Bianjibu, ed. *Dangdai Zhongguo de Qinghai*. 2 vols. Beijing: Dangdai Zhongguo Chubanshe, 1991.

FDXZ   Gansu Sheng Minzu Shiwu Weiyuanhui, ed. *Fandui Difangzhuyi Xuexi Ziliao*. Lanzhou: n.p., 1958.

GDXZ   Guide Xian Difangzhi Bianzuan Weiyuanhui, ed. *Guide Xianzhi*. Xi'an: Shaanxi Renmin Chubanshe, 1995.

GNZZ   Gannan Zangzu Zizhizhou Difang Shizhi Bianzuan Weiyuanhui, ed. *Gannan Zanzgu Zizhi Zhouzhi*. 2 vols. Beijing: Renmin Chubanshe, 1999.

GSSZ JSZ   Gansu Sheng Difang Shizhi Bianzuan Weiyuanhui and Gansu Sheng Junqu Junshi Lingdao Xiaozu, eds. *Gansu Shengzhi*. Vol. 10, *Junshizhi*. Lanzhou: Gansu Renmin Chubanshe, 2001.

HNGK   "Huangnan Zangzu Zizhizhou Gaikuang" Bianxiezu, ed. *Huangnan Zangzu Zizhizhou Gaikuang*. Rev. ed. Beijing: Minzu Chubanshe, 2009.

HNZZ   Huangnan Zangzu Zizhizhou Difangzhi Bianzuan Weiyuanhui, ed. *Huangnan Zangzu Zizhi Zhouzhi*. 2 vols. Lanzhou: Gansu Renmin Chubanshe, 1999.

HZZZ   Hainan Zangzu Zizhizhou Difang Zhibian Zuanwen Yuanhui. *Hainan Zangzu Zizhi Zhouzhi*. Beijing: Minzu Chubanshe, 1997.

JFQH   Zhonggong Qinghai Shengwei Dangshi Ziliao Zhengji Weiyuanhui and Zhonggong Renmin Jiefangjun Qinghai Sheng Junqu Zhengzhibu, eds. *Jiefang Qinghai*. Xining: Qinghai Renmin Chubanshe, 1987.

JQHC   Zhonggong Qinghai Shengwei Dangshi Ziliao Zhengji Weiyuanhui and Zhonggong Renmin Jiefangjun Qinghai Sheng Junqu Zhengzhibu, eds. *Jiefang Qinghai Huace*. Xining: Qinghai Renmin Chubanshe, 1989.

JQSX   Zhonggong Qinghai Shengwei Dangshi Ziliao Zhengji Weiyuanhui and Zhonggong Renmin Jiefangjun Qinghai Sheng Junqu Zhengzhibu, eds. *Jiefang Qinghai Shiliao Xuanbian*. Xining: Qinghai Xinhua Chubanshe, 1990.

JZXZ   Jianzha Xian Difangzhi Bianzuan Weiyuanhui. *Jianzha Xianzhi*. Lanzhou: Gansu Renmin Chubanshe, 2003.

LQXZ   Luqu Xian Difangzhi Bianzuan Weiyuanhui. *Luqu Xianzhi*. Lanzhou: Gansu Wenhua Chubanshe, 2006.

MQXZ   "Maqu Xianzhi" Bianzuan Weiyuanhui, ed. *Maqu Xianzhi*. Lanzhou: Gansu Renmin Chubanshe, 2001.

MZGWH   [Zhonggong Qinghai Shengwei Tongzhanbu], ed. *Minzu Zongjiao Gongzuo Wenjian Huiji*. Xining: n.p., 1959.

NJZWH   Zhonghua Renmin Gongheguo Guojia Nongye Weiyuanhui Bangongting, ed. *Nongye Jitihua Zhongyao Wenjian Huibian: 1949–1981*. 2 vols. Beijing: Zhonggong Zhongyang Dangxiao Chubanshe, 1982.

QHSZ DSJ   Qinghai Sheng Difangzhi Bianzuan Weiyuanhui, ed. *Qinghai Shengzhi*. Vol. 2, *Dashiji*. Xining: Qinghai Renmin Chubanshe, 2001.

QHSZ FLZ   Qinghai Sheng Difangzhi Bianzuan Weiyuanhui, ed. *Qinghai Shengzhi*. Vol. 81, *Fuluzhi*. Xining: Qinghai Renmin Chubanshe, 2003.
QHSZ JSZ   Qinghai Sheng Difangzhi Bianzuan Weiyuanhui, and "Qinghai Shengzhi Junshizhi" Bianzuan Weiyuanhui, eds. *Qinghai Shengzhi*. Vol. 56, *Junshizhi*. Xining: Qinghai Renmin Chubanshe, 2001.
QHSZ NYZ   Qinghai Sheng Difangzhi Bianzuan Weiyuanhui, ed. *Qinghai Shengzhi*. Vol. 12, *Nongyezhi, Yuyezhi*. Xining: Qinghai Renmin Chubanshe, 1993.
QHSZ RWZ   Qinghai Sheng Difangzhi Bianzuan Weiyuanhui. *Qinghai Shengzhi*. Vol. 80, *Renwuzhi*. Hefei: Huangshan Shushe, 2001.
QHSZ XMZ   Qinghai Sheng Difangzhi Bianzuan Weiyuanhui, ed. *Qinghai Shengzhi*. Vol. 14, *Xumuzhi*. Hefei: Huangshan Shushe, 1998.
QHSZ ZSZ   Qinghai Sheng Difangzhi Bianzuan Weiyuanhui. *Qinghai Shengzhi*. Vol. 48, *Zhengshizhi, Sheng Zhengfu*. Xining: Qinghai Renmin Chubanshe, 2001.
QNHJS   "Qinghai Nongmuqu Hezuo Jingji Shiliao" Bianji Weiyuanhui, ed. *Qinghai Nongmuqu Hezuo Jingji Shiliao*. Xining: Qinghai Renmin Chubanshe, 1993.
SZJS   "Salazu Jianshi" Bianxiezu. *Salazu Jianshi*. Rev. ed. Beijing: Renmin Chubanshe, 2008.
TRXZ   Tongren Xianzhi Bianzuan Weiyuanhui. *Tongren Xianzhi*. 2 vols. Xi'an: Sanqin Chubanshe, 2001.
XHXZ   Gansu Sheng Xiahe Xianzhi Bianzuan Weiyuanhui, ed. *Xiahe Xianzhi*. Lanzhou: Gansu Wenhua Chubanshe, 1999.
XSMG   Guojia Minzu Shiwu Weiyuanhui and Zhonggong Zhongyang Wenxian Yanjiushi, eds. *Xin Shiqi Minzu Gongzuo Wenxian Xuanbian*. Beijing: Zhongyang Wenxian Chubanshe, 1990.
ZCPC   Zeku County Party Committee Archives.
ZCPG   Zeku County People's Government Archives.
ZFYS   Zhongguo Fanyou Yundong Shujuku, 1957–. Zhongguo Dangdai Zhengzhi Yundong Lishi Shujuku, 1949–. Xianggang Zhongwen Daxue Zhongguo Yanjiu Fuwu Zhongxin.
ZGGL   Zhonggong Gannan Zhouwei Dangshi Yanjiushi. *Zhongguo Gongchandang Gannan Lishi, 1921.7–2003.7*. Lanzhou: Gansu Minzu Chubanshe, 2003.
ZGHN LD   Zhonggong Huangnan Zangzu Zizhi Zhouwei Dangshi Yanjiushi, ed. *Zhongguo Gongchandang Huangnan Zangzu Zizhizhou Lishi Dashiji: 1949.8–1999.12*. Xining: n.p., 2001.
ZGHN ZZ   Zhonggong Huangnan Zhouwei Zuzhibu, Zhonggong Huangnan Zhouwei Dangshi Yanjiushi, and Huangnan Zangzu Zizhizhou Dang'anju. *Zhongguo Gongchandang Qinghai Sheng Huangnan Zangzu Zizhizhou Zuzhishi Ziliao: 1953–1987*. Xining: n.p., 1993.
ZGQH ZZ   Zhonggong Qinghai Shengwei Zuzhibu, Zhongong Qinghai Shengwei Dangshi Yanjiushi, and Qinghai Sheng Dang'anju, eds. *Zhongguo Gongchandang Qinghai Sheng Zuzhishi Ziliao: 1949.9–1987.10*. Xining: n.p., 1995.
ZKXZ   Zeku Xianzhi Bianzuan Weiyuanhui, ed. *Zeku Xianzhi*. Beijing: Zhongguo Xianzhen Nianjian Chubanshe, 2005.

A NOTE ON SOURCES, TRANSLITERATION, AND NOMENCLATURE

1. This is not to say that I made the only correct or moral decision. There are several excellent studies of the Sino-Tibetan borderlands that make conscientious, judicious, and successful use of oral sources, including Makley, *Violence of Liberation*; Makley, *Battle for Fortune*; Mortensen, "Historical Amnesia in Gyalthang"; Meriam, *China's "Tibetan" Frontiers*.

2. Pirie, "Feuding, Mediation and the Negotiation of Authority," 12. See also Langelaar, "Historical Social Organisation," 25–32.

3. For example, see Makley, *Violence of Liberation*, 64–65.

4. Sneath, *Headless State*. Sneath notes that another misconception in Western colonial literature on nomadic peoples is the assumption that nomadic societies were free of vertical impositions of state power common to sedentary societies. Sneath, 66–71.

5. According to Paul Nietupski, for example, in the Labrang region the largest unit normatively is the shokwa, which may contain multiple tsowa. *Labrang*, 56–60. See also Ekval, *Fields on the Hoof*, 28–29; Carrasco, *Land and Polity in Tibet*, 155–59; Clarke, "Social Organisation of Tibetan Pastoralists"; Pirie, "Feuding, Mediation and the Negotiation of Authority," 11–12; and Langelaar, "Descent and Houses in Rebgong." In farming communities, dewa most often refers to a group of villages. In Zeku, the CCP used the term (C. *tawa*) to refer to the small communities that grew up alongside the larger monastic institutions.

6. The Chinese ethnologist and historian Chen Qingying has admitted that researchers still do not understand what distinguishes the many variable terms Tibetans use to describe their "tribal organization" and that Chinese glosses such as zu, bu, and buluo are insufficient representations. Chen and He, *Zangzu Buluo Zhidu Yanjiu*, 140–44.

7. Leibold, *Reconfiguring Chinese Nationalism*, 8. The Japanese neologism *minzoku* was itself a rough translation of the German word *volk*.

8. Mullaney, *Coming to Terms with the Nation*, 11. See also Xiaoyuan Liu, *Frontier Passages*, and Minglang Zhou, "Nation-State Building and Multiculturalism," 117–25. For an overview of Soviet nationality policies, see Suny, *Revenge of the Past*.

9. See, for example, Ma Rong, "New Perspective on Guiding Ethnic Relations," 3–5. For an overview, see Elliot, "Case of the Missing Indigene."

INTRODUCTION

1. Ekvall, *Fields on the Hoof*, 31–39; Tan, *In the Circle of White Stones*, 36–62.

2. *ZKXZ*, 411–12.

3. In February 2008, several weeks before the better-known disturbances erupted in Lhasa, a riot that initially pitted Tibetans against Hui Muslims broke out in Qinghai's Tongren County. See Makley, "Ballooning Unrest."

4. For a sample of the literature on these issues, see the contributions to the special edition of *Central Asian Survey* edited by Joanne Smith Finley, "Securitization, Insecurity and Conflict in Contemporary Xinjiang"; contributions to Hillman and Tuttle, *Ethnic Conflict and Protest in Tibet and Xinjiang*; contributions to McGranahan and Litzinger, "Self-Immolation as Protest in Tibet"; Barnett, "Tibet Protests of Spring, 2008"; Makley, *Battle for Fortune*; and Roberts, "Biopolitics of China's 'War on Terror.'"

5. Fischer, *Disempowered Development of Tibet*, 9.

6. On Xinjiang, see McMillen, *Chinese Communist Power*; Bovingdon, *Uyghurs*; and Thum, "Uyghurs in Modern China."

7. Schwartz, *Circle of Protest*.

8. Winichakul, *Siam Mapped*, 12–14; Renan, "What Is a Nation?"; Duara, *Rescuing History from the Nation*.

9. Yeh, *Taming Tibet*, 1–2.

10. ZCPG, folder 2, folio 1.

11. *ZKXZ*, 1.

12. ZCPC, folder 1, folios 7–8. Eight of the monasteries were Geluk, while six, including the largest, Hor Monastery, were Nyingma. On trülku, see chapter 1.

13. Zeku's total area covers 2,570 square miles, or 6,658 square kilometers. Ninety-eight percent is classified as grassland.

14. Weiner, "Tibet in China?"; Gruschke, *Cultural Monuments*, 1:9. Both activists and scholars often gloss the Tibetan phrase *"chölkha sum"* as the "three provinces" of Tibet. However, a more precise and politically neutral translation would render it something akin to the "three regions."

15. Shakya, "Whither the Tsampa Eaters?" For an illustration of the parochial nature of identity in 1950s Amdo, see Naktsang Nulo, *My Tibetan Childhood*. For a dissenting perspective, see Dreyfus, "Proto-Nationalism in Tibet."

16. Carrasco, *Land and Polity in Tibet*; Clarke, "Social Organisation of Tibetan Pastoralists."

17. See, for example, Lipman, *Familiar Strangers*, 159–66; Cooke, "Becoming and Un-becoming Tu"; Dwyer, *Salar*; and Roche, "Tibetanization of Henan's Mongols."

18. Adelman and Aron, "From Borderlands to Borders," 815. For a thoughtful consideration of the use of the conceptual category "frontier" as a way to analyze Kham as a historical and spatial entity, see Gros, "Frontier (of) Experience."

19. Huber, "A Mdo and Its Modern Transition," xiii.

20. Stoler and McGranahan employ the term "imperial formation as a critical analytic to underscore not the inevitable rise and fall of empires, but the active and contingent process of their making and unmaking." In "Refiguring Imperial Terrains," 8.

21. Perdue, "Comparing Empires"; Sperling, "Tibet and China," 34.

22. On "multiple sovereignties" and "shared sovereignty" in premodern Southeast Asia, see Winichakul, *Siam Mapped*, 81–88.

23. Tambiah, *World Conqueror and World Renouncer*; Dreyfus, "Law, State, and Political Ideology in Tibet," 133.

24. Samuel, "Tibet as a Stateless Society," 215; Cooke and Goodman, "Idea of Qinghai."

25. Michaud, "Zomia and Beyond," 187. For critiques of Zomia in the context of Tibet, see Shneiderman, "Are the Central Himalayas in Zomia?," 290; Giersch, "Across Zomia with Merchants, Monks, and Musk"; and Samuel, "'Zomia.'"

26. Nietupski, "Understanding Religion and Politics in A Mdo," 70.

27. Sulek and Ptácková, "Mapping Amdo," 11–12; Rieber, *Struggle for the Eurasian Borderlands*, 38–9; Hayes, *Change in Worlds*, 13–30.

28. Oidtmann, *Forging the Golden Urn*; Nietupski, "Understanding Sovereignty in Amdo."

29. Pagden, *Lords of All the World*, 12–19; Lieven, *Empire*, 7–26.

30. Barkey, *Empire of Difference*, 4.

31. Esherick, Kayah, and Van Young, introduction to *Empire to Nation*, 2; Perdue, "Empire and Nation in Comparative Perspective," 301–2.

32. Suny, *Revenge of the Past*, 3. The phrase "prison house of nations" was coined in 1839 by the Marquis de Custine in reference to the Russian Empire. It has since been used to describe polities as diverse as the Hapsburg and Ottoman Empires, the USSR, Yugoslavia and the post–Cold War United States.

33. Formative works include Weber, *Peasants into Frenchmen*, and Gellner, *Nations and Nationalism*.

34. Rieber, *Struggle for the Eurasian Borderlands*, 532.

35. Rieber, 532.

36. Pye, "How China's Nationalism Was Shanghaied." Cited in Perdue, "Where Do Incorrect Political Ideas Come From?" 188.

37. Foundational works in this Manchu turn include Rawski, *Last Emperors*; Millward, *Beyond the Pass*; Crossley, *Translucent Mirror*; and Elliott, *Manchu Way*.

38. Crossley, *Translucent Mirror*, 11, 38, 44.

39. DiCosmo, "Qing Colonial Administration in Inner Asia," 288.

40. See, for example, Tuttle, *Tibetan Buddhists*; Lin, *Tibet and Nationalist China's Frontier*; Brophy, *Uyghur Nation*; Jacobs, *Xinjiang and the Modern Chinese State*; and Hammond, *China's Muslims and Japan's Empire*.

41. Important exceptions include volumes 2 through 4 of Melvyn Goldstein's series on the political history of twentieth-century Central Tibet and the work of Uradyn Bulag. Goldstein, *History of Modern Tibet*; Bulag, *Mongols at China's Edge*; and Bulag, *Collaborative Nationalism*.

42. Doyle, *Empires*, 19, 30–34 (italics added).

43. Lieven, *Empire*, 25.

44. Tilly, "How Empires End," 3.

45. Tilly, 4.

46. Barkey, *Empire of Difference*, 10.

47. Barkey, 10; Esherick, Kayah, and Van Young, introduction to *Empire to Nation*, 6–7; Stoler and McGranahan, "Refiguring Imperial Terrains."

48. Burbank and Cooper, *Empires in World History*, 12.

49. Burbank and Cooper, 9–10. See also Crossley, *Translucent Mirror* 12, 38. Of course, the reality is often far messier. For example, see Bulag, *Collaborative Nationalism*, 67–69; Kang and Sutton, *Contesting the Yellow Dragon*, especially 88–94; and Milward, *Beyond the Pass*.

50. Barkey, *Empire of Difference*, 4, 12–14; Burbank and Cooper, *Empires in World History*, 12; Rieber, *Struggle for the Eurasian Borderlands*, 9, 533.

51. Barkey, *Empire of Difference*, 10.

52. Walzer, "Politics of Difference"; Burbank and Cooper, *Empires in World History*, 8; Crossley, "Nationality and Difference in China," 139–40.

53. Suny, "Empire Strikes Out," 30. See, for example, Rhoads, *Manchus and Han*, and Karpat, "*Millets* and Nationality."

54. Anderson, *Imagined Communities*, 86.

55. Esherick, "How the Qing Became China," 243, 247–52; Crossley, "Nationality and Difference in China," 145–48. The reasons for this reversal were multiple, but an important consideration was the justifiable fear of the further encroachment of European and Japanese imperialism into the former dominions of the Qing.

56. Perdue, "Erasing Empire."

57. Cited in Esherick, "How the Qing Became China," 245.

58. Esherick, 246–47.

59. Rieber, *Struggle for the Eurasian Borderlands*, 9, 293.

60. Leibold, *Reconfiguring Chinese Nationalism*, 13. See also Tuttle, *Tibetan Buddhists*, 9.

61. Bulag, "Going Imperial"; Bulag, *Collaborative Nationalism*, 67.

62. For example, see Tuttle, *Tibetan Buddhists*, and Bulag, "Going Imperial."

63. Goldstein, *Snow Lion and the Dragon*.

64. The significant exception was the former Qing dependency of Outer Mongolia, then the Mongolian People's Republic, which under the patronage of the Soviet Union had long since established its independence.

65. Chang, *Party and the National Question*, 36–37, 39. Chang wrote of the GMD, "It does not admit the existence of national minorities within the frontiers of China, but, on the contrary, looks upon the nationalities as merely branches—or clans—of the Han people" (p. 46). This widely accepted characterization is taken from *China's Destiny*, ghostwritten for Chiang Kaishek in 1943. For a critique, see Leibold, *Reconfiguring Chinese Nationalism*, 52.

66. Makley, *Violence of Liberation*, 78–79.

67. Chang, *Party and the National Question*, 43, 71–73. This difference is used to explain the USSR's federalism versus the PRC's unitary structure and denial of the right to succession. See also Bulag, "Good Han, Bad Han." On great Russian chauvinism, see Martin, *Affirmative Action Empire*, 2–9.

68. This perspective is perhaps most fully laid out in Jianglin Li, *Tibet in Agony*.

69. Although the United Front is active in numerous countries, it is in Australia that its efforts have raised the greatest alarm. See for example, Groot, "China's United Front Work," and Dreyer, "Weapon without War."

70. Van Slyke, *Enemies and Friends*, 2, 208; Groot, "Self-Defeating Secret Weapon?" 29. Although usually translated as "magic weapon," Groot glosses *fabao* as "secret weapon," and Van Slyke more prosaically as the "three fundamental problems" and "the three main weapons." The original meaning refers to the "three jewels" of Buddhism: the Buddha, the dharma, and the sangha, or monastic community.

71. Van Slyke, *Enemies and Friends*, 7–9; Suny, *Revenge of the Past*, 93–95.

72. Van Slyke, *Enemies and Friends*, 255.

73. Van Slyke, 103.

74. Groot, "Self-Defeating Secret Weapon?," 31.

75. Xiaoyuan Liu, *Frontier Passages*, 127–57.

76. Groot, *Managing Transitions*, 67; Van Slyke, *Enemies and Friends*, 208.

77. Van Slyke, *Enemies and Friends*, 208.

78. Mao penned "On New Democracy" in 1939, the same year he first spotlighted the CCP's "three magic weapons." This was no coincidence. Groot writes, "'On New Democracy' provided united front work with a full theoretical framework." *Managing Transitions*, 19. See also Van Slyke, *Enemies and Friends*, 111–12.

79. Groot, "Self-Defeating Secret Weapon?," 34.

80. Groot, *Managing Transitions*, 57.

81. Van Slyke, *Enemies and Friends*, 208.

82. See also Seymour, *China's Satellite Parties*.

83. Groot, *Managing Transitions*, xiv.

84. Groot, 70–75; Van Slyke, *Enemies and Friends*, 208–19.

85. On CCP activity in the Labrang region prior to 1949, see Nietupski, *Labrang Monastery*, 185–89.

86. *DZMG*, 1:71–84. The other two tasks were making immediate improvements to local economies and training minority cadres.

87. Hirsch, *Empire of Nations*, 5.

88. Groot, *Managing Transitions*, xvii.

89. *DZMG*, 1:82.

90. Groot allows that "interest *intermediation*" rather than "interest *representation*" better describes a process by which the "transmission of information" through United Front operatives is not neutral but is "influenced by organizational structures and the state's influence on them." *Managing Transitions*, xxii (italics in original).

91. *JQSX*, 307. See also *DZMG*, 1:82, 1:323.

92. Dreyer, *China's Forty Millions*, 94; *DZMG*, 1:324.

93. *JQSX*, 307.

94. From the CCP's "Common Program," reproduced in *Chinese Law and Government* 14, no. 4 (1981–82): 31.

95. Dirlik, *Marxism in the Chinese Revolution*, 144.

96. See Lin Chun, "Mass Line," 123.

97. Similar accusations were launched against United Front work in other arenas. Groot, *Managing Transitions*, 69.

98. Scott, *Seeing like a State*, 4.

99. Scott, 4–5.

1. AMDO AT THE EDGE OF EMPIRE

1. *JFQH*, 5, 484; *DZQH*, 1:40–41; Qinghai Sheng Junqu Silingbu and Zhengzhibu, "Wo Jun Jiefang Qinghai," 1–2. Xunhua is the center of the Turkic-speaking Salar community but also has a significant Tibetan population. See chapter 2.

2. Zhaxi Anjia and Duojie. "Tongren Jiefang Qianhou," 171–72; Duojie and Zhao, "Aiguo Minzhu Renshi Xiaricang Shengping," 93; Stevenson, "Role of the Traditional Tibetan Tribal Leadership," 2–3. The Shartsang lineage is more properly referred to as the Rongwo Drupchen lineage.

3. *TRXZ*, 923–25. See also Zhao Qingyang, "Tongren Zongqianhu Jiawu Duojie Pianduan," 157. On the nangso and zongqianhu titles, see below.

4. Zhaxi Anjia and Duojie, "Tongren Jiefang Qinliji," 55. See also Duojie, "Jianli Tongren Xian Renmin," 256, and Zhao Long, "Yi Tongren Jiefang Jingguo," 260–61.

5. Zhaxi Anjia and Duojie, "Tongren Jiefang Qinliji," 56; Duojie and Zhao, "Aiguo Minzhu Renshi Xiaricang Shengping," 93–94; Zhao Long, "Yi Tongren Jiefang Jingguo," 261; Zhao Qingyang, "Ji Yiwei yu Dang," 151; *TRXZ*, 29, 709–10.

6. Duojie and Zhao, "Aiguo Minzhu Renshi Xiaricang Shengping," 93–94.

7. *JQSX*, 76; Xin and Wang, "Huiyi Jingye Wang Zheng Silingyuan," 134–36.

8. Bulag, *Collaborative Nationalism*, 67.

9. Makley, *Violence of Liberation*, 99. Makley is specifically referring to the Labrang region.

10. Schwieger, *Dalai Lama and the Emperor*, 11.

11. Schwieger, 17–18; Van der Kuijp, "Dalai Lamas," 343–46; Gamble, *Reincarnation in Tibetan Buddhism*; Oidtmann, *Forging the Golden Urn*, 24–29, 50.

12. Yang Hongwei refers to the historical intersection of "tribal," religious, and state power in Amdo as "society's operational mechanism of authority" (*shehui de quanli yunzuo jizhi*). Yang, "Xunhua Zangqu Quanli," 1–6.

13. Franke, *Tribal Chieftain to Universal Emperor*, 300; Petech, "Tibetan Relations with Sung China," 180–81.

14. In current administrative terms, the pacification commission had authority over not only the "Tibetan regions of Gansu and Qinghai [not including present-day Yushu Prefecture] and a small part of the Tibetan regions of Sichuan" but also "neighboring areas of China proper [*neidi*] and regions of mixed Tibetan and Han inhabitants." Wu Chengyi, "Lidai Wangchao Jinglue Qinghai," 35. See also Chen Qingying, "Year of the Establishment."

15. *HNZZ*, 1317.

16. Li and Li, *Anduo Zangzu Shilue*, 101; *HNGK*, 80; *HNZZ*, 155.

17. Sonam Tsering, "Historical Polity of Repgong."

18. Sonam Tsering; Dhondup, "Reb Kong," 37.

19. Qin, *Qinghai Longwusi*, 92. See also Dhondup, "Reb Kong," 39–42.

20. Sonam Tsering, "Historical Polity of Repgong"; Zhiguanba Gongquehudanbaraoji, *Anduo Zhengjiaoshi*, 292; Qin, *Qinghai Longwusi*, 20; Dhondup, "Reb Kong," 38–39; Tuttle, "Overview of Amdo." "Tabéhu" is a transliteration of a Chinese-language title meaning "Great Baihu." In all, six nangso houses would be established in eastern Amdo, four south of the Yellow River and two north of the river in present-day Hualong County. Danzhu Angben, *Zangzu Dacidian*, 554.

21. Sperling, " 'Divide and Rule' Policy in Tibet?," 351; Wei Xinchun, "Qinghai Zangqu Qianbaihu Zhidu," 54; Wang Jiguang, "Mingdai Biliwei Xinkao," 151; Kang and Sutton, *Contesting the Yellow Dragon*, 16–68.

22. *ZKXZ*, 9, *HNGK*, 80.

23. Sonam Tsering, "Historical Polity of Repgong"; Zhiguanba Gongquehudanbaraoji, *Anduo Zhengjiaoshi*, 293; Dhondup, "Reb Kong," 41–42.

24. Qin, *Qinghai Longwusi*, 93. For similar dynamics in Ming-era Songpan/Sharkhok, see Kang and Sutton, *Contesting the Yellow Dragon*, 24–32.

25. For examples of some of the less seismic changes, see Kang and Sutton, *Contesting the Yellow Dragon*.

26. Gray Tuttle suggests that it was only from "the rise of Gelukpa religious tradition since the 17th century" that both the term "Amdo" and its territorial extent came into being. "Overview of Amdo."

27. On the Lubsang-Danzin Rebellion and its consequences, see Katō, "Lobjang Danjin's Rebellion of 1723"; Katō, "Warrior Lamas"; and Perdue, "Empire and Nation in Comparative Perspective," 288–96.

28. See, for example, Sullivan, "Qing Regulation of the Sangha in Qinghai."

29. Dhondrup, "Reb Kong," 45–46; Dhondup and Diemberger, "Tashi Tsering." The qinwang were especially important as principal sponsors of Labrang Monastery.

30. See Sonam Tsering, "Historical Polity of Repgong"; Qin, *Qinghai Longwusi*, 82–90; and Dhondup, "Reb Kong," 45.

31. Dhondup, "Reb Kong." In addition to several Nyingma monasteries, Repgong is well known for its communities of lay Nyingma tantric practitioners (*ngakpa*).

32. Lipman, *Familiar Strangers*, 120–37.

33. *ZKXZ*, 540. On the late eighteenth- and early nineteenth-century disruptions in Amdo, see Cui, Zhang and Du, *Qinghai Tongshi*, 369–72.

34. Tilly, "How Empires End," 4.

35. Cooke, "Surviving State and Society," 404. On the genesis of Muslim power during the late Qing period and the subsequent relationships between branches of the Ma family and the Republican and Nationalist governments, see Lipman, *Familiar Strangers*.

36. Cooke, "Surviving State and Society," 406.

37. Fischer, "Close Encounters," 10.

38. Goodman, "Qinghai and the Emergence of the West," 386.

39. For example, see Horlemann, "Tibetans and Muslims in Northwest China," and Nietupski, *Labrang Monastery*, 177.

40. On the Ma Bufang regime, see Hunsberger, "Ma Pu-fang in Chinghai Province."

41. Barnett, *China on the Eve of Communist Takeover*, 185.

42. Roderick, *Covering China*, 104, 106.

43. Clark, *Marching Wind*, 13.

44. Lindbeck, "Communism, Islam and Nationalism in China," 485–86. The Ma family adopted and championed the Yihewani (Arabic: Ikhwan) order against the more established Islamic orders. The Yihewani was founded by Ma Wanfu in Gansu during the late nineteenth century as a scriptural fundamentalist movement. However, in the course of the early twentieth century, it became a socially conservative institution that, with patronage by the Ma family, advocated for Chinese national unity. See Lipman, *Familiar Strangers*, 200–11.

45. For example, see Horlemann, "Tibetans and Muslims in Northwest China," 154–62.

46. Bulag, *Mongols at China's Edge*, 43–44, 50–54; Hunsberger, "Ma Pu-fang in Chinghai Province," 150–53. On the GMD's hopes that the ceremony could help convince Mongol and Tibetan headmen to join the GMD in anti-Japanese resistance, see AAH, Xingzhengyuan, "Qinghai Juxing Haidianli," 014-010604-0014.

47. Tilly, "How Empires End," 4.

48. On the Guomindang's policies in Tibetan areas, both of which emphasize the regime's reliance on various forms of negotiation and compromise, see Tuttle, *Tibetan Buddhists*, and Lin, *Tibet and Nationalist China's Frontiers*.

49. Kimura and Berry, *Japanese Agent in Tibet*, 57.

50. Located north of Repgong in a wooded, hilly area on the southern bank of the Yellow River, with a population of over eight thousand, the Nangra was the largest chiefdom in the region that makes up today's Jianzha (T. Chentsa) County. Chen Qingying, *Zhongguo Zangzu Buluo*, 266–67; *JZXZ*, 685.

51. Zhao Qingyang, "Ji Yiwei yu Dang," 197; Zhang and Guo, "Junshi Xiaomie Canfei," 416; *HNZZ*, 1529. After 1949, both the Gurong Gyelsé Rinpoché and Kangtsé Welzang would become important United Front figures.

52. Chen Bingyuan, *Ma Bufang Jiazu*, 98–99. In response to the Japanese invasion, in 1938 the Guomindang ordered the establishment of ad hoc provincial advisory committees (*linshi canyihui*) as a means to rally support for the regime. They were made permanent in 1945 and extended to the county level. It is unclear whether Wangchen Döndrup's appointment as canyi was mostly ceremonial or if he was an active member of the advisory committee. For instance, neither Wangchen Döndrup or any of the headmen from the Repgong region who were also appointed as canyi (see below), appear in admittedly incomplete records of Qinghai's Provincial Advisory Committee from 1947. By contrast, both the Gurong Gyelsé Rinpoché and Zongqianhu Kangtsé Welzang are listed as committee members. See AAH, Neizhengbu, "Qinghai Linshi Canyihui An," 026000010674A.

53. Zhaxi Anjia, "Yi Wo Jiefang Qianhou," 243–44.

54. Qieben Jia, "Xinghai Aquhu Buluo Qianhu," 117. On the Mongol-Tibet School and for brief comments on Ma's strategy of hostage taking, see Bulag, *Mongols at China's Edge*, 51.

55. Zhaxi Anjia, "Yi Wo Jiefang Qianhou," 244. The position was not necessarily passed down from father to son, nor did it remain within a single patriline. Instead, the nangso was chosen from among the several branches of the clan, often leading to succession struggles. See Qin, *Qinghai Longwusi*, and Sonam Tsering, "Historical Polity of Repgong."

56. Horlemann, "Victims of Modernization?"

57. Duojie and Zhao, "Aiguo Minzhu Renshi Xiaricang Shengping," 90.

58. Deng Jingsheng, "Ma Bufang Liyong Zongjiao," 208–9; Cui, Zhang, and Du, *Qinghai Tongshi*, 550–51; Gedun Rabsal, "Reb kong gyi nyi ma nub pa."

59. *TRXZ*, 1088; Zhao Qingyang, "Tongren Zongqianhu Jiawu Duojie Pianduan," 157.

60. *TRXZ*, 1090; Zhaxi Anjia, "Yi Wo Jiefang Qianhou," 245–46.

61. Zhouta, *Gansu Zangzu Buluo*, 146–47.

62. According to most PRC sources, Ma played both sides in order to sabotage nationality unity. See Huangnan Zhou Zhengxie, "Huangnan Tiaojie," 266–67; Ruan, "Huigu Tiaojie Tongren Xian"; and Xibei Junzheng Weiyuanhui and Minzu Shiwu Weiyuanhui, "Huzhu Hurang."

63. *ZKXZ*, 55–56; *TRXZ*, 78. Prior to 1929, Qinghai had been administered under Gansu Province.

64. Hunsberger, "Ma Pu-fang in Chinghai Province," 145. On the organization and implementation of the baojia system in Qinghai, see Niu, "Ma Bufang de Baojia Zhidu."

65. *JZXZ*, 685; *HNZZ*, 980; *TRXZ*, 683–84.

66. *TRXZ* 80; *ZKXZ*, 56.

67. *ZKXZ*, 403.

68. *HNZZ*, 1549; *ZKXZ*, 403, 529.

69. This assumption is supported by the recollections of a headman from neighboring Guide County, Lhündrup Gyel, who in 1936 was dispatched to the Zeku region with his own "militia" at the behest of one of Ma Bufang's generals. See chapter 2.

70. See *ZKXZ*, 526, 543.

71. Chen Qingying, *Zhongguo Zangzu Buluo*, 253. A different chronology is provided in the *Zeku County Gazetteer*, which claims that Lubum served as disciplinary head of Gartsé Monastery from 1933 to 1936. In 1936, he traveled with Gyelwo Dorjé to Xining, where he was "appointed" qianhu. He is then said to have joined the GMD in 1940. *ZKXZ*, 528.

72. *ZKXZ*, 540, 543.

73. Lipman, *Familiar Strangers*, 166.

74. Bulag, *Mongols at China's Edge*, 49–51.

75. Tilly, "How Empires End," 4.

76. [Zhao] Qingyang, "Yiwei Jiujing Kaoyan de Minzhu Renshi," 165; Zhao Qingyang, "Tongren Zongqianhu Jiawu Duojie Pianduan," 157; *ZKXZ*, 530–31.

77. Wei Xinchun, "Qinghai Zangqu Qianbaihu Zhidu," 57; Qinghai Sheng Bianjizu, *Qinghai Sheng Zangzu Mengguzu*, 56.

78. Huang Wenyuan (T. Gönpo Namgyel) was a scion of Labrang's leading family and husband of the last qinwang, the "Mongol female prince" Trashi Tséring. See Chen and Zhouta, *Labulengsi yu Huangshi Jiazu*, 409, and Dhondup and Diemberger, "Tashi Tsering."

79. [Zhao] Qingyang, "Yiwei Jiujing Kaoyan de Minzhu Renshi," 165.

80. Wajia and Lajia, "Tongren Decang Buluo," 134–35; *ZKXZ*, 411.

81. Wajia and Lajia, 134–35.

82. Wajia and Lajia, 135; [Zhao] Qingyang, "Yiwei Jiujing Kaoyan de Minzhu Renshi," 165.

83. *ZKXZ*, 526.

84. Mitter, *Manchurian Myth*, 17.

85. Mitter, 19. Mitter is borrowing from Ronald Robinson's "Excentric Idea of Imperialism."

2. IF YOU KILL THE COUNTY HEAD, HOW WILL I EXPLAIN IT TO THE COMMUNIST PARTY?

1. Dongshan Lanzhou, "Wo de Guanren Shijia," 155.

2. *GDXZ*, 598–99.

3. Dongshan Lanzhou, "Wo de Guanren Shijia," 158–59.

4. *HZZZ*, 831; Ermu, "'Guide Wang' Ma Yuanhai," 251–52. After initially fleeing toward Xinjiang, Ma Yuanhai surrendered on October 25. He was escorted to the provincial capital under military guard, allegedly for his own protection. Ma died in January 1951. The official cause was illness.

5. Brook, "Collaboratist Nationalism in Occupied Wartime China," 162.

6. Duoji, "Jianli Tongren Xian Renmin," 257; Zhaxi Anjia and Duojie, "Tongren Jiefang Qianhou," 173. Despite the different characters used to transliterate Dorjé's name in these two works, it appears that Duoji and Duojie is the same person. See also *HZZG*, 87, and *TRXZ*, 29.

7. Born in the Kardzé area of Kham (C. Ganzi, Sichuan), Trashi Wangchuk joined the Red Army during the Long March. After arriving at the CCP's wartime base of Yan'an, he attended the newly established Nationalities Institute and was among the first group of Tibetans to join the CCP. On Trashi Wangchuk's career after 1949, see chapter 8.

8. Duoji, "Jianli Tongren Xian Renmin," 257.

9. Duojie and Zhao, "Aiguo Minzhu Renshi Xiaricang Shengping," 94. Dexinghai was one of several official trading concerns set up in 1926 by the Xining regime to levy taxes and monopolize the market for animal and agricultural products. In grassland regions, pastoral goods would be exchanged for tea and grains at what are described as artificially low prices and then exported to coastal markets at significant profit. Hunsberger, "Ma Pu-fang in Chinghai Province," 177; Zhang, Lei, and Tian, *Qinghai Xumu*, 27–28; *QHSZ XMZ*, 7.

10. Zhao Long, "Yi Tongren Jiefang Jingguo," 262. See also Duojie and Zhao, "Aiguo Minzhu Renshi Xiaricang Shengping," 94–95.

11. Duojie and Zhao, 94.

12. Duojie and Zhao, 94; Zhao Qingyang, "Tongren Zongqianhu Jiawu Duojie Pianduan," 158. Gyelwo Dorjé's son commanded this force.

13. Duoji, "Jianli Tongren Xian Remnin," 257.

14. *JQSX*, 84; Dreyer, "China's Minority Nationalities," 511.

15. Duoji, "Jianli Tongren Xian Remnin," 257; *TRXZ*, 29, 573, 608–9, 710–11.

16. Duoji, "Jianlin Tongren Xian Remnin," 258–59. See also Duojie and Zhao, "Aiguo Minzhu Renshi Xiaricang Shengping," 95, and Zhao Qingyang, "Ji Yiwei yu Dang," 152.

17. On the "coercive power exercised by hereditary leaders and monastic representatives" as a built-in mechanism for the de-escalation of violent confrontation in Amdo, see Pirie, "Feuding, Mediation, and Negotiation," 20.

18. Wajia and Lajia, "Tongren Decang Buluo," 132–33.

19. Duojie and Zhao, "Aiguo Minzhu Renshi Xiaricang Shengping," 95.

20. Zhang and Yao, "Qinghai Gezu Renmin Lianyihui," 243.

21. Zhaxi Anjia, "Yi Wo Jiefang Qianhou," 252.

22. Zhang and Yao, "Qinghai Gezu Renmin Lianyihui," 243.

23. Zhang and Yao, 245. It appears that the majority of delegates did eventually arrive in Xining. After Han Chinese (260 representatives), Tibetans (155) made up the conference's largest contingent, followed by Mongols (50), Hui (38), Monguor (Tu) (6), and Salar (3).

24. Cited in Zhaxi Anjia, "Yi Wo Jiefang Qianhou," 252–53.

25. Liao Hansheng, "Guanche Zhixing Minzu Pingdeng," 105–6.

26. Zhang and Yao, "Qinghai Gezu Renmin Lianyihui," 245.

27. Zhang and Yao, 244–45. The executive committee was made up of fifteen "Party/government/army representatives," plus six Tibetans, three Mongols, three Hui, one Salar, one Monguor, and three Han Chinese. Twelve of the fifteen state representatives appear to have been Han. Although himself a Labrang Tibetan, Huang Wenyuan, husband of the Mongol qinwang Trashi Tséring and son of Labrang's Apa Alo, was chosen one of the three "Mongol" chairmen. On the marriage alliance between Trashi Tséring and Huang Wenyuan, see Dhondup and Diemberger, "Tashi Tsering," 207–11.

28. Zhang and Yao, 249. The authors are paraphrasing rather than quoting Liao's speech.

29. Zhaxi Anjia, "Yi Wo Jiefang Qianhou," 253.

30. Duojie, "Jiefang Chu Xiaricang Huofo," 126–30; Wang and Zhao, "Xiaricang Huofo," 112–18. The Southwest Military Region was simultaneously organizing its own mission to Lhasa led by the Gétak Rinpoché of Kham's Béri Monastery. See Shakya, *Dragon in the Land of Snows*, 40–41.

31. On the endemic intercommunity violence that often permeated Amdo, particularly in pastoral areas, see Ekvall, "Peace and War among Tibetan Nomads."

32. Zhao Qingyang, "Ji Yiwei yu Dang," 153.

33. Even today, grassland disputes tend to be mediated by religious authorities and community leaders. In some cases, as both Emily Yeh and Fernanda Pirie have noted, the state actively cedes its legal and administrative responsibilities to these nonstate or quasi-state actors. Yeh, "Tibetan Range Wars," 514–20; Pirie, "Segmentation within the State," 90–94.

34. Zhaxi Anjia, "Yi Wo Jiefang Qianhou," 245. Other sources depict a far more protracted process of negotiation in which Trashi Namgyel played a less central role and that instead involved a host of Party, state, and indigenous actors. See, for example, Huangnan Zhou Zhengxie, "Huangnan Tiaojie," 266–67, and Ruan, "Huigu Tiaojie Tongren Xian."

35. Details of the resolution can be found in Xibei Junzheng Weiyuanhui and Minzu Shiwu Weiyuanhui, "Huzhu Hurang." Apa Alo's authority was based on his familial connections to two of the major trülku lineages at Labrang Monastery, those of the Fifth Jamyang Shepa and the Fourth Welmang, which he parlayed into becoming the region's paramount military and political leader. After a brief post-1949 flirtation with GMD-affiliated

insurgencies, Apa Alo joined the new state, serving in several senior provincial positions in the local government. See Nietupski, *Labrang*, 81–93.

36. Zhaxi Anjia, "Yi Wo Jiefang Qianhou," 246–47.

37. Reprinted in *JQSX*, 92–103. The report was originally published on January 7, 1950, days before the opening of the Friendship and Unity Conference.

38. *JQSX*, 45; Zhao Long, "Yi Tongren Jiefang Jingguo," 260.

39. *JQSX*, 20–21. See also speeches by Peng Dehuai and Qinghai Party Secretary Zhang Zhongliang in *JQSX*, 104–7, 125–27, 141–53.

40. *JQSX*, 45–6, 49–52; Rohlf, *Building New China*, 9.

41. *JQSX*, 45–46.

42. *JQSX*, 49–50.

43. *JQSX*, 49–50.

44. Dreyer, "China's Minority Nationalities," 517.

45. Zhang Zhongliang, "Ba Dang de Minzu Zhengce," 142.

46. For example, see the November 30, 1949, editorial in the *Qinghai Daily*, reprinted in *JQSX*, 206–7.

47. Li and Xu, *Datong Xianzhi*, 106, 477–80. The Datong uprising was led by the Eighth Brigade's former commander, General Ma Ying. According to the county gazetteer, during the nine-day insurrection, security forces killed 837 combatants and either captured or accepted the surrender of over one thousand more. See also *JQSX*, 211, 213, 229.

48. Wei Cong, *Xunhua Salazu Zizhixian Zhi*, 37, 599, 855, 89. See also Weiner, "In the Footsteps of Garaman," 50.

49. See the speech by Liao Hansheng excerpted in the *Qinghai Daily* on October 24, 1950, reprinted in *JQSX*, 252–53.

50. Li Xibo, "Lu'ershi zai Guide Jiaofei," 14.

51. Zhang and Guo, "Jiefang Qinghai Chuqi," 416–17. See also Yang Jiuce, "Weijiao Angla Gufei de Huiyi," 431–32.

52. *JZXZ*, 511.

53. Zhang and Guo, "Junshi Xiaomie Canfei," 416; Zhao Qingyang, "Yiwei Jingli Quzhe de Minzhu Renshi," 197–98; *JQSX*, 247; *JZXZ*, 685.

54. Zhang and Guo, "Junshi Xiaomie Canfei," 415–19.

55. Zhang and Guo, "Jiefang Qinghai Chuqi," 33.

56. Zhang and Guo, "Junshi Xiaomie Canfei," 417–19; *JZXZ*, 511. The Second Army had two regiments raised from among the Nangra and a third from elsewhere in Guide.

57. Dongshan Lanzhou, "Wo de Guanren Shijia," 138.

58. Dongshan Lanzhou, 139. Makley documents abuses committed by overambitious (and possibly corrupt) cadres in the Labrang region. *Violence of Liberation*, 49–52.

59. *JQSX*, 214.

60. *JQSX*, 208.

61. Reproduced in *JQSX*, 269–72, and *Qinghai Wenshi Ziliao Xuanji* 15 (1987), 53–55.

62. Liao Hansheng, "Qinghai Sheng Renmin Junzheng," 96.

63. Short descriptions of all seventeen missions are found in Zhang and Guo, "Junshi Xiaomie Canfei," 420–23, and Zhang and Guo, "Jiefang Qinghai Chuqi," 37–40.

64. Zhang and Guo, "Junshi Xiaomie Canfei," 423–24; Yang Jiuce, "Weijiao Angla Gufei de Huiyi," 432–34. According to official sources, 264 defenders were killed in the assault, along with 467 captured and another 864 surrendered. The PLA suffered eighty-nine deaths and seventy-one injured. Wang Danzheng, "Yi Jiefang Jianzha Angla Er San Shi," 42. For detailed descriptions of the military campaign, see *JQSX*, 276–95.

65. The announcement is reproduced in *JQSX*, 273–74.

66. *JQSX*, 275. Despite these assurances, a contemporary report from the First Regiment, First Army, admits (without much elaboration) that the "organizational discipline" displayed by its soldiers was "very poor." See *JQSX*, 294.

67. Zhang and Guo, "Junshi Xiaomie Canfei," 423–27. On a roughly parallel rebellion in the Songpan/Sharkhok region of Ngawa (northern Sichuan), see Kang and Sutton, *Contesting the Yellow Dragon*, 232–34.

68. Wangchen Döndrup had been hiding in a forested area of neighboring Tongren County. For a Nangra guerrilla's description of the hardships they experienced while in the mountains, see Information and Publicity Office of His Holiness the Dalai Lama, *Tibet under Chinese Communist Rule*, 18–19.

69. Zhang and Guo, "Junshi Xiaomie Canfei," 428–30; Xibeiju Tongzhanbu and Xibei Minwei Dangzu, "Guanyu Pingxi Angla," 301.

70. Reproduced in *Qinghai Wenshi Ziliao Xuanji* 15 (1987), 56–59.

71. Xibeiju Tongzhanbu and Xibei Minwei Dangzu, "Guanyu Pingxi Angla," 305.

72. Xibeiju Tongzhanbu and Xibei Minwei Dangzu, 300, 306. These were rebellions among the Labrang area Achok Tibetans and Hui Muslims in Xiji (present-day Ningxia Hui Autonomous Region).

73. Cited in Zhang and Guo, "Jiefang Qinghai Canfei," 52.

74. Stevenson, "Role of the Traditional Tibetan Tribal Leadership," 6n7 (emphasis added).

75. Zhou Renshan, "Jixu Kaizhan Minzu Quyu Zizhi Yundong," 644. Zhou specifically cited the contiguous territories of present-day Zeku and Henan Counties and Guoluo Prefecture. On the Ma regime's defensive arrangements in southern Amdo, see Ma Letian, "Ma Bufang zai Qinghai," 63–65; *HNZZ*, 980–1; and Dhondup and Diemberger, "Tashi Tsering," 205–7.

76. Li and Zhang, "Ma Yuanxiang Gufei de Fumie," 435–36. *HNZZ* (p. 1026) and its abbreviated version, *HNGK* (p. 90), agree with Li and Zhang, claiming that Ma was originally a Tibetan named Labuzang.

77. *HNGK*, 90.

78. Xibeiju Tongzhanbu and Xibei Minwei Dangzu, "Guanyu Pingxi Angla," 310–11. The admission that Ma was essentially forced to take up arms was made by the Northwest Bureau in December 1952 and offered as an example of the consequences of poor nationalities work.

79. *JQSX*, 329–32.

80. Li and Zhang, "Ma Yuanxiang Gufei de Fumie," 436; Xibeiju Tongzhanbu and Xibei Minwei Dangzu, "Guanyu Pingxi Angla," 309–11. In addition to Ma Yuanxiang and Ma Liang, the Guomindang leadership sought to enlist Labrang's Apa Alo and two headmen from Ngawa to lead a rear-guard guerrilla movement that might aid GMD efforts to recapture the Chinese mainland. See the proposal submitted by Mao Renfeng to Chiang Kaishek on February 29, 1952, and related documents in AAH, Jiang Zhongzheng Zongtong Dang'an, 002-080102-00103-001. See also Lin, *Modern China's Ethnic Frontiers*, xxi–xxii, and Kang and Sutton, *Contesting the Yellow Dragon*, 232–35. On the airdrops, see *JQSX*, 360–66.

81. *JQSX*, 311–12, 316. According to the Qinghai Party Committee, Ma Yuanxiang's agents were active in Tongren (including Zeku), Tongde, Jianzha, Guide, Hualong, Xinghai, Xunhua, and Guoluo.

82. *JQSX*, 318. See also instructions by the Qinghai Military District's Political Department, in *JQSX*, 322–23.

83. Ma was shot in the stomach during a skirmish on May 7. His body was found ten days later and brought to Ragya Monastery for identification. On the military operations, see Li and Zhang, "Ma Yuanxiang Gufei de Fumie," 437–40, and related documents in *JQSX*, 329–55.

84. *JFQH*, 507. The Qinghai Military District proclaimed Ma's defeat the "elimination of the last remnant political bandits on the Mainland." Qinghai Sheng Junqu Silingbu and Zhengzhibu, "Wo Jun Jiefang Qinghai," 9.

85. See the introduction to part 3 in *JQHC*.

86. Bulag, "Models and Moralities," 24; Abu-Lughod, "The Romance of Resistance."

3. BECOMING MASTERS OF THEIR OWN HOME

1. ZCPG, folder 2, folio 7; ZCPG, folder 7, folio 5.

2. ZCPG, folder 2, folio 13.

3. Mosely, introduction to *Party and the National Question*, 17; Heberer, *China and Its National Minorities*; Phan, "Autonomous Areas of the PRC?"; Smith, *Tibetan Nation*, 348–51. See also Zang, *Ethnicity in China*, 97–103.

4. Gladney, "Internal Colonialism and China's Uyghur," 20. See also Winichakul, *Siam Mapped*, 16–17, and Adelman and Aron, "From Borderlands to Borders," 840.

5. This summary is drawn from Zhou Renshan's speeches collected in *MZGWH*. I am grateful to Jianglin Li for sharing selections from this very important source.

6. Huang Jingbo, "Wuyi Wanghuai Zhou Renshan," 52–53; *ZGQH ZZ*, 18, 308. On Zhou's career in Central Tibet, particularly his fall during the Cultural Revolution, see Weiner, "When 'the Sky Fell to the Earth.'"

7. Goldstein has documented discord in both Central Tibet and Kham areas of Sichuan over the pace of socialist reforms. My contention is not that similar dynamics necessarily were absent from Qinghai—it is that these debates were not relayed to lower-level administrations. When policy did shift, as described in later chapters, it appears to have followed the pattern described by Frederick Teiwes and Warren Sun as a "shifting consensus." Goldstein, *History of Modern Tibet*, vol. 3; Teiwes and Sun, "Editors' Introduction," 2, 19.

8. Mao, "Some Questions Concerning Methods of Leadership," 114.

9. *TRXZ*, 551.

10. *ZKXZ*, 15; Jiayong, "Zai Muqu Congshi Yiliao Weisheng," 275. Gyelyön claims that they left on September 1. However, he is almost certainly mistaken. There is no record of a similar force departing at the start of September.

11. Jiayong, "Zai Muqu Congshi Yiliao Weisheng," 269–70.

12. Jiayong, 272.

13. Jiayong, 275

14. According to Bianca Horlemann, when a similar but much larger work group was sent into the Golok region in summer 1952, arrangements had been made in advance of their arrival, including an agreement with a local headman on where their base of operations would be located. Although not mentioned by Gyelyön—who as a low-level cadre perhaps was not privy to all of the details of the assignment—it seems likely that similar preparations had been made in Zeku. See Horlemann, "'Liberation' of Golog."

15. According to the county gazetteer, the average September temperature in the county seat is forty degrees Fahrenheit (4.2 degrees Celsius). By October, it drops to thirty degrees Fahrenheit (minus 1.5 degrees Celsius) and continues to fall, not approaching the freezing point again until April. *ZKXZ*, 60, 76.

16. Jiayong, "Zai Muqu Congshi Yiliao Weisheng," 278.

17. ZCPG, folder 2, folio 15. The documents only refer to the Chinese toponym "Zeku." It is not clear whether the headmen were only objecting to the Chinese name or the proposed Tibetan county name, Tsékhok, as well. On Du Hua'an, see Ruan, "Wo Xinmu zhongde Xianwei Shuji."

18. *ZKXZ*, 1.

19. Hor gtsan Jigs med, *Mdo smad lo rgyus chen mo*. Hortsang Jigme instead refers to a region known as Tsézhung, which appears to have referred to the lands belonging to the Mongol qinwang, including parts of the future Zeku County.

20. For example, in a speech delivered to a pastoral work conference in summer 1952, Zhou Renshan referred to Zeku County alongside other extant county administrations. Zhou, "Jixu Kaizhan Minzu Quyu Zizhi Yundong," 644, 51.

21. ZCPG, folder 2, folio 1. See also *ZKXZ*, 332.

22. On debates among early Soviet social scientists, theorists, and planners over the characteristics of nomadism and its position within Marxist paradigms of social evolution, see Cameron, *Hungry Steppe*, 60–69.

23. *TRXZ*, 551.

24. "Zhou Renshan Tongzhi Di'erzi Dangdaihui," 629–30. Even in the "eastern agricultural areas" north of the Yellow River, land reform was not implemented in Tibetan agricultural regions, places in which Tibetans lived intermixed with other communities, or where agriculture and pastoralism coexisted. *QHSZ NYZ*, 65.

25. Bulag, *Mongols at China's Edge*, 120. The Three Nos, and its corollary, the "Two Benefits" (*liangli*) first became official policy at a 1948 meeting of CCP leaders of Inner Mongolia. Promising to promote the "mutual benefit of herdlord and herd laborer," in Qinghai the Two Benefits was described as "a policy to aid poor pastoralists develop production"—for example, by pressuring wealthy herdsmen to *voluntarily* reduce interest rates on loaned animals and to pay higher wages to hired workers. *QHSZ XMZ*, 66. On the Three Nos and Two Benefits, see also Ling, *Tibet*, 83–85; Bensen and Svanberg, *China's Last Nomads*, 113–14.

26. Zhang, Lei, and Tian, *Qinghai Xumu*, 66; *QNHJS*, 227–28, 31.

27. See "Summary of Basic Expressions in Promoting Regional Autonomy among Minority Nationalities," reproduced and translated in Ling, *Tibet*, 79.

28. Zhou Renshan, "Guanyu Jiji Tuixing Minzu Quyu Zizhi," 623.

29. Zhou Renshan, "Jixu Kaizhan Minzu Quyu Zizhi Yundong," 637–38.

30. "Zhou Renshan Tongzhi Di'erzi Dangdaihui," 634.

31. Zhou Renshan, "Guanyu Jiji Tuixing Minzu Quyu Zizhi," 623.

32. Zhou Renshan, "Jixu Kaizhan Minzu Quyu Zizhi Yundong," 637–38.

33. Chen Sigong, "Qinghai Sheng Tuixing Minzu Quyu Zizhi," 657. Chen would remain a senior member of the Qinghai leadership into the 1960s, serving as a standing committee member of the provincial Party committee for much of that time and leading several Party organs, including the powerful Organization Department and Disciplinary Inspection Committee.

34. Zhou Renshan, "Jixu Kaizhan Minzu Quyu Zizhi Yundong," 649.

35. Zhou Renshan, 644. See also "Zhou Renshan Tongzhi Di'erzi Dangdaihui," 630–31.

36. Zhe Wu, "Caught between Opposing Han Chauvinism," 309. See, for example, the directive issued by the NAC in 1953, "Summary of Basic Expressions in Promoting Regional Autonomy among Minority Nationalities," reproduced and translated in Ling, *Tibet*, 36–48, especially 38–42. See also Mao Zedong's comments on the relationship between the Han and minority nationalities in his 1956 address "On the Ten Major Relationships" (Lun Shida Guanxi), Ling, 55–56.

37. Zhou Renshan, "Jixu Kaizhan Minzu Quyu Zizhi Yundong," 648–49. In 1922, Vladimir Lenin remarked on the need to "distinguish between the nationalism of oppressor nations and the nationalism of oppressed nations, the nationalism of large nations and the nationalism of small nations," concluding that "in almost all historical practice, we nationals of the large nations are guilty, because of an infinite amount of violence [committed against smaller nations]." Quoted in Martin, *Affirmative Action Empire*, 7. See also Hirsch, *Empire of Nations*, 29.

38. *MZGWH*, 485. The Northwest Bureau was referencing Mao Zedong's 1953 directive, "Criticize Han Chauvinism" (Pipan Da Hanzu Zhuyi), translated in Ling, *Tibet*, 53–54.

39. On these ornate headdresses (*rawa*) and the role they play in coming-of-age rituals and gendered dimensions of life cycles, see Makley, *Violence of Liberation*, 117–18.

40. *MZGWH*, 483.

41. "Zhou Renshan Tongzhi Di'erzi Dangdaihui," 628.

42. Bulag, *Collaborative Nationalism*, 67.

43. These critiques were not confined to Amdo. See, for example, NAC vice chairman Ulanhu's address to the state council, reproduced as "Report on the General Program for the Implementation of Regional Autonomy for Minorities," translated in Ling, *Tibet*, 23.

44. "Zhou Renshan Tongzhi Di'erzi Dangdaihui," 634.

45. "Zhou Renshan Tongzhi Di'erzi Dangdaihui," 636.

46. "Zhou Renshan Tongzhi Di'erzi Dangdaihui," 628 (emphasis added).

47. Zhou Resnshan, "Jixu Kaizhan Minzu Quyu Zizhi Yundong," 646.

48. Zhou, 649 (emphasis added).

49. Zhou, 647–48.

50. Zhou, 652.

51. *MZGWH*, 620–21.

52. Chen Sigong, "Qinghai Sheng Tuixing Minzu Quyu Zhizhi," 656.

53. Zhou Renshan, "Jixu Kaizhan Minzu Quyu Zizhi Yundong," 647–48.

54. Zhou, 639.

55. Zhou, 648.

56. Zhou, 641, 55.

57. Zhou, 645.

58. Zhou, 655.

59. "Zhou Renshan Tongzhi Di'erzi Dangdaihui," 629.

60. Zhou Renshan, "Jixu Kaizhan Minzu Quyu Zizhi Yundong," 655. According to Zhou, this period would last two years.

61. "Zhou Renshan Tongzhi Di'erzi Dangdaihui," 628 (emphasis added).

62. Bulag, "Ethnic Resistance with Socialist Characteristics," 185–86; Gladney, "Representing Nationality in China," 100; Harrell, "Introduction," 19, 26.

63. "Zhou Renshan Tongzhi Di'erzi Dangdaihui," 634 (emphasis added).

64. Zhou Renshan, "Jixu Kaizhan Minzu Quyu Zizhi Yundong," 639–40.

65. *MZGWH*, 617.

66. *MZGWH*, 483–84.

67. ZCPG, folder 2, folio 12.

68. *TRXZ*, 578.

69. *TRXZ*, 578–79; *ZGHN LD*, 13.

70. *ZKXZ*, 305.

71. ZCPG, folder 2, folios 2, 16.

72. "Zhou Renshan Tongzhi Di'erzi Dangdaihui," 629. When referring to transnationality sentiments within a unified nation-state, rather than speaking of minzu tuanjie, the documents more often employ the phrase *aiguozhuyi*, literally "love-of-country-ism" or more commonly "patriotism." By contrast, nationalism, or *minzuzhuyi*, held the negative connotation of single-nationality parochialism at the expense of broad multi-nationality unity.

73. ZCPG, folder 2, folios 68–70.

74. *ZKXZ*, 550.

75. ZCPG, folder 2, folio 13. Party guidelines dictated that a "nationality representative" (i.e., a minority elite) be put in charge of autonomous region governments while an "outside cadre" (i.e., a Party representative) serve as second-in-command. See "Zhou Renshan Tongzhi Di'erzi Dangdaihui," 627; Zhou Renshan, "Jixu Kaizhan Minzu Quyu Zizhi Yundong," 640.

76. ZCPG, folder 2, folio 3; ZCPG, folder 4, folio 94.

77. According to the Chinese sociologist Pu Wencheng, in 1949 the two largest fixed-place monasteries in the region each had fewer than two hundred resident monks. Many of the others were mobile "tent monasteries." Pu, *Gan Qing Zangchuan Fojiao Siyuan*,

481–89. See also Nian and Bai, *Qinghai Zangchuan Fojiao Siyuan Mingjian*, 169–73, 299–301, and *ZKXZ*, 498–503.

78. ZCPC, folder 1, folio 11. See also ZCPG, folder 2, folio 5.

79. ZCPG, folder 2, folios 5–6.

80. ZCPG, folder 4, folio 94.

81. ZCPG, folder 4, folios 95–96. See also ZCPG, folder 4, folio 134.

82. ZCPG, folder 2, folio 3.

83. ZCPG, folder 1, folio 5. An appendix with the names of the delegates and comments from the masses is missing.

84. ZCPC, folder 1, folio 9.

85. ZCPC, folder 1, folio 9.

86. ZCPG, folder 2, folio 5.

87. ZCPC, folder 1, folio 6.

88. ZCPG, folder 2, folio 14.

89. ZCPG, folder 4, folio 140.

90. ZCPG, folder 4, folio 140.

91. ZCPC, folder 1, folio 5.

92. ZCPG, folder 2, folios 6–7; ZCPG, folder 4, folio 140.

93. ZCPC, folder 1, folio 6.

94. ZCPG, folder 2, folio 7.

95. Xi Chen, *Social Protest and Contentious Authoritarianism*, 90.

96. ZCPG, folder 2, folio 17. See also ZCPG, folder 2, folios 220–32. Neither the blueprint nor the budget is available.

97. ZCPC, folder 1, folio 135.

98. ZCPG, folder 4, folio 108. See also ZCPG, folder 4, folios 89, 137.

99. ZCPG, folder 4, folio 109; ZCPG, folder 15, folio 69; *ZKXZ*, 364.

100. ZCPG, folder 2, folio 68.

101. ZCPG, folder 4, folios 121–22.

102. ZCPG, folder 4, folio 137.

103. See Huangnan Zhou Zengxie, "Minzu Tuanjie Hao," 63–67.

104. ZCPG, folder 4, folio 136. See also ZCPG, folder 4, folio 108.

105. ZCPC, folder 5, folio 78. See also ZCPG, folder 15, folios 62–63.

106. ZCPC, folder 1, folios 10–11. Not all were technically grassland disputes. For example, they included cases of banditry and even domestic disputes.

107. ZCPC, folder 15, folio 69.

108. See, for example, ZCPC, folder 6, folio 78.

109. ZCPG, folder 2, folio 70; ZCPC, folder 6, folios 68, 79. In response, Serökyap was fined a total of 570 yuan.

110. ZCPC, folder 8, folios 7–8; ZCPC, folder 9, folio 10. To this day, grassland disputes continue to be a semiregular occurrence in Amdo. Emily Yeh and Fernanda Pirie have both written on the occurrence of grassland feuds during the reform era. Yeh asserts that the imposition of state territoriality has caused an increase in their frequency, while Pirie sees these disputes as a continuation of pre-1949 patterns of violence largely dictated by the segmented nature of "tribal" society and a culture in which male honor is tied to "ideologies of loyalty and revenge." Yeh, "Tibetan Range Wars," 515–20; Pirie, "Order, Individualism and Responsibility," 62–69; Pirie, "Feuding, Mediation and Negotiation.

111. ZCPG, folder 2, folio 19.

112. ZCPG, folder 2, folio 19. Because most of China's hard currency reserves had been shipped to Taiwan and its economy substantially delinked form the global economy, it is difficult to determine a meaningful value for the renminbi during the 1950s. A new renminbi would be issued in 1955 and valued at a rate of 1:10,000 to the old currency. See ZKX, 262.

113. ZCPG, folder 1, folio 6.

114. ZCPG, folder 1, 6; ZCPG, folder 2, folios 19–20.

115. Ling, *Tibet*, 82.

116. As of February 1954, women made up just seventeen of the 144 CCP and government cadres working in Zeku County. ZCPG, folder 1, folio 4.

117. ZCPG, folder 3, folios 2, 10. Population figures were calculated by assuming four people per household. On the allotment policy, see Guo Min's pronouncement in ZCPG, folder 2, folio 4, and *ZKXZ*, 324.

118. ZCPG, folder 2, folios 10, 13; ZCPG, folder 3, folio 10.

119. ZCPG, folder 3, folios 10–12; ZCPC, folder 3, folio 1; *ZKXZ*, 333.

120. ZCPG, folder 4, folio 121.

121. ZCPG, folder 3, folio 103. Several pages including the title page are missing, making the author unidentifiable.

122. ZCPG, folder 1, folio 11.

123. The Zeku County Party Committee would be officially established in February 1954, replacing the Zeku County Work Committee, which on December 1 had replaced the County Establishment Preparatory Work Group. Guo Min served as secretary of all three.

124. At the time Huangnan was called an "area" (*qu*). Following new constitutional guidelines, in 1955 it was rechristened a "prefecture" (*zhou*). The remaining vice chairman was the Eighth Lamo Sertri, an important trülku from Lhamo Dechen Monastery in Jianzha County. Wagya was the lowest-ranking of the six.

125. ZCPG, folder 3, folio 12.

4. ESTABLISHING A FOUNDATION AMONG THE MASSES

1. ZCPG, folder 4, folio 124; ZCPG, folder 3, folio 8. For example, to Zeku's south in the future Henan Mongolian Autonomous County, residual Ma Yuanxiang–affiliated "counterrevolutionary" activity prevented preparatory work from beginning until October 1953. *HNGK*, 89.

2. *ZKXZ*, 382.

3. Shue, *Peasant China in Transition*, 195–96; Teiwes and Sun, "Editor's Introduction," 8.

4. *QNHJS*, part 1; *DZQH*, 1:70. Basic-level cooperatives had been established in some of Qinghai's agricultural areas as early as 1952.

5. ZCPG, folder 2, folios 73–74. See also ZCPG, folder 2, folios 75–88, and ZCPG, folder 14, folios 11–17.

6. ZCPG, folder 5, folio 28.

7. Scott, *Seeing like a State*, 183–84.

8. ZCPG, folder 7, folios 2–3.

9. ZCPC, folder 8, folio 11; ZCPG, folder 5, folio 76. The five work teams were organized as follows: Hor, Shawonar, Gönshül (including Shisa), Sonak (including Wöngya and Gartsé), and Méshül (including Khéri Chunga and Ködé Karing).

10. ZCPG, folder 7, folio 91; ZCPG, folder 7, folios 1–3.

11. ZCPG, folder 1, folios 21–3, 27–28, 43–45.

12. Ling, *Tibet*, 90–91.

13. ZCPG, folder 1, folios 19–20.

14. ZCPC, folder 8, folio 11.

15. ZCPC, folder 8, folio 21. On Nyingma practice in the Repgong region, see Dhondup, "Reb Kong," and Dhondup, "Rules and Regulations."

16. ZCPC, folder 8, folios 20–21.

17. ZCPG, folder 7, folio 39. See also ZCPG, folder 2, folio 97.

18. ZCPG, folder 8, folio 12.

19. ZCPG, folder 7, folio 36.

20. ZCPG, folder 1, folios 16–29. For comparison, see ZCPG, folder 1, folios 35–40, which were filed by the Hor Work Group.

21. ZCPG, folder 5, folios 3–5. Documents dated May 13 to May 18 show that much of what was discussed after the formal opening of the conference had already been worked out during preliminary meetings. Although I refer in this passage to the Second Joint Committee, I do not distinguish between the interim period discussions for which detailed transcripts and reports exist and the formal conference for which there are only summary reports.

22. ZCPG, folder 5, folio 3.

23. ZCPG, folder 5, folios 58–59. The Gurong Gyelsé Rinpoché had been a member of the third North Korea Greetings and Solicitude Delegation (Chaoxian Weiwentuan). He would serve on the first three provincial government committees (1955–66) before being purged at the start of the Cultural Revolution, making him one of the few Tibetan leaders to retain his position through the 1958 Amdo Rebellion. Nian and Bai, *Qinghai Zangchuan Fojiao Siyuan Mingyuan*, 302; *ZGQH ZZ*, 299–303, 598–603.

24. ZCPG, folder 5, folios 58–59. On the juvenilization of minority peoples as younger siblings in need of guidance from their Han elder brothers, see Borchigud, "Impact of Urban Ethnic Education," and Bulag, "Ethnic Resistance with Socialist Characteristics," 8–9.

25. Bulag refers to these tours as "political tourism." Bulag, "Seeing like a Minority." See also Mortensen, "Harnessing the Power of Tibetan Elites," and Kang and Sutton, *Contesting the Yellow Dragon*, 234.

26. ZCPG, folder 5, folio 53.

27. ZCPG, folder 5, folios 52–53.

28. ZCPG, folder 5, folio 129.

29. ZCPG, folder 5, folio 57. See also ZCPG, folder 5, folios 54, 135, 136. On the evolution of criticism and self-criticism as mechanisms of revolutionary discipline and then mass mobilization, see Dittmer, *Liu Shao-Ch'i and the Chinese Cultural Revolution*, 336–58.

30. ZCPG, folder 14, folio 4.

31. ZCPG, folder 5, folio 54.

32. ZCPG, folder 5, folio 131.

33. ZCPG, folder 5, folios 54–57.

34. ZCPG, folder 14, folio 4; ZCPG, folder 5, folio 28.

35. *MZGWH*, 484.

36. ZCPG, folder 5, folio 133.

37. ZCPG, folder 5, folios 55, 57.

38. ZCPG, folder 5, folio 56 (emphasis added).

39. ZCPG, folder 5, folio 133.

40. *HNZZ*, 847–48, 1537–39; Stevenson, "Role of the Traditional Tibetan Tribal Leadership," 15–16; Zhao Qingyang, "Ji Yiwei yu Dang," 155. In 1958, Gélek Gyatso married a Tibetan woman with whom he had two children.

41. ZCPC, folder 6, folio 86; ZCPG, folder 5, folios 48–49, 64; ZCPC, folder 8, folios 22–23.

42. ZCPG, folder 1, folios 19–20.

43. *ZKXZ*, 351.

44. ZCPG, folder 2, folio 28. More than 36 million yuan was allocated to the Hor chiefdom, while the Khéri Chunga, Ködé Karing and Shisa received between 2.7 and 4.7 million each. According to the county gazetteer, during the early years of the PRC the silver dollar (*yinyuan*) remained the primary currency of exchange on Zeku's grasslands. One silver dollar was worth 10,000 yuan, meaning that when the new renminbi was introduced in 1955 it was theoretically equal in value to a silver dollar. *ZKXZ*, 262.

45. ZCPG, folder 2, folios 28–30. See also *ZKXZ*, 351. One hundred and fifty-six families received between 20 to 140 jin (ten to seventy kilograms) of grain per household. According to a contemporary report, in 1953 and 1954 the central government provided Qinghai with over fourteen billion yuan to be dispensed as pastoral loans and another sixteen billion for emergency relief. Ling, *Tibet*, 96.

46. ZCPG, folder 2, folios 31–32.

47. ZCPG, folder 5, folios 64, 71, 130; ZCPC, folder 6, folio 84.

48. ZCPG, folder 5, folios 48–49.

49. ZCPG, folder 5, folios 50, 51. According to reports, the entire prefecture was given 830 million yuan in relief funds. Given its much smaller population, the 230 million allocated to Zeku County was actually a rather large per capita percentage of the funding.

50. ZCPG, folder 5, folio 56.

51. ZCPC, folder 15, folio 19. In September 1953, the NAC outlined the pastoral sector's role within this triad of mutual support. See Ling, *Tibet*, 86–87.

52. ZCPG, folder 1, folio 20.

53. ZCPG, folder 5, folios 48–50.

54. ZCPG, folder 5, folios 49–52.

55. ZCPG, folder 5, folio 78.

56. ZCPG, folder 5, folios 48, 50.

57. ZCPG, folder 1, folio 20.

58. ZCPG, folder 14, folio 19.

59. ZCPG, folder 5, folio 127.

60. ZCPG, folder 5, folio 128.

61. ZCPG, folder 5, folio 126. As noted in chapter 3, a new renminbi, was introduced in 1955 at a rate of 1:10,000 to the old currency.

62. ZCPG, folder 5, folio 129.

63. ZCPG, folder 7, folio 109.

64. ZCPG, folder 7, folio 130.

65. ZCPG, folder 7, folio 131.

66. The method of pressure most often cited was levying fines. See ZCPG, folder 15, folio 71; ZCPG, folder 5, folio 123.

67. ZCPG, folder 7, folio 20.

68. ZCPG, folder 7, folio 110.

69. ZCPG, folder 5, folio 131.

70. ZCPG, folder 5, folio 75.

71. ZCPG, folder 5, folio 63. The first constitution of the PRC was formally enacted on September 20, 1954.

72. ZCPG, folder 14, folios 44–45.

73. ZCPG, folder 5, folios 63–64.

74. ZCPG, folder 2, folio 65 (emphasis added).

75. ZCPG, folder 5, folio 70.

76. ZCPG, folder 5, folio 70. The NAC had made these points in its 1953 directive on pastoral regions. See Ling, *Tibet*, 86–87.

77. ZCPG, folder 5, folio 70. As the largest chiefdom, the Hor was to provide the largest share of animals—357 head of cattle and 6,013 sheep. By comparison, the next largest quota was given to the Méshül (40 head of cattle and 542 sheep), then the Shawonar (39 and 516), Gönshül (29 and 406), and so on.

78. ZCPG, folder 5, folios 62–63.

79. ZCPG, folder 1, folios 24–25.

80. ZCPG, folder 7, folios 97–98.

81. ZCPG, folder 5, folio 70.

82. *ZKXZ*, 254.

83. ZCPG, folder 1, folio 23.

84. ZCPG, folder 1, folio 24.

85. ZCPG, folder 8, folios 41–43.

86. ZCPG, folder 1, folios 23–24, 29.

87. ZCPG, folder 8, folio 43 (emphasis added). See also ZCPG, folder 10, folios 3, 59.

88. ZCGC, folder 1, folio 25. See also ZCPG, folder 8, folios 41–43. On tax policy and tax evasion in agricultural regions of China, where an initial reliance on self-reporting also proved inadequate, see Shue, *Peasant China in Transition*, 99–143.

89. ZCPG, folder 2, folio 97.

90. ZCPG, folder 2, folio 99; ZCPG, folder 10, folio 47; ZCPG, folder 15, folio 66. The Hor Work Group's 1954 work report estimated that more animals actually died in 1954 than were added to the Hor's herds. Considering that the Hor accounted for upward of one third of Zeku's population, this puts the county's statistics into further question. See ZCPG, folder 2, folio 74; ZCPG, folder 1, folios 28–29.

91. ZCPG, folder 2, folio 97–99.

92. ZCPG, folder 1, folios 35, 38, 41, 44–45.

93. *ZKXZ*, 344, 347.

94. ZCPG, folder 1, folio 34.

95. ZCPG, folder 2, folio 69; ZCPG, folder 10, folio 38.

96. ZCPG, folder 1, folio 30; ZCPG, folder 5, folio 27. The grain problem would continue to plague Zeku. See, for example, the county grain office's 1955 summary report discussing difficulties related to planning, propaganda, oversight, transport, theft, hording, and black markets. ZCPG, folder 13, folios 26–30.

97. ZCPG, folder 15, folios 67–68.

98. ZCPG, folder 1, folios 16, 54.

99. ZCPG, folder 15, folios 70–71.

100. ZCPG, folder 2, folios 97–99, 102; ZCPG, folder 15, folios 66–71.

101. ZCPG, folder 1, folios 54–55.

5. HIGH TIDE ON THE HIGH PLATEAU

1. ZCPG, folder 15, folio 32.

2. ZCPG, folder 15, folios 68–75.

3. ZCPG, folder 15, folios 32–33.

4. ZCPG, folder 15, folios 70–71.

5. ZCPC, folder 9, folio 10. Language courses were slated to begin in November. It is not clear if the program was ever launched or to what effect.

6. ZCPG, folder 15, folios 32–33; ZCPG, folder 15, folio 110.

7. *DZQH*, 1:56–9, 68–71; *QHSZ NYZ*, 69–71.

8. ZCPC, folder 14, folio 19.

9. ZCPG, folder 14, folio 1.

10. ZCPC, folder 15, folio 39.

11. ZCPC, folder 15, folio 39.

12. ZCPG, folder 15, folios 62–63.

13. *NJZWH*, 283.

14. Cited in *QNHJS*, 235–36. A veteran cadre who joined the CCP in 1933, to that point Gao Feng had served his entire career in China's northwest. In 1952, he was transferred from Xinjiang to Qinghai, where he became vice secretary of the provincial Party committee. At the time of Gao's appointment as Qinghai first Party secretary, his predecessor, Zhang Zhongliang, assumed the same position atop Gansu's Party organization.

15. *DZQH*, 1:71. For an overview of the rationale, organization, and implementation of agricultural MATs during the High Tide, see Walker, "Collectivisation in Retrospect"; Shue, *Peasant China in Transition*, 144–91, 275–317, and Bernstein, "Leadership and Mass Mobilisation."

16. ZCPG, folder 15, folios 66–73; *QHSZ XMZ*, 68–69.

17. ZCPC, folder 6, folio 8 (emphasis added).

18. *QNHJS*, 232.

19. ZCPC, folder 6, folios 8–9.

20. ZCPC, folder 6, folio 9. The exception was Guoluo Prefecture, which was instructed to choose two sites.

21. ZCPC, folder 6, folios 19, 34, 44.

22. ZCPC, folder 6, folios 11–12.

23. ZCPC, folder 6, folios 21–24. Scott, *Seeing like a State*, 4, 89–90.

24. ZCPC, folder 6, folio 23.

25. ZCPC, folder 6, folio 14.

26. *QNHJS*, 239. Party planners did express concern that extant class and power relationships might be replicated in the new cooperatives. On the employment of existing forms of rural cooperation on agricultural MATs, see Shue, *Peasant China in Transition*, 149–56.

27. ZCPC, folder 6, folios 36–37 (emphasis added). Similar pronouncements can be found in a report from a work team investigating conditions among Chöbum Gyel's Atsok chiefdom in Xinghai (T. Drakkar) County. *QNHJS*, 238–39.

28. ZCPC, folder 6, folio 31.

29. ZCPC, folder 6, folio 33.

30. ZCPC, folder 6, folios 32–33.

31. ZCPC, folder 6, folio 68.

32. ZCPC, folder 6, folios 67–68.

33. ZCPC, folder 6, folio 67. This "partial report" was submitted December 4. The county Party committee did not submit its final report until January 18, 1956, well after Xining's mid-December deadline. See ZCPC, folder 6, folios 69–94.

34. ZCPC, folder 6, folio 68.

35. ZCPC, folder 6, folios 78–79 (emphasis added).

36. ZCPC, folder 11, folios 36–37.

37. ZCPC, folder 6, folios 88–89.

38. ZCPC, folder 6, folio 78.

39. ZCPC, folder 11, folio 36.

40. ZCPC, folder 6, folios 75–76. On collectivization in Inner Mongolia, see Sneath, *Changing Inner Mongolia*, 62–102, and Bulag, *Mongols at China's Edge*, 114–25.

41. ZCPC, folder 6, folio 68.

42. ZCPC, folder 6, folios 91–92.

43. ZCPC, folder 6, folio 64.

44. ZCPC, folder 6, folio 79.

45. *DZQH*, 1:73; *QHSZ XMZ*, 68–69; Zhang, Lei, and Tian, *Qinghai Xumu*, 122–23.

46. *QHSZ XMZ*, 70.

47. *QNHJS*, 240–42. These four stipulations can also be found in a March 1954 report by Zhou Renshan. At the time, however, Zhou categorically stated that the conditions had not yet been met. *QNHJS*, 235. See also *QHSZ XMZ*, 68–71, and *TRXZ*, 268.

48. *DZQH*, 1:73.

49. *QHSZ XMZ*, 70.

50. *QNHJS*, 244. These orders were initially announced at the end of December and then reissued on March 3 as part of a provincial Party committee report. See also *DZQH*, 1:73.

51. *QNHJS*, 245.

52. *DZQH*, 1:73–74.

53. ZCPC, folder 13, folios 1–2. See also *ZKXZ*, 17.

54. ZCPC, folder 13, folio 3.

55. ZCPC, folder 6, folios 75–76.

56. ZCPC, folder 6, folios 75–76.

57. ZCPC, folder 13, folio 27; *ZKXZ*, 296, 313. At the beginning of 1956, Zeku County had a total of 58 CCP members and 70 CYL members. By the end of the year, the numbers had risen to 127 and 74, respectively. Of these, just 28 CCP and 12 CYL members were Tibetan.

58. ZCPC, folder 13, folios 3–4.

59. *QHSZ XMZ*, 69.

60. ZCPC, folder 13, folios 4–6. See also *QHSZ XMZ*, 70.

61. ZCPC, folder 13, folio 5.

62. *QHSZ XMZ*, 69–70. See also *ZKXZ*, 115; Ling, *Tibet*, 89–90; and *QNHJS*, 238.

63. ZCPC, folder 13, folio 5.

64. ZCPC, folder 13, folios 5–8. Yearly production targets for the traditional animals again were surprisingly moderate: an increase of 7 percent for horses, 9 percent for cattle, and 16.5 percent for sheep and goats.

65. *QHSZ XMZ*, 69.

66. ZCPC, folder 13, folios 8–9. The plan called for the construction of two mid-sized and fourteen smaller reservoirs.

67. ZCPC, folder 13, folios 12–13. On state-owned pastoral farms, see Ling, *Tibet*, 92. In Qinghai, see Zhang, Lei, and Tian, *Qinghai Xumu*, 264–88; *QHSZ XMZ*, 230–40; and *QNHJS*, 265–73.

68. ZCPC, folder 13, folio 8.

69. On the link between collectivization and sedentarization in Soviet Kazakhstan, see Pianciola, "Famine in the Steppe," especially 154–56.

70. ZCPC, folder 11, folio 54.

71. ZCPC, folder 11, folio 53.

72. ZCPC, folder 11, folio 54.

73. Rohlf, *Building New China*, 4, 69–77, 130–52. The program was called "Support the Construction of the Frontier" (Zhibian Bianjiang Jianshe).

74. Ling, *Tibet*, 88. See also Zhang, Lei, and Tian, *Qinghai Xumu*, 124–25.

75. ZCPC, folder 13, folios 13–14.

76. ZCPC, folder 13, folios 127, 131.

77. ZCPC, folder 13, folios 132–34.

78. ZCPC, folder 13, folios 127–28.

79. *ZKXZ*, 148.

80. Rohlf, *Building New China*, 70. Rohlf notes that one hundred thousand youth volunteers were brought to Qinghai in the late 1950s and early 1960s. A main purpose was to feed the region's other new residents, many of whom had been sent to exploit Qinghai's natural resources, especially in the Tsadam Basin. See Rohlf, "Dreams of Oil and Fertile Fields," 455–63.

81. Rohlf, *Building New China*, 249–56.

82. *ZKXZ* 149–51.

83. ZCPC, folder 13, folio 17.

84. ZCPC, folder 7, folio 40.

85. ZCPC, folder 7, folio 78.

86. ZCPC, folder 7, folios 51–54.

87. ZCPG, folder 1, folio 156.

88. ZCPC, folder 7, folio 44.

89. ZCPC, folder 7, folio 44.

90. *QNHJS*, 243; Goldstein, *History of Modern Tibet*, 3:124–40; Kang and Sutton, *Contesting the Yellow Dragon*, 248–49.

91. ZCPC, folder 7, folio 44.

92. *QNHJS*, 241.

93. ZCPC, folder 7, folios 74–75 (emphasis added).

94. *ZKXZ*, 17, 115. At the time of its founding, Guanghui Cooperative was made up of seventeen households. This would grow to twenty-eight households with 119 members, sixty-five of whom were classified as laborers.

95. ZCPC, folder 7, folio 74. Over the course of the spring, opposition to the High Tide had been building among some segments of the CCP leadership. See Teiwes and Sun, *China's Road to Disaster*, 20–31.

96. *QNHJS*, 243.

97. *QNHJS*, 243; *HNGK*, 96–97; *TRXZ*, 698–99; *QHSZ JSZ*, 514; Chen Yunfeng, *Dangdai Qinghai Jianshi*, 150.

98. *QNHJS*, 243.

99. *QNHJS*, 243.

100. Wang Haiguang, "Radical Agricultural Collectivization," 283.

101. *QNHJS*, 246–47.

102. *QNHJS*, 243.

103. *QNHJS*, 243–44.

104. *QNHJS*, 242–43.

105. ZCPC, folder 16, folio 46; *DZQH*, 1:74; *QNHJS*, 237.

106. In agricultural regions of Hubei and Hunan Provinces, Shue asserts, "At the bottom level there had been pressure for a top-level go-ahead to permit the quick, final expropriation [of the wealth] of upper-middle and rich peasants." *Peasant China in Transition*, 330–31. See also Goldstein, *History of Modern Tibet*, 3:88–89.

107. See, for example, Bernstein, "Leadership and Mass Mobilisation," and Yu, "Why Did It Go So High?" 56. For examples of strategies of resistance to the High Tide among Han peasants, see Friedman, Pickowicz, and Selden, *Chinese Village, Socialist State*, 185–213, and Perry, *Challenging the Mandate of Heaven*, 281–85.

108. Wang Haiguang, "Radical Agricultural Collectivization," 282. On the Khampa Rebellion, see Goldstein, *History of Modern Tibet*, vol. 3; McGranahan, *Arrested Histories*; and Jianglin Li, *Tibet in Agony*, 1–20.

109. *DZQH*, 1:74; *QNHJS*, 247.

6. TIBETANS DO THE HOUSEWORK, BUT HAN ARE THE MASTERS

1. MacFarquhar, *Origins of the Cultural Revolution*, 1:99–138. MacFaquhar translates *jizao maojin* as "impetuosity and adventurism."

2. For an overview, see Zhou Zhongyu, "Dang de Bada yu Muyequ de Shehuizhuyi Gaizao."

3. *Zhongguo Gongchandang Dibaci Quanguo Daibiao Dahui Wenxian*, 367–69; Zhou Zhongyu, "Dang de Bada yu Muyequ de Shehuizhuyi Gaizao," 61.

4. Jianglin Li, *Tibet in Agony*, 46–47, 64–65.

5. *Zhongguo Gongchandang Dibaci Quanguo Daibiao Dahui Wenxian*, 368–69.

6. Teiwes and Sun, *China's Road to Diasaster*, 20.

7. Dreyer, *China's Forty Millions*, 149–50. See, for example, the documents translated in Ling, *Tibet*, 190–96, 266–70.

8. Deng's address was delivered at a special meeting of the NAC convened in Qingdao, discussed later in the chapter.

9. Mosely, introduction to Chang, *The Party and the Nationality Question*, 24–25; McMillen, *Chinese Communist Power*, 113; Teiwes, *Politics and Purges in China*, 290–93; Smith, "Nationalities Policy of the Chinese Communist Party," 60; Goldstein, Sherap, and Siebenschuh, *Tibetan Revolutionary*, 224.

10. Dreyer, "China's Minority Nationalities," 520.

11. In 1959, Guo Min resurfaced as a vice secretary of the Hualong County Party Committee, serving in that capacity until May 1963. *ZGQH ZZ*, 112.

12. *ZGHN ZZ*, 34; *ZKXZ*, 17, 278–79, 282.

13. *ZKXZ*, 18.

14. ZCPC, folder 13, folio 160. On Party building, see also ZCPC, folder 9, folio 10, and ZCPC, folder 13, folios 25–30.

15. ZCPC, folder 11, folios 33, 39–46, 58; ZCPC, folder 16, folios 42–8; *ZKXZ*, 143. The outbreak was blamed on the introduction of diseased animals from Central Tibet.

16. ZCPC, folder 11, folios 33–34.

17. ZCPC, folder 11, folio, 37; ZCPC, folder 16, folios 41, 43; ZCPG, folder 1, folio 13.

18. ZCPC, folder 16, folio 43.

19. ZCPC, folder 16, folio 47.

20. ZKPC, folder 16, folio 70.

21. ZKPC, folder 16, folio 68.

22. ZKPC, folder 16, folio 69.

23. ZKPC, folder 16, folio 67.

24. ZKPC, folder 16, folios 70–71.

25. ZKPC 16, folio 34.

26. ZKPC 19, folio 65.

27. ZKPC 19, folio 67. For parallel accusations published in national propaganda outlets, see Lo Ping-cheng, "What Is Great Hanism," in Ling, *Tibet*, 269.

28. ZCPC, folder 19, folio 67.

29. In Ling, *Tibet*, 192–93.

30. ZCPC, folder 19, folios 68–69.

31. ZCPC, folder 19, folios 68–69.

32. Zhe Wu, "Caught between Opposing Han Chauvinism," 317–19, 37; Brophy, "1957–59 Xinjiang Committee Plenum."

33. ZCPC, folder 20, folio 5.

34. ZCPC, folder 20, folios 2–3.

35. *ZKXZ*, 272; *TRXZ*, 543; *HNZZ*, 807. All twenty-four cadres targeted in Tongren were later cleared.

36. "Zhonggong guanyu zai Shaoshu Minzu," 3–4.

37. Dreyer, *China's Forty Millions*, 151. A report issued in January 1958 indicates that across Qinghai, only fifty-one people identified as a member of a minority nationality were ultimately confirmed as rightists. "Qinghai Sheng ji yishang Jiguang Zhengfeng Yundong de Jinzhang Qingkuang he Anpai" (January 10, 1958), in ZFYS.

38. ZCPC, folder 19, folios 69–70.

39. ZCPC, folder 17, folio 39.

40. ZCPC, folder 17, folios 4, 2–3. On the extent of the ongoing damage brought on by natural disaster and livestock epidemics, see ZCPC, folder 16, folios 5–7.

41. ZCPC, folder 17, folio 44.

42. ZCPC, folder 17, folio 45. While both the Zeku County Party Committee and Huangnan Prefecture expressed general agreement with Li's findings, they admitted that because Li and his team only visited sixteen families, it was far from comprehensive. See ZCPC, folder 17, folios 39–41.

43. *QNHJS*, 247.

44. *QNHJS*, 247–48.

45. *QNHJS*, 247.

46. See Dreyer, *China's Forty Millions*, 150–51; Minglang Zhou, "Politics of Bilingual Education," 150; Smith, *Tibetan Nation*, 429–32; *DZMG*, 1:258–71.

47. Teiwes, *Politics and Purges in China*, 261.

48. Teiwes, *Politics and Purges in China*, 264–65; Teiwes and Sun, *China's Road to Disaster*, 66–72; MacFarquhar, *Origins of the Cultural Revolution*, 1:1, 311–17. An example can be found in January instructions issued by the Qinghai Provincial Party Committee's Rectification Small Group. See "Qinghai Sheng ji yishang Jiguang Zhengfeng Yundong de Jinzhang Qingkuang he Anpai" (January 10, 1958) in ZFYS.

49. Teiwes and Sun, *China's Road to Disaster*, 71.

50. MacFarquhar, *Origins of the Cultural Revolution*, 1:4.

51. *QHSZ ZSZ*, 211. The speech was delivered at the closing of the Fourth Plenum of the Second Qinghai Party Committee.

52. *QNHJS*, 248–50.

53. *QNHJS*, 248–50; *DZQH*, 1:75.

54. *QNHJS*, 248.

55. "Zhonggong guanyu zai Shaoshu Minzu," 2.

56. Peng, "Qinghai Shengwei dui Guanche Zhixing Zhonggong," 22.

57. ZCPC, folder 16, folio 8. The three PPCs were to be built in the Hor, Shawonar, and Duofudun (Méshül, Ködé Karing, and Khéri Chunga chiefdoms) Districts. Joint-ownership pastoral cooperative farms were described as a "form of national capitalism" expressly appropriate for reforming herdlords during the transition to socialism. In Liu Zexi's Beijing speech, he called for 80 percent of Qinghai's herdlords (1,080 households) to be enrolled on one of 216 joint-ownership pastoral farms by the end of the Third Five-Year Plan. See *QNHJS*, 250–51, 265–68.

58. ZCPC, folder 23, folio 102.

59. ZCPC, folder 16, folios 8, 11–2.

60. ZCPC, folder 16, folio 23. For the central UFWD's orders outlining these policies, see "Zhonggong guanyu zai Shaoshu Minzu," 3–4.

61. *ZKXZ*, 306.

7. REACHING THE SKY IN A SINGLE STEP

1. *ZKXZ*, 411; *HNGK*, 101.

2. Scott, *Weapons of the Weak*.

3. See, for example, Zhaxi Anjia, "Yi Wo Jiefang Qianhou," 244; ZCPG, folder 4, folio 124; and *ZKXZ*, 382.

4. *GSSZ JSZ*, 804. The UFWD director's name was Cao Xueyan.

5. Scott, *Art of Not Being Governed*.

6. Sutton, "Ngaba in the 1950s," 285–86; Zhang Wu, "Gannan Zangqu 'Shuanggai'" Jingguo," 15.

7. *QHSZ JSZ*, 514; Chen Yunfeng, *Dangdai Qinghai Jianshi*, 151.

8. *LQXZ*, 21–23, 327–29; *HNGK*, 96–97; Robin, "Uneasy Incorporation of a Tibeto-Mongolian Community." Robin reports that prior to the massacre, a Shitsang headman named Kelzang Rachu hid himself among the Serlung. The *Luqu County Gazetteer* claims that 137 rebels were killed, 72 wounded, and 230 captured in a final battle on June 24.

9. *HNGK*, 96–97; *QHSZ JSZ*, 514; Chen Yunfeng, *Dangdai Qinghai Jianshi*, 158.

10. *HNGK*, 97.

11. *TRXZ*, 698; *HNGK* 98. Gyelwo Dorjé purportedly traveled to Central Tibet with 150 people, including his entire family and many close acquaintances. See also *ZGGL*, 218–19.

For a wonderful first-person account of a large caravan traveling from Amdo to Lhasa during this time period, see Nakstang Nulo, *My Tibetan Childhood*.

12. See, for example, the instructions issued in June 1958 by the Qinghai Provincial Party Committee (and personally approved by Mao Zedong), in *QHSZ FLZ*, 647–50. Sources out of Gannan are more likely to cast blame on instigation by Guomindang spies and their purported American backers. See *ZGGL*, 217–25; Zhang Wu, "Gannan Zangqu 'Shuanggai' Jingguo," 13–14; and Xin and Zhao, "Jianzheng 'Amang Shijian," 304. There is little evidence of direct outside involvement. However, records found in the national archives in Taiwan show that the GMD government maintained hope that ethnic rebellion in western China could help destabilize the Communist regime. See AAH, Guomindang Wenzhuanhui Dangshiguan, Tejiao Dang'an, Feiqing Baogao (601), 002-080300-00067, files 001-009 and 021.

13. See *QHSZ FLZ*, 742–50, and *QHSZ JSZ*, 515.

14. *QHSZ XMZ*, 75; *DZQH*, 1:75; Zhonggong Huangnan Zhouwei, "Huangnan Diqu Pingxi Panluan," 1046.

15. *QHSZ FLZ*, 648–49, 52. See also Peng, "Xunhua Salazu Zizhixian," 15.

16. *DZQH*, 1:75; *QHSZ DSJ*, 234. On the central policies and elite rivalries that helped lead to the Great Leap Forward, see Teiwes and Sun, *China's Road to Disaster*, and MacFarquhar, *Origins of the Cultural Revolution*, vol. 2.

17. ZCPC, folder 23, folios 99–105.

18. ZCPC, folder 23, folio 105.

19. ZCPC, folder 23, folios 105–7.

20. In Li Jianglin, *Dang Tieniao zai Tiankong Feixiang*, 218.

21. *QHSZ DSJ*, 233–34. See also Li, *Dang Tieniao zai Tiankong Feixiang*, 212–17.

22. In Luo Guanwu, *Xin Zhongguo Minzu Gongzuo Dashi Gailan*, 285–86. See also the documents compiled by Gansu's NAC as study material for the campaign against local nationalism, in *FDXZ*.

23. Huihuiguo alludes to a Japanese plot during the Sino-Japanese War to establish a Muslim puppet state in northern China. See Lin, *Tibet and Nationalist China's Frontier*, 107–8, and Hammond, *China's Muslims and Japan's Empire*.

24. Zhang Wu, "Gansu Dangbiaohui Jiefa," 3–7. See also "Zhonggong guanyu zai Shaoshu Minzu," 3. These types of accusations were common in campaigns against local nationalism. See Teiwes, *Politics and Purges in China*, 290–93.

25. Wang Feng, "Guanyu Shaoshu Minzu zhong Jinxing Zhengfeng," 11.

26. Xie, "Ba Fandui Minzuzhuyi," 39.

27. Xie, 44–46.

28. *QNHJS*, 275.

29. ZCPG, folder 34, folio 101.

30. ZCPC, folder 23, folios 142–44, 158, 167.

31. *QNHJS*, 251.

32. Gai, "Qinghai Muqu Ge Jiceng," 12; Peng, "Qinghai Jiasu dui Xumuye," 14.

33. Nie, "Jianjue ba Qinghai Muqu Shehuizhuyi," 5.

34. *QHSZ DSJ*, 234. Sun was one of three governors ousted in the early stages of the Great Leap Forward. Teiwes, *Politics and Purges in China*, 278, 285–86. For the charges against Sun and three others in Qinghai, see Zhonggong Gongchandang Qinghaisheng Di'erjie Daibiaohui Di'erci Huiyi guanyu Tongyi Qingqu Youpaifenzi Sun Zuobin deng Chudang de Hueyi (June 20, 1958), in ZFYS.

35. *ZKXZ*, 286. Chen was from Shandong Province.

36. One internally circulated report notes that Gannan experienced rebellion in 1953, was "*relatively* calm" from 1954 to 1955, saw rebellion again in 1956, was again "*relatively*

calm" in 1957, and finally exploded in "all-out rebellion" in 1958. Zhang Wu, "Gannan Zangqu 'Shuanggai' Jingguo," 15 (italics added).

37. *LQXZ*, 329. See also *ZGGL*, 217–18; 222–23.

38. Zhang Wu, "Gannan Zangqu 'Shuanggai' Jingguo," 15; *MQXZ*, 676. The Maqu County gazetteer suggests that the leadership of Labrang Monastery orchestrated the attack, a "detail" not found in contemporary accounts.

39. *ZGGL*, 225.

40. The Dongxiang are a small Mongol-speaking Muslim community designated as one of China's fifty-six official minzu.

41. Zhang Wu, "Gannan Diqu Fasheng Wuzhuang Panluan," 3–4. See also "Gan Qing Diqu Kangbao Zhuangkuang," in AAH, Guomindang Wenzhuanhui Dangshiguan, Tejiao Dang'an, Feiqing Baogao (601), 002-080300-00067-008, 52-3.

42. Zhang Wu, "Gannan Zangqu 'Shuanggai' Jingguo," 15–17. See also *GSSZ JSZ*, 805; *ZGGL*, 226; and Pieragastini, "Regulating Religion."

43. Peng, "Huangnan Zangzu Zizhizhou," 3; Chen Yunfeng, *Dangdai Qinghai Jianshi*, 152. The Fifth District includes the territories of the Dowa chiefdom just to the north of Zeku County.

44. Zhonggong Huangnan Zhouwei, "Huangnan Diqu Pingxi Panluan," 1046–47. See also *HNGK*, 98–99, and *TRXZ*, 698–99.

45. *QHSZ JSZ*, 51; *HNGK*, 98–9; Jianglin Li, *Tibet in Agony*, 48. According to a contemporary but unsubstantiated charge, in December 1957, the Gyanak Weltsang Rinpoché and others sent representatives to Huangnan and Gannan Prefectures to coordinate plans for an uprising. Allegedly, local cadres and activists discovered the plot, but their report failed to get the attention of their superiors. Peng, "Xunhua Salazu Zizhixian," 15.

46. Peng, "Qinghai Huangnan Dengdi Fasheng Wuzhuang Panluan," 3–4;

47. Han, *Yichang bei Yinmoliao de Guonei Zhanzheng*, 5.

48. Wei Cong, *Xunhua Salazu Zizhixhian Zhi*, 47, 600, 890; *QHSZ FLZ*, 652–54; Peng, "Qinghai Huangnan Dengdi Fasheng Wuzhuang Panluan," 3–4; *QHSZ JSZ*, 514, 519, 525.

49. Jianglin Li, *Tibet in Agony*, 49.

50. Wei Cong, *Xunhua Salazu Zizhixhian Zhi*, 855. Li reports that 435 were killed in the initial assault and another 284 wounded. In the rebellion's immediate aftermath, twenty-five hundred people were imprisoned. Of those, nearly two-thirds were Salar. Jianglin Li, *Tibet in Agony*, 48–49; Li Jianglin, "Qinghai 'Xunhua Shijian' Shimo"; Weiner, "In the Footsteps of Garaman."

51. Peng, "Huangnan Zangzu Zizhizhou," 3. See also *HNZZ*, 1032–33.

52. *QHSZ DSJ*, 237. See also "Gan Qing Diqu Kangbao Zhuangkuang," in AAH, Guomindang Wenzhuanhui Dangshiguan, Tejiao Dang'an, Feiqing Baogao (601), 002-080300-00067-008, 57-60.

53. *QHSZ JSZ*, 515.

54. Zhang Wu, "Gannan Zangqu 'Shuanggai' Jingguo," 16.

55. *QNHJS*, 277. See also *ZGGL*, 233, 165–66; Chen Yunfeng, *Dangdai Qinghai Jianshi*, 159; and Jianglin Li, *Tibet in Agony*, 56.

56. Peng, "Qinghai Muyequ Wuzhuang Panluan de Qingkuang," 14.

57. On the rebellion in Linxia, see Pieragastini, "Regulating Religion"; *GSSZ JSZ*, 806–7.

58. *QHSZ FLZ*, 648–49. See also Peng, "Muqian Qinghai Shehui Zhian Qingkuang," 10–11.

59. Huang Jing, "Gansu Renda Wuci Huiyi," 16; Peng, "Qinghai Huangnan Dengdi Fasheng Wuzhuang Panluan," 5. On the debate over the virtues of various Islamic practices, including the idhn/kouhuan, see Huang Jing, "Gansu Sheng Gezu Daibiao dui Minzu Zongjiao Wenti," 19–20.

60. *QHSZ FLZ*, 654–57; Peng, "Qinghai Sheng Shaoshu Minzu Dangyuan," 16.

61. Zhang Wu, "Gannan Diqu Fasheng Wuzhuang Panluan," 3–4. The Sixth Gungtang Lama, Jikmé Tenpé Wangchuk (1926–2000), was in many ways a paradigmatic subimperial operative. According to Paul Nietupski, "Always exhibiting the flexibility necessary for survival in this region, [prior to 1949] he worked as a diplomat and intermediary between Tibetan and Chinese authorities." After 1949, he served within the new provincial government while also attending to his duties at Labrang. See Nietupski, *Labrang Monastery*, 146–47. For a brief overview of the Sixth Gungtang Lama's life, including his arrest and imprisonment, see Samten Chhosphel, http://treasuryoflives.org/biographies/view/Jigme-Tenpai-Wangchuk/8128.

62. *QHSZ FLZ*, 658–59.

63. *QHSZ FLZ*, 653–54; Peng, "Xunhua Salazu Zizhixian," 15.

64. Zhonggong Huangnan Zhouwei, "Huangnan Diqu Pingxi Panluan," 1045–46.

65. *ZGHN ZZ*, 160; *ZGHN LD*, 50. For the manner in which the Shartsang Lama was used in the subsequent propaganda campaigns, see ZCPC, folder 30, folio 207.

66. *ZKXZ*, 19.

67. See Zhonggong Huangnan Zhouwei, "Huangnan Diqu Pingxi Panluan," 1045–46, and *QHSZ JSZ*, 513–17.

68. *ZGHN LD*, 50. On the "one-sided battle"—known to locals as the "massive massacre on the banks of the Machu River"—between the Datsen and other chiefdoms of Sogpo (Henan) and the PLA, see Lama Jabb, *Oral and Literary Continuities*, 119–22. For a brief Chinese account of the rebellion in Henan, see *HNZZ*, 1032.

69. ZCPC, folder 24, folio 7.

70. *QHSZ DSJ*, 240.

71. See, for example, Peng, "Qinghai Sheng Jiang Kaishi," 7–8.

72. Anagnost, "Who Is Speaking Here?," 263. Anagnost notes that due to its "deeply emotional content," Speaking Bitterness was not simply a unidirectional process imposed or scripted by the Party-state but instead might unleash many potential outcomes.

73. Makley, "'Speaking Bitterness,'" 47. See also Javed, "Speaking Bitterness," and Bulag, "Can the Subalterns Not Speak?," 100.

74. Zhonggong Huangnan Zhouwei, "Huangnan Diqu Pingxi Panluan," 1046.

75. Zhonggong Huangnan Zhouwei, 1046. The implication is that individuals participated in multiple Speaking Bitterness struggle sessions and against multiple targets.

76. *ZKXZ* 411; *HNGK*, 101; *QHSZ JSZ*, 525.

77. ZCPC, folder 24, folios 7–8.

78. ZCPC, folder 24, folio 8.

79. ZCPC, folder 24, folios 21–22. Execution was reserved for "those reactionary herdlords and headmen who took advantage of their power to kill without cause." It is not clear if or how often capital punishment was carried out in Zeku.

80. *ZKXZ*, 306.

81. ZCPC, folder 24, folio 1.

82. ZCPC, folder 24, folio 6. The Zeku County Party Committee would also report that by the end of summer, 64 percent of Zeku's male population had "cut their braids and shaved their heads" and 49 percent of women had cut their hair. However, only 8.4 percent of the latter had yet shed their traditional dress.

83. *ZKXZ*, 306.

84. Pu, *Gan Qing Zangchuan Fojiao Siyuan*, 481

85. Zhongyang Minzu Shiwu Weiyuanhui Dangzu, "Guanyu Dangqian Yisilanjiao Lamajiao Gongzuo," 7–9.

86. "Zhongyang Pizhuan Minwei Dangzu," 6.

87. "Gansu Zangqu Jiben Qingkuang," 5–6. A Party history of Gannan boasts that of the prefecture's 242 monasteries and mosques in existence prior to 1958, all but six were demolished. *ZGGL*, 235.

88. Wang Tiqiang, "Linxia Jiaofei he Fanfengjian Tequan," 8–19.

89. Cited in Jianglin Li, *Tibet in Agony*, 58.

90. ZCPC, folder 24, folio 21.

91. Zhonggong Huangnan Zhouwei, "Huangnan Diqu Pingxi Panluan," 1046. See also *QHSZ FLZ*, 648–49.

92. Nie, "Jianjue ba Qinghai Muqu Shehuizhuyi," 5.

93. Peng, "Qinghai Jiasu dui Xumuye," 15.

94. *DZQH*, 1:75.

95. *QHSZ XMZ*, 72.

96. *TRXZ*, 269.

97. *QNHJS*, 275–76; *ZKXZ*, 414–15.

98. ZCPC, folder 24, folio 22. That owners did sometimes kill their animals rather than give them to the cooperatives is confirmed in the archival sources. For example, see ZCPC, folder 30, folio 209.

99. ZCPC, folder 24, folio 5.

100. *QHSZ FLZ*, 671–75. Party secretary Gao Feng had first announced the policy at an August 24 gathering with provincial leaders and then in a series of telephone meetings with prefectural and county officials. Guang, "Qinghai Sheng Shi Zheyang Ban Renmin Gongshe de," 3.

101. Chen Yunfeng, *Dangdai Qinghai Jianshi*, 142; *QHSZ XMZ*, 76; *ZKXZ*, 115. For instructions on the organization and administration of pastoral people's communes, see *QHSZ FLZ*, 676–701.

102. Animals of herdlords and headmen accused of participating in the rebellion were confiscated, while those not alleged to have rebelled purportedly received compensation. Given that the majority of Amdo's traditional elite were accused of counterrevolutionary crimes, it is unclear how often the latter occurred. *ZKXZ*, 115. See also *QHSZ XMZ*, 75–76.

103. *HNZZ*, 1032–33.

104. *ZKXZ*, 20, 412; *HNZZ*, 1032–33; *HNGK*, 101–2.

105. For a brief update on the military situation as of May 1959, see *QHSZ FLZ*, 713–22.

106. Peng, "Qinghai Panfei Yinmou," 6. See also Peng, "Qinghai Feiqing jiqi Huodong Tedian," 15–17, and Peng, "Qinghai Muqu Panfei Huodong Youqu Xiaozhang," 13–4.

107. Xin and Zhao, "Jianzheng 'Amang Shijian,'" 304–11.

108. *HNGK*, 102.

109. *QHSZ JSZ*, 519–25.

110. *QHSZ FLZ*, 650 (emphasis added).

111. "Yuan Renyuan Tongzhi," 725.

112. ZCPC, folder 24, folio 7 (emphasis added). See also Zhonggong Huangnan Zhouwei, "Huangnan Diqu Pingxi Panluan," 1052.

113. Nie, "Jianjue ba Qinghai Muqu Shehuizhuyi," 6.

114. Nie, 6.

115. Xie, "Ba Fandui Minzuzhuyi," 45.

8. EMPTY STOMACHS AND UNFORGIVABLE CRIMES

1. Cui, *Qinghai Shihua*, 56.

2. Han Youren has made the most concerted attempted to document the course of the Amdo Rebellion and scale of violence. Han, *Yichang bei Yinmoliao de Guonei Zhanzheng*. See also Li Jianglin, *Dang Tieniao zai Tiankong Feixiang*, 169–252.

3. Zhonggong Huangnan Zhouwei, "Huangnan Diqu Pingxi Panluan," 1047.

4. *ZKXZ*, 414. See also, *HNGK*, 105.

5. Zhonggong Huangnan Zhouwei, "Huangnan Diqu Pingxi Panluan," 1048.

6. *QNHJS*, 277. See also "Qinghai Shengwei guanyu Muyequ Shehuizhuyi Geming de Chubu Zongjie," 2–5, and Nie, "Jianjue ba Qinghai Muqu Shehuizhuyi," 5.

7. Huangnan Zangzu Zizhizhou Gaikuang Bianji Weiyuanhui, *Qinghai Sheng Huang-nan Zangzu Zizhizhou Gaikuang (Chugao)*, 48.

8. Huangnan Zangzu Zizhizhou Gaikuang Bianji Weiyuanhui, 51.

9. Chen Yunfeng, *Dangdai Qinghai Jianshi*, 155–56.

10. Zhou Wei, "Gannan Zangzu Renmin Fandui Zongjiaojie," 17.

11. Starting in November 1958, senior leaders gathered at Zhengzhou to confront serious problems that had accompanied the rapid establishment of the people's communes. See Teiwes, *Politics and Purges in China*, 306–7.

12. *QHSZ FLZ*, 715–22.

13. "Yuan Renyuan Tongzhi," 725.

14. "Yuan Renyuan Tongzhi," 726–27.

15. *QHSZ FLZ*, 718.

16. "Yuan Renyuan Tongzhi," 726–28.

17. "Yuan Renyuan Tongzhi," 727.

18. *QHSZ FLZ*, 720–21.

19. *QNHJS*, 279. See also "Qinghai Shengwei guanyu Muyequ Shehuizhuyi de Chubu Zongjie," 2–7, and Nie, "Jianjue ba Qinghai Muqu Shehuizhuyi," 5–7.

20. *QHSZ FLZ*, 708–9. See also the 1959 directive, quoted in Jianglin Li, *Tibet in Agony*, 51–52.

21. *QHSZ FLZ*, 721.

22. "Yuan Renyuan Tongzhi," 726.

23. "Yuan Renyuan Tongzhi," 729.

24. "Yuan Renyuan Tongzhi," 726.

25. *QHSZ FLZ*, 721.

26. "Zhonggong Qinghai Shengwei guanyu Jinyibu Jiaqiang Zongjiao Gongzuo de Zhi-shi," 13–16.

27. See Nags tshang Nus blos, *Nags tshang zhi lu'i skyid sdug*. In addition to Nakstang Nulo's account, there are at least two collections of interviews with those who lived through Amdo '58, both published in China through unofficial channels. The first is a Tibetan-language collection of interviews from Hainan Prefecture. The book was banned, and the author, Chamdo Rinzang, arrested. According to Lama Jabb, "the prison experience left him with incapacitating physical and psychological damages." The second book, published in Chinese, consists of interviews conducted among Mongol, Yugur, and Tibetan inhabitants of the Qilian Mountain region of northern Qinghai and neighboring Gansu. In addition, under the pseudonym Orgyan Nyima, an unknown compiler has self-published seventeen English translations of oral histories conducted with Tibetan residents of the Nangchen region of Yushu Prefecture. Several of the interviews include accounts of 1958. Bya mdo Rin bzan, *Nga'i pha yul dang zhi ba'i bcings grol*; Tiemuer, *Zai Kukunaoer Yibei*; Orgyan Nyima, *Living and Dying in Modern Tibet*. On the treatment of Chamdo Rinzang while in prison, see Lama Jabb, *Oral and Literary Continuities*, 118.

28. *QNHJS*, 277. The report claims that over ninety thousand people participated in open rebellion.

29. *QHSZ FLZ*, 718.

30. *QHSZ FLZ*, 744.

31. Lama Jabb, *Oral and Literary Continuities*, 94. A separate contemporary source maintains that thirty-two thousand people, nearly 20 percent of Gannan Prefecture's Tibetan population, joined the rebellion. "Gansu Zangqu Jiben Qingkuang," 6.

32. Jianglin Li, *Tibet in Agony*, 51 (emphasis added).

33. Cited in Han, *Yichang bei Yinmoliao de Guonei Zhanzheng*, 47.

34. Chen Yunfeng, *Dangdai Qinghai Jianshi*, 162–63. A contact in Amdo informs me that after authorities realized that the volume contained these figures, it was withdrawn from circulation.

35. This is based on a Tibetan population in 1957 of 513,415. Notably, by 1964, the Tibetan population of Qinghai had officially dropped to 422,662, a remarkable 18 percent decrease. See Qinghai Sheng Renkou Pucha Bangongshi, *Qinghai Zangzu Renkou*, 17.

36. Panchen Lama, *Panchen Lama Speaks*, 16–17.

37. For example, David Goodman reports that upward of 10 percent of the male Salar population was sent to labor camps. "Exiled by Definition," 332.

38. Dali Yang, *Calamity and Reform in China*, 43; MacFarquhar, *Origins of the Cultural Revolution*, 3:7–8.

39. Yuan, *Zhengtu Jishi*, 197–98. Yuan, who also made a self-criticism, claims that he was the meeting's real, unnamed target. On the Lushan Conference and its immediate consequences, see MacFarquhar, *Origins of the Cultural Revolution*, 2:187–251; Teiwes, *Politics and Purges in China*, 301–44; and Dali Yang, *Calamity and Reform in China*, 51–54.

40. Yuan, *Zhengtu Jishi*, 194–206.

41. Yuan, 203; *ZGQH ZZ*, 10. The Northwest Bureau had been disbanded in 1954. It was officially reconstituted in January 1961. However, a preparatory committee had begun work the previous August.

42. Frederick Teiwes writes that while the campaign mainly focused on grassroots cadres, Gao was one of five provincial Party secretaries to lose his position. A common denominator appears to have been their zeal for the Great Leap and, perhaps relatedly, particularly poor economic performance and high levels of famine. Teiwes, *Politics and Purges in China*, 351–58.

43. The "three levels" refers to provincial, prefectural, and county-level cadres. Wang Zhao arrived in Qinghai in March, initially serving as its second-ranking Party secretary. Gao, who made a self-criticism at the conference, officially remained a member of the Party committee's secretariat until April 1962. Yuan, *Zhengtu Jishi*, 204; *ZGQH ZZ*, 10–11.

44. Wang Zhao, "Shengwei Sanji Ganbu Huiyi Zongjie Fayan," 775.

45. Wang, 775, 778. Wang Zhao claimed that the percent of urban and township inhabitants had grown from 17.5 percent in 1957 to 28.8 percent in 1960.

46. Teiwes describes a "Communist wind" as a tendency that "affected cadres who were unable to distinguish between the utopian vision of the people's commune trumpeted in 1958 and concrete measures subsequently adopted for commune management." It was one of "five winds" (*wufeng*) that despite "good intentions" lent themselves to leftist deviation. Teiwes, *Politics and Purges in China*, 352–53; Yuan, *Zhengtu Jishi*, 199–200.

47. Wang Zhao, "Shengwei Sanji Ganbu Huiyi Zongjie Fayan," 776–77.

48. *QHSZ FLZ*, 720. See also Jianglin Li, *Tibet in Agony*, 53–55.

49. *QHSZ FLZ*, 795.

50. "Qinghai Shengwei guanyu Muyequ Shehuizhuyi Geming de Chubu Zongjie," 5.

51. Wang Zhao, "Shengwei Sanji Ganbu Huiyi Zongjie Fayan," 778.

52. *QHSZ FLZ*, 796.

53. Chen Yunfeng, *Dangdai Qinghai Jianshi*, 161.

54. Groot, who dates the Second Hundred Flowers as running from 1960 to 1964, is referring to its effects on intellectuals and the minority democratic parties. In Qinghai, this period of relaxation was far shorter, lasting from perhaps early 1961 through summer 1962. Groot, *Managing Transitions*, 110–14; MacFarquhar, *Origins of the Cultural Revolution*, 3:69–70.

55. *QHSZ FLZ*, 802–7.

56. Wang Zhao, "Shengwei Sanji Ganbu Huiyi Zongjie Fayan," 778.

57. Han, *Yichang bei Yinmoliao de Guonei Zhanzheng*, 154; Chen Yunfeng, *Dangdai Qinghai Jianshi*, 164.

58. Wang Zhao, "Shengwei Sanji Ganbu Huiyi Zongjie Fayan," 778.

59. *QHSZ FLZ*, 796. For regulations on correcting mistakes made during the two Anti-Rightist Campaigns, see *QHSZ FLZ*, 759–63.

60. MacFarquhar, *Origins of the Cultural Revolution*, 3:45–8.

61. *QNHJS*, 284–93.

62. *ZKXZ*, 344–47.

63. *QNHJS*, 288–89.

64. Cited in Han, *Yichang bei Yinmoliao de Guonei Zhanzheng*, 154. See also Chen Yunfeng, *Dangdai Qinghai Jianshi*, 164.

65. *TRXZ*, 1092.

66. Stevenson, "Role of the Traditional Tibetan Tribal Leadership," 17.

67. Zhonggong Huangnan Zhouwei, "Huangnan Diqu Pingxi Panluan," 1045–47.

68. *TRXZ*, 1086, 1095; *HNZZ*, 1546.

69. *QHSZ RWZ*, 264–65.

70. *JZXZ*, 686.

71. Nian and Bai, *Qinghai Zangchuan Fojiao Siyuan Mingjian*, 299.

72. *ZKXZ*, 526–28.

73. *ZKXZ*, 415. According to the gazetteer, no one in Zeku belonged to the fifth category: *rightists*.

74. *ZKXZ*, 306. Pu Wencheng writes that after 1958, only 11 of Qinghai's 772 Tibetan Buddhist monasteries remained active. Now, an additional 126 were reopened. *Gan Qing Zangchuan Fojiao Siyuan*, 4.

75. Groot, *Managing Transitions*, 108–13; MacFarquhar, *Origins of the Cultural Revolution*, 3:261–69.

76. See Robert Barnett's preface followed by a translation of the petition in Panchen Lama, *Poisoned Arrow*.

77. Groot, *Managing Transitions*, 113; Minglang Zhou, *Multilingualism in China*, 72–73; Chu, "Peiping's Nationality Policy in the Cultural Revolution." Vice Premier Xi Zhongxun, father of Xi Jinping, was also criticized and demoted.

78. *HNZZ*, 1549.

79. *ZKXZ*, 528.

80. *ZKXZ*, 531.

81. Others include Sherab Gyatso, the Mongol qinwang Trashi Tséring, the Gurong Gyalsé Rinpoché, and Chöbum Gyel. However, each was purged at the start of the Cultural Revolution or, in the case of Sherab Gyatso, even earlier.

82. Zhao Qingyang, "Ji Yiwei yu Dang," 155. During the Cultural Revolution, rebel Red Guards accused Wang Zhao of being Qinghai's "biggest capitalist roader." He died in prison in 1970 at the age of fifty-three. Wang was posthumously rehabilitated in January 1978. See *QHSZ RWZ*, 251–52, and Weiner, "When 'the Sky Fell to the Earth.'" On Cultural Revolution–era accusations against Wang, see Qinghai Ribao Bianjibu, *Dadao Fangeming Xiuzhengzhuyi Fenzi Wang Zhao*.

83. *ZKXZ*, 529–31.

84. Fromm, "Producing History through 'Wenshi Ziliao,'" 5. See also Weiglin-Schwiedrzik, "In Search of a Master Narrative," 1076.

85. "Resolution on Certain Questions," 41.

86. *XSMG*, 21–22; *DZMG*, 1:161.

87. Deng Xiaoping, "Xin Shiqi de Tongyi Zhanxian," 16.

88. Fromm, "Producing History through 'Wenshi Ziliao,'" 5–7.

89. Reproduced in *XSMG*, 19–20.

90. *XSMG*, 21–22. See also *DZMG*, 1:165–66.

91. Mackerras, *China's Minorities*, 153–54; *DZMZ*, 1:164–65. An abridged version can be found as "Some Questions on Policy towards Nationalities," *Beijing Review* 33, nos. 9/10 (1980): 14–23/23–28.

92. Wulanfu, "Minzu Quyu Zizhi de Guanghui Licheng," 134.

93. Reproduced in *XSMG*, 52. See also Mackerras, *China's Minorities*, 155.

94. Lai, "Ethnic Autonomous Regions," 149–50. These provisions were elaborated in 1984's Law of Regional Ethnic Autonomy.

95. Zhang Zhongliang, "Zhong Tuanjie, Jiang Zhengce," 10; Liao, "Re'ai Qinghai, Jianshe Qinghai."

96. Both Wagya and Lhagyel served as members of the Huangnan Prefectural People's Consultative Conference, and Wagya later accepted positions as vice chairman of the prefectural government committee as well as on the Qinghai Provincial People's Consultative Conference's standing committee. On the latter committee with Wagya was a who's who of surviving actors from the "early Liberation period," including cadres such as Du Hua'an (former Huangnan Prefecture Party secretary and United Front director) and pre-1949 elites such as the Rongwo nangso Trashi Namgyel, the Gurong Gyelsé Rinpoché, and the Atsok's Chöbum Gyel. See *ZGQH ZZ*, 597–601.

97. Zhao Qingyang, "Ji Yiwei yu Dang," 155; Stevenson, "Role of the Traditional Tibetan Tribal Leadership," 15–16; Han, *Yichang bei Yinmoliao de Guonei Zhanzheng*, 162–63; *HNZZ*, 847–88. A fourth honoree was the Eighth Lamo Sertri, the Geluk lama and former vice chairman of Huangnan Prefecture who died in prison in 1961.

98. Weiner, "Aporia of Re-Remembering."

99. Arjia Luosang Tudan, preface to *1959 Lhasa*, 5.

100. Longbian Jiacuo, "Zangzu Laohongjun Zhanshi Zhaxi Wangxu," 65–67.

101. Arjia Luosang Tudan, preface to *1959 Lhasa*, 5. Arjia Rinpoché is relaying information passed on to him by a Hui Muslim acquaintance, Ma Hailin, who at the time was a UFWD cadre and accompanied Trashi Wangchuk on at least one of his trips to lobby Beijing. Although based on hearsay, his account is supported by other sources. See Ma Wanli, *Zhaxi Wangxu Jinian Wenji*.

102. Han Youren reports that 16,700,000 yuan was set aside as compensation for individuals and dependents of those erroneously harmed during the "expansion of the rebellion pacification." Yushu, which experienced the most violence during the rebellion and its aftermath, received nearly a third of the overall pool of money. Two million, six hundred thousand yuan was earmarked for Huangnan Prefecture. According to Françoise Robin, however, in Henan County the compensation paid to the victims or their heirs was just three hundred yuan each. Han, *Yichang bei Yinmoliao de Guonei Zhanzheng*, 162; Robin, "Uneasy Incorporation of a Tibeto-Mongolian Community."

103. Longbian Jiacuo, "Zangzu Laohongjun Zhanshi Zhaxi Wangxu," 67–68; Ma Mingshan, "Ge Minzu Quzhong de Tiexinren," 104; Gesang Duojie, "Xueshan Weibei, Fengfan Yongcun," 39.

104. Chen Yunfeng, *Dangdai Qinghai Jianshi*, 162–63. The rehabilitations were not limited to Tibetans. For instance, 85 percent of Salar arrested in the wake of the 1958 rebellion were exonerated, while an additional 10 percent had their punishments retroactively reduced. Wei Cong, *Xunhua Salazu Zizhixian Zhi*, 573; *SZJS*, 109–10.

105. Based on the internal 1982 report by Qinghai's Party committee, Han Youren writes that 78,147 of the more than 85,000 people (92 percent) punished during the expansion of rebellion pacification efforts were eventually rehabilitated. Han, *Yichang bei Yinmoliao de Guonei Zhanzheng*, 47, 163.

106. Chen Yufeng, *Dangdai Qinghai Jianshi*, 163.

107. These advocates framed the championing of minority rights as a core component for promoting the Four Modernizations (modernizing agriculture, industry, defense, and science and technology) and economic development. See, for example, *XSMG*, 52

108. See Foreign Broadcast Information Service, "NPC Deputies Nagpoi, Benqen Meet Press," and Panchen Lama, *Panchen Lama Speaks*. On monastic revival, see Kolås and Thowsen, *On the Margins of Tibet*, and Caple, "Remembering Monastic Revival."

109. Chen Yunfeng, *Dangdai Qinghai Jianshi*, 162 (emphasis added).

110. *QHSZ JSZ*, 513–14.

111. Chen Yunfeng, *Dangdai Qinghai Jianshi*, 162.

CONCLUSION

1. Petech, "Notes on Tibetan History," 227; Katō, "Lobjang Danjin's Rebellion of 1723," 57.

2. Robin, "Events of Amdo '58"; Makley, *Battle for Fortune*, 12; Makley, *Violence of Liberation*, 104.

3. Cited in De Heering, "Re-Remembering the Day 'Times Turned Around.'"

4. Naktsang Nulo, *My Tibetan Childhood*, 7.

5. Pirie, "Limits of the State," 73. See also Makley, *Violence of Liberation*, 104.

6. Lama Jabb, *Oral and Literary Continuities*, 95. See also Robin, "Events of Amdo '58."

7. Robin, "Events of Amdo '58." See also Robin, "Révolte en Amdo en 1958."

8. See, for example, Goldstein, *Snow Lion and the Dragon*; Shakya, *Dragon in the Land of the Snows*; Smith, *Tibetan Nation*.

9. Shakya, "Genesis of the Sino-Tibetan Agreement."

10. Quoted in Goldstein, *Snow Lion and the Dragon*, 47.

11. Goldstein, 48.

12. Goldstein, *History of Modern Tibet*, 3:87–195, 306–34. According to Goldstein, similar dynamics had been afoot in Central Tibet. There, Fan Ming, a rival of regional strongman General Zhang Guohua, took advantage of the latter's absence in 1955 to launch reforms in the Shigatse area. In this case, however, Beijing censored Fan, removing him from his post, and no uprising occurred.

13. Scott, *Seeing like a State*, 89–90.

14. Mitter, *Manchurian Myth*; Duara, *Sovereignty and Authenticity*; Hotta, *Pan-Asianism and Japan's War*. In the preface to Hotta's book, Mitter refers to pan-Asianism as a "defeated ideology."

15. Groot, "Self-Defeating Secret Weapon?," 29–30.

16. Referring to the "post-Mao response to the Cultural Revolution" as an attempt to legitimize the new regime through an exercise in "transitional justice," Alex Cook nonetheless notes the Party's "substantial failures to fully redress past injustices or prevent future ones." Susanne Wieglin-Schwiedrzik likewise argues that despite its best efforts the CCP has failed to make its "master narrative" for post-1949 history hegemonic. Cook, *Cultural Revolution on Trial*, 21–24; Wieglin-Schwiedrzik "In Search of a Master Narrative," 1076.

17. Weiner, "Aporia of Re-Remembering." In the Reform Era, the Party-state produced a number of serialized publications focusing on recent history. These include local gazetteers (*difangzhi*), regional overviews (*gaikuang*), the Contemporary China (Dangdai Zhongguo) series and corollary Brief History of Contemporary China (Dangdai Zhongguo Jianshi), chronologies of major events (*dashiji*), Communist Party organizational histories (*zuzhishi ziliao*), and wenshi ziliao (cultural and historical material).

18. This has included adding individual bureaus dedicated to work in Tibet (2006) and Xinjiang (2017) and placing the NAC under the formal leadership of the UFWD. See Groot, "Expansion of the United Front," and Joske, "Reorganizing the United Front."

19. On the debate over whether the granting of "ethnoterritorial" autonomy most often leads to increased or decreased likelihoods for ethnopolitical conflict and demands for

succession, see Cornell, "Autonomy as a Source of Conflict." See also Crossley, "Nationality and Difference in China," 151–53.

20. Makley, *Violence of Liberation*, 115–16. See also, Mortensen, "Historical Amnesia in Gyelthang"; Goldstein, *On the Cultural Revolution in Tibet*; and Mueggler, *Age of Wild Ghosts*.

21. On the Great Western Development Campaign in Qinghai, see Goodman, "Qinghai and the Emergence of the West." For a more general discussion of the campaign, including its use as an instrument of state and nation building, see Goodman, "Campaign to 'Open up the West,'" 317–34 (especially 324–30), and Minglang Zhou, "Nation-State Building and Multiculturalism," 130–31.

22. Hillman, "Money Can't Buy Tibetans' Love"; Barnett, *Lhasa*; Yeh, *Taming Tibet*; Fischer, *Disempowered Development of Tibet*; Makley, *Battle for Fortune*.

23. Panchen Lama, *Panchen Lama Speaks*, 14–15.

24. Renan, "What Is a Nation?," 53.

25. Renan, 45.

26. Lama Jabb, *Oral and Literary Continuities*, esp. chap. 4. See also Pirie, "Limits of the State," 73; Makley, *Violence of Liberation*, 49; and the contributions by Benno Weiner, Charlene Makley, Françoise Robin, Xenia de Heering, Nicole Willock, Maria Turek, and Geoffrey Barstow in Barnett, Weiner, and Robin, *Conflicting Memories*.

27. Beissinger, "Demise of an Empire-State," 101–2.

28. Beissinger, "Persisting Ambiguity of Empire," 157.

29. Suny, "Empire Strikes Out," 26–27; Lieven, *Empire*, 6–7.

30. Khalid, "Soviet Union as an Imperial Formation," 114.

31. Elliot, "Case of the Missing Indigene"; Leibold, "Preferential Policies," 182–87; Leibold, "China's Ethnic Policy under Xi Jinping"; Minglang Zhou, "Nation-State Building and Multiculturalism," 128–35; Smith Finley, introduction to "Securitization, Insecurity and Conflict in Contemporary Xinjiang," 9–12.

32. Barnett, "Revolution at the Grassroots"; Zenz and Leibold, "Chen Quanguo"; Zenz, "China's Securitization Drive."

33. See, for example, Li and Chen, "Xi Zhongxun Zongjiao Gongzuo," and Liu Lijun, "Xi Zhongxun yu Tongyi Zhanxian," 349–51. See also Leibold, "China's Ethnic Policy under Xi Jinping."

34. Gladney, "Introduction: Making and Marking Majorities."

Bibliography

Abu-Lughod, Lila. "The Romance of Resistance: Tracing Transformations of Power through Bedoin Women." *American Ethnologist* 17, no. 1 (1990): 41–55.

Adelman, Jeremy, and Stephen Aron. "From Borderlands to Borders: Empires, Nation-States, and the Peoples in between in North American History." *American Historical Review* 104, no. 3 (1999): 814–41.

Anagnost, Ann. "Who Is Speaking Here? Discursive Boundaries and Representation in Post-Mao China." In *Boundaries in China*, edited by John Hay, 257–79. London: Reaktion Books, 1994.

Anderson, Benedict. *Imagined Communities: Reflections on the Origin and Spread of Nationalism*. Rev. and extended ed. London: Verso, 1991.

Arjia Luosang Tudan. Preface to *1959 Lhasa*, by Li Jianglin, 3–6. Hong Kong: New Media Publishing and Consulting, 2010.

Atwill, David G. "A Tibetan by Any Other Name: The Case of Muslim Tibetans and Ambiguous Ethno-Religious Identities." *Cahiers d'Extrême-Asie* 23 (2014): 33–61.

Atwood, Christopher Pratt, ed. *Encyclopedia of Mongolia and the Mongol Empire*. New York: Facts On File, 2004.

Barkey, Karen. *Empire of Difference: The Ottomans in Comparative Perspective*. Cambridge: Cambridge University Press, 2008.

Barnett, A. Doak. *China on the Eve of Communist Takeover*. New York: Praeger, 1963.

Barnett, Robert. "Beyond the Collaborator-Martyr Model: Strategies of Compliance, Opportunism, and Opposition within Tibet." In *Contemporary Tibet: Politics, Development, and Society in a Disputed Region*, edited by Barry Sautman and June Teufel Dreyer, 25–66. Armonk, NY: M. E. Sharpe, 2006.

——. *Lhasa: Streets with Memories*. New York: Columbia University Press, 2006.

——. Preface to *A Poisoned Arrow: The Secret Petition of the 10th Panchen Lama*, by Tenth Panchen Lama, xi–xxii. London: Tibet Information Network, 1998.

——. "Revolution at the Grassroots: Changes in Village-Level Administration in the TAR, 2011-19." Paper presented at the Fifteenth Seminar of the International Association for Tibetan Studies, Paris, July 2019.

——. "The Tibet Protests of Spring, 2008: Conflict between the Nation and State." *China Perspectives*, no. 3 (2009): 6–23.

Barnett, Robert, Benno Weiner, and Françoise Robin, eds. *Conflicting Memories: Tibet under Mao Retold*. Leiden: Brill, forthcoming.

Beissinger, Mark R. "The Demise of an Empire-State: Identity, Legitimacy and the Deconstruction of Soviet Politics." In *The Rising Tide of Cultural Pluralism: The Nation-State at Bay?*, edited by Crawford Young, 93–115. Madison: University of Wisconsin Press, 1993.

——. "The Persisting Ambiguity of Empire." *Post-Soviet Affairs* 11, no. 2 (1995): 149–84.

Benson, Linda, and Ingvar Svanberg. *China's Last Nomads: The History and Culture of China's Kazaks*. Armonk, NY: M. E. Sharpe, 1998.

Bernstein, Thomas P. "Leadership and Mass Mobilisation in the Soviet and Chinese Collectivisation Campaigns of 1929–30 and 1955–56: A Comparison." *China Quarterly*, no. 31 (1967): 1–47.

Borchigud, Wurling. "The Impact of Urban Ethnic Education on Modern Mongolian Ethnicity, 1949–1966." In *Cultural Encounters on China's Ethnic Frontiers*, edited by Stevan Harrell, 278–300. Seattle: University of Washington Press, 1995.

Bovingdon, Gardner. *The Uyghurs: Strangers in Their Own Land*. New York: Columbia University Press, 2010.

Brook, Timothy. "Collaboratist Nationalism in Occupied Wartime China." In *Nation Work: Asian Elites and National Idenitities*, edited by André Schmind and Timothy Brook, 159–90. Ann Arbor: University of Michigan Press, 2010.

Brophy, David. "The 1957–59 Xinjiang Committee Plenum and the Attack on 'Local Nationalism.'" *Sources and Methods* (blog). Wilson Center. December 11, 2017. https://www.wilsoncenter.org/blog-post/ the-1957-58-xinjiang-committee-plenum-and-the-attack-local-nationalism.

——. *Uyghur Nation: Reform and Revolution on the Russia-China Frontier*. Cambridge, MA: Harvard University Press, 2016.

Brown, Jeremy, and Matthew D. Johnson, eds. *Maoism at the Grassroots: Everyday Life in China's Era of High Socialism*. Cambridge, MA: Harvard University Press, 2015.

Bulag, Uradyn E. "Can the Subalterns Not Speak? On the Regime of Oral History in Socialist China." *Inner Asia* 12, no. 1 (2010): 95–111.

——. *Collaborative Nationalism: The Politics of Friendship on China's Mongolian Frontier*. Lanham, MD: Rowman & Littlefield, 2010.

——. "Ethnic Resistance with Socialist Characteristics." In *Chinese Society: Change, Conflict and Resistance*, edited by Elizabeth J. Perry and Mark Selden, 178–97. New York: Routledge, 2000.

——. "Going Imperial: Tibeto-Mongolian Buddhism and Nationalisms in China and Inner Asia." In *Empire to Nation: Historical Perspectives on the Making of the Modern World*, edited by Joseph W. Esherick, Hasan Kayali, and Eric Van Young, 260–95. Lanham, MD: Rowman & Littlefield, 2006.

——. "Good Han, Bad Han: The Moral Parameters of Ethnopolitics in China." In *Critical Han Studies: The History, Representation, and Identity of China's Majority*, edited by Thomas S. Mullaney, James Leibold, Stéphane Gros, and Eric Vanden Bussche, 92–109. Berkeley: University of California Press, 2012.

——. "Models and Moralities: The Parable of the Two 'Heroic Little Sisters of the Grassland.'" *China Journal*, no. 42 (1999): 21–41.

——. *The Mongols at China's Edge: History and the Politics of National Unity*. Lanham, MD: Rowman & Littlefield, 2002.

——. "Seeing like a Minority: Political Tourism and the Struggle for Recognition in China." *Journal of Current Chinese Affairs* 41, no. 4 (2012): 133–58.

Burbank, Jane, and Frederick Cooper. *Empires in World History: Power and the Politics of Difference*. Princeton, NJ: Princeton University Press, 2010.

Bya mdo Rin bzan. *Nga'i pha yul dang zhi ba'i bcings grol*. N.p., ca. 2008.

Cameron, Sarah I. *The Hungry Steppe: Famine, Violence, and the Making of Soviet Kazakhstan*. Ithaca, NY: Cornell University Press, 2018.

Caple, Jane. "Remembering Monastic Revival: Stories from Reb Kong and Its Neighboring Places." In *Monastic and Lay Traditions in North-Eastern Tibet*, edited by Yangdon Dhondup, Ulrich Pagel, and Geoffrey Samuel, 23–47. Leiden: Brill, 2013.

Carrasco, Pedro. *Land and Polity in Tibet*. Seattle: University of Washington Press, 1959.

Chang Chih-i. *The Party and the National Question in China*. Translated and edited by George Mosely. Cambridge: MIT Press, 1966.

Chen Bingyuan. *Ma Bufang Jiazu Tongzhi Qinghai Sishi Nian*. Xining: Qinghai Renmin Chubanshe, 1986.

Chen Qingying. "The Year of the Establishment and the Naming of the Domed (Mdo Smad) Pacification Commission of the Yuan Dynasty." *China Tibetology*, no. 1 (2003): 9–14.

——, ed. *Zhongguo Zangzu Buluo*. 2nd ed. Beijing: Zhongguo Zangxue Chubanshe, 2004.

Chen Qingying and He Feng, eds. *Zangzu Buluo Zhidu Yanjiu*. Beijing: Zhongguo Zangxue Chubanshe, 1995.

Chen Sigong. "Qinghai Sheng Tuixing Minzu Quyu Zizhi de Jingyan ji Jinhou Yijian." In *Minzu Zongjiao Gongzuo Wenjian Huiji*, edited by Zhonggong Qinghai Shengwei Tongzhanbu, 656–61. [Xining]: n.p., 1959.

Chen, Xi. *Social Protest and Contentious Authoritarianism in China*. New York: Cambridge University Press, 2012.

Chen Yunfeng, ed. *Dangdai Qinghai Jianshi*. Beijing: Dangdai Zhongguo Chunbanshe, 1996.

Chen Zhongyi and Zhouta, eds. *Labulengsi yu Huangshi Jiazu*. Lanzhou: Gansu Minzu Chubanshe, 1995.

Chu, Wen-lin. "Peiping's Nationality Policy in the Cultural Revolution." *Issues and Studies*, nos. 8/9 (1969): 12–23/26–41.

Clark, Leonard. *The Marching Wind: A Mounted Explorer Rides into Forbidden Tibet*. La Vergne, TN: Long Riders' Guild Press, 2001.

Clarke, Graham E. "Aspects of Social Organisation of Tibetan Pastoralists." In *Tibetan Studies: Proceedings of the 5th Seminar of the International Association for Tibetan Studies, Narita 1989*, edited by Ihara Shōren and Zuihō Yamaguchi, 393–412. Tokyo: Naritasan Shinshoji, 1992.

Cook, Alexander C. *The Cultural Revolution on Trial: Mao and the Gang of Four*. Cambridge: Cambridge University Press, 2016.

Cooke, Susette. "Becoming and Unbecoming Tu: Nation, Nationality and the People's Republic of China." In *Exile Cultures, Misplaced Identities*, edited by Paul Allatson and Jo McCormack, 34–56. Amsterdam: Rodopi, 2008.

——. "Surviving State and Society in Northwest China: The Hui Experience in Qinghai Province under the PRC." *Journal of Muslim Minority Affairs* 28, no. 3 (2008): 401–20.

Cooke, Susette, and David S. G. Goodman. "The Idea of Qinghai, 1910–2010: State Formation and Competing Identities." Paper presented at the Regional China Workshop, Pousada de Mong-Há, Macau, 2010.

Cornell, Svante E. "Autonomy as a Source of Conflict: Caucasian Conflicts in Theoretical Perspective." *World Politics* 54, no. 2 (2002): 245–76.

Crossley, Pamela Kyle. "Nationality and Difference in China: The Post-Imperial Dilemma." In *The Teleology of the Modern Nation-State: Japan and China*, edited by Joshua A. Fogel, 138–58. Philadelphia: University of Pennsylvania Press, 2005.

——. *A Translucent Mirror: History and Identity in Qing Imperial Ideology*. Berkeley: University of California Press, 1999.

Cui Yonghong. *Qinghai Shihua*. Xining: Qinghai Renmin Chubanshe, 2004.

Cui Yonghong, Zhang Dezu, and Du Changshun, eds. *Qinghai Tongshi*. Xining: Qinghai Renmin Chubanshe, 1999.

Danzhu Angben, ed. *Zangzu Dacidian*. Lanzhou: Gansu Renmin Chubanshe, 2003.

de Heering, Xénia. "Re-Remembering the Day 'Times Turned Around': The Arrival of 'Chinese Soldiers' at Chukhama." In *Conflicting Memories: Tibet under Mao Retold*, edited by Robert Barnett, Benno Weiner, and Françoise Robin. Leiden: Brill, forthcoming.

Deng Jingsheng. "Ma Bufang Liyong Zongjiao Tongzhi Gezu Renmin." *Qinghai Wenshi Ziliao Xuanji*, no. 10 (1982): 199–210.

Deng Xiaoping. "Xin Shiqi de Tongyi Zhanxian he Renmin Zhengxie de Renwu." In *Xin Shiqi Minzu Gongzuo Wenxian Xuanbian*, edited by Guojia Minzu Shiwu Weiyuanhui and Zhonggong Zhongyang Wenxian Yanjiushi, 14–17. Beijing: Zhongyang Wenxian Chubanshe, 1990.

Dhondup, Yangdon. "Reb Kong: Religion, History and Identity of a Sino-Tibetan Borderland Town." *Revue d'Études Tibétaines*, no. 20 (2011): 33–59.

——. "Rules and Regulations of the Reb Kong Tantric Community." In *Monastic and Lay Traditions in North-East Tibet*, edited by Yangdon Dhondup, Ulrich Pagel, and Geoffrey Samuel, 117–40. Leiden: Brill, 2013.

Dhondup, Yangdon, and Hildegard Diemberger. "Tashi Tsering: The Last Mongol Queen of Sogpo (Henan)." *Inner Asia* 4, no. 2 (2002): 197–224.

DiCosmo, Nicola. "Qing Colonial Administration in Inner Asia." *International History Review* 20, no. 2 (1998): 287–309.

Dirlik, Arif. *Marxism in the Chinese Revolution*. Lanham, MD: Rowman & Littlefield, 2005.

Dittmer, Lowell. *Liu Shao-Ch'i and the Chinese Cultural Revolution: The Politics of Mass Criticism*. Berkeley: University of California Press, 1974.

Dongshan Lanzhou. "Wo de Guanren Shijia." *Guide Wenshi Ziliao*, no. 1 (2000): 128–43.

Doyle, Michael W. *Empires*. Ithaca, NY: Cornell University Press, 1986.

Dreyer, June Teufel. *China's Forty Millions: Minority Nationalities and National Integration in the People's Republic of China*. Cambridge, MA: Harvard University Press, 1976.

——. "China's Minority Nationalities: Traditional and Party Elites." *Pacific Affairs* 43, no. 4 (1970): 506–30.

——. "China's Minority Peoples." *Humboldt Journal of Social Relations* 19, no. 2 (1993): 331–58.

——. "A Weapon without War: China's United Front Strategy." Foreign Policy Research Institute, February 6, 2018. https://www.fpri.org/article/2018/02/weapon-without-war-chinas-united-front-strategy/?fbclid=IwAR1Qe4i8gC9Cs hE19Z1Vymqi5q9RZiJUpniAE5PXw18KC2bC_BTphJ3-CEo.

Dreyfus, Georges. "Law, State, and Political Ideology in Tibet." *Journal of the International Association of Buddhist Studies* 18, no. 1 (1995): 117–38.

——. "Proto-Nationalism in Tibet." In *Tibet Studies: Proceedings of the 6th Seminar of the International Association for Tibetan Studies*, edited by Per Kvaerne. Oslo: Institute for Comparative Research in Human Culture, 1994.

Duara, Prasenjit. *Rescuing History from the Nation: Questioning Narratives of Modern China*. Chicago: University of Chicago Press, 1996.

——. *Sovereignty and Authenticity: Manchukuo and the East Asian Modern*. Lanham, MD: Rowman & Littlefield, 2003.

Duoji. "Jianli Tongren Xian Renmin Zhengquan Jingguo Pianduan." *Huangnan Wenshi Ziliao*, no. 2 (1994): 256–59.

Duojie. "Jiefang Chu Xiaricang Huofo Shouming Puzang Cunjin he Tan Jingguo." *Qinghai Wenshi Ziliao Xuanji*, no. 15 (1987): 126–30.

Duojie and Zhao Qingyang. "Aiguo Minzhu Renshi Xiaricang Shengping." *Huangnan Wenshi Ziliao*, no. 2 (1994): 90–103.

Dwyer, Arienne M. *Salar: A Study in Inner Asian Language Contact Processes.* Weisbaden: Harrassowitz, 2007.

Ekvall, Robert B. *Fields on the Hoof: Nexus of Tibetan Nomadic Pastoralism.* New York: Holt, Rinehart and Winston, 1968.

——. "Peace and War among Tibetan Nomads." *American Anthropologist* 66, no. 5 (1964): 1119–48.

Elliott, Mark C. "The Case of the Missing Indigene: Debate over a 'Second Generation' Ethnic Policy." *China Journal*, no. 73 (2016): 186–213.

——. *The Manchu Way: The Eight Banners and Ethnic Identity in Late Imperial China.* Stanford, CA: Stanford University Press, 2001.

Ermu. "'Guide Wang' Ma Yuanhai." *Guide Wenshi Ziliao*, no. 1 (2000): 240–52.

Esherick, Joseph W. "How the Qing Became China." In *Empire to Nation: Historical Perspectives on the Making of the Modern World*, edited by Joseph W. Esherick, Hasan Kayah, and Eric Van Young, 229–59. Lanham, MD: Rowman & Littlefield, 2006.

Esherick, Joseph W., Hasan Kayah, and Eric Van Young. Introduction to *Empire to Nation: Historical Perspectives on the Making of the Modern World*, edited by Joseph W. Esherick, Hasan Kayah, and Eric Young, 1–31. Lanham, MD: Rowman & Littlefield, 2006.

Fischer, Andrew Martin. "Close Encounters of an Inner Asian Kind: Tibetan-Muslim Co-Existence and Conflict in Tibet Past and Present." Crisis States Research Centre Working Paper no. 68 (2005).

——. *The Disempowered Development of Tibet in China: A Study in the Economics of Marginalization.* Lanham, MD: Lexington Books, 2014.

Foreign Broadcast Information Service. "NPC Deputies Nagpoi, Benqen Meet Press." Beijing Television Service in Mandarin. April 4, 1988, FBIS-CHI-99-064, 25–29.

Franke, Herbert. *From Tribal Chieftain to Universal Emperor and God: The Legitimation of the Yuan Dynasty.* Munich: Verlag der Baerischen Akademie der Wissenschaften, 1978.

Friedman, Edward, Paul Pickowicz, and Mark Selden. *Chinese Village, Socialist State.* New Haven, CT: Yale University Press, 1991.

Fromm, Martin. "Producing History through 'Wenshi Ziliao': Personal Memory, Post-Mao Ideology, and Migration to Manchuria." PhD diss., Columbia University, 2010.

Gai Qingqi. "Qinghai Muqu Ge Jiceng dui Shehuizhuyi Gaizao de Taidu." *Neibu Cankao*, no. 2457 (April 14, 1958): 12–14.

Gamble, Ruth. *Reincarnation in Tibetan Buddhism: The Third Karmapa and the Invention of a Tradition.* New York: Oxford University Press, 2018.

"Gansu Zangqu Jiben Qingkuang." *Neibu Cankao*, no. 2757 (April 23, 1959): 2–6.

Gedun Rabsal. "Reb kong gyi nyi ma nub pa: Shar skal ldan rgya mtsho sku phreng dbun pa'i sku tshe: 1916–1978." In *Monastic and Lay Traditions in North-Eastern Tibet*, edited by Yangdon Dhondup, Ulrich Pagel, and Geoffrey Samuel, 49–65. Leiden: Brill, 2013.

Gellner, Ernest. *Nations and Nationalism.* Ithaca, NY: Cornell University Press, 1983.

Gesang Duojie. "Xueshan Weibei, Fengfan Yongcun." In *Zhaxi Wangxu Jinian Wenji*, edited by Ma Wanli, 31–41. Xining: Qinghai Minzu Chubanshe, 2007.

Giersch, C. Patterson. "Across Zomia with Merchants, Monks, and Musk: Process Geographies, Trade Networks, and the Inner-East-Southeast Asian Borderlands." *Journal of Global History* 5, no. 2 (2010): 215–39.

Gladney, Dru C. "Internal Colonialism and China's Uyghur Muslim Minority." *International Institute for the Study of Islam in the Modern World*, no. 1 (1998): 20.

——. "Introduction: Making and Marking Majorities." In *Making Majorities: Constituting the Nation in Japan, Korea, China, Malaysia, Fiji, Turkey, and the United States*, edited by Dru C. Gladney, 1–9. Stanford, CA: Stanford University Press, 1998.

——. "Representing Nationality in China: Refiguring Majority/Minority Identities." *Journal of Asian Studies* 53, no. 1 (1994): 92–123.

Goldstein, Melvyn C. *A History of Modern Tibet*. Vol. 2, *The Calm before the Storm, 1951–1955*. Berkeley: University of California Press, 2007.

——. *A History of Modern Tibet*. Vol. 3, *The Storm Clouds Descend, 1955–1957*. Berkeley: University of California Press, 2014.

——. *A History of Modern Tibet*. Vol. 4, *In the Eye of the Storm, 1958–1959*. Berkeley: University of California Press, 2019.

——. *The Snow Lion and the Dragon: China, Tibet, and the Dalai Lama*. Berkeley: University of California Press, 1997.

Goldstein, Melvyn C., Ben Jiao, and Tanzen Lhundrup. *On the Cultural Revolution in Tibet: The Nyemo Incident of 1969*. Berkeley: University of California Press, 2009.

Goldstein, Melvyn C., Dawei Sherap, and William R. Siebenschuh. *A Tibetan Revolutionary: The Political Life and Times of Bapa Phüntso Wangye*. Berkeley: University of California Press, 2004.

Goodman, David S. G. "The Campaign to 'Open up the West': National, Provincial-Level and Local Perspectives." *China Quarterly*, no. 178 (2004): 317–34.

——. "Exiled by Definition: The Salar and Economic Activism in Northwest China." *Asian Studies Review*, no. 29 (2005): 325–43.

——. "Qinghai and the Emergence of the West: Nationalities, Communal Interaction and National Integration." *China Quarterly*, no. 178 (2004): 379–99.

Groot, Gerry. "China's United Front Work: Propaganda and Policy." Interview by Mercy A. Kuo. *The Diplomat*, February 14, 2018. https://thediplomat.com/2018/02/chinas-united-front-work-propaganda-as-policy/.

——. "The Expansion of the United Front under Xi Jinping." *China Story Yearbook* (2015): 168–78.

——. *Managing Transitions: The Chinese Communist Party, United Front Work, Corporatism, and Hegemony*. New York: Routledge, 2004.

——. "A Self-Defeating Secret Weapon? The Institutional Limitations of Corporatism on United Front Work." In *The Chinese Corporatist State: Adaption, Survival and Resistance*, edited by Jennifer Y. J. Hsu and Reza Hasmath, 29–49. New York: Routledge, 2013.

Gros, Stéphane. "Frontier (of) Experience: An Introduction." In *Frontier Tibet: Patterns of Change in the Sino-Tibetan Borderlands*, edited by Stéphane Gros. Amsterdam: Amsterdam University Press, 2019.

Gruschke, Andreas. *The Cultural Monuments of Tibet's Outer Provinces: Amdo*. 2 vols. Bangkok: White Lotus Press, 2001.

Guang Yuan. "Qinghai Sheng Shi Zheyang Ban Renmin Gongshe de." *Neibu Cankao*, no. 2571 (September 1, 1958): 3–6.

Hammond, Kelly A. *China's Muslims and Japan's Empire*. Chapel Hill: University of North Carolina Press, 2020.

Han Youren. *Yichang bei Yinmoliao de Guonei Zhanzheng: Ji 1958 Nian Qinghai Pingpan Kuodahua jiqi Jiuzheng Shimo*. Hong Kong: Tianyuan Shuwu, 2013.

Harrell, Stevan. "L'état c'est nous, or We Have Met the Oppressor and He Is Us: The Predicament of Minority Cadres in the PRC." In *The Chinese State at the Borders*, edited by Diana Lary, 221–39. Vancouver: UBC Press, 2007.

——. "Introduction: Civilizing Projects and the Reaction to Them." In *Cultural Encounters on China's Ethnic Frontiers*, edited by Stevan Harrell, 3–36. Seattle: University of Washington Press, 1995.

Hayes, Jack Patrick. *A Change in Worlds on the Sino-Tibetan Borderlands: Politics, Economies, and Environments in Northern Sichuan*. Lanham, MD: Lexington Books, 2014.

Heberer, Thomas. *China and Its National Minorities: Autonomy or Assimilation?* Armonk, NY: M. E. Sharpe, 1989.

Hillman, Ben. "Money Can't Buy Tibetans' Love." *Far Eastern Economic Review*, April 4, 2008, 8–12.

Hillman, Ben, and Gray Tuttle, eds. *Ethnic Conflict and Protest in Tibet and Xinjiang: Unrest in China's West*. New York: Columbia University Press, 2016.

Hirsch, Francine. *Empire of Nations: Ethnographic Knowledge and the Making of the Soviet Union*. Ithaca, NY: Cornell University Press, 2005.

Hor gtsan Jigs med. *Mdo smad lo rgyus chen mo*. [Dharamsala]: Bod kyi dpe mdzod khan, 2009.

Horlemann, Bianca. "The 'Liberation' of Golog as Reflected in the Memoir of Wang Yuying." In *Conflicting Memories: Tibet under Mao Retold*, edited by Robert Barnett, Benno Weiner, and Françoise Robin. Leiden: Brill, forthcoming.

——. "Tibetans and Muslims in Northwest China: Economic and Political Aspects of a Complex Historical Relationship." *Asian Highlands Perspectives*, no. 21 (2012): 141–86.

——. "Victims of Modernization? Struggles between the Goloks and the Muslim Ma Warlords in Qinghai, 1917–1942." In *Muslims in Amdo Tibetan Society: Multidisciplinary Approaches*, edited by Marie-Paule Hille, Bianca Horlemann, and Paul K. Nietupski, 153–77. Lanham, MD: Lexington Books, 2015.

Hotta, Eri. *Pan-Asianism and Japan's War 1931–1945*. New York: Palgrave Macmillan, 2007.

Huang Jing. "Gansu Renda Wuci Huiyi dui Gannan, Zhangjiachuan Panluan Shijian Zhankai Zhengbian." *Neibu Cankao*, no. 2478 (May 13, 1958): 16–18.

——. "Gansu Sheng Gezu Daibiao dui Minzu Zongjiao Wenti, Shaoshu Minzu Diqu Jinxing Minzhu Gaige Wenti de Zhengbian." *Neibu Cankao*, no. 2484 (May 20, 1958): 18–21.

Huang Jingbo. "Wuyi Wanghuai Zhou Renshan." *Zhongguo Minzu*, February 2006, 52–56.

Huangnan Zangzu Zizhizhou Gaikuang Bianji Weiyuanhui, ed. *Qinghai Sheng Huangnan Zangzu Zizhizhou Gaikuang (Chugao)*. N.p., 1963.

Huangnan Zhou Zengxie. "Huangnan Tiaojie Minzu Jiufen Jishi." In *Qinghai Wenshi Ziliao Jicui: Jianguohoujuan*, edited by Qinghai Sheng Zhengxie Xuexi he Wenshi Weiyuanhui, 266–69. Xining: Qinghaisheng Zhengxie Xuexi he Wenshi Weiyuanhui, 2001.

——. "Minzu Tuanjie Hao, Caoyuan Qixiang Xin." *Qinghai Wenshi Ziliao Xuanji*, no. 12 (1984): 63–67.

Huber, Toni. "A Mdo and Its Modern Transition." In *Amdo Tibetans in Transition: Society and Culture in the Post-Mao Era*, edited by Toni Huber, xi–xxiii. Leiden: Brill, 2002.

Hunsberger, Merrill. "Ma Pu-fang in Chinghai Province, 1931–1949." PhD. diss., Temple University, 1978.

Information and Publicity Office of His Holiness the Dalai Lama, ed. *Tibet under Chinese Communist Rule: A Compilation of Refugee Statements, 1958–1975.* Dharamsala: Information and Publicity Office of His Holiness the Dalai Lama, 1976.

Jacobs, Justin M. *Xinjiang and the Modern Chinese State.* Seattle: University of Washington Press, 2016.

Javed, Jeffrey. "Speaking Bitterness." In *Afterlives of Chinese Communism*, edited by Christian Sorace, Ivan Franceschini, and Nicholas Loubere, 257–61. Canberra: ANU Press, 2019.

Jiayong. "Zai Muqu Congshi Yiliao Weisheng Gongzuo de Huiyi." *Huangnan Wenshi Ziliao*, no. 2 (1994): 269–85.

Joske, Alex. "Reorganizing the United Front Work Department: New Structures for a New Era of Diaspora and Religious Affairs Work." *China Brief* 19, no. 9 (2019).

Kang, Xiaofei, and Donald S. Sutton. *Contesting the Yellow Dragon: Ethnicity, Religion, and the State in the Sino-Tibetan Borderland, 1379–2009.* Leiden: Brill, 2016.

Karpat, Kemal H. "*Millets* and Nationality: The Roots of the Incongruity of Nation and State in the Post-Ottoman Era." In *Christians and Jews in the Ottoman Empire: The Functioning of a Plural Society*, edited by Benjamin Braude and Bernard Lewis, 141–69. New York: Holmes and Meier, 1982.

Katō Naota. "Lobjang Danjin's Rebellion of 1723." *Acta Asiatica: Bulletin of the Institute of Eastern Culture*, no. 64 (1993): 57–80.

——. "Warrior Lamas: The Role of Lamas in Lobjang Danjin's Unprising in Kokonor, 1723–1724." *Memoirs of the Research Department of the Toyo Bunko*, no. 62 (2004): 29–43.

Khalid, Adeeb. "The Soviet Union as an Imperial Formation: A View from Central Asia." In *Imperial Formations*, edited by Ann Laura Stoler, Carole McGranahan, and Peter C. Perdue, 113–39. Santa Fe, NM: School for Advanced Research Press, 2007.

Kimura, Hisao, and Scott Berry. *Japanese Agent in Tibet: My Ten Years of Travel in Disguise.* London: Serindia, 1990.

Kolås, Åshild, and Monika P. Thowsen. *On the Margins of Tibet: Cultural Survival on the Sino-Tibetan Frontier.* Seattle: University of Washington Press, 2005.

Lai, Hongyi. "Ethnic Autonomous Regions and the Unitary Multi-Ethnic State." In *Handbook on Ethnic Minorities in China*, edited by Xiaowei Zang, 138–64. Cheltenham, UK: Edward Elgar Publishing, 2016.

Lama Jabb. *Oral and Literary Continuities in Modern Tibetan Literature: The Inescapable Nation.* Lanham, MA: Lexington Books, 2015.

Langelaar, Reinier J. "Descent and Houses in Rebgong (Reb gong): Group Formation and Rules of Recruitment among Eastern Tibetan *tsho ba*." In *Mapping Amdo: People and Places in an Ongoing Transition*, edited by Jarmila Ptáčková and Adrian Zenz, 155–83. Prague: Oriental Institute, 2017.

——. "Historical Social Organisation on the Eastern Tibetan Plateau: The Territorial Origins and Etymology of *tsho-ba*. *Inner Asia* 21, no. 1 (20019): 7–37.

Leibold, James. "China's Ethnic Policy under Xi Jinping." *China Brief* 15, no. 20 (2015): 6–10.

——. "Preferential Policies for Ethnic Minorities in China." In *Handbook on Ethnic Minorities in China*, edited by Xiaowei Zang, 165–88. Cheltenham, UK: Edward Elgar Publishing, 2016.

———. *Reconfiguring Chinese Nationalism: How the Qing Frontier and Its Indigenes Became Chinese*. New York: Palgrave Macmillan, 2007.

Li, Jianglin. *Tibet in Agony: Lhasa 1959*. Translated by Susan Wilf. Cambridge, MA: Harvard University Press, 2016.

Li Jianglin. *Dang Tieniao zai Tiankong Feixiang: 1956–1962 Qingzang Gaoyuan shangde Mimi Zhanzheng*. Taibei: Lianjing Chuban, 2012.

———. "Qinghai 'Xunhua Shijian' Shimo." *Zhongguo Renquan Shuang Zhoukan*. http://biweeklyarchive.hrichina.org/article/307.html.

Li Shumao and Zhang Zhixin. "Ma Yuanxiang Gufei de Fumie." In *Jiefang Qinghai*, edited by Zhonggong Qinghai Shengwei Dangshi Ziliao Zhengji Weiyuanhui and Zhonggong Renmin Jiefangjun Qinghai Sheng Junqu Zhengzhibu, 435–40. Xining: Qinghai Renmin Chubanshe, 1987.

Li Wenshan and Chen Yi'ou. "Xi Zhongxun Zongjiao Gongzuo Celue Sixiang Xilun." In *Zai Xibeiju de Rizi li*, edited by Shi Jie and Si Zhihao, 339–44. Xi'an: Shaanxi Shifan Daxue Chubanshe Youlian Gongsi, 2013.

Li Xibo. "Lu'ershi zai Guide Jiaofei." *Guide Xian Wenshi Ziliao*, no. 1 (2000): 14–19.

Li Zhongfu and Xu Dianxi, eds. *Datong Xianzhi*. Xi'an: Shaanxi Renmin Chubanshe, 1993.

Li Zonghua and Li Yankai. *Anduo Zangzu Shilue*. Xining: Qinghai Minzu Chubanshe, 1992.

Liao Hansheng. "Guanche Zhixing Minzu Pingdeng he Minzu Tuanjie wei Qinghai Sheng Renmin Zhengfu de Jiben Zhengce." In *Jiefang Qinghai Shiliao Xuanbian*, edited by Zhonggong Qinghai Shengwei Dangshi Ziliao Zhengji Weiyuanhui and Zhonggong Renmin Jiefangjun Qinghai Sheng Junqu Zhengzhibu, 104–7. Xining: Qinghai Xinhua Chubanshe, 1990.

———. "Qinghai Sheng Renmin Junzheng Weiyuanhui Gongzuo Baogao." In *Jiefang Qinghai Shiliao Xuanbian*, edited by Zhonggong Qinghai Shengwei Dangshi Ziliao Zhengji Weiyuanhui and Zhonggong Renmin Jiefangjun Qinghai Sheng Junqu Zhengzhibu, 92–103. Xining: Qinghai Xinhua Chubanshe, 1990.

———. "Re'ai Qinghai, Jianshe Qinghai." *Qinghai Wenshi Ziliao Xuanji*, no. 6 (1980): 1–6.

Lieven, Dominic. *Empire: The Russian Empire and Its Rivals*. New Haven, CT: Yale University Press, 2001.

Lin Chun. "Mass Line." In *Afterlives of Chinese Communism*, edited by Christian Sorace, Ivan Franceschini, and Nicholas Loubere, 121–26. Canberra: ANU Press, 2019.

Lin, Hsiao-ting. *Modern China's Ethnic Frontiers: A Journey to the West*. New York: Routledge, 2011.

———. *Tibet and Nationalist China's Frontier: Intrigues and Ethnopolitics, 1928–49*. Vancouver: UBC Press, 2006.

Lindbeck, John M. H. "Communism, Islam and Nationalism in China." *Review of Politics* 12, no. 4 (1950): 473–88.

Ling, Nai-min, ed. *Tibet, 1950–1967*. Hong Kong: Union Research Institute, 1968.

Lipman, Jonathan N. *Familiar Strangers: A History of Muslims in Northwest China*. Seattle: University of Washington Press, 1997.

Liu Lijun. "Xi Zhongxu yu Tongyi Zhanxian." In *Zai Xibeiju de Rizi li*, edited by Shi Jie and Si Zhihao, 345–55. Xi'an: Shaanxi Shifan Daxue Chubanshe Youlian Gongsi, 2013.

Liu, Xiaoyuan. *Frontier Passages: Ethnopolitics and the Rise of Chinese Communism, 1921–1945*. Stanford, CA: Stanford University Press, 2004.

Liu, Yu. "Why Did It Go So High? Political Mobilization and Agricultural Collectivization in China." *China Quarterly*, no. 187 (2006): 732–42.

Longbian Jiacuo. "Zangzu Laohongjun Zhanshi Zhaxi Wangxu." In *Zhaxi Wangxu Jinian Wenji*, edited by Ma Wanli, 42–69. Xining: Qinghai Minzu Chubanshe, 2007.

Luo Guanwu, ed. *Xin Zhongguo Minzu Gongzuo Dashi Gailan*. Beijing: Huawen Chubanshe, 2001.

Ma Letian. "Ma Bufang zai Qinghai Henan Mengqi Bushu Fangyu Hongjun de Jingguo." *Qinghai Wenshi Ziliao Xuanji*, no. 3 (1964): 63–65.

Ma Mingshan. "Ge Minzu Quzhong de Tiexinren." In *Zhaxi Wangxu Jinian Wenji*, edited by Ma Wanli, 100–7. Xining: Qinghai Minzu Chubanshe, 2007.

Ma Rong. "A New Perspective in Guiding Ethnic Relations in the 21st Century: 'De-Politicization' of Ethnicity in China." In *De-Politicization of Ethnic Questions in China*, edited by Lizhong Xie, 1–27. Singapore: World Scientific, 2014.

Ma Wanli, ed. *Zhaxi Wangxu Jinian Wenji*. Xining: Qinghai Minzu Chubanshe, 2007.

MacFarquhar, Roderick. *The Origins of the Cultural Revolution*. Vol. 1, *Contradictions among the People 1956–1957*. New York: Columbia University Press, 1974.

——. *The Origins of the Cultural Revolution*. Vol. 2, *The Great Leap Forward 1958–60*. New York: Columbia University Press, 1983.

——. *The Origins of the Cultural Revolution*. Vol. 3, *The Coming of the Cataclysm 1961–1966*. New York: Columbia University Press, 1997.

Mackerras, Colin. *China's Minorities: Integration and Modernization in the Twentieth Century*. Oxford: Oxford University Press, 1994.

Makley, Charlene E. *The Battle for Fortune: State-Led Development, Personhood, and Power among Tibetans in China*. Ithaca, NY: Cornell University Press, 2018.

——. "Ballooning Unrest: Tibet, State Violence, and the Incredible Lightness of Knowledge." In *China in 2008: A Year of Great Significance*, edited by Kate Merkel-Hess, Kenneth Pomeranz, and Jeffrey N. Wasserstrom, 44–55. Lanham, MD: Rowman & Littlefield, 2009.

——. "'Speaking Bitterness': Autobiography, History, and Mnemonic Politics on the Sino-Tibetan Frontier." *Comparative Studies in Society and History* 47, no. 1 (2005): 40–78.

——. *The Violence of Liberation: Gender and Tibetan Buddhist Revival in Post-Mao China*. Berkeley: University of California Press, 2007.

Mao Zedong. "Some Questions Concerning Methods of Leadership." In *Selected Works*. Vol. 3, 117–22. Beijing: Foreign Language Press, 1965.

Martin, Terry. *The Affirmative Action Empire: Nations and Nationalism in the Soviet Union, 1923–1939*. Ithaca, NY: Cornell University Press, 2001.

McGranahan, Carole. *Arrested Histories: Tibet, the CIA, and Memories of a Forgotten War*. Durham, NC: Duke University Press, 2010.

McGranahan, Carole, and Ralph Litzinger, eds. "Self-Immolation as Protest in Tibet." Hot Spots, *Fieldsights*, April 9, 2012. https://culanth.org/fieldsights/series/self-immolation-as-protest-in-tibet.

McMillen, Donald Hugh. *Chinese Communist Power and Policy in Xinjiang, 1949–1977*. Boulder, CO: Westview, 1979.

Meriam, Beth. *China's "Tibetan" Frontiers: Sharing the Contested Ground*. Leiden: Global Oriental, 2012.

Michaud, Jean. "Zomia and Beyond." *Journal of Global History* 5, no. 2 (2010): 187–214.

Millward, James A. *Beyond the Pass: Economy, Ethnicity, and Empire in Qing Central Asia, 1759–1864*. Stanford, CA: Stanford University Press, 1998.

Mitter, Rana. *The Manchurian Myth: Nationalism, Resistance and Collaboration in Modern China*. Berkeley: University of California Press, 2000.

Mortensen, Dáša Pejchar. "Harnessing the Power of Tibetan Elites: Political Persuasion and the Consolidation of Communist Party Rule in Gyelthang." In *Frontier Tibet: Patterns of Change in the Sino-Tibetan Borderlands*, edited by Stéphane Gros. Amsterdam: Amsterdam University Press, 2019.

——. "Historical Amnesia in Gyalthang: The Legacy of Tibetan Participation in the Cultural Revolution." In *Re-Remembered Meetings: Post-Mao Retellings of Early Tibetan Encounters with the Chinese Communist Party*, edited by Robert Barnett, Benno Weiner, and Françoise Robin. Leiden: Brill, forthcoming.

Mosely, George. Introduction to *The Party and the National Question in China*, by Chang Chih-i. Cambridge, MA: MIT Press, 1966.

Mueggler, Erik. *The Age of Wild Ghosts: Memory, Violence, and Place in Southwest China*. Berkeley: University of California Press, 2001.

Mullaney, Thomas S. *Coming to Terms with the Nation: Ethnic Classification in Modern China*. Berkeley: University of California Press, 2011.

Nags tshang Nus blos. *Nags tshang zhi lu'i skyid sdug*. Xining: Qinghai Xining Yinshuchang, 2007.

Naktsang Nulo. *My Tibetan Childhood: When Ice Shattered Stone*. Translated by Angus Cargill and Sonam Lhamo. Durham, NC: Duke University Press, 2014.

Nian Zhihai and Bai Gengdeng, eds. *Qinghai Zangchuan Fojiao Siyuan Mingjian*. Lanzhou: Gansu Minzu Chubanshe, 1993.

Nie Jingde. "Jianjue ba Qinghai Muqu Shehuizhuyi Geming Jingxing Daodi." *Minzu Tuanjie*, no. 3 (March 1959): 5–7.

Nietupski, Paul Kocot. *Labrang: A Tibetan Buddhist Monastery at the Crossroads of Four Civilizations*. Ithaca, NY: Snow Lion Publications, 1999.

——. *Labrang Monastery: A Tibetan Buddhist Community on the Inner Asian Borderlands, 1709–1958*. Lanham, MD: Lexington Books, 2011.

——. "Understanding Religion and Politics in A Mdo: The Sde Khri Estate at Bla Brang Monastery." In *Monastic and Lay Traditions in North-East Tibet*, edited by Yangdon Dhondup, Ulrich Pagel, and Geoffrey Samuel, 67–86. Leiden: Brill, 2013.

——. "Understanding Sovereignty in Amdo." *Revue d'Études Tibétaines*, no. 31 (2015): 217–32.

Niu Huaimin. "Ma Bufang de Baojia Zhidu He Zhuangding Xunlian." *Qinghai Wenshi Ziliao Xuanji*, no. 11 (1983): 150–52.

Oidtmann, Max. *Forging the Golden Urn: The Qing Empire and the Politics of Reincarnation in Tibet*. New York: Columbia University Press, 2018.

Orgyan Nyima, *Living and Dying in Modern Tibet*. N.p., 2016.

Pagden, Anthony. *Lords of All the World: Ideologies of Empire in Spain, Britain and France c. 1500–c.1800*. New Haven, CT: Yale University Press, 1995.

Panchen Lama, Tenth. *The Panchen Lama Speaks*. Dharamsala: Department of Information and International Relations, Central Tibetan Administration of His Holiness the Dalai Lama, 1991.

——. *A Poisoned Arrow: The Secret Petition of the 10th Panchen Lama*. London: Tibet Information Network, 1997.

Peng Xue. "Huangnan Zangzu Zizhizhou Tongren Xian Qingjiao Panfei Gongzuo Qude Henda Chengji." *Neibu Cankao*, no. 2499 (June 6, 1958): 3–4.

——. "Muqian Qinghai Shehui Zhian Qingkuang." *Neibu Cankao*, no. 2515 (June 27, 1958): 10–11.

——. "Qinghai Feiqing Jiqi Huodong Tedian." *Neibu Cankao*, no. 2800 (June 17, 1959): 15–17.

——. "Qinghai Huangnan Dengdi Fasheng Wuzhuang Panluan." *Neibu Cankao*, no. 2480 (May 13, 1958): 3–5.

——. "Qinghai Jiasu dui Xumuye de Shehuizhuyi Gaizao." *Neibu Cankao*, no. 2478 (May 13, 1958): 13–15.

——. "Qinghai Muqu Panfei Huodong Youqu Xiaozhang." *Neibu Cankao*, no. 2722 (March 1959): 13–14.

——. "Qinghai Muyequ Wuzhuang Panluan de Qingkuang." *Neibu Cankao*, no. 2540 (July 26, 1958): 14–16.

——. "Qinghai Panfei Yinmou Zaici Zuzhi Wuzhuang Panluan." *Neibu Cankao*, no. 2740 (March 31, 1959): 6–7.

——. "Qinghai Sheng Jiang Kaishi Jinxing Zongjiao Zhidu de Gaige Gongzuo." *Neibu Cankao*, no. 2560 (August 19, 1958): 5–9.

——. "Qinghai Sheng Shaoshu Minzu Dangyuan de Zongjiao Guannian Reng Hen Nonghou." *Neibu Cankao*, no. 2556 (August 14, 1958): 16–17.

——. "Qinghai Shengwei dui Guanche Zhixing Zhonggong guanyu zai Shaoshu Minzu zhong Jinxing Zhengfeng he Shehuizhuyi Jiaoyu de Zhishi Yi Zuochu Juti Anpai." *Neibu Cankao*, no. 2375 (December 5, 1957): 22–26.

——. "Xunhua Salazu Zizhixian Fasheng Wuzhuang Panluan de Jiaoxun." *Neibu Cankao*, no. 2504 (June 12, 1958): 14–17.

Perdue, Peter C. "Comparing Empires: Manchu Colonialism." *International History Review* 20, no. 2 (1998): 255–62.

——. "Empire and Nation in Comparative Perspective: Frontier Administration in Eighteenth-Century China." *Journal of Early Modern History* 5, no. 4 (2001): 282–304.

——. "Erasing Empire, Re-Racing the Nation: Racialism and Culturalism in Imperial China." In *Imperial Formations*, edited by Ann Laura Stoler, Carole McGranahan, and Peter C. Perdue, 141–69. Santa Fe, NM: School for Advanced Research Press, 2007.

——. "Where Do Incorrect Political Ideas Come From? Writing History of the Qing Empire and the Chinese Nation." In *The Teleology of the Modern Nation-State: Japan and China*, edited by Joshua A. Fogel, 174–99. Philadelphia: University of Pennsylvania Press, 2005.

Perry, Elizabeth J. *Challenging the Mandate of Heaven: Social Protest and State Power in China*. Armonk, NY: M. E. Sharpe, 2002.

Petech, Luciano. "Notes on Tibetan History of the 18th Century." *T'oung-pao* 52, no. 4 (1966): 262–93.

——. "Tibetan Relations with Sung China and with the Mongols." In *China among Equals: The Middle Kingdom and Its Neighbors, 10th–14th Centuries*, edited by Morris Rossabi, 173–201. Berkeley: University of California Press, 1983.

Phan, Binh G. "Autonomous Areas of the PRC? An Analysis of Documents and Cases." *Issues and Studies* 32, no. 7 (1996): 83–108.

Pianciola, Niccolò. "Famine in the Steppe: The Collectivization of Agriculture and the Kazak Herdsmen, 1928–1934." *Cahiers du monde russe* 45, no. 1–2 (2004): 137–92.

Pieragastini, Steven. "Regulating Religion in China's 'Little Mecca': Confrontation and Negotiation in Linxia." Paper presented at the Annual Meeting of the Association for Asian Studies, Washington, DC, March 2018.

Pirie, Fernanda. "Feuding, Mediation and the Negotiation of Authority among the Nomads of Eastern Tibet." Max Plank Institute for Social Anthropology Working Papers, no. 72, 2005.

——. "The Limits of the State: Coercion and Consent in Chinese Tibet." *Journal of Asian Studies* 72, no. 1 (2013): 69–89.

———. "Order, Individualism and Responsibility: Contrasting Dynamics on the Tibetan Plateau." In *Order and Disorder: Anthropological Perspectives*, edited by Keebet von Benda-Beckmann and Fernanda Pirie, 54–73. New York: Berghahn, 2007.

———. "Segmentation within the State: The Reconfiguration of Tibetan Tribes in China's Reform Period." *Nomadic Peoples* 9, nos. 1–2 (2005): 83–102.

Pu Wencheng, ed. *Gan Qing Zangchuan Fojiao Siyuan*. Xining: Qinghai Renmin Chubanshe, 1990.

Pye, Lucian W. "How China's Nationalism Was Shanghaied." *Australian Journal of Chinese Affairs*, no. 29 (1993): 107–33.

Qieben Jia. "Xinghai Aquhu Buluo Qianhu Xiangsongmu Fajia Shi." *Qinghai Wenshi Ziliao Xuanji*, no. 3 (1964): 109–20.

Qin Shijin. *Qinghai Longwusi Zhengjiao Heyi Tizhi zhi Lishi Yanjiu*. Xining: n.p., 1992.

Qinghai Ribao Bianjibu, ed. *Dadao Fangeming Xiuzhengzhuyi Fenzi Wang Zhao*. 1967.

Qinghai Sheng Bianjizu, ed. *Qinghai Sheng Zangzu Mengguzu Shehui Lishi Diaocha*. Beijing: Minzu Chubanshe, 1985.

Qinghai Sheng Junqu Silingbu and Zhengzhibu. "Wo Jun Jiefang Qinghai de Zhandou Licheng." *Qinghai Wenshi Ziliao Xuanji*, no. 9 (1982): 1–12.

Qinghai Sheng Renkou Pucha Bangongshi, ed. *Qinghai Zangzu Renkou*. Beijing: Zhongguo Tongji Chubanshe, 1994.

"Qinghai Shengwei guanyu Muyequ Shehuizhuyi Geming de Chubu Zongjie." *Tongyi Zhanxian Gongzuo*, no. 79 (March 24, 1960): 2–7.

Rawski, Evelyn S. *The Last Emperors: A Social History of Qing Imperial Institutions*. Berkeley: University of California Press, 1998.

Renan, Ernest. "What Is a Nation?" In *Becoming National: A Reader*, edited by Geoff Eley and Ronald Grigor Suny, 42–55. New York: Oxford University Press, 1996.

"Resolution on Certain Questions in the History of Our Party since the Founding of the People's Republic of China." In *The China Reader: The Reform Era*, edited by Orville Schell and David L. Shambaugh, 37–49. New York: Vintage Books, 1999.

Rhoads, Edward J. M. *Manchus and Han: Ethnic Relations and Political Power in Late Qing and Early Republican China, 1861–1928*. Seattle: University of Washington Press, 2000.

Rieber, Alfred J. *The Struggle for the Eurasian Borderlands: From the Rise of Early Modern Empires to the End of the First World War*. Cambridge: Cambridge University Press, 2014.

Roberts, Sean R. "The Biopolitics of China's 'War on Terror' and the Exclusion of the Uyghurs." *Critical Asian Studie* 50, no. 2 (2018): 232–58.

Robin, Françoise. "The Events of Amdo '58 and the Emergence of Literary Postmemory among Tibetans." In *Conflicting Memories: Tibet under Mao Retold*, edited by Robert Barnett, Benno Weiner, and Françoise Robin, Leiden: Brill, forthcoming.

———. "Le révolte en Amdo en 1958." In *L'histoire du Tibet du XVIIème au XXIème siècle*, Rapport de groupe interparlementaire d'amitié 104, June 18, 2012. https://www.senat.fr/ga/ga104/ga104.html#toc4.

———. "The Uneasy Incorporation of a Tibeto-Mongolian Community of Amdo with the Chinese State: The 1956 and 1958 Uprising in Gser lung and Their Aftermaths." Paper presented at the Fifteenth Seminar of the International Association for Tibetan Studies, Paris, July 2019.

Robinson, Ronald. "The Excentric Idea of Imperialism, with or without Empire." In *Imperialism and After*, edited by Wolfgang J. Mommsen and Jürgen Osterhammel, 267–89. London: Allen & Unwin, 1986.

Roche, Gerald. "The Tibetanization of Henan's Mongols: Ethnicity and Assimilation on the Sino-Tibetan Frontier." *Asian Ethnicity* 17, no. 1 (2016): 128–49.

Roderick, John. *Covering China: The Story of an American Reporter from the Revolutionary Days to the Deng Era*. Chicago: Imprint Publications, 1993.

Rohlf, Gregory. *Building New China, Colonizing Kokonor: Resettlement to Qinghai in the 1950s*. Lanham, MD: Lexington Books, 2016.

——. "Dreams of Oil and Fertile Fields: The Rush to Qinghai in the 1950s." *Modern China* 29, no. 4 (2003): 455–89.

Ruan Hai. "Huigu Tiaojie Tongren Xian Jiawu Buluo yu Xiahe Xian Ganjia Buluo Lishi Yiliu Caoshan Jiufen zhong Guanche Zhixing Minzu Zhengce de Jingguo." *Huangnan Wenshi Ziliao*, no. 5 (2001): 1–7.

——. "Wo Xinmu zhongde Xianwei Shuji: Du Hua'an." *Huangnan Wenshi Ziliao*, no. 6 (2006): 239-244.

Samuel, Geoffrey. "Tibet as a Stateless Society and Some Islamic Parallels." *Journal of Asian Studies* 41, no. 2 (1982): 215–29.

——. "'Zomia': New Constructions of the Southeast Asian Highlands and Their Tibetan Implications." *Asian Highlands Perspectives* 37, no. 1 (2015): 221–49.

Schwartz, Ronald D. *Circle of Protest: Political Ritual in the Tibetan Uprising*. New York: Columbia University Press, 1994.

Schwieger, Peter. *The Dalai Lama and the Emperor of China: A Political History of the Tibetan Institution of Reincarnation*. New York: Columbia University Press, 2014.

Scott, James C. *The Art of Not Being Governed: An Anarchist History of Upland Southeast Asia*. New Haven, CT: Yale University Press, 2009.

——. *Seeing like a State: How Certain Schemes to Improve the Human Condition Have Failed*. New Haven, CT: Yale University Press, 1998.

——. *Weapons of the Weak: Everyday Forms of Peasant Resistance*. New Haven, CT: Yale University Press, 1985.

Seymour, James D. *China's Satellite Parties*. Armonk, NY: M. E. Sharpe, 1987.

Shakya, Tsering. *The Dragon in the Land of Snows: A History of Modern Tibet since 1947*. New York: Columbia University Press, 1999.

——. "The Genesis of the Sino-Tibetan Agreement of 1951." In *The Tibetan History Reader*, edited by Gray Tuttle and Kurtis R. Schaeffer, 609–36. New York: Columbia University Press, 2013.

——. "Whither the Tsampa Eaters?" *Himal* (September/October 1993): 8–11.

Shneiderman, Sara. "Are the Central Himalayas in Zomia? Some Scholarly and Political Considerations across Time and Space." *Journal of Global History* 5, no. 2 (2010): 289–312.

Shue, Vivienne. *Peasant China in Transition: The Dynamics of Development toward Socialism, 1949–1956*. Berkeley: University of California Press, 1980.

Smith, Warren W. "The Nationalities Policy of the Chinese Communist Party and the Socialist Transformation of Tibet." In *Resistance and Reform in Tibet*, edited by Robert Barnett, 51–75. Bloomington: Indiana University Press, 1994.

——. *Tibetan Nation: A History of Tibetan Nationalism and Sino-Tibetan Relations*. Boulder, CO: Westview, 1996.

Smith Finley, Joanne, ed. "Securitization, Insecurity and Conflict in Contemporary Xinjiang." *Central Asian Survey* 38, no. 1 (2019).

Sneath, David. *Changing Inner Mongolia: Pastoral Mongolian Society and the Chinese State*. Oxford: Oxford University Press, 2000.

——. *The Headless State: Aristocratic Orders, Kinship Society, and Misrepresentations of Nomadic Inner Asia*. New York: Columbia University Press, 2007.

Sonam Tsering. "The Historical Polity of Repgong." Tibetan and Himalayan Library. July 6, 2011. http://places.thlib.org/features/23751/descriptions/1225.

Sperling, Elliot. "Did the Early Ming Emperors Attempt to Implement a 'Divide and Rule' Policy in Tibet?" In *Contributions on Tibetan Language, History and Culture: Proceedings of the Csoma de Kőrös Symposium Held at Velm-Vienna, Austria, 13–19 September 1981*, edited by Ernst Steinkellner, 339–56. Vienna, 1983.

——. "Tibet and China: The Interpretation of History since 1950." *China Perspectives*, no. 3 (2009): 25–37.

Stevenson, Mark. "The Role of the Traditional Tibetan Tribal Leadership in A Mdo Reb Gong (Huangnan) after 1949." Paper presented at Amdo Conference, Department of Sanskrit and Indian Studies, Harvard University, 1997.

Stoler, Ann Laura, and Carole McGranahan. "Refiguring Imperial Terrains." In *Imperial Formations*, edited by Ann Laura Stoler, Carole McGranahan, and Peter C. Perdue, 3–42. Santa Fe, NM: School for Advanced Research Press, 2007.

Sulek, Emilia Róża, and Jarmila Ptáčková. "Mapping Amdo: Dynamics of Change." In *Mapping Amdo: People and Places in an Ongoing Transition*, edited by Jarmila Ptáčková and Adrian Zenz, 9–21. Prague: Oriental Institute, 2017.

Sullivan, Brenton. "The Qing Regulation of the Sangha in Qinghai." Unpublished manuscript.

Suny, Ronald Grigor. "The Empire Strikes Out: Imperial Russia, 'National' Identity, and Theories of Empire." In *A State of Nations: Empire and Nation-Making in the Age of Lenin and Stalin*, edited by Ronald Grigor Suny and Terry Martin, 23–66. Oxford: Oxford University Press, 2001.

——. *The Revenge of the Past: Nationalism, Revolution, and the Collapse of the Soviet Union*. Stanford, CA: Stanford University Press, 1993.

Sutton, Donald. "Ngaba in the 1950s: The United Front to Democratic Reform on the Pastoral Frontier." In *Papers from the Fourth International Conference on Sinology: Shaping Frontier History and Its Subjectivity*. Taipei: Academica Sinica, 2013.

Tambiah, Stanley Jeyaraja. *World Conqueror and World Renouncer: A Study of Buddhism and Polity in Thailand against a Historical Background*. Cambridge: Cambridge University Press, 1976.

Tan, Gillian G. *In the Circle of White Stones: Moving through Seasons with Nomads of Eastern Tibet*. Seattle: University of Washington Press, 2016.

Teiwes, Frederick C. *Politics and Purges in China: Rectification and the Decline of Party Norms, 1950–1965*. 2nd ed. Armok, NY: M. E. Sharpe, 1993.

Teiwes, Frederick C., and Warren Sun. *China's Road to Disaster: Mao, Central Politicians, and Provincial Leaders in the Unfolding of the Great Leap Forward, 1955–1959*. Armonk, NY: M. E. Sharpe, 1999.

——. "Editor's Introduction." In *The Politics of Agricultural Cooperativization in China: Mao, Deng Zihui, and the "High Tide" of 1955*, edited by Frederick C. Teiwes and Warren Sun, 5–27. Armonk, NY: M. E. Sharpe, 1993.

Thum, Rian. "The Uyghurs in Modern China." In *Oxford Research Encyclopedia of Asian History*, 2018. https://oxfordre.com/asianhistory/abstract/10.1093/acrefore/9780190277727.001.0001/acrefore-9780190277727-e-160?rskey=uJmeSY&result=6.

Tiemuer. *Zai Kukunaoer Yibei*. N.p., 2015.

Tilly, Charles. "How Empires End." In *After Empire: Multiethnic Societies and Nation-Building: The Soviet Union and the Russian, Ottoman, and Habsburg Empires*, edited by Karen Barkey and Mark Von Hagen, 1–11. Boulder, CO: Westview, 1997.

Tuttle, Gray. "An Overview of Amdo (Northeastern Tibet) Historical Polities." Tibetan Himalayan Library. https://collab.its.virginia.edu/wiki/aboutthl/

An%20Overview%20of%20Amdo%20%28Northeastern%20Tibet%29%20 Historical%20Polities.html.

———. *Tibetan Buddhists in the Making of Modern China*. New York: Columbia University Press, 2005.

van der Kuijp, Leonard W. J. "The Dalai Lamas and the Origins of Reincarnate Lamas." In *The Tibetan History Reader*, edited by Gray Tuttle and Kurtis R. Schaeffer, 335–47. New York: Columbia University Press, 2013.

Van Slyke, Lyman P. *Enemies and Friends: The United Front in Chinese Communist History*. Stanford, CA: Stanford University Press, 1967.

Wajia and Lajia. "Tongren Decang Buluo bei Jiaosha de Jingguo." *Qinghai Wenshi Ziliao Xuanji*, no. 10 (1982): 219–23.

Walker, Kenneth R. "Collectivisation in Retrospect: The 'Socialist High Tide' of Autumn 1955–Spring 1956." *China Quarterly*, no. 26 (1966): 1–43.

Walzer, Michael. "The Politics of Difference: Statehood and Toleration in a Multicultural World." In *The Morality of Nationalism*, edited by Robert McKim and Jeff McMahan, 245–57. New York: Oxford University Press, 1997.

Wang Danzheng. "Yi Jiefang Jianzha Angla Er San Shi." *Huangnan Wenshi Ziliao*, no. 7 (2010): 40–44.

Wang Feng. "Guanyu Shaoshu Minzu zhong Jinxing Zhengfeng he Shehuizhuyi Jiaoyu Wenti de Baogao." In *Fandui Difangzhuyi Xuexi Ziliao*, edited by Gansu Sheng Minzu Shiwu Weiyuanhui, 11–37. Lanzhou: n.p., 1958.

Wang Haiguang. "Radical Agricultural Collectivization and Ethnic Rebellion: The Communist Encounter with a 'New Emperor' in Guizhou's Mashan Region, 1956." In *Maoism at the Grassroots: Everyday Life in China's Era of High Socialism*, edited by Jeremy Brown and Matthew D. Johnson, 281–305. Cambridge: Harvard University Press, 2015.

Wang Jiguang. "Mingdai Biliwei Xinkao." *Xibei Minzu Yanjiu*, no. 1 (1993): 149–56.

Wang Rongde and Zhao Qingyang. "Xiaricang Huofo wei Xizang de Heping Jiefang Xiexiale Guanghui de Yiye." *Huangnan Wenshi Ziliao*, no. 2 (1994): 112–18.

Wang Tiqiang. "Linxia Jiaofei he Fanfengjian Tequan, Zongjiao Yapo de Qingkuang." *Neibu Cankao*, no. 2624 (October 31, 1958): 18–20.

Wang Zhao. "Shengwei Sanji Ganbu Huiyi Zongjie Fayan." In *Qinghai Shengzhi*, vol. 81 *Fuluzhi*, edited by Qinghai Sheng Difangzhi Bianzuan Weiyuanhui, 772–93. Xining: Qinghai Renmin Chubanshe, 2003.

Weber, Eugen. *Peasants into Frenchmen: The Modernization of Rural France, 1870–1914*. Stanford, CA: Stanford University Press, 1976.

Wei Cong, ed. *Xunhua Salazu Zizhixian Zhi*. Beijing: Zhonghua Shuju, 2001.

Wei Xinchun. "Qinghai Zangqu Qianbaihu Zhidu Chansheng he Cunzai de Yuanyin Qianxi." *Qinghai Minzu Yanjiu*, no. 1 (1989): 53–58.

Weiglin-Schwiedrzik, Susanne. "In Search of a Master Narrative for 20th-Century Chinese History." *China Quarterly*, no. 188 (2006): 1070–91.

Weiner, Benno. "The Aporia of Re-Remembering: Amdo's Early-Liberation Period in Qinghai's *Wenshi Ziliao*." In *Conflicting Memories: Tibet under Mao Retold*, edited by Robert Barnett, Benno Weiner, and Françoise Robin, Leiden: Brill, forthcoming.

———. "In the Footsteps of Garaman or Han Yinu? Rebellion, Nationality Autonomy, and Popular Memory among the Salar of Xunhua County." In *Muslims in Amdo Tibetan Society: Multidisciplinary Approaches*, edited by Marie-Paule Hille, Bianca Horlemann, and Paul K. Nietupski, 47–65. Lanham, MD: Lexington Books, 2015.

———. "Tibet in China? China in Tibet: An Historical Overview." In *Handbook on Ethnic Minorities in China*, edited by Xiaowei Zang, 83–110. Cheltenham, UK: Elgar, 2016.

———. "When 'the Sky Fell to the Earth': The Great Proletarian Cultural Revolution in the Tibetan Autonomous Region, 1966–71." MA thesis, Columbia University, 2002.

Winichakul, Thongchai. *Siam Mapped: A History of the Geo-Body of a Nation.* Honolulu: University of Hawai'i Press, 1994.

Wu Chengyi. "Lidai Wangchao Jinglue Qinghai Ge Minzu Zhengcu Shiyao." *Xibei Shidi*, no. 2 (1991): 34–41.

Wu, Zhe. "Caught between Opposing Han Chauvinism and Opposing Local Nationalism: The Drift toward Ethnic Antagonism in Xinjiang Society, 1952–1963." In *Maoism at the Grassroots: Everyday Life in China's Era of High Socialism*, edited by Jeremy Brown and Matthew D. Johnson, 306–39. Cambridge: Harvard University Press, 2015.

Wulanfu. "Minzu Quyu Zizhi de Guanghui Licheng." In *Xin Shiqi Minzu Gongzuo Wenxian Xuanbian*, edited by Guojia Minzu Shiwu Weiyuanhui and Zhonggong Zhongyang Wenxian Yanjiushi, 121–46. Beijing: Zhongyang Wenxian Chubanshe, 1990.

Xibei Junzheng Weiyuanhui and Minzu Shiwu Weiyuanhui. "Huzhu Hurang, Jiaqiang Tuanjie: Zangzu Ganjia, Jiawu Buluo Caoshan Jiufen Tiaojie Huajie Xuanchuan Gangyao." *Huangnan Wenshi Ziliao*, no. 5 (2001): 8–13.

Xibeiju Tongzhanbu and Xibei Minwei Dangzu. "Guanyu Pingxi Angla, Xiji Deng Shaoshu Minzu Diqu Panluan de Baogao." In *Jiefang Qinghai Shiliao Xuanbian*, edited by Zhonggong Qinghai Shengwei Dangshi Ziliao Zhengji Weiyuanhui and Zhonggong Renmin Jiefangjun Qinghaisheng Junqu Zhengzhibu, 300–10. Xining: Qinghai Xinhua Chubanshe, 1990.

Xie Fumin. "Ba Fandui Minzuzhuyi de Douzheng Jinxing Daodi." In *Fandui Difangzhuyi Xuexi Ziliao*, edited by Gansu Sheng Minzu Shiwu Weiyuanhui, 38–50. Lanzhou: n.p.,1958.

Xin Jianping and Zhao Shunlu. "Jianzheng 'Amang Shijian.'" *Huangnan Wenshi Ziliao*, no. 7 (2010): 304–11.

Yang, Dali L. *Calamity and Reform in China: State, Rural Society, and Institutional Change since the Great Leap Famine.* Stanford, CA: Stanford University Press, 1996.

Yang Hongwei. "Xunhua Zangqu Quanli Yuanzuo Jizhi de Wenhua Kaocha: Yi Guangxu Chao wei Zhongxin." PhD diss., Lanzhou University, 2009.

Yang Jiuce. "Weijiao Angla Gufei de Huiyi." In *Jiefang Qinghai*, edited by Zhonggong Qinghai Shengwei Dangshi Ziliao Zhengji Weiyuanhui and Zhonggong Renmin Jiefangjun Qinghai Sheng Junqu Zhengzhibu, 431–34. Xining: Qinghai Renmin Chubanshe, 1987.

Yeh, Emily T. *Taming Tibet: Landscape Transformation and the Gift of Chinese Development.* Ithaca, NY: Cornell University Press, 2013.

———. "Tibetan Range Wars: Spatial Politics and Authority on the Grasslands of Amdo." *Development and Change*, no. 34 (2003): 499–523.

Yuan Renyuan. *Zhengtu Jishi.* Changsha: Hunan Renmin Chubanshe, 1985.

"Yuan Renyuan Tongzhi zai Tongzhan Gongzuo Huiyi shangde Jianghua." In *Qinghai Shengzhi*, vol. 81, *Fuluzhi*, edited by Qinghai Sheng Difangzhi Bianzuan Weiyuanhui, 723–32. Xining: Qinghai Renmin Chubanshe, 2003.

Zang, Xiaowei. *Ethnicity in China: A Critical Introduction.* Malden, MA: Polity Press, 2015.

Zenz, Adrian. "China's Securitization Drive in Tibet and Xinjiang." *Asia Dialogue*, February 14, 2018.

Zenz, Adrian, and James Leibold. "Chen Quanguo: The Strongman behind Beijing's Securitization Strategy in Tibet and Xinjiang." *China Brief* 17, no. 12 (2017): 16–24.

Zhang Bo and Yao Xiuchuan. "Qinghai Gezu Renmin Lianyihui Shengkuang Zhuishu." In *Qinghai Wenshi Ziliao Jicui: Jianguo Houjuan*, edited by Qinghai Sheng Zhengxie Xuexi he Wenshi Weiyuanhui, 242–50. Xining: Qinghaisheng Zhengxie Xuexi he Wenshi Weiyuanhui, 2001.

Zhang Fengxu, Lei Daheng, and Tian Zhengxiong, eds. *Qinghai Xumu*. Xining: Qinghai Renmin Chubanshe, 1987.

Zhang Shaowu and Guo Suqiang. "Jiefang Qinghai Chuqi Pingxi Angla Diqu Panluan yu Zhengqu Zangzu Touren Xiangqian de Jingguo." *Qinghai Wenshi Ziliao Xuanji*, no. 15 (1987): 31–52.

——. "Junshi Xiaomie Canfei, Zhengzhi Zhengqu Xiangqian." In *Jiefang Qinghai*, edited by Zhonggong Qinghai Shengwei Dangshi Ziliao Zhengji Weiyuanhui and Zhonggong Renmin Jiefangjun Qinghai Sheng Junqu Zhengzhibu, 415–30. Xining: Qinghai Renmin Chubanshe, 1987.

Zhang Wu. "Gannan Diqu Fasheng Wuzhuang Panluan." *Neibu Cankao*, no. 2461 (April 21, 1958): 3–4.

——. "Gannan Zangqu 'Shuanggai' Jingguo." *Neibu Cankao*, no. 2624 (November 4, 1958): 13–18.

——. "Gansu Dangbiaohui Jiefa, Pipan Difang Minzuzhuyi." *Neibu Cankao*, no. 2420 (February 13, 1958): 3–7.

Zhang Zhongliang. "Ba Dang de Minzu Zhengce Guanche Dao Gexian Gongzuo zhong Qu." In *Jiefang Qinghai Shiliao Xuanbian*, edited by Zhonggong Qinghai Shengwei Dangshi Ziliao Zhengji Weiyuanhui and Zhonggong Renmin Jiefangjun Qinghai Sheng Junqu Zhengzhibu, 141–54. Xining: Qinghai Xinhua Chubanshe, 1990.

——. "Zhong Tuanjie, Jiang Zhengce, Shenshen Zhagen yu Qunzhong." *Qinghai Wenshi Ziliao Xuanji*, no. 6 (1980): 7–12.

Zhao Long. "Yi Tongren Jiefang Jingguo." *Huangnan Wenshi Ziliao*, no. 2 (1994): 260–62.

Zhao Qingyang. "Ji Yiwei yu Dang Zhencheng Hezuo de Haopengyou." *Huangnan Wenshi Ziliao*, no. 2 (1994): 151–56.

——. "Tongren Zongqianhu Jiawu Duojie Pianduan." *Huangnan Wenshi Ziliao*, no. 2 (1994): 157–59.

——. "Yiwei Jingli Quzhe de Minzhu Renshi: Ji Angla Qianhu Xiangqian." *Huangnan Wenshi Ziliao*, no. 2 (2004): 196–203.

[Zhao] Qingyang. "Yiwei Jiujing Kaoyan de Minzhu Renshi: Ji Wajia Xiansheng." *Huangnan Wenshi Ziliao*, no. 2 (2004): 165–68.

Zhaxi Anjia. "Yi Wo Jiefang Qianhou de Jingli he Gongzuo Pianduan." *Huangnan Wenshi Ziliao*, no. 2 (1994): 243–55.

Zhaxi Anjia and Duojie. "Tongren Jiefang Qianhou." *Qinghai Wenshi Ziliao Xuanji*, nos. 10–12 (1984): 171–75.

——. "Tongren Jiefang Qinliji." In *Qinghai Wenshi Ziliao Jicui: Jianguohoujuan*, 55–58. Xining: Qinghaisheng Zhengxie Xuexi he Wenshi Ziliao Weiyuanhui, 2001.

Zhiguanba Gongquehudanbaraoji. *Anduo Zhengjiaoshi*. Translated by Wu Jun, Mao Jizu, and Ma Shilin. 2 vols. Lanzhou: Gansu Sheng Minzu Chubanshe, 1989.

"Zhonggong guanyu zai Shaoshu Minzu zhong Jinxing Zhengfeng he Shehuizhuyi Jiaoyu de Zhishi." *Tongyi Zhanxian Gongzuo*, no. 23 (December 5, 1957): 2–6.

Zhonggong Huangnan Zhouwei. "Huangnan Diqu Pingxi Panluan, Fadong Qunzhong Kaizhan Suku Yundong Qingkuang de Baogao." In *Minzu Zongjiao Gongzuo*

Wenjian Huiji, edited by Zhonggong Qinghai Shengwei Tongzhanbu, 1045–54. Xining: n.p., 1959.

"Zhonggong Qinghai Shengwei guanyu Jinyibu Jiaqiang Zongjiao Gongzuo de Zhishi." *Tongyi Zhanxian Gongzuo*, no. 76 (March 23, 1960): 13–16.

Zhongguo Gongchandang Dibaci Quanguo Daibiao Dahui Wenxian. Beijing: Renmin Chubanshe, 1956.

Zhongyang Minzu Shiwu Weiyuanhui Dangzu. "Guanyu Dangqian Yisilanjiao Lamajiao Gongzuo de Qingkuang Wenti he Yijian." *Tongyi Zhanxian Gongzuo*, no. 54 (Feburary 6, 1959): 7–9.

"Zhongyang Pizhuan Minwei Dangzu guanyu Dangqian Yisilanjiao Lamajiao Gongzuo de Qingkuang Wentide Baogao." *Tongyi Zhanxian Gongzuo*, no. 54 (February 6, 1958): 5–6.

Zhou, Minglang. *Multilingualism in China: The Politics of Writing Reforms for Minority Languages, 1949–2002*. Berlin: Mouton de Gruyter, 2003.

——. "Nation-State Building and Multiculturalism in China." In *Handbook on Ethnic Minorities in China*, edited by Xiaowei Zang, 111–37. Cheltenham, UK: Elgar, 2016.

——. "The Politics of Bilingual Education in the People's Republic of China since 1949." *Bilingual Research Journal* 25, no. 1/2 (2001): 147–71.

Zhou Renshan. "Guanyu Jiji Tuixing Minzu Quyu Zizhi de Yijian: Zhou Renshan Tongzhi yu Yijiuwuyi Nian Wu Yue Shiwu Ri zai Muyequ Gongzuo Huiyi shang de Fayan Tigang." In *Minzu Zongjiao Gongzuo Wenjian Huiji*, edited by Zhonggong Qinghai Shengwei Tongzhanbu, 623–26. Xining: n.p., 1959.

——. "Jixu Kaizhan Minzu Quyu Zizhi Yundong: Zhou Renshan Tongzhi yu Yijiuwu'er Nian Liu Yue Qi Ri zai Muyequ Gongzuo Huiyi shang de Fayan Tigang." In *Minzu Zongjiao Gongzuo Wenjian Huiji*, edited by Zhonggong Qinghai Shengwei Tongzhanbu, 637–56. Xining: n.p., 1959.

"Zhou Renshan Tongzhi Di'erzi Dangdaihui shang guangyu Minzu yu Tongzhan Gongzuo de Fayan Tigang." In *Minzu Zongjiao Gongzuo Wenjian Huiji*, edited by Zhonggong Qinghai Shengwei Tongzhanbu, 628–37. Xining: n.p., 1959.

Zhou Wei. "Gannan Zangzu Renmin Fandui Zongjiaojie Fangeming Fenzi he Huaifenzi de Douzheng Huode Da Shengli." *Minzu Tuanjie*, no. 1 (1959): 17.

Zhou Zhongyu. "Dang de Bada yu Muyequ de Shehuizhuyi Gaizao." *Qinghai Minzu Xueyuan Xuebao*, no. 3 (1997): 56–61.

Zhouta. *Gansu Zangzu Buluo de Shehui yu Lishi Yanjiu*. Lanzhou: Gansu Minzu Chubanshe, 1996.

Index

Studies of the Weatherhead East Asian Institute, Columbia University

Selected Titles

(Complete list at: http://weai.columbia.edu/publications/studies-weai/)

Fighting for Virtue: Justice and Politics in Thailand, by Duncan McCargo. Cornell University Press, 2020.

Beyond the Steppe Frontier: A History of the Sino-Russian Border, by Sören Urbansky. Princeton University Press, 2020.

Pirates and Publishers: A Social History of Copyright in Modern China, by Fei-Hsien Wang. Princeton University Press, 2019.

The Typographic Imagination: Reading and Writing in Japan's Age of Modern Print Media, by Nathan Shockey. Columbia University Press, 2019.

Down and Out in Saigon: Stories of the Poor in a Colonial City, by Haydon Cherry. Yale University Press, 2019.

Beauty in the Age of Empire: Japan, Egypt, and the Global History of Aesthetic Education, by Raja Adal. Columbia University Press, 2019.

Mass Vaccination: Citizens' Bodies and State Power in Modern China, by Mary Augusta Brazelton. Cornell University Press, 2019.

Residual Futures: The Urban Ecologies of Literary and Visual Media of 1960s and 1970s Japan, by Franz Prichard. Columbia University Press, 2019.

The Making of Japanese Settler Colonialism: Malthusianism and Trans-Pacific Migration, 1868–1961, by Sidney Xu Lu. Cambridge University Press, 2019.

The Power of Print in Modern China: Intellectuals and Industrial Publishing from the End of Empire to Maoist State Socialism, by Robert Culp. Columbia University Press, 2019.

Beyond the Asylum: Mental Illness in French Colonial Vietnam, by Claire E. Edington. Cornell University Press, 2019.

Borderland Memories: Searching for Historical Identity in Post-Mao China, by Martin Fromm. Cambridge University Press, 2019.

Sovereignty Experiments: Korean Migrants and the Building of Borders in Northeast Asia, 1860–1949, by Alyssa M. Park. Cornell University Press, 2019.

The Greater East Asia Co-Prosperity Sphere: When Total Empire Met Total War, by Jeremy A. Yellen. Cornell University Press, 2019.

Thought Crime: Ideology and State Power in Interwar Japan, by Max Ward. Duke University Press, 2019.

Statebuilding by Imposition: Resistance and Control in Colonial Taiwan and the Philippines, by Reo Matsuzaki. Cornell University Press, 2019.

Nation-Empire: Ideology and Rural Youth Mobilization in Japan and Its Colonies, by Sayaka Chatani. Cornell University Press, 2019.

Fixing Landscape: A Techno-Poetic History of China's Three Gorges, by Corey Byrnes. Columbia University Press, 2019.

The Invention of Madness: State, Society, and the Insane in Modern China, by Emily Baum. University of Chicago Press, 2018.

Japan's Imperial Underworlds: Intimate Encounters at the Borders of Empire, by David Ambaras. Cambridge University Press, 2018.

Heroes and Toilers: Work as Life in Postwar North Korea, 1953–1961, by Cheehyung Harrison Kim. Columbia University Press, 2018.

Electrified Voices: How the Telephone, Phonograph, and Radio Shaped Modern Japan, 1868–1945, by Kerim Yasar. Columbia University Press, 2018.

Making Two Vietnams: War and Youth Identities, 1965–1975, by Olga Dror. Cambridge University Press, 2018.

Playing by the Informal Rules: Why the Chinese Regime Remains Stable Despite Rising Protests, by Yao Li. Cambridge University Press, 2018.

Raising China's Revolutionaries: Modernizing Childhood for Cosmopolitan Nationalists and Liberated Comrades, by Margaret Mih Tillman. Columbia University Press, 2018.

Buddhas and Ancestors: Religion and Wealth in Fourteenth-Century Korea, by Juhn Y. Ahn. University of Washington Press, 2018.

Idly Scribbling Rhymers: Poetry, Print, and Community in Nineteenth Century Japan, by Robert Tuck. Columbia University Press, 2018.

China's War on Smuggling: Law, Economic Life, and the Making of the Modern State, 1842–1965, by Philip Thai. Columbia University Press, 2018.

Forging the Golden Urn: The Qing Empire and the Politics of Reincarnation in Tibet, by Max Oidtmann. Columbia University Press, 2018.

The Battle for Fortune: State-Led Development, Personhood, and Power among Tibetans in China, by Charlene Makley. Cornell University Press, 2018.

Aesthetic Life: Beauty and Art in Modern Japan, by Miya Elise Mizuta Lippit. Harvard University Asia Center, 2018.

Where the Party Rules: The Rank and File of China's Communist State, by Daniel Koss. Cambridge University Press, 2018.

Resurrecting Nagasaki: Reconstruction and the Formation of Atomic Narratives, by Chad R. Diehl. Cornell University Press, 2018.

China's Philological Turn: Scholars, Textualism, and the Dao in the Eighteenth Century, by Ori Sela. Columbia University Press, 2018.

Making Time: Astronomical Time Measurement in Tokugawa Japan, by Yulia Frumer. University of Chicago Press, 2018.

Mobilizing Without the Masses: Control and Contention in China, by Diana Fu. Cambridge University Press, 2018.

Post-Fascist Japan: Political Culture in Kamakura after the Second World War, by Laura Hein. Bloomsbury, 2018.

China's Conservative Revolution: The Quest for a New Order, 1927–1949, by Brian Tsui. Cambridge University Press, 2018.

Promiscuous Media: Film and Visual Culture in Imperial Japan, 1926–1945, by Hikari Hori. Cornell University Press, 2018.

The End of Japanese Cinema: Industrial Genres, National Times, and Media Ecologies, by Alexander Zahlten. Duke University Press, 2017.

The Chinese Typewriter: A History, by Thomas S. Mullaney. The MIT Press, 2017.

Forgotten Disease: Illnesses Transformed in Chinese Medicine, by Hilary A. Smith. Stanford University Press, 2017.

Borrowing Together: Microfinance and Cultivating Social Ties, by Becky Yang Hsu. Cambridge University Press, 2017.

Food of Sinful Demons: Meat, Vegetarianism, and the Limits of Buddhism in Tibet, by Geoffrey Barstow. Columbia University Press, 2017.

Youth For Nation: Culture and Protest in Cold War South Korea, by Charles R. Kim. University of Hawaii Press, 2017.

Printed in the USA
CPSIA information can be obtained
at www.ICGtesting.com
LVHW091643250823
756268LV00025B/611/J